Critical Acclaim for *Solaris® System Administrator's Guide*

"A solid book, with all the important system administrati
—**Bill Joy, Vice President, F**

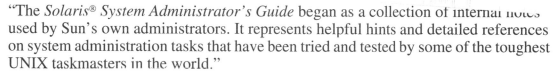

"The *Solaris® System Administrator's Guide* began as a collection of internal notes used by Sun's own administrators. It represents helpful hints and detailed references on system administration tasks that have been tried and tested by some of the toughest UNIX taskmasters in the world."

—**Ed Zander, President**
SunSoft, Inc.

"This small book is a perfect mix of quick-and-easy tasks and timely reference material. A must for novices and experts."

—**Steve Hanlon, Product Marketing Manager**
SunSoft, Inc.

"...[I] was having a problem with my workstation, so I used the *Solaris® System Administrator's Guide* and it got me up and running in no time at all! It's a very handy desktop reference."

—**Bob McInroy, Manager, Developer Marketing Programs**
SunSoft, Inc.

"Our system administrators are using the *Solaris® System Administrator's Guide* internally to make the transition to Solaris 2.0 and find it a helpful reference for anyone to have next to the workstation. Especially helpful is the thorough index that allows you to clue into the task at hand. The guide is useful because it is not only compact, but is also a clearly written reference."

—**Bill Prouty, Chair, Sun Solaris 2.0**
Internal Migration Committee, SunSoft, Inc.

Solaris® System Administrator's Guide offers a sane, well-written alternative to the documentation which is supplied with the Solaris system. . . .What makes this book different from similar publications is the concise description and syntax of command and procedures needed to smoothly operate a Solaris system. . . .The book immediately gives readers what they need—a plain English explanation of how to start up the system, shut the system down, send messages to users, and control and monitor processes. . . .*Solaris® System Administrator's Guide* is an exceptional book for both Unix newcomers and experienced Unix users alike. . ."

—**Paul Paradigm,** *Australian Personal Computer*

Solaris® Advanced System Administrator's Guide

SunSoft Press

Solaris®
Advanced System
Administrator's
Guide

Janice Winsor

Ziff-Davis Press
Emeryville, California

Senior Development Editor	Melinda Levine
Copy Editor	Ellen Falk
Technical Reviewers	Tom Kessler, Vipin Samar, Brent Callaghan, Patrick Moffitt, Steve Shumway, and Sam Cramer
Project Coordinator	A. Knox
Proofreader	Cort Day
Cover Design	Carrie English
Book Design	Laura Lamar/MAX, San Francisco
Technical Illustration	Cherie Plumlee Computer Graphics & Illustration
Word Processing	Howard Blechman, Cat Haglund, and Allison Levin
Page Layout	Tony Jonick, Anna L. Marks, and M.D. Barrera
Indexer	Valerie Robbins

Ziff-Davis Press books are produced on a Macintosh computer system with the following applications: FrameMaker®, Microsoft® Word, QuarkXPress®, Adobe Illustrator®, Adobe Photoshop®, Adobe Streamline™, MacLink®*Plus*, Aldus® FreeHand™, Collage Plus™.

Ziff-Davis Press
5903 Christie Avenue
Emeryville, CA 94608
1-800-688-0448

CONTENTS AT A GLANCE

TABLE OF CONTENTS

Part 2   NIS+

Part 3   Automounter Services

Part 4   Service Access Facility

Part 5   Application Software

Part 6   Introduction to Shell Programming

ACKNOWLEDGMENTS

MANY PEOPLE CONTRIBUTED TO THE DESIGN, WRITING, AND PRODUCtion of this book. SunSoft would particularly like to acknowledge the following people for their contributions.

Connie Howard and Mike Rogers, SunSoft Information Technology and Products managers, and Bridget Burke for their support and encouragement.

Karin Ellison, SunSoft Press, deserves special thanks for her can-do attitude and her willingness to help out with all kinds of issues related to this book.

Don Charles, SunSoft Engineering Services Organization, for help in setting up a two-SPARCstation network for this project, and for general system administration support.

Lori Reid, SunSoft Engineering Services Organization, for providing a Solaris® 2.1 CD-ROM disc.

Because this book contains so many different subject areas, specific acknowledgments are listed by part.

Part 1: Mail Services

Tom Kessler, SunSoft Engineering, for technical review and helpful discussions about different mail services configurations.

Dave Miner, SunSoft Engineering, for help with information about the Aliases database in Administration Tool.

Mike Gionfriddo, SunSoft Engineering, for answering questions about Administration Tool.

Don Brazell for technical review.

Part 2: NIS+

Rick Ramsey, SunSoft Information Technology and Products, for writing a great book about NIS+, providing me with background information, and answering many questions about NIS+.

Vipin Samar, SunSoft Engineering, for providing the engineering perspective for NIS+ and for technical review.

Saqib Jang, SunSoft Marketing, for providing the marketing perspective and information about the benefits of NIS+.

Bob LeFave, SunSoft Engineering Services Organization, for last-minute technical input and technical review.

John Auer, SMCC Enterprise Information Services, for additional technical review.

Don Brazell for technical review.

Scott Mann and SunU for permission to sit in on lab classes about NIS+.

Part 3: Automount Services

Brent Callaghan, SunSoft Engineering, for background information and technical review.

Don Brazell for technical review.

Part 4: Service Access Facility

Patrick Moffitt, SunSoft Training, for technical review.

Scott Mann and SunU for permission to sit in on lab classes about the SAF.

Neil Groundwater, SunSoft Engineering, for answering questions about modem connections and for technical review.

Tom Fowler, SunSoft Technical Marketing, for spending lots of time and effort figuring out how printing works in the Solaris 2.*x* releases, and for providing most of the printing troubleshooting examples.

Mary Morris, SunSoft Engineering, for technical review.

Bruce Sesnovich, SunSoft Information Technology and Products, for providing background information about the SAF and modem procedures.

Tom Amiro, SunSoft Information Technology and Products, for providing background information about administering user accounts and printers.

Part 5: Application Software

Steve Shumway, SunSoft Marketing, for technical review.

Davis Weatherby, Sun Information Resources systems engineer, for taking time off from his vacation to provide excellent background information on implementing wrapper-based application servers.

Wayne Thompson, Sun Information Resources systems engineer, for technical review and contributing to the background on application servers.

Rob Goodman, Sun Information Resources software distribution manager, for technical review and for facilitating the quality technical input on Sun's implementation of application servers.

Scott Mann and SunU for permission to sit in on lab classes about pkgadd and Software Manager.

Charla Mustard-Foote, SunSoft Information Technology and Products, for providing me with a CD-ROM of SearchIt™ software to use in the examples, and for answering questions about Software Manager.

MacDonald King Aston and Julie Bettis, SunSoft Information Technology and Products, for patiently answering questions about Software Manager.

Keith Palmby, SunSoft Information Technology and Products, for providing background information about the Online: DiskSuite™ product.

Terry Gibson, SunTech Technical Publications, for providing background information about software licensing.

Dan Larson, SunTech Engineering Support Organization, for discussions about the engineering implementation of application servers.

Bill Petro, SunSoft Marketing, for background information about installing application software.

Linda Ries, SunSoft Engineering, for answering questions about the package commands and Software Manager.

Part 6: Introduction to Shell Programming

Sam Cramer, SunSoft Engineering, for doing two technical reviews of this part, even though his newest family member arrived right in the middle of the review cycle.

Ellie Quigly, Learning Enterprises; Chico, California; for providing me with her class notes for the Bourne, Korn, and C shells, and for permission to use examples from her course notes.

Wayne Thomson, SMCC Sun Information Resources, for technical review and for providing sample scripts for Chapter 16.

Appendix A: Volume Management

Howard Alt, SunSoft Engineering, for background information and for technical review.

Lynn Rohrer, SunSoft Information Technology and Products, for background information and for technical review.

Robert Novak, SunSoft Marketing, for technical review.

Mary Lautner, SunSoft Information Technology and Products, for letting me use her system to test the remote CD-ROM procedures.

Appendix B: Serial Port Manager

Neil Groundwater, SunSoft Engineering, for background information and for technical review.

Lynn Rohrer, SunSoft Information Technology and Products, for background information and for technical review.

Robert Novak, SunSoft Marketing, for technical review.

Glossary

Craig Mohrman, SunSoft Engineering, for technical review.

Thanks are also due to the following people at Ziff-Davis Press for being so easy to work with: senior development editor Melinda Levine, copyeditor Ellen Falk, managing editor Cheryl Holzaepfel, and project coordinator Ami Knox.

The author would like to thank her husband for his love and patience, and her three cats for lap sitting, keyboard walking, and general company keeping while this book was in progress.

INTRODUCTION

THIS BOOK IS FOR SYSTEM ADMINISTRATORS WHO ARE FAMILIAR WITH basic system administration and with the tasks described in the *Solaris System Administrator's Guide*, cited in the bibliography at the back of this book.

A Quick Tour of the Contents

This book is divided into six parts, two appendixes, a glossary, and a bibliography.

Part 1, "Mail Services," describes the Solaris 2.*x* mail services in four chapters. Refer to the chapters in this part if you need to set up a new mail service or expand an existing one.

Chapter 1, "Understanding Mail Services," describes the components of the mail service, defines mail service terminology, and explains how the programs in the mail service interact.

Chapter 2, "Planning Mail Services," describes several common mail configurations and provides guidelines for how to set up each configuration.

Chapter 3, "Setting Up and Administering Mail Services," describes how to set up, test, administer, and troubleshoot mail services.

Chapter 4, "Customizing sendmail Configuration Files," describes the sendmail configuration file and how to customize it if you need a more complex configuration file for your mail system.

Part 2, "NIS+," introduces the NIS+ naming service environment. Refer to the chapters in this part if you want to familiarize yourself with the basics of the NIS+ naming service and its administrative commands, and for instructions on how to set up an NIS+ client. This part does not provide in-depth information for a system administrator who must set up and support an NIS+ environment.

Chapter 5, "Introducing the NIS+ Environment," provides an overview of NIS+, explains how NIS+ differs from the Solaris 1.*x* NIS naming service and introduces the NIS+ commands.

Chapter 6, "Setting Up NIS+ Clients," describes how to set up a SunOS 5.*x* system as an NIS+ client when NIS+ servers are set up and running.

Part 3, "Automount Services," describes the Solaris 2.*x* automount services. Refer to the chapters in this part if you need to set up a new automount service or modify an existing one.

Chapter 7, "Understanding the Automounter," describes automount terminology and the components of automounting, explains how the automounter works, recommmends automounting policies, and tells you how to plan your automount services.

Chapter 8, "Setting Up the Automounter," describes how to set up and administer automount maps.

Part 4, "Service Access Facility," describes the Solaris 2.x Service Access Facility (SAF). Refer to the chapters in this part if you need to set up a new SAF service for terminals, modems, or printers or to modify an existing one. Also refer to Appendix B, "Serial Port Manager," for information about a graphical user interface tool, available with Solaris 2.3 system software, which you can use to configure character terminals and modems.

Chapter 9, "Understanding the Service Access Facility," provides an overview of the SAF and describes the port monitors and services used by the SAF.

Chapter 10, "Setting Up Modems and Character Terminals," describes how to set up and administer the SAF for modems and terminals.

Chapter 11, "Setting Up Printing Services," describes how to set up and administer the SAF for printers and how to troubleshoot printing problems.

Part 5, "Application Software," describes how to install and delete application software. Refer to this part for guidelines on how to set up an application server, and for information on how to install and remove application software.

Chapter 12, "Installing and Managing Application Software," provides an overview of the installation process, introduces the package commands and the Software Manager for installation, recommends policy for installing software on an application server, and describes how to access files from a CD-ROM drive.

Chapter 13, "Package Commands," describes how to use the package commands to administer application software, and how to set up the users' environment.

Chapter 14, "Software Manager," describes how to use the Software Manager to administer application software.

Part 6, "Introduction to Shell Programming," introduces shell programming. Refer to this part if you want to familiarize yourself with the basics of shell programming and to decide which shell language you want to use to perform a specific task. This part does not provide in-depth instructions for writing scripts in the three shells.

Chapter 15, "Writing Shell Scripts," introduces the basic concepts of shell programming and the three shells available with Solaris 2.x system software. It describes how shells work, and describes the programming elements.

Chapter 16, "Reference Tables and Example Scripts," provides reference tables comparing shell syntax and contains examples of shell scripts.

Appendix A, "Volume Management," describes a new feature with Solaris 2.2 system software. Volume management automates mounting of CD-ROMs and diskettes. You no longer need to have superuser permission to mount a CD-ROM or a diskette.

Appendix B, "Serial Port Manager," introduces a tool new with Solaris 2.3 system software and describes how to use it. You can use the Administration Tool Serial Port Manager to easily set up and configure the SAF for character terminals and for modems.

The glossary contains basic system administration terms and defines their meanings.

The bibliography contains a list of books on related system administration topics.

Important: Read This Before You Begin

Because we assume that the root path includes the /sbin, /usr/sbin, /usr/bin, and /etc directories, the steps show the commands in these directories without absolute path names. Steps that use commands in other, less common directories show the absolute path in the example.

The examples in this book are for a basic Solaris 2.x system software installation without the Binary Compatibility Package installed and without /usr/ucb in the path.

CAUTION! *If /usr/ucb is included in a search path, it should always be at the end. Commands such as ps and df are duplicated in /usr/ucb with different formats and options from the SunOS 5.x commands.*

This book describes six different system administration areas in depth; however, a given section may not contain all the information you need to administer systems. Refer to the complete system administration documentation set for complete information.

Because the Solaris 2.x system software provides the Bourne (default), Korn, and C shells, examples in this book show prompts for each of the shells. The default Bourne and Korn shell prompt is $. The default C shell prompt is *system-name%*. The default root prompt for all shells is a pound sign (#). In examples that affect more than one system, the C shell prompt (which shows the system name) is used to make it clearer when you change from one system to another.

Because Solaris 2.x system software is evolving, procedures may be different depending on the system software that is installed on the system you are administering. For example, with the advent of Solaris 2.2 volume management, procedures for accessing files on CD-ROM discs and on diskettes are different for Solaris 2.2 and later releases. The old procedures will not work on the new software. To help you understand how Solaris is evolving, Table I.1 provides a list of the major system administration feature differences for each release. Table I.2 describes three new NIS+ scripts.

Table I.1 **Solaris System Software Evolution**

Release	New Features
Solaris 1.0	Berkeley (BSD) UNIX with Solaris 4.*x* functionality.
Solaris 2.0 (SunOS 5.0)	A merger of AT&T System V Release 4 (SVR4) and BSD UNIX. To facilitate customer transition, Solaris uses SVR4 as the default environment, with BSD commands and modes as an option. Administration Tool provides a graphical user interface Database Manager and Host Manager. (Refer to the *Solaris System Administrator's Guide*.)
Solaris 2.1 (SunOS 5.1)	Administration Tool adds a graphical user interface Printer Manager and User Account Manager. (Refer to Appendix B in the *Solaris System Administrator's Guide*.)
Solaris 2.2 (SunOS 5.2)	Volume management integrates access to CD-ROM and diskette files with the File Manager, and provides a command-line interface. Users no longer need superuser privileges to mount CD-ROMs and diskettes. (Solaris 2.0 and 2.1 procedures do not work with volume management because volume management controls and owns the devices. Refer to Appendix A.)
Solaris 2.3 (SunOS 5.3)	Volume management changes Solaris 2.2 mount point naming conventions. (Refer to Appendix A.)
	Administration Tool adds a graphical user interface Serial Port Manager with templates that provide default settings, which makes adding character terminals and modems much easier. (Refer to Appendix B.)
	The automounter is split into two programs: an automounted daemon and a separate automount program. Both are run when the system is booted. The /tmp_mnt mount point is not displayed as part of the path name, and the local path is displayed as /home/*username*. Additional predefined automount map variables are provided. (Refer to Part 3.)
	Online: Backup 2.1 is included with the release (Not documented in this book.)
	Pluggable Authentication Model (PAM) is included with the release. PAM provides a consistent framework to allow access control applications, such as login, to be able to choose any authentication scheme available on a system, without concern for implementation details of the scheme. (Not documented in this book.)
	C2 Security is included in this release. (Not documented in this book.)
	Format(1) changes for SCSI disks. (Not documented in this book.)
	PPP network protocol product that provides IP network connectivity over a variety of point-to-point connections is included in this release. (Not documented in this book.)
	Cache File System (CacheFS) for NFS is included in this release. CacheFS is a generic, nonvolatile caching mechanism to improve performance of certain file systems by using a small, fast, local disk. (Not documented in this book.)

Table I.1	**Solaris System Software Evolution (Continued)**
	New NIS+ setup scripts are included in this release. The nisserver(1M), nispopulate(1M), and nisclient(1M) scripts described in Table I.2 let you set up an NIS+ domain much more quickly and easily than if you used the individual NIS+ commands to do so. With these scripts you can avoid a lengthy manual process.

Table I.2 **The NIS+ Scripts**

NIS+ Script	What It Does
nisserver(1M)	Sets up the root master, nonroot master, and replica servers with level 2 security (DES)
nispopulate(1M)	Populates NIS+ tables in a specified domain from their corresponding system files or NIS maps
nisclient(1M)	Creates NIS+ credentials for hosts and users; initializes NIS+ hosts and users; restores the network service environment

Refer to the nisserver(1M), nispopulate(1M), and nisclient(1M) manual pages for more information.

Conventions Used in This Book

Commands

In the steps and examples, the commands to be entered are in bold type. For example: "Type **su** and press Return." When following steps, press Return only when instructed to do so, even if the text in the step breaks at the end of a line.

Variables

Variables are in *italic* typeface. When following steps, replace the variable with the appropriate information. For example, to tell a printer to accept print request, the step instructs you to "type **accept** ***printer-name*** and press Return." To substitute the printer named pinecone for the ***printer-name*** variable, type **accept pinecone** and press Return.

Mouse Button Terminology

This book describes mouse buttons by function. The default mapping of mouse buttons in a three-button mouse is:

- SELECT is left.

- ADJUST is middle.

- MENU is right.

Use the SELECT mouse button to select unselected objects and to activate controls. Use the ADJUST mouse button to adjust a selected group of objects, either adding to the group or deselecting part of the group. Use the MENU mouse button to display and choose from menus.

Storage-Medium Terminology

This book distinguishes among different types of media storage terminology in this way:

- *Disc* is used for an optical disc or CD-ROM.

- *Disk* is used for a hard-disk storage device.

- *Diskette* is used for a floppy diskette storage device. (Note that sometimes screen messages and mount points use the term *floppy*.)

Refer to the chapters in this part if you need to set up a new mail service or expand an existing one.

This part describes the Solaris 2.*x* mail services in four chapters. Chapter 1 describes the components of the mail service, defines mail service terminology, and explains how the programs in the mail service interact. Chapter 2 describes several common mail configurations and provides guidelines for how to set up each configuration. Chapter 3 describes how to set up and administer mail services. Chapter 4 describes the sendmail configuration file and how to customize it if you need a more complex configuration file for your mail system.

PART

1

Mail Services

Understanding Mail Services

THE SUNOS™ 5.*X* MAIL SERVICES USE THE SUNOS 4.*X* SENDMAIL MAIL-ROUTING program—which came from 4.3 BSD UNIX®—with some minor modifications; SunOS 5.*x* does not use the AT&T mail-routing program. If you are familiar with SunOS 4.*x* mail services, you will be able to easily set up and administer mail services for SunOS 5.*x* systems. You will also find that it is easy to administer mail services on a network that has some systems running SunOS 4.*x* system software and others running SunOS 5.*x* system software. To help you find the modifications, information that is new to the SunOS 5.*x* sendmail program has an icon in the margin and is labeled "New with SVR4."

As system administrator, you may need to expand an existing mail service or set up a new one. To help you with these tasks, this chapter defines mail services terminology and describes the components of the mail service.

Mail Services Terminology

This section defines the following terms and describes how they are used as part of the mail services:

- Systems in a mail configuration

  - Relay host

  - Gateway

  - Mailhost

  - Mail server

  - Mail client

- User agent (UA)

- Mail transport agent (MTA)

- Domains

- Mail addressing

- Mailbox

- Aliases

Systems in a Mail Configuration

A mail configuration requires three elements, which can be combined on the same system or provided by separate systems: a mailhost, at least one mail server, and mail clients. When you want users to be able to communicate with networks outside your domain, you must also have a relay host or a gateway.

Figure 1.1 shows a typical electronic mail configuration, using all four elements. Each of these elements is identified and described in the following sections.

Figure 1.1

A typical electronic mail configuration

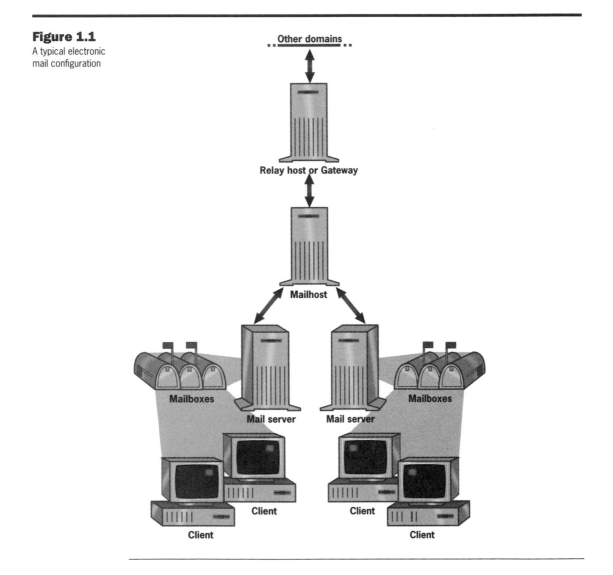

Relay Host

A *relay host* is a system that runs at least one mail-related protocol, called a *mailer*. Each mailer specifies a policy and the mechanics to be used when delivering mail. The relay host handles unresolved mail—mail with an address for which sendmail could not find a recipient in your domain. If a relay host exists, sendmail uses it for sending and receiving mail outside your domain.

The mailer on the sending relay host must be compatible with the mailer on the receiving system, as shown in Figure 1.2. You specify the mailer for your domain in the sendmail.cf file. The default sendmail.cf file defines several *mailer specifications,* such as smartuucp, ddn, ether, and uucp. You can define others.

The relay host can be the same system as the mailhost, or you can configure another system as the relay host, as shown in Figure 1.3. You may, in fact, choose to configure more than one relay host for your domain if you have several connections outside of your site. If you have uucp or Internet connections, configure the system with those connections as the relay host.

Gateway

A *gateway* is a system that handles connections between networks running different communications protocols, as shown in Figure 1.4. A relay host and the system it is connected to must use matching mailers. A gateway can handle connections to systems with unmatched mailers. You must customize the sendmail.cf file on the gateway system, which can be a difficult and time-consuming process.

If you have to set up a gateway, find a gateway configuration file that is close to what you need, and modify it to fit your situation. For example, you can modify the default /etc/mail/main.cf file to use on a gateway system.

Mailhost

A *mailhost* is a system that you designate as the main mail system on your network. The mailhost is the system to which other systems at the site forward mail that they cannot deliver. You designate a system as a mailhost by adding the word *mailhost* to the Aliases line for the system entry in the Hosts database, or by adding the word *mailhost* to the Internet Protocol (IP) address line in the system's /etc/hosts file. You should also use the main.cf file as the mail configuration file on the mailhost system.

A good candidate for mailhost is a system that is attached to an Ethernet and to phone lines, or a system configured as a router to the Internet. If you have a stand-alone system that is not networked but is in a time-sharing configuration, you can treat the stand-alone as the mailhost of a one-system network. Similarly, if you have several systems on an Ethernet and none have phones, designate one as the mailhost.

Figure 1.2

Compatible mailers on a relay host and on the receiving system

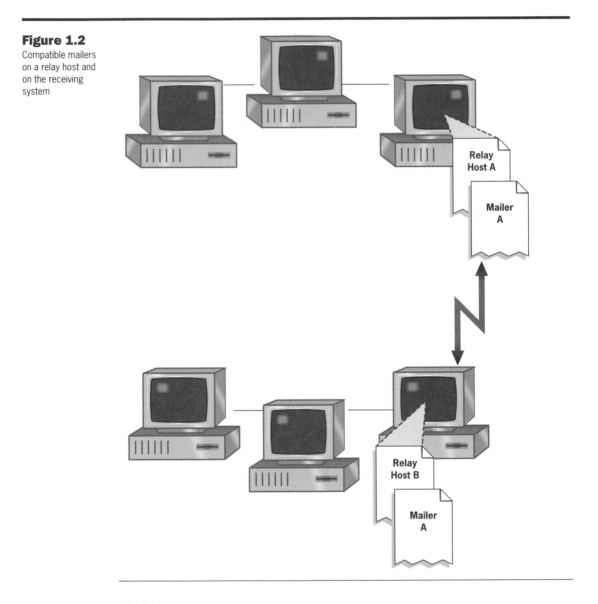

Mail Server

A *mail server* is any system that stores mailboxes in the /var/mail directory. The mail server is responsible for routing all mail from a client. When a client sends mail, the mail server puts it in a queue for delivery. Once the mail is in the queue, the client can reboot or turn off the system without losing those mail messages. When the recipient gets mail from a client, the path in the

"From:" line of the message contains the name of the mail server. If the recipient chooses to respond, the response goes to the user's mailbox on the server.

Figure 1.3
The relay host and the mailhost can be on the same system or on different systems.

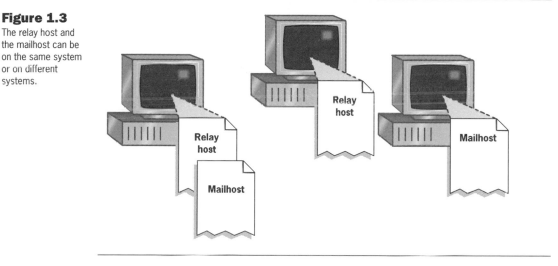

When the mailbox is on a mail server, messages are delivered to the server, and not directly to the client's system. When the mailbox is on the user's local system, the local system acts as its own mail server if it does not mount /var/mail from another system.

If the mail server is not the user's local system, users with NFS can mount the /var/mail directory in the /etc/vfstab file, use the automounter, or log into the server to read their mail.

NOTE. *If you automount the /var/mail directory, you may have problems with mail on heterogeneous networks that have SunOS 4.x mail clients.*

Good candidates for mail servers are systems that provide a home directory for users, or that are backed up on a regular basis.

Table 1.1 shows some sample statistics about the size of mail messages and mail traffic at a computer company with about 12,000 employees.

NOTE. *The information in Table 1.1 is valid for ASCII messages only. With the advent of multimedia mail, which lets users transmit any type of data (not just ASCII text), the average size of an e-mail message is likely to grow enormously. In the future, system administrators will need to allocate more spooling space for multimedia mailboxes.*

Figure 1.4

A gateway can
handle connections
between different
communications
protocols.

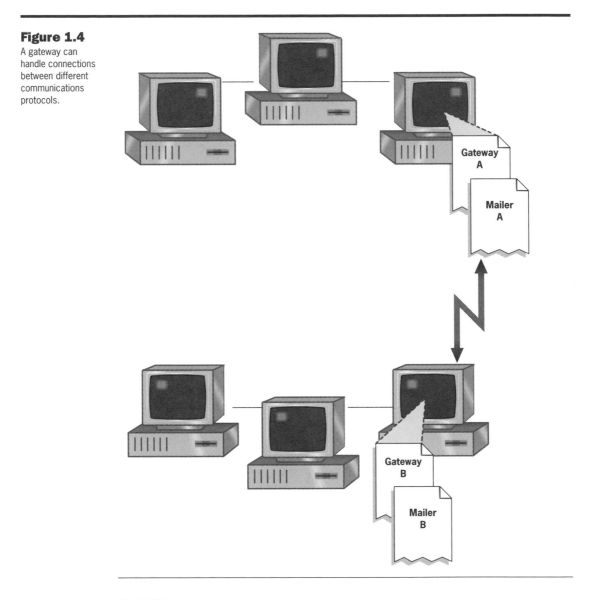

Mail Client

A *mail client* is any system that receives mail on a mail server and does not
have a local /var/mail directory, but instead mounts /var/mail using NFS. You
must make sure the mail client has the appropriate entry in the /etc/vfstab file
and a mount point to mount the mailbox from the mail server.

Table 1.1 **Sample Statistics for Mail Messages and Traffic**

Statistic	Description
6,500 bytes	Average size of an e-mail message
140 kilobytes	Amount of mail received by an average user in one day
15 kilobytes	Small mailbox size (user reads mail regularly and stores messages elsewhere)
40 megabytes	Large mailbox size (user stores long-term mail in /var/mail mailbox)
18,000 messages	Average number of messages per day sent outside the company
55,000 messages	Average number of messages per day received from outside the company
2 megabytes	Recommended spooling space to allocate for each user's mailbox, based on the figures in this table

User Agent

The *user agent* is the program that acts as the interface between the user and the sendmail program. The user agents for SunOS 5.*x* system software are /usr/bin/mail, /usr/bin/mailx, and $OPENWINHOME/bin/mailtool.

Mail Transport Agent

The *transport agent* is responsible for actually receiving and delivering messages. The transport agent for SunOS 5.*x* system software is sendmail. The transport agent performs these functions:

- Accepts messages from the user agent

- Understands destination addresses

- Delivers mail originating on the local system to the proper mailbox(es) if local, or to a delivery agent if not local

- Receives incoming mail from other delivery agents and delivers it to local users

Mailers

A *mailer* is a protocol that specifies the policy and mechanics used by sendmail when it delivers mail. You need to specify a mailer in the sendmail.cf file of a relay host or a gateway. The mailer for a relay host must match the

mailer on the system outside of your domain. A gateway is a more complicated relay host (alternatively, you can think of a relay host as a simple gateway) and can communicate with more than one type of mailer.

The mailers provided with SunOS 5.*x* system software are:

- smartuucp (the default relay mailer) uses uux to deliver messages but formats headers with a domain-style address, and the To: and CC: lines are
formatted by domain. For example, if winsor in the eng.sun.com domain
sends mail to guy at auspex using smartuucp, the headers look like this:

```
To: guy@auspex.com
From: winsor@Eng.Sun.COM
```

Use smartuucp for uucp mail to systems that can handle and resolve
domain-style names. The sender also must be able to handle domain-
style names and be able to receive replies from the Internet.

- uucp uses uux to deliver mail but uses route-based addressing in the headers, where part or all of the address route is specified by the sender. See
"Route-Based Addressing" later in this chapter for more information. For
example, if winsor in domain sun.eng.sun.com sends mail to guy@auspex
using the uucp mailer, the headers look like this:

```
To: auspex!guy
From: sun!winsor
```

The exclamation point (bang) in the address means that it is route based.
Use uucp for uucp connections to systems that need a bang-style path.

- ddn uses SMTP (simple mail transport protocol) on TCP port 25 to connect to the remote host. ddn inverts aliases and adds a domain name. For
example, if winsor in domain eng.sun.com sends mail to paul@phoenix.-
princeton.edu, the headers look like this:

```
To: paul@phoenix.princeton.edu
From: Janice.Winsor@Eng.Sun.COM
```

If winsor sends mail to irving@sluggo (both users in the eng.sun.com
domain) and is using the main.cf configuration file, the header looks like this:

```
To: Irving.Who@Eng.Sun.Com
From: Janice.Winsor@Eng.Sun.COM
```

Use ddn for sending mail outside of your domain, especially for mailers
that you must reach through a relay.

- ether uses the SMTP protocol on port 25 to connect to the remote host; ether does not invert aliases or append a domain name. Use ether for systems in your dns domain that users can reach directly.

You can define other mailers by providing a mailer specification in the sendmail.cf file. See Chapter 4 for more information.

Domains

A *domain* is a directory structure for electronic mail addressing and network address naming. The domain address has this format:

```
mailbox@subdomain. . . . . subdomain2.subdomain1.top-level-domain
```

The part of the address to the left of the @ sign is the local address, as shown in Figure 1.5. The local address may contain information about routing using another mail transport (for example, bob::vmsvax@gateway or smallberries%mill.uucp@physics.uchicago.edu), an alias (iggy.ignatz), or a token that resolves to the name of a mailbox (ignatz--> /var/mail/ignatz). The receiving mailer is responsible for determining what the local part of the address means.

Figure 1.5
Domain address
structure

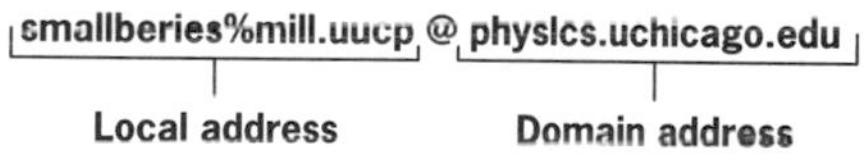

```
|smallberies%mill.uucp|@|physics.uchicago.edu|
          Local address         Domain address
```

The part of the address to the right of the @ sign shows the domain address where the local address is located. A dot separates each part of the domain address. The domain can be an organization, a physical area, or a geographic region. Domain addresses are case insensitive. It makes no difference whether you use upper, lower, or mixed case in the domain part of an address.

The order of domain information is hierarchical, with the locations more specific and local the closer they are to the @ sign (although certain British and New Zealand networks reverse the order). Note that most gateways automatically translate the reverse order of British and New Zealand domain names into the commonly used order. The larger the number of subdomains, the more detailed the information that is provided about the destination. Just as a subdirectory or a file in a file system hierarchy is inside the directory above, each subdomain is considered to be inside the one located to its right.

Table 1.2 shows the top-level domains in the United States.

Table 1.2   **Top-Level Domains in the United States**

Domain	Description
Com	Commercial sites
Edu	Educational sites
Gov	Government installations
Mil	Military installations
Net	Networking organizations
Org	Nonprofit organizations

Table 1.3 shows the top-level domains for the United States and European countries. The book *!%@:: A Directory of Electronic Mail Addressing and Networks,* written by Donnalyn Frey and Rick Adams, contains a complete list of domain addresses and is updated periodically. See the bibliography for a complete reference.

Table 1.3   **Top-Level Country Domains**

Domain	Description
AT	Austria
BE	Belgium
CH	Switzerland
De	West Germany
DK	Denmark
ES	Spain
FI	Finland
FR	France
GR	Greece
IE	Ireland
IS	Iceland
IT	Italy

Table 1.3	**Top-Level Country Domains (Continued)**

Domain	Description
LU	Luxembourg
NL	The Netherlands
NO	Norway
PT	Portugal
SE	Sweden
TR	Turkey
UK	United Kingdom
US	United States

Here are some examples of education, commercial, and government domain addresses:

```
roy@shibumi.cc.columbia.edu
rose@haggis.ssctr.bcm.tmc.edu
smallberries%mill.uucp@physics.uchicago.edu
day@concave.convex.com
paul@basic.ppg.com
angel@enterprise.arc.nasa.gov
```

Here is a French domain address:

```
hobbit@ilog.ilog.fr
```

and here is a British one:

```
fred@uk.ac.aberdeen.kc
```

Note that some British and New Zealand networks write their mail addresses from top level to lower level, but most gateways automatically translate the address into the commonly used order (that is, lower level to higher).

Mail Addressing

The *mail address* contains the name of the recipient and the system where the mail message is delivered. When you are administering a small mail system that does not use a naming service, addressing mail is easy: Login names uniquely identify users.

When, however, you are administering a mail system that has more than one system with mailboxes or has one or more domains, or when you have a uucp (or other) mail connection to the outside world, mail addressing becomes more complex. Mail addresses can be route-based, route-independent, or a mixture of the two.

Route-Based Addressing

Route-based addressing requires the sender of an e-mail message to specify not only the local address (typically a user name) and its final destination, but the route that the message must take to reach its final destination. Route-based addresses are fairly common on uucp networks and have this format:

    host!path!user

Whenever you see an exclamation point (bang) as part of an e-mail address, all (or some) of the route was specified by the sender. Route-based addresses are always read from left to right.

For example, an e-mail address that looks like this:

    castle!sun!sierra!hplabs!ucbvax!winsor

reached user winsor on the system named ucbvax by going first from castle to the address sun, then to sierra, then to hplabs, and finally to ucbvax. (Note that this is an example and not an actual route.) If any of the four mail handlers is out of commission, the message will be delayed or returned as undeliverable.

Route-Independent Addressing

Route-independent addressing requires the sender of an e-mail message to specify the name of the recipient and the final destination address. Route-independent addresses usually indicate the use of a high-speed network such as Internet. In addition, newer uucp connections frequently use domain-style names. Route-independent addresses have this format:

    user@host.domain

Increased popularity of the domain hierarchical naming scheme for computers across the country is making route-independent addresses more common. In fact, the most common route independent address omits the host name from the address and relies on the domain-naming service to properly identify the final destination of the e-mail message:

    user@domain

Route-independent addresses are read by searching for the @ sign, then reading the domain hierarchy from the right (the highest level) to the left (the most specific address to the right of the @ sign).

Mailbox

A *mailbox* is a directory on a mail server that is the final destination for e-mail messages. The name of the mailbox may be the username, a group of users, or a place to put mail for someone with a specific function, such as the postmaster. Mailboxes can be in the /var/mail/*username* directory on either the user's local system or on a mail server.

Mail should always be delivered to a local file system so that the user agent can pull mail from the mail spool and store it readily in the local mailbox.

Do not use NFS-mounted file systems as the destination for a user's mailbox. NFS-mounted file systems cause problems with mail delivery and handling if the server fails.

The Aliases database, the /etc/mail/aliases file, and naming services such as NIS and NIS+ provide mechanisms for creating aliases for electronic mail addresses so that users do not need to know the precise local name of a user's mailbox. DNS provides aliases only for systems and domains. You cannot use DNS to maintain user or mailing list aliases.

Some common naming conventions for special-purpose mailboxes are shown in Table 1.4.

Table 1.4 **Conventions for the Format of Mailbox Names**

Format	Description
username	User names are frequently the same as mailbox names.
Firstname.Lastname, *Firstname_Lastname,* *Firstinitial.Lastname,* or *Firstinitial_Lastname*	User names may be identified as full names with a dot (or an underscore) separating the first and last names or by a first initial with a dot (or an underscore) separating the initial and the last name.
postmaster	Each site and domain should have a postmaster mailbox. Users can address questions and report problems with the mail system to the postmaster mailbox.
MAILER-DAEMON	Any mail addressed to the MAILER-DAEMON is automatically routed to the postmaster by sendmail.
x-interest	Names with dashes are likely to be a distribution list or a mailing list. This format is commonly used for net mail groups.
x-interest-request	Names ending in -request are administrative addresses for distribution lists.
owner-*x*-interest	Names beginning with owner- are administrative addresses for distribution lists.

Table 1.4	Conventions for the Format of Mailbox Names (Continued)

Format	Description
local%domain	The percent sign (%) shows a local address that is expanded when the message arrives at its destination. Most mail systems interpret mailbox names with % characters as full mail addresses. The % is replaced with an @ and the mail is redirected accordingly. Note that although many people use the % convention, it is not a formal standard. In the e-mail community, it is referred to as the "% hack."

Aliases

An *alias* is an alternative name. For electronic mail, you can use aliases to assign additional names to a user, route mail to a particular system, or define mailing lists.

You need to create a mail alias for each user at your site to point to where the mail is stored. Providing a mail alias is like providing a mail stop as part of the address for an individual at a large corporation. If you do not provide the mail stop, the mail is delivered to a central address. Extra effort is required to determine where within the building the mail is to be delivered, and the possibility of error increases. For example, if there are two people named Kevin Smith in the same building, the probability is high that each Kevin will receive mail intended for the other.

Use domains and location-independent addresses as much as possible when you create alias files. To enhance portability and flexibility of alias files, make your alias entries as generic and system-independent as possible. For example, if you have a user named ignatz on system oak in domain Eng.sun.com, create the alias as ignatz instead of ignatz@Eng or ignatz@oak. If user ignatz changes the name of his system but remains within the engineering domain, you do not need to update any alias files to reflect the change in system name.

When creating aliases that include users outside of your domain, create the alias with the username and the domain name. For example, if you have a user named smallberries on system privet in domain Corp.sun.com, create the alias as smallberries@Corp.

You can sct an option in the sendmail.cf file to translate the e-mail address to a fully qualified domain name when mail goes outside of the user's domain. See Chapter 4 for more information.

Uses for Alias Files

You create mail aliases for global use in the NIS+ mail_aliases table, in the NIS aliases map, or, if your site does not use a naming service, in local /etc/mail/aliases files. You can also create and administer mailing lists using the same alias files.

Depending on the configuration of your mail services, you may administer aliases by using the NIS or NIS+ naming service to maintain a global aliases database, or by updating all of the local /etc/mail/aliases files to keep them in sync. See Chapter 3 for information on how to create aliases.

Users can also create and use aliases. They can create aliases either in their local .mailrc file, which only they can use, or in their local /ctc/mail/aliases file, which can be used by anyone. Users cannot create or administer NIS or NIS+ alias files.

Syntax of Aliases

The following paragraphs describe the syntax of NIS+, NIS, and .mailrc aliases.

NIS+ Aliases The NIS+ aliases table contains all names by which a system or person is known, except for private aliases listed in users' local .mailrc files. The sendmail program can use the NIS+ Aliases database instead of the local /etc/mail/aliases files to determine mailing addresses. See the aliasadm(8) and nsswitch.conf(4) manual pages for more information.

The NIS+ aliases table has four columns, as described in Table 1.5.

Table 1.5 **Columns in the NIS+ Aliases Database**

Column	Description
alias	The name of the alias
expansion	The value of the alias as it would appear in a sendmail /etc/aliases file
options	Reserved for future use
comments	Can be used to add specific comments about an individual alias

Aliases use the format of the NIS+ aliases table:

```
alias: expansion   [options#   "comments"]
```

The NIS+ Aliases database should contain entries for all mail clients. You list, create, modify, and delete entries in the NIS+ Aliases database using the Administration Tool's Database Manager or the aliasadm command. If you are creating a new NIS+ aliases table, you must initialize the table before you create the entries. If the table already exists, no initialization is needed.

When creating alias entries, enter one alias per line. You should only have one entry that contains the user's system name. For example, you could create the following entries for one user named winsor:

```
winsor: janice.winsor
jwinsor: janice.winsor
janicew: janice.winsor
janice.winsor: winsor@castle
```

You can create an alias for local names or domains. For example, an alias entry for user fred who has a mailbox on the system oak and who is in the domain Trees could have this entry in the NIS+ aliases table:

```
fred: fred@Trees
```

To use the Administration Tool's Database Manager to edit the Aliases database, you must be a member of the sysadmin group (GID 14) and have create and delete permissions for the NIS+ Aliases database.

To use the aliasadm command, you must be root, be a member of the NIS+ group that owns the Aliases database, or be the person who created the database.

NIS Aliases   Aliases in the NIS aliases map use this format:

```
name: name1, name2, . . .
```

.mailrc Aliases   Aliases in a .mailrc file use this format:

```
alias aliasname value value value . . .
```

/etc/mail/aliases Aliases   Distribution list formats in a local /etc/mail/aliases file use this format:

```
aliasname: value,value,value . . .
```

The aliases in the /etc/mail/aliases file are stored in text form. When you edit the /etc/mail/aliases file, run the newaliases program to rehash the database and make the aliases available in binary form to the sendmail program.

See Chapter 3 for information about how to create NIS+ alias tables.

Components of Mail Services

Mail services are composed of a number of programs and daemons that interact with one another. The following sections introduce the programs, along with a number of terms and concepts related to administration of electronic mail.

The Mail Services Programs

Table 1.6 lists the mail services programs.

Table 1.6 **The Components of Mail Services**

Command	Description
/usr/bin/mailx	Mail program described in the mailx(1) manual page
/usr/bin/mail	Mailer that delivers mail to mailboxes
$OPENWINHOME/bin/mailtool	Window-based interface to the sendmail program
/usr/lib/sendmail	Mail-routing program
/usr/lib/sendmail.mx	Mail-routing program linked with the domain name service resolver
/etc/mail/main.cf	Sample configuration file for main systems
/etc/mail/sendmail.subsidiary.cf	Sample configuration file for subsidiary systems
/etc/mail/sendmail.cf	Configuration file for mail routing
/etc/mail/aliases	Mail-forwarding information
/etc/mail/sendmailvars	Table that stores macro and class definitions for lookup from sendmail.cf file
.sendmailvars.org_dir	NIS+ version of sendmailvars table
/usr/bin/newaliases	Symbolic link to /usr/lib/sendmail
/usr/bin/mailq	Symbolic link to /usr/lib/sendmail
/usr/bin/mailstats	File used to store mail statistics generated by /etc/mail/sendmail.st (if present)
/usr/bin/mconnect	Connects to the mailer for address verification and debugging
/usr/sbin/in.comsat	Mail notification daemon
/usr/sbin/syslogd	Error message logger, used by sendmail

NEW

New with SVR4.

Mail services are provided by a combination of these programs that interact as shown by the simplified diagram in Figure 1.6.

Users send messages using programs such as /bin/mailx or mailtool. See the manual pages for information about these programs.

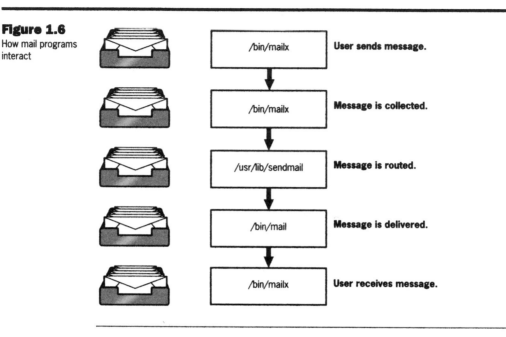

Figure 1.6
How mail programs interact

/bin/mailx	**User sends message.**
/bin/mailx	**Message is collected.**
/usr/lib/sendmail	**Message is routed.**
/bin/mail	**Message is delivered.**
/bin/mailx	**User receives message.**

The message is collected by the program that was used to generate it and is passed to the sendmail daemon. The sendmail daemon *parses* (divides into identifiable segments) the addresses in the message, using information from the configuration file /etc/mail/sendmail.cf to determine network name syntax, aliasing, forwarding information, and network topology. Using this information, sendmail determines the route a message must take to get to a recipient.

The sendmail daemon passes the message to the appropriate system. The /bin/mail program on the local system delivers the mail to the mailbox in the /var/mail/*username* directory of the recipient of the message.

The user is notified that mail has arrived and retrieves it using /bin/mail, /bin/mailx, mailtool, or a similar program.

The Sendmail Program

SunOS 5.*x* system software uses sendmail as a mail router. The sendmail program is responsible for receiving and delivering electronic mail messages. It is an interface between mail-reading programs such as mail, mailx, and mailtool, and mail-transport programs such as uucp. The sendmail program controls e-mail messages that users send, understands the recipients' addresses, chooses an appropriate delivery program, rewrites the addresses in a format that the delivery agent understands, reformats the mail headers as required, and, finally, passes the transformed message to the mail program for delivery.

Figure 1.7 shows how sendmail uses aliases. Programs that read mail, such as /usr/bin/mailx, can have aliases of their own, which are expanded before the message reaches sendmail.

As system administrator, you should decide on a policy for updating aliases and for forwarding mail messages. You might set up an aliases mailbox as a place for users to send requests for mail forwarding and for changes to their default mail alias. If your system uses NIS or NIS+, you can administer forwarding rather than forcing users to manage it themselves. A common mistake users make is to put a .forward file in the home directory of Host A that forwards mail to user@host-b. When the mail gets to Host B, sendmail looks up user in the NIS or NIS+ aliases and sends the message back to user@host-a, resulting in a loop and more bounced mail.

The sendmail Configuration File (sendmail.cf)

A *configuration file* controls the way that sendmail performs its functions. The configuration file determines the choice of delivery agents, address-rewriting rules, and the format of the mail header.

The sendmail program uses the information from the /etc/mail/sendmail.cf file to perform its functions. Each system has a default sendmail.cf file installed in the /etc/mail directory. You do not need to edit or change the default configuration file for mail servers or mail clients. The only systems that require a customized configuration file are the mailhost, a relay host, or a gateway. See "Mail Services Terminology" earlier in this chapter, or the glossary at the back of this book, for descriptions of each of these types of systems.

SunOS 5.x system software provides two default configuration files, which are also in the /etc/mail directory:

- A configuration file, named main.cf, for the system (or systems) you designate as the mailhost, a relay host, or a gateway

- A configuration file, named subsidiary.cf (a duplicate copy of the default sendmail.cf file)

Which configuration file you use on any individual system depends on the role the system plays in your mail service.

- For mail clients or mail servers, you do not need to do anything to set up or edit the default configuration file.

- To set up a mailhost, a relay host, or a gateway, copy the main.cf file and rename it sendmail.cf (in the /etc/mail directory). Then edit the sendmail.cf file to set these parameters needed for your mail configuration: relay mailer and relay host.

Figure 1.7

How sendmail uses
aliases

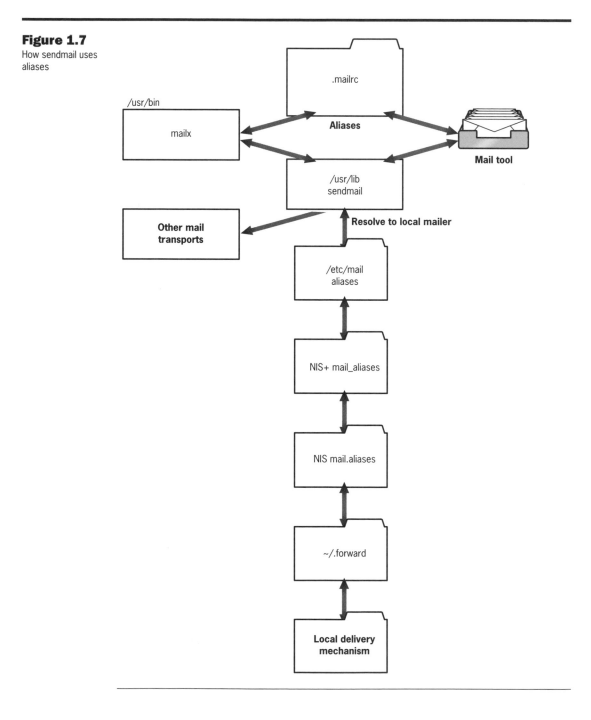

The following list describes some configuration parameters you may want to change, depending on the requirements of your site:

- Time values.

  - Specify how often sendmail runs the queue. The interval is typically set to between 15 minutes and 1 hour.

  - Specify read timeouts.

  - Specify how long a message remains in the queue before it is returned to the sender.

- Delivery modes specify how quickly mail will be delivered.

- Load limiting prevents wasted time during loaded periods by not attempting to deliver large messages, messages to many recipients, or messages to sites that have been down for a long time.

- Log level specifies what kinds of problems are logged.

- File modes.

  - setuid for sendmail.

  - Temporary file modes.

  - /etc/mail/aliases permissions.

See Chapter 3 for information on setting up the sendmail.cf files. See Chapter 4 for a detailed description of each of these parameters.

NEW

New with SVR4.

The sendmail Configuration Table

The sendmail program can define macros and classes in response to commands from the sendmail.cf file by looking up values in the sendmailvars configuration table. The sendmail.cf file can contain two such commands:

- Lines that begin with the L key letter are macro definitions, where the values assigned to the specified variable are obtained from the configuration table.

- Lines that begin with the G key letter are class definitions, where the values assigned to the specified variable are obtained from the configuration table.

The L command has the following syntax:

```
LXsearch_key
```

For example: Lm maildomain.

In this example, the search key maildomain is used to look up a value in the configuration table to assign to the variable *m*. Most often the single-letter variable name is uppercase, but for internal variables (such as m for the mail domain name), it is lowercase.

NOTE. *Lowercase variables are reserved for use by sendmail and may have special meanings to the sendmail program.*

The G command sets a class. It permits multiple entries, and has the following syntax:

```
GCsearch_key
```

For example: GVuucp-list.

In this example, the search key uucp-list is used to look up a value in the configuration table to assign to the class V.

In both cases, matching of the search key is case sensitive. Both commands have counterparts for defining macros or classes within the sendmail.cf file, rather than using the lookup table. D is the counterpart of L; C is the counterpart of G.

If NIS+ is used to administer the network, you can maintain a global version of the table sendmailvars.org_dir. In addition to the NIS+ table (or as an alternative), the table can be maintained in /etc/mail/sendmailvars files. The order in which these sources are searched by sendmail is controlled by the sendmailvars entry in the /etc/nsswitch.conf file. By default, the search order is files nisplus, which means that sendmail looks for information in the local table before going to the NIS+ table.

Entries in an /etc/mail/sendmailvars file have the following format:

```
search_key [value1 value2 value3 . . . ]
```

The search key may be followed by a Tab or a number of spaces; values are separated by a single space.

The NIS+ sendmailvars table has two columns: a Key column and a Value column. The Value column can have one or more values, each separated by a space, as shown in Table 1.7.

Table 1.7 **Examples of Key and Value Columns in an NIS+ sendmailvars Table**

Key Column	Value Column
maildomain	Eng.Sun.COM
uucp-list	castle oak cinderella

The names in the Value column are systems that uucp can access.

You should define most nondefault mail variables in the NIS+ table. However, in special cases—such as when a system has a local uucp connection or is a gateway between two Internet domains—you can override the global setting for a variable on a system by including the variable in the system's local /etc/mail/sendmailvars file.

.forward Files

Users can create a .forward file in their home directory that sendmail uses to temporarily redirect mail or send mail to a custom set of programs without bothering a system administrator. When troubleshooting mail problems, particularly problems of mail not being delivered to the expected address, always check the user's home directory for a .forward file.

An Overview of the Mail Service

The following sections describe the directory structure and files of the mail service and explain how the sendmail program and mail addressing work.

The Anatomy of the Mail Service

Files for the mail service are located in three directories: /bin, /etc/mail, and /usr/lib. Users' mailboxes are located in the /var/mail directory.

Table 1.8 shows the contents of the /bin directory that are used for mail services.

Table 1.8   **Contents of the /bin Directory That Are Used for Mail**

Name	Type	Description
mail	File	A user agent
mailcompat	File	A filter to store mail in 4.x mailbox format
mailq	Link	Link to /usr/lib/sendmail
mailstats	File	A file used to store mail statistics generated by the /etc/mail/sendmail.st file (if present)
mailx	File	A user agent
newaliases	Link	Link to /usr/lib/sendmail

Table 1.9 shows the contents of the /etc/mail directory.
Table 1.10 shows the contents of the /usr/lib directory.

Table 1.9 **Contents of the /etc/mail Directory**

Name	Type	Description
Mail.rc	File	Default settings for the mailtool user agent
aliases	File	Mail-forwarding information
aliases.dir	File	Binary form of mail-forwarding information (created by running newaliases)
aliases.pag	File	Binary form of mail-forwarding information (created by running newaliases)
mailx.rc	File	Default settings for the mailx user agent
newaliases	File	Command that creates the binary form of the aliases file
main.cf	File	Sample configuration file for main systems
sendmail.cf	File	Configuration file for mail routing
sendmail.fc	File	Frozen configuration file
sendmail.hf	File	Help file used by the SMTP HELP command
sendmail.st	File	The sendmail statistics file (If this file is present, sendmail logs the amount of traffic through each mailer.)
sendmailvars	File	Table that stores macro and class definitions for lookup from sendmail.cf
sendmailvars.org_dir	Table	NIS+ version of sendmailvars table
sendmail.subsidiary.cf	File	Sample configuration file for subsidiary systems

NEW
New with SVR4.

Table 1.10 **Contents of the /usr/lib Directory**

Name	Type	Description
sendmail	File	The routing program, also known as the mail transport agent
sendmail.mx	File	Mail-routing program linked with the domain name service

Spooling directories for delivered mail are located in the /var/mail directory, as shown in Table 1.11. Mail that has not been delivered is stored in the /var/spool/mqueue directory.

Table 1.11   **Contents of the /var/mail Directory**

Name	Type	Description
mailbox1	File	Mailboxes for delivered mail
mailbox2	File	Mailboxes for delivered mail
mailbox3	File	Mailboxes for delivered mail

How the Mail Service Works

Figure 1.8 shows how sendmail interacts with the other programs in the mail system. The user interacts with a mail generating and sending program. When the mail is submitted, the generator calls sendmail, which routes the message to the correct mailer(s).

How sendmail Works

The sendmail program collects a message from a program such as mailx or mailtool, edits the message header as required by the destination mailer, and calls appropriate mailers to do delivery or queuing for network transmission.

NOTE.   *The sendmail program never edits or changes the body of a message. Any changes that it makes to interpret e-mail addresses are made only in the header of the message.*

Argument Processing and Address Parsing

When sendmail receives input, it collects recipient names (either from the command line or from the SMTP protocol) and generates two files. One is an envelope that contains a list of recipients and information about delivery. The other file contains the header and the body of the message. The sendmail program expands aliases, including mailing lists, and validates as much as possible of the remote recipient; sendmail checks syntax and verifies local recipients. Detailed checking of host names is deferred until delivery. As local recipients are verified, messages are forwarded to them.

After parsing the recipient lists, sendmail appends each name to both the envelope and the header of the message. When a name is aliased or forwarded, it retains the old name in the list and sets a flag to tell the delivery phase to ignore this recipient. The lists are kept free from duplicates, preventing alias loops and duplicate messages delivered to the same recipient, which can occur if a recipient is in two different alias groups.

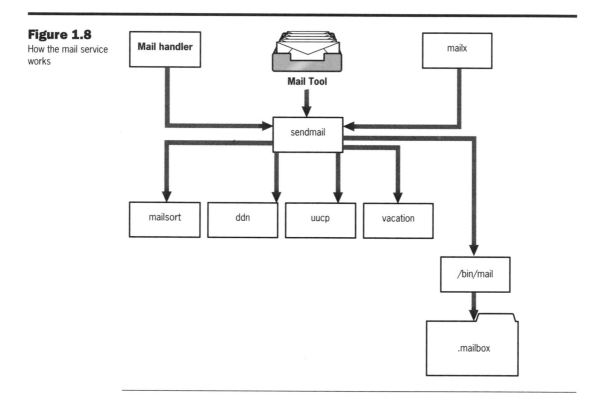

Figure 1.8

How the mail service works

NOTE.   *Users may receive duplicate copies of the same message when alias lists contain e-mail addresses for the same person using different syntax. The sendmail program cannot always match the e-mail addresses as duplicates of one another.*

Message Collection

The sendmail program then collects the message. The message should have a header at the beginning. The header and the body of the message must be separated by a blank line. No formatting requirements are imposed on the message body except that they must be lines of text no longer than 1024 bytes. The sendmail program stores the header in memory and stores the body of the message in a temporary file. To simplify the program interface, the message is collected, even if no names are valid. The message is returned with an error.

NOTE.   *Until now, sendmail could not transmit binary data as part of mail messages. With the advent of multimedia mailtool, users now can transmit binary data. It must, however, be encoded by mailtool. Sendmail does not do any automatic encoding of binary data. Refer to the documentation for Mail Tool for information on how to encode and decode electronic mail messages.*

Message Delivery

For each unique mailer and host in the recipient list, sendmail calls the appropriate mailer. Each invocation of a mailer sends a message to all users on one host. Mailers that accept only one recipient at a time are handled properly.

The sendmail program sends the message to the mailer using one of the same interfaces used to submit a message to sendmail (using the conventional UNIX argument vector/return status, speaking over a pair of UNIX pipes, and speaking SMTP over a TCP connection). Each copy of the message has a customized header attached to the beginning of it. The mailer catches and checks the status code, and a suitable error message is given as appropriate. The exit code must conform to a system standard. If a nonstandard exit code is used, the message "Services unavailable" is used.

Queuing for Retransmission

When the mailer returns a status that shows it might be able to handle the mail later (for example, the next host is down, or the phone is busy for uucp), sendmail queues it and tries again later.

Return to Sender

If errors occur during processing, sendmail returns the message to the sender for retransmission. The letter may be mailed back or written to the dead.letter file in the sender's home directory.

How Mail Addressing Works

Assuming that you are using the default rule set in the sendmail.cf file, the following examples show the route an e-mail message takes, depending on how it is addressed.

Mail within a domain addressed with only the user's login name goes to the aliases file on the mailhost (or to the Aliases database) and is sent to the address found in the database. In the example shown in Figure 1.9, mail addressed to user winsor goes to the mailhost and is forwarded to the host named castle.

Mail within a domain addressed with the user's login name and host name goes directly to the host system without any additional processing. In the example shown in Figure 1.10, mail addressed to user winsor at the host named castle goes directly to the host named castle.

Figure 1.9
Delivery path for mail addressed with username only

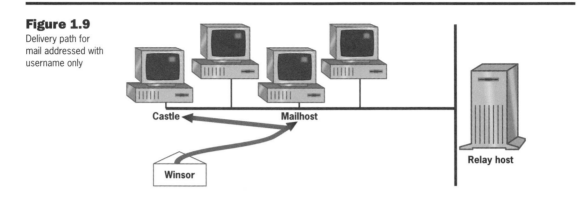

Figure 1.10
Delivery path for mail addressed with username and host name

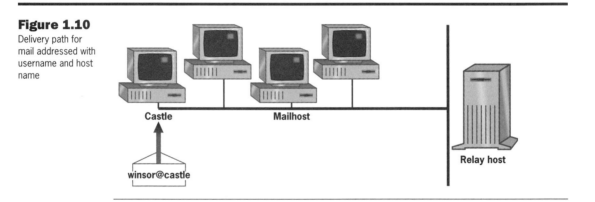

Mail within a domain addressed with the user's login name and domain name goes to the aliases file on the mailhost (or to the Aliases database). If the mailhost has an alias, it redirects the message to the host system. In the example shown in Figure 1.11, mail addressed to user winsor@Eng goes to the mailhost and is then forwarded to the host named castle.

Mail addressed with the user's name and a fully qualified domain name goes to the mailhost, which sends it to the relay host. The relay host sends the message to the host system. When the mail comes from within the recipient's domain, however, the mailhost recognizes the domain name and does not send the message to the relay host. In the example shown in Figure 1.12, mail addressed to user ignatz@Eng.sun.com from outside the engineering domain goes to the sender's mailhost, then to the sender's relay host, and is then forwarded to the recipient's relay host, the recipient's mail host, and finally to the host named oak.

Figure 1.11

Delivery path for mail addressed with username and domain name

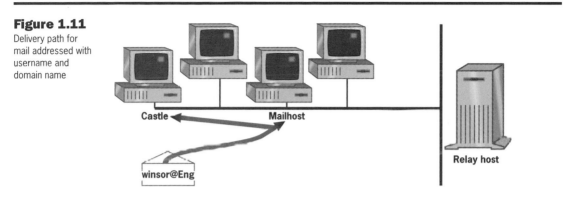

Figure 1.12

Delivery path for mail addressed with username and fully qualified domain name

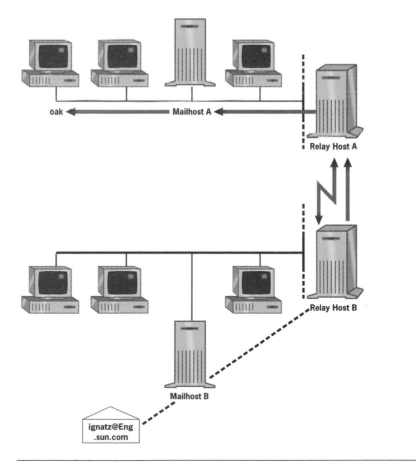

When a recipient responds to a message that was sent within a domain not running NIS or NIS+, without /etc/aliases files on each system, and using only the login name as an address, the sender's host name is appended to the address. If a recipient responds to such a message, the message is routed to the named system, then to the mailhost. If the named host system is not available, the message is delayed until the host responds, or the message bounces after three days of trying. In the example shown in Figure 1.13, if winsor@castle sent a copy to fred, and the recipient uses the information in the message header to reply, a message to fred@castle goes first to castle, then to the mailhost, and finally to fred@ash, Fred's real mail destination.

Figure 1.13

Delivery path for mail addressed with username and the sender's host name

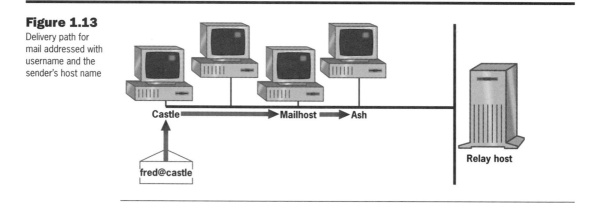

2

Planning Mail Services

Planning Your Mail System

THIS CHAPTER DESCRIBES FOUR BASIC MAIL CONFIGURATIONS AND briefly outlines the tasks required to set up each configuration. You may find the following sections useful if you need to set up a new mail system or are expanding an existing one. The configurations start with the most basic case (mail completely local, no connection to the outside world) and increase in complexity to a two-domain configuration with a gateway. More complex systems are beyond the scope of this book.

Planning Your Mail System

To set up a mail system, regardless of its configuration, you need these elements:

- A sendmail.cf configuration file on each system

- Alias files with an alias for each user to point to the place where mail is stored

- A mailbox to store (or spool) mail files for each user

- A postmaster alias for the person who administers mail services

See Chapter 3 for detailed information on how to set up these elements.

How you set up the configuration file and the alias file and where you put the mailboxes depends on the configuration you choose.

Local Mail Only

The simplest mail configuration, shown in Figure 2.1, is one mail server with a number of workstations connected to it. Mail is completely local. One system is both the mail server (providing mail spooling for client mailboxes) and the mailhost. Mail addresses are parsed using the /etc/mail/aliases files. No naming service is used.

To set up this kind of a local mail configuration, assuming that the mail clients mount their mail files from /var/mail on the mailhost, you need:

- The default sendmail.cf file in the /etc/mail directory on each system (no editing required)

- A server designated as the mailhost (Add mailhost to the /etc/hosts file on the mailhost.)

- The mailhost IP address line added to the /etc/hosts file of each mail client

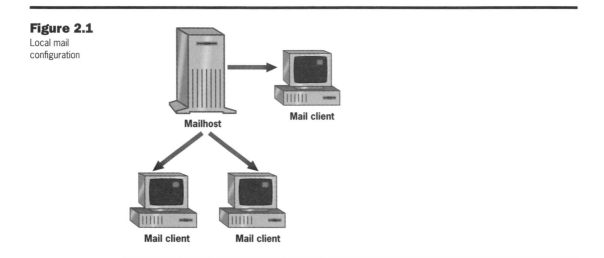

Figure 2.1
Local mail
configuration

- Entries in each mail client's /etc/vfstab file to mount the /var/mail directory when mailboxes are located on the mail server

See Chapter 3 for detailed information on how to set up mail services.

Local Mail and a uucp Connection

The most common mail configuration in a small network is shown in Figure 2.2. One system is the mail server, the mailhost, and also the relay host to the outside world. Mail is distributed using the /etc/mail/aliases files. No naming service is required.

To set up this kind of a mail configuration, assuming that the mail clients mount their mail files from /var/mail on the mailhost, you need:

- The main.cf file on the mailhost. You must edit the file to select a major relay mailer.

- The default subsidiary.cf file on each mail client system (no editing required).

- A server designated as the mailhost. (Add mailhost to the /etc/hosts file on the mailhost; add the mailhost IP address line to the /etc/hosts file of all mail clients.)

- Matching /etc/mail/aliases files on any system that has a local mailbox.

Figure 2.2

Local mail
configuration with a
uucp connection

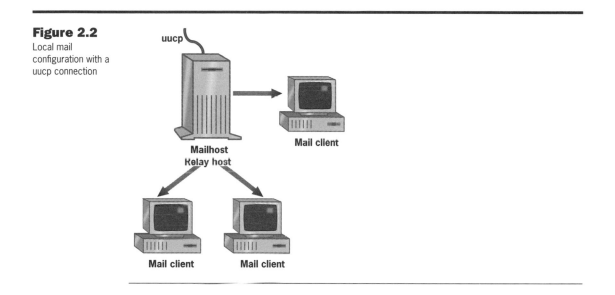

- Entries in each mail client's /etc/vfstab file to mount the /var/mail directory when mailboxes are located on the mail server.

See Chapter 3 for detailed information on how to set up mail services.

One Domain, Two Networks, and a Router

The mail configuration shown in Figure 2.3 has one domain, two networks, and a router. In this configuration, the mail server, the mailhost, and the relay host (or hosts) are likely to be different systems. To make administering and distributing mail easier, a naming service is used.

To set up this kind of a mail configuration, assuming that the mail clients may have local or remote /var/mail files, you need everything specified in Table 2.1.

Two Domains and a Gateway

The mail configuration shown in Figure 2.4 has two domains and a gateway. In this configuration, the mail server, the mailhost, and the relay host (or hosts) for each domain are likely to be different systems. To make administering and distributing mail easier, a naming service is used.

Table 2.2 lists the requirements for this mail configuration.

Figure 2.3

One domain, two networks, a router, and multiple uucp connections

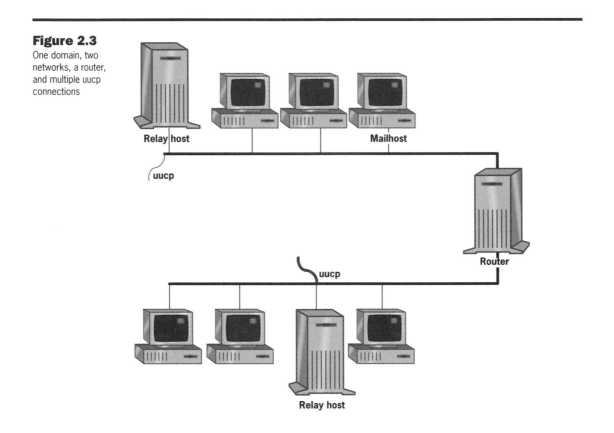

Table 2.1   Requirements for One-Domain, Two-Network Mail Configuration

Category	Requirements
Relay host	The main.cf file on the relay hosts—the systems with uucp connections. You must edit the file to select a major relay connector. You may want to define a mail relay host that knows about all connections. Special rules added to the sendmail.cf file are nice but are not mandatory.
Mailhost	One system designated as the mailhost. (Add mailhost to the Hosts data-base on the mailhost system.)
Mail server	Adequate spooling space for client mailboxes.
Mail client	The subsidiary.cf file on each mail client system (no editing required). Entries in each mail client's /etc/vfstab file to mount the /var/mail directory.
NIS+ tables	mail_aliases.org_dir tables for NIS+ with a mail alias entry for all users to point to where their mail is stored.

New to SVR4.

Figure 2.4

Two domains with a gateway

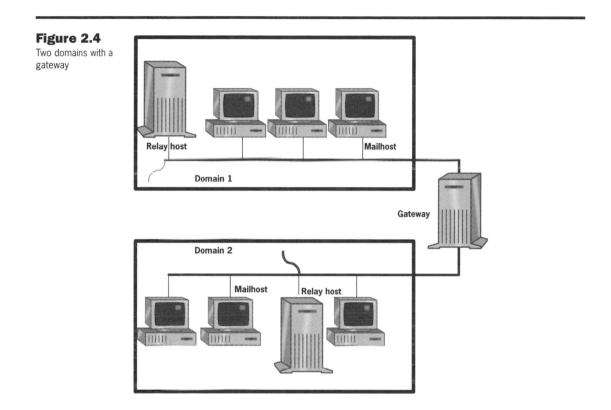

Relay host · Mailhost · Domain 1 · Gateway · Domain 2 · Mailhost · Relay host

Table 2.2   Requirements for Two Domains, One Route Configuration

Category	Requirements
Gateway	Complex gateway systems usually need a customized sendmail.cf file with special rules added.
Relay host	The main.cf file on the relay hosts—the systems with uucp connections. (You must edit the file to select a major relay mailer.) It might be useful to define a mail relay host that knows about all connections. (Special rules added to the sendmail.cf file are nice but are not mandatory.) **NOTE:** The subsidiary.cf file has an entry (the CV class) that you can use to define "local" uucp connections (such as the system at the left of Domain 1 in Figure 2.4). If you define such a local uucp connection, users must address mail using the format uucphost!remote-system!address.
Mailhost	One system designated as the mailhost. (Add mailhost to the Hosts database on the mailhost system.)

Table 2.2   **Requirements for Two Domains, One Route Configuration (Continued)**

Category	Requirements
Mail server	Adequate spooling space for client mailboxes.
Mail client	The sendmail.cf file on each mail client system (no editing required). Entries in each mail client's /etc/vfstab file to mount the /var/mail directory.
NIS+ tables	mail_aliases.org_dir tables for NIS+ with a mail alias entry for each user to point to NIS+ tables.

New to SVR4.

C H A P T E R

Setting Up and Administering Mail Services

Preparing to Set Up Mail Services

Setting Up Mail Services

Testing Your Mail Configuration

Administering Your Mail Configuration

Troubleshooting Your Mail Configuration

T HIS CHAPTER DESCRIBES HOW TO SET UP, TEST, ADMINISTER, AND troubleshoot mail services. If you are not familiar with administering mail services, read Chapter 1 for an introduction to the terminology and structure of the mail services. Read Chapter 2 for descriptions of several mail services configurations.

Preparing to Set Up Mail Services

You can set up a mail service relatively easily if your site does not provide connections to electronic mail services outside your company, or if your company is in a single domain. Setting up complicated sites with multiple domains is beyond the scope of this book. Chapter 4 contains information about how to create the more complicated configuration files required for sites with multiple domains.

Mail requires three types of configurations for local mail and a fourth for communication with networks outside of your domain. These configurations can be combined on the same system or provided by separate systems. A fifth, optional type of mail configuration is called a gateway. Table 3.1 describes each of these configurations.

Table 3.1 **Mail Configurations**

Configuration	Description
Mail server	You need to have at least one mail server. The mail server stores mailboxes in the /var/mail directory.
Mailhost	You need at least one mailhost. The mailhost resolves difficult e-mail addresses and reroutes mail within your domain.
Mail client	Mail clients are users who have mailboxes either locally or on a mail server.
Relay host	A relay host manages communication with networks outside of your domain.
Gateway	A gateway is a connection between different communications networks. A relay host may also act as a gateway. You must add rules to the sendmail.cf file to set up a gateway. See Chapter 4 for information about adding rules. Another helpful reference is Chapter 15 of the *UNIX System Administration Handbook*, published by Prentice-Hall. (See the bibliography at the back of this book for more information.) If you have to set up a gateway, find a gateway configuration file that is close to what you need, and modify it to fit your situation.

Before you begin to set up your mail service, choose the systems that will act as mail servers, mailhosts, and relay hosts. You should also make a list of all the mail clients you will be providing service for, and include the location of their mailboxes. This list will help you when you are ready to create mail aliases for your users. See Chapter 1 for more information about the function each of these systems provides. For your convenience, guidelines about which systems are good candidates for mail server, mailhost, and relay host are described in the following sections.

Setting Up Mail Services

To simplify the setup instructions, the following sections tell you what you need to do to set up individual mail servers, mailhosts, mail clients, and relay hosts. If a system in your mail services configuration is acting in more than one capacity, simply follow the appropriate instructions for each type of system. For example, if your mailhost and mail server are the same system, follow the directions for setting up that system as a mailhost and then follow the directions for setting up the same system as a mail server.

NOTE.   *The following procedures for setting up a mail server and mail client apply when mailboxes are NFS-mounted. You do not need to follow these procedures when mailboxes are maintained in locally mounted /var/mail directories.*

Setting Up a Mail Server

The *mail server* is responsible for routing all mail from a client. The only resource requirement for a mail server is that it have adequate spooling space for client mailboxes. See Chapter 1 for recommendations about spooling space.

New to SVR4.

To set up a mail server, the /var directory must be exported. On SunOS 5.*x* systems, type **share** and press Return to check whether the /var directory is exported. In this example, the /var/mail directory is not exported:

```
cinderella% share
cinderella%
```

If the /var directory is not exported, become superuser, then type **share -F nfs -o rw /var/mail** and press Return. You can type **share** with no arguments to verify that the directory is exported. You should also add the line to the /etc/dfs/dfstab file so that the file system is shared when the system is rebooted.

```
cinderella% share
cinderella% su
Password:
cinderella# share -F nfs -o rw /var/mail
cinderella# share
```

```
-              /var/mail    rw  ""
cinderella# vi /etc/dfs/dfstab
Add the line:
share -F nfs -o rw /var/mail
```

NOTE. *The sendmail program automatically creates mailboxes in the /var/mail directory the first time a message is delivered. You do not need to create individual mailboxes for your mail clients.*

Setting Up a Mail Client

A *mail client* is a user of mail services, with a mailbox on a mail server and a mail alias in the Aliases database or local /etc/mail/aliases file to point to the location of the mailbox.

NOTE. *You will use Administration Tool as part of the steps for setting up a mail client. Before you can use Administration Tool to edit the Hosts and Aliases databases, you must be a member of the sysadmin group (GID 14). If the system is running NIS+, you must also have the appropriate create and delete permissions for each NIS+ database. See the* Solaris® System Administrator's Guide *for information on how to set up Administration Tool security. See Part II of this book for more information about NIS+ security, or refer to* All about Administering NIS+. *The bibliography at the back of this book has complete references for these sources*

Follow these steps to set up a SunOS 5.*x* mail client with a mailbox on a mail server. (When instructions for setting up a SunOS 4.*x* mail client are different, the SunOS 4.*x* instructions are included in parentheses.)

1. Become superuser on the mail client's system.

2. Create a /var/mail mount point on the mail client's system.

3. Edit the /etc/vfstab file and add an entry to mount the /var/mail directory from the mail server on the local /var/mail directory. With an entry in the client system's /etc/vfstab file, the client's mailbox automatically will be mounted any time that system is rebooted. (To set up a SunOS 4.*x* mail client, edit the client's /etc/fstab file.)

4. Type **mountall** to mount the mailbox. The client's mailbox is mounted. (On SunOS 4.*x* mail clients, type **mount -a** to mount the mailbox.)

5. Use the Administration Tool to edit the Hosts database and add an entry for the mail server. (For SunOS 4.*x* systems, edit the /etc/hosts file and add an entry for the mail server.)

6. Add the user accounts for the client system to the Aliases database. See "Creating Mail Aliases" later in this chapter for information about how to create mail aliases for different types of mail configurations. (For SunOS 4.*x* systems, add the client to the /etc/aliases file.)

NOTE. *The sendmail program automatically creates mailboxes in the /var/mail directory the first time a message is delivered. You do not need to create individual mailboxes for your mail clients.*

This example sets up the SunOS 5.*x* system newton as a mail client of the system cinderella:

```
newton% su
Password:
newton# mkdir /var/mail
newton# vi /etc/vfstab
Add the line:
cinderella:/var/mail  -  /var/mail  nfs  -  yes  rw
newton# mountall
newton# admintool&
```

Figures 3.1 through 3.12 show the Administration Tool screens and steps for adding user accounts to the Aliases database.

Figure 3.1

Open the Administration Tool window.

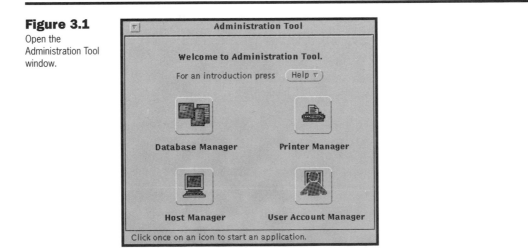

Figure 3.2

Display the Database Manager window.

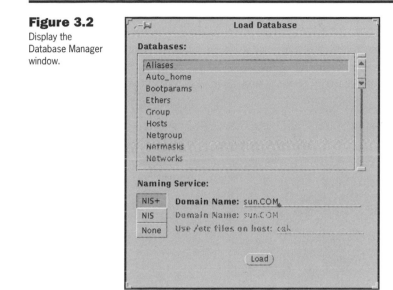

Figure 3.3

Click SELECT on the pushpin in the upper-left corner of the window.

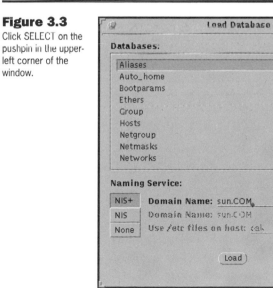

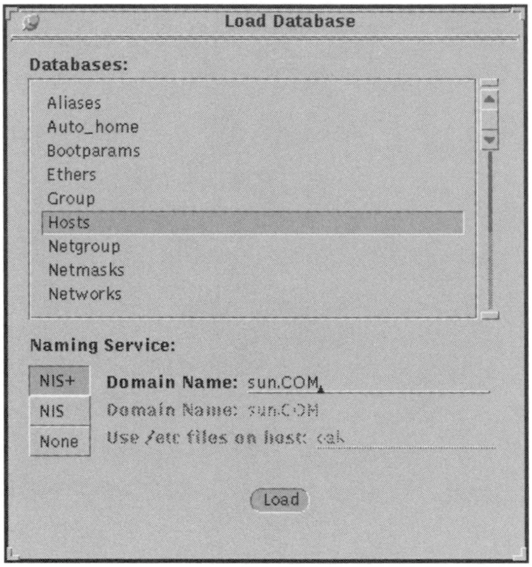

Figure 3.4

Choose the Hosts database and click SELECT on Load.

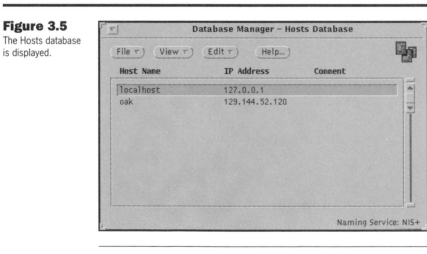

Figure 3.5

The Hosts database is displayed.

Figure 3.6

Choose Add Entry from the Edit menu.

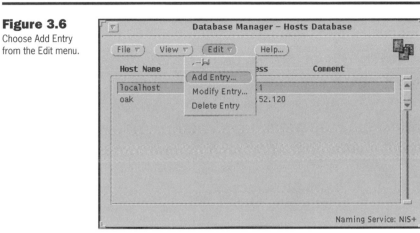

Figure 3.7

Type entry in the Add Entry window.

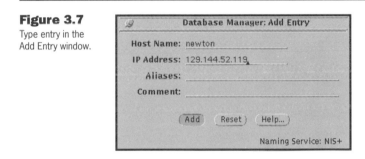

Figure 3.8

The hosts entry is added to the Hosts database.

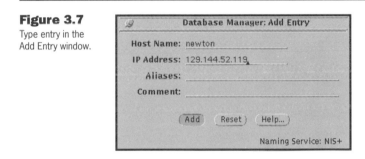

Figure 3.9

From the Database Manager window, display the Aliases Database window.

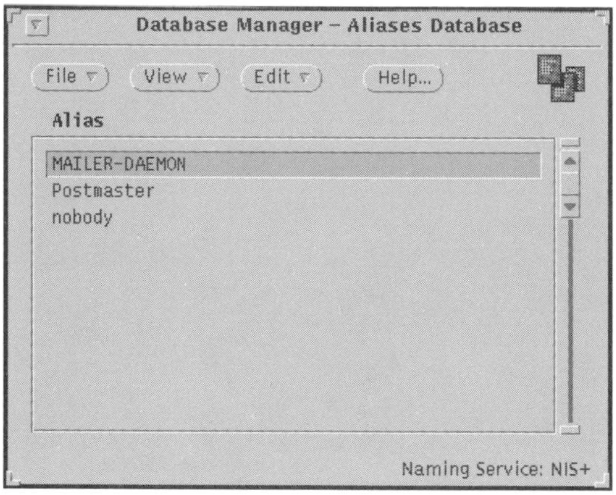

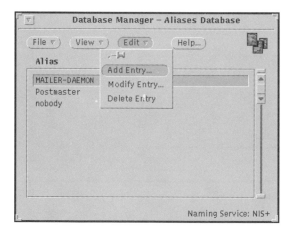

Figure 3.10

Choose Add Entry from the Edit menu.

Figure 3.11

Type entries into the Add Entry window.

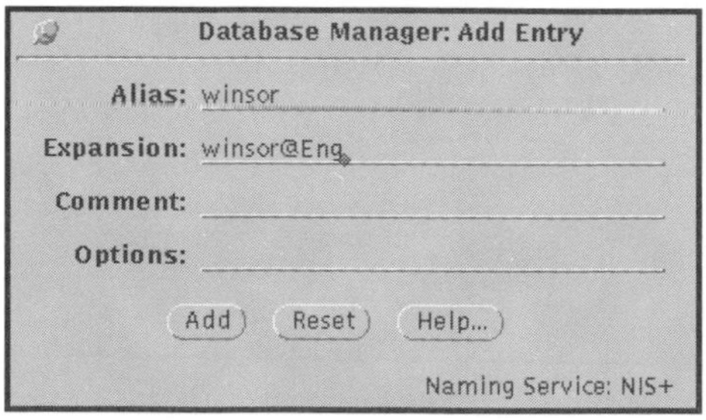

Figure 3.12

The entry is added to the Aliases database.

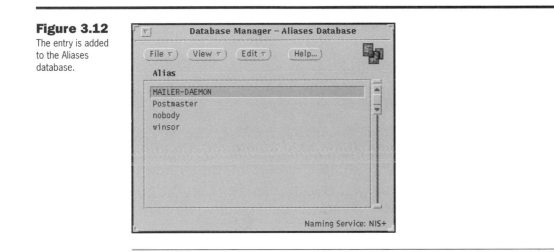

Setting Up a Mailhost

A mailhost resolves difficult e-mail addresses and reroutes mail within your domain. A good candidate for a mailhost is a system that connects you to the outside world or to a parent domain. Before you begin this task, you must be a member of the UNIX group sysadmin (GID 14) and have the appropriate NIS+ read and write permissions for the Hosts database.

1. Log into the mailhost system as yourself.

2. Use Administration Tool's Database Manager to edit the Hosts database, and type **mailhost** in the Aliases field of the mailhost system, as shown in the example in Figure 3.13. The system is designated as a mailhost. If you are not using NIS+, NIS, or DNS, you must create an entry in the /etc/hosts file for each system on the network. The /etc/hosts entry should use this format: *IP address mailhost_name* mailhost.

   NOTE. *Aliases are not automatically displayed as part of the Hosts database information, although you can find them by using the Show Entries that Match item from the View menu. Comments, however, are always displayed. If you want to easily identify mailhosts when you list information in the Hosts database, type* **mailhost** *in both the Comment and the Aliases fields for mailhost systems.*

Figure 3.13
Type **mailhost** in the Aliases and Comment text fields.

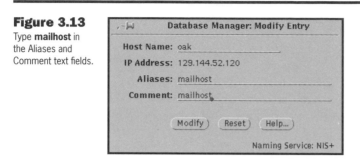

3. Type **cp /etc/mail/main.cf /etc/mail/sendmail.cf** and press Return. The main.cf file is copied and renamed sendmail.cf.

```
# cp /etc/mail/main.cf /etc/mail/sendmail.cf
#
```

4. Reboot the mailhost and test your mail configuration. See "Testing Your Mail Configuration" later in the chapter for more information.

```
# init 6
```

Setting Up a Relay Host

A *relay host* manages communications with networks outside of your domain that use the same relay mailer. The mailer on the sending relay host must match the mailer on the receiving system.

A good candidate for a relay host is a system attached to an Ethernet and to phone lines or a system configured as a router to the Internet. You may want to configure the mailhost as the relay host or configure another system as relay host. You may choose to configure more than one relay host for your domain. Each relay host you configure must use a mailer that matches the mailer on the connecting system. If you have uucp connections, you should configure the system (or systems) that have the uucp connections as the relay host.

1. Become superuser on the relay host system.

2. Type **cp /etc/mail/main.cf /etc/mail/sendmail.cf** and press Return. The main.cf file is copied and renamed sendmail.cf.

3. Edit the /etc/mail/sendmail.cf file and make the following changes:

   a. If your relay mailer is uucp, you do not need to change this entry. If your relay mailer is not uucp, change the default entry (DMsmartuucp) to the entry that is appropriate for your relay mailer. Available mailers are smartuucp (the default), ddn, ether, and uucp. You can specify a different relay mailer for each relay host (if appropriate). You can define rule sets for other relay mailers in the sendmail.main.cf file. See "Mailers" in Chapter 1 for a description of each of the default relay mailers.

b. In the entry DR ddn-gateway, replace *ddn-gateway* with the name of your relay host. The DR entry defines the relay host.

c. In the entry CR ddn-gateway, replace *ddn-gateway* with the name of your relay host. The CR entry defines the class of the relay host. You can designate one or more hosts as a member of this class.

d. (Optional) Add a Dmmail_domain or Lmmaildomain entry to define the mail domain name. If the macro is not defined, the naming service domain name is used, with the first component stripped off. For example, Ecd.East.Sun.COM becomes East.Sun.Com. If you use the L command, sendmail looks up the name to use in the sendmailvars table, using maildomain as the search key.

e. Save the edits.

4. Reboot the mailhost and test your mail configuration.

In this example, the system oak is set up as a relay host:

```
castle% rlogin oak
oak% su
Password:
# cp /etc/mail/main.cf /etc/mail/sendmail.cf
# vi /etc/mail/sendmail.cf
Replace DR ddn-gateway and CR ddn-gateway with:
DR oak
CR oak
Save changes and quit.
# init 6
```

Setting Up a Gateway

A *gateway* is a connection between different communications networks. A relay host may also act as a gateway. You must add rules to the sendmail.cf file to set up a gateway. Adding rules to the sendmail.cf file is beyond the scope of this chapter. See Chapter 4 for information about adding rules. Another helpful reference is the *UNIX System Administration Handbook,* Chapter 15; see the bibliography at the back of this book for the complete reference.

If you have to set up a gateway, your best bet is to find a gateway configuration file that is close to what you need and modify it to fit your situation. Most gateway files must be customized for each site. The main.cf file is a good place to start.

Creating Mail Aliases

This section describes how to use the Database Manager to create, modify, and delete aliases in the Aliases database. If you do not want to use Administration Tool to create aliases, you can use the aliasadm command to create, modify, and delete aliases from a command line. See the aliasadm(1M) manual page for more information.

Adding Aliases to an NIS+ Alias Database Using the Database Manager

New to SVR4.

To add aliases to an NIS+ Alias database using the Database Manager, follow these steps:

1. If necessary, type **admintool&** and press Return to start the Administration Tool. The Administration Tool window is displayed, as shown in Figure 3.14.

Figure 3.14
The Administration
Tool window

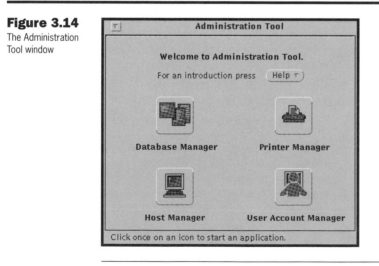

2. Click SELECT on the Database Manager icon. The Database Manager window is displayed, as shown in Figure 3.15. Because the Aliases database is the first database listed, it is automatically selected.

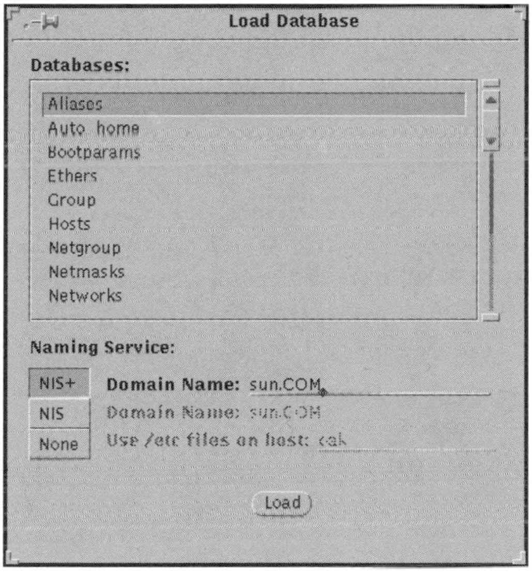

Figure 3.15
The Database
Manager window

3. Choose the naming service you want to use and click SELECT on Load. The Aliases database for the naming service you choose is displayed. In the example shown in Figure 3.16, the default list of aliases—MAILER-DAEMON, Postmaster, and nobody—is shown.

4. Choose Add Entry from the Edit menu, as shown in Figure 3.17. The Add Entry window is displayed, as shown in Figure 3.18.

5. Type the alias in the Alias text field and the expansion for the alias in the Expansion field. In the example shown in Figure 3.19, the alias is winsor and the expanded name is winsor@Eng.

6. When the information is entered correctly, click SELECT on Add. The information is added to the Aliases database, as shown in Figure 3.20.

Figure 3.16

The Aliases
Database window
with the default list
of aliases

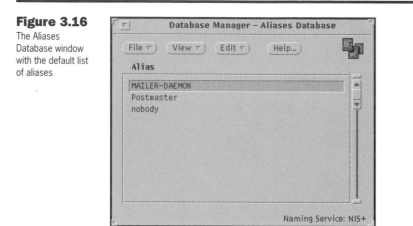

Figure 3.17

Choose Add Entry
from the Edit menu.

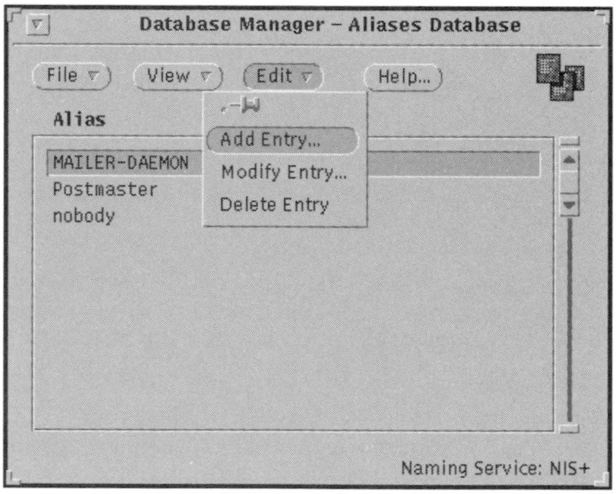

Changing Entries in an NIS+ Aliases Database

New to SVR4.

This section describes how to change entries in an NIS+ Aliases database using the Database Manager. The steps in this section start from the Aliases Database window. If you need instructions for how to display the Aliases Database window, see "Adding Aliases to an NIS+ Alias Database Using the Database Manager," just preceding this section.

1. Click SELECT on the entry you want to modify. The entry is highlighted, as shown in Figure 3.21.

Figure 3.18
The Add Entry
window

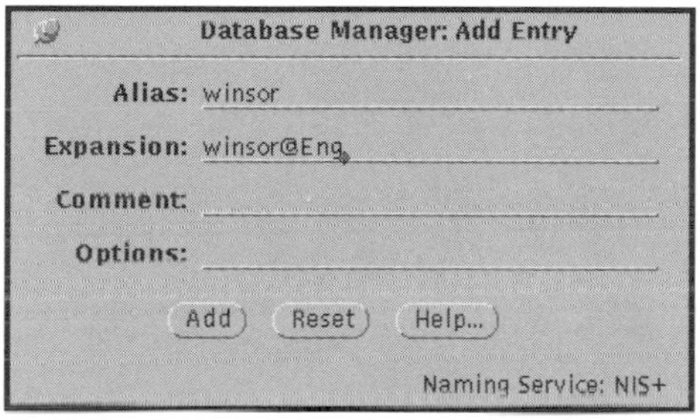

Figure 3.19
Type the information
in the text fields in
the Add Entry
window.

Figure 3.20
The Aliases
Database window
shows the new entry.

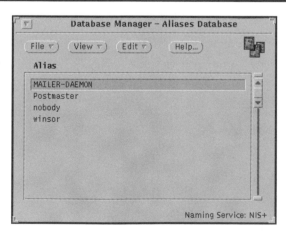

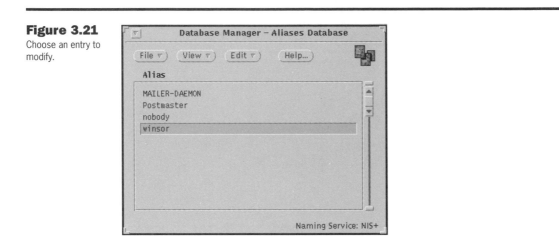

Figure 3.21
Choose an entry to modify.

2. Choose Modify Entry from the Edit menu. The Modify Entry window is displayed, with the current information about the alias displayed in the text fields, as shown in Figure 3.22.

Figure 3.22
Current information about the alias is displayed.

3. Change the entry as needed. You can edit existing information in the text field or add new expansions to the Expansion text field. In the example shown in Figure 3.23, the current alias is edited to add jwinsor to the Expansion field.

4. When the entry is modified, click SELECT on Modify. The information for the entry is modified. The information in the Aliases Database window is modified only if you changed the alias name itself. Changed expansion information is not displayed.

Figure 3.23

Modify the Aliases Database entry.

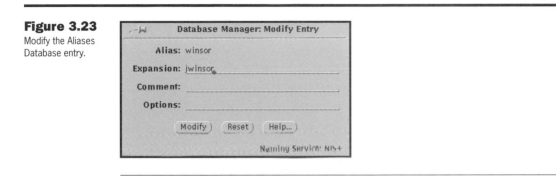

Deleting Entries from an NIS+ Aliases Database

This section describes how to delete entries from an NIS+ Aliases database using the Database Manager. The steps in this section start from the Aliases Database window. If you need instructions for how to display the Aliases Database window, see "Adding Aliases to an NIS+ Alias Database Using the Database Manager" earlier in this chapter.

Follow these steps to delete an alias entry from the Aliases database:

1. Click SELECT on the entry in the Aliases Database window that you want to delete. The entry is highlighted, as shown in Figure 3.24.

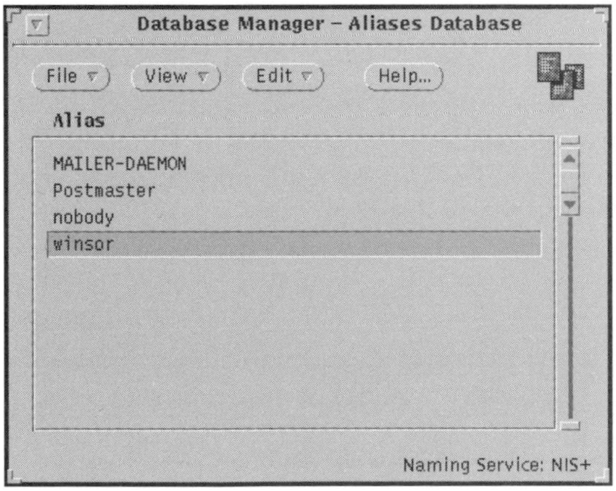

Figure 3.24

Choose an entry to delete.

2. Choose Delete Entry from the Edit menu. A notice is displayed, shown in Figure 3.25, asking you to confirm deletion of the entry.

Figure 3.25
The Delete Aliases
Notice window

3. If you do not want to delete the entry, click SELECT on Cancel. To delete the entry, click SELECT on Delete. The entry is deleted from the Aliases database and is removed from the list of aliases displayed in the Aliases Database window.

Setting Up NIS Alias Files

It is likely that you have a network that has a mixture of systems running SunOS 4.*x* and SunOS 5.*x* system software. To help you administer networks with systems running different versions of SunOS system software, this section describes how to set up mail aliases on a SunOS 4.*x* NIS master server.

NOTE. *On SunOS 4.*x* systems, the aliases file is located in the /etc directory, not in /etc/mail.*

The /etc/aliases file on an NIS master contains all names by which a system or person is known. The NIS master is searched if there is no match in the local /etc/aliases (for SunOS 4.*x* systems) or /etc/mail/aliases (for SunOS 5.*x* systems) file. The sendmail program uses the NIS master file to determine mailing addresses. See the aliases(5) manual page for more information.

The /etc/aliases file on the NIS master should contain entries for all mail clients. You can either edit the file on each system or edit the file on one system and copy it to each of the other systems.

Aliases are of the form:

```
name: name1, name2,...
```

You can alias local names or domains. For example, an alias entry for user fred who has a mailbox on the system oak and who is in the domain Trees would have this entry in the /etc/aliases file:

```
fred: fred@Trees
```

NOTE. *Because Administration Tool is new with SunOS 5.*x* system software, it is not available on SunOS 4.*x* systems. Therefore, you must edit the /etc/aliases file on SunOS 4.*x* systems manually.*

Follow these steps to set up NIS mail aliases files:

1. Compile a list of each of your mail clients, the locations of their mailboxes, and the names of the mail server systems.

2. Become superuser on the NIS master server.

3. Edit the /etc/aliases file and make the following entries:

   a. Add an entry for each mail client.

   b. Change the entry "Postmaster: root" to the mail address of the person who is designated as postmaster. See "Setting Up the Postmaster Alias" later in the chapter for more information.

   c. If you have created a mailbox for administration of a mail server, create an entry for "root: *mailbox@mailserver.*"

   d. Save the changes.

4. Edit the /etc/hosts file on the NIS master server and create an entry for each mail server.

5. Type **cd /var/yp** and press Return.

6. Type **make** and press Return. The changes in the /etc/hosts and /etc/aliases files are propagated to NIS slave systems. It takes a few minutes, at most, for the aliases to take effect.

Setting Up Local Mail Alias Files

The /etc/mail/aliases file on a local SunOS 5.*x* system contains all names by which a system or person is known. The sendmail program uses this file to determine mailing addresses. See the aliases(5) manual page for more information.

The /etc/mail/aliases file of each system should contain entries for all mail user accounts. You can either edit the file on each system or edit the file on one system and copy it to each of the other systems.

You can use Administration Tool to edit local /etc/mail/aliases files.

NOTE. *Before you can use Administration Tool to edit a local /etc/mail/aliases file, you must either have superuser access to the local system or be a member of the sysadmin group (GID 14).*

It is a good idea to create an administrative account for each mail server. You do this by assigning root a mailbox on the mail server and adding an entry to the /etc/mail/aliases file for root. For example, if the system oak is a mailbox server, add the entry "root: sysadmin@oak" to the /etc/mail/aliases file.

To set up local mail aliases files:

1. Compile a list of each of your mail clients and the locations of their mailboxes.

2. Become superuser on the mail server.

3. Using the Database Manager's Aliases Database window, make the following entries:

   a. Add an entry for each mail user account.

   b. Change the entry "Postmaster: root" to the mail address of the person who is designated as postmaster. See "Setting Up the Postmaster Alias" later in the chapter for more information.

   c. If you have created a mailbox for administration of a mail server, create an entry for "root: *mailbox@mailserver*".

   d. Save the changes.

4. To re-create the same information on each of the other systems, you can enter it again using the Database Manager's Aliases Database window. Alternatively, you can copy the /etc/mail/aliases, /etc/mail/aliases.dir, and /etc/mail/aliases.pag files to each of the other systems. You can copy the file by using the rcp or rdist command or by using a script that you create for this purpose. Remember that you must update all the /etc/mail/aliases files each time you add or remove a mail client.

Setting Up DNS Alias Files

The DNS naming service does not use aliases for individuals. It does use aliases for hosts or domains, called Mail Exchange (MX) records. These MX records are set in the /etc/named.boot file on the DNS server(s) for the domain or subdomain. You can specify host names or domain names in this file. Domain names can contain wildcards; for example, *.sun.com is an acceptable domain name.

You must use the sendmail.mx program with the DNS naming service. When you use the sendmail.mx program, the ${name} rule, which creates fully qualified host names, is activated in the sendmail.cf file. You do not need to edit the configuration file to activate this rule.

Follow these steps to set up the sendmail.mx program:

1. Type **mv /usr/lib/sendmail /usr/lib/sendmail.nomx** and press Return. The current sendmail program is renamed.

2. Type **mv /usr/lib/sendmail.mx /usr/lib/sendmail** and press Return. The sendmail.mx file gets host names directly from DNS.

3. Make sure there is an entry for mailhost in the DNS /etc/named.boot file on the DNS server (or servers).

Setting Up the Postmaster Alias

Every system should be able to send mail to a postmaster. You can create an NIS or NIS+ alias for postmaster or create one in each local /etc/mail/aliases file. Here is the default /etc/mail/aliases entry:

```
# Following alias is required by the mail protocol, RFC 822
# Set it to the address of a HUMAN who deals with this system's mail problems.
Postmaster: root
```

To create the postmaster alias, edit each system's /etc/mail/aliases file and change root to the mail address of the person who will act as postmaster.

You may want to create a separate mailbox for the postmaster to keep postmaster mail separate from personal mail. If you create a separate mailbox, use the mailbox address instead of the postmaster's mail address when you edit the /etc/mail/aliases files.

Follow these steps to create a separate mailbox for postmaster:

1. Create an account named postmaster and put an asterisk (*) in the password field of the /etc/shadow file.

2. Type **mail -f postmaster** and press Return. Mail will be able to read and write to the mailbox name.

Follow these steps to add the postmaster mailbox to the alias:

1. Become superuser and edit the /etc/mail/aliases file on each system. If your network runs NIS or NIS+, use the Database Manager to edit the Aliases database.

2. Change the postmaster alias from root to postmaster:

    postmastermailbox@postmasterhost.

    Save the changes.

3. On the postmaster's local system, create an entry in the /etc/mail/aliases file that defines the name of the alias (postmaster, for example) and includes the path to the local mailbox.

4. Type **newaliases** and press Return.

Alternatively, you could change the "postmaster:" entry in the aliases file to "postmaster: */usr/somewhere/somefile*".

Testing Your Mail Configuration

When you have all the systems in your mail configuration set up, use the suggestions in this section to test the setup to be sure mail messages can be sent and received.

1. Reboot any system for which you have changed a configuration file.

2. Send test messages from each system by typing **/usr/lib/sendmail -v </dev/null** *names* and press Return. Specify a recipient's e-mail address in place of the *names* variable. This command sends a null message to the specified recipient and displays messages while it runs.

3. Run the following tests:

   a. Send mail to yourself or other people on the local system by addressing the message to a regular user name.

   b. If you are on an Ethernet, send mail to someone on another system. Do this in three directions: from the main system to a subsidiary system, from a subsidiary system to the main system, and from a subsidiary system to another subsidiary system.

   c. If you have a relay host, send mail to another domain from the mailhost to ensure that the relay mailer and host are configured properly.

   d. If you have set up a uucp connection on your phone line to another host, send mail to someone at that host, and have him or her send mail back or call you when the message is received.

   e. Ask someone to send you mail over the uucp connection. The sendmail program cannot tell whether the message gets through, because it hands the message to uucp for delivery.

   f. Send a message to postmaster on different systems and make sure that it comes to your postmaster's mailbox.

Administering Your Mail Configuration

The following sections describe how to keep mail services running smoothly.

Duties of Postmaster

Your responsibilities for administering mail include the following tasks:

■ Check the mail queues to be sure mail is flowing in and out.

- Check any downed systems where mail is backing up. If the system is not needed, delete it from the mail system, or bring the system up to keep mail moving.

- Fix personal aliases, as requested.

- Administer Aliases databases as people move in and out of the domain.

- Set up temporary forwarding files.

- Contact owners of mailing lists and help them to fix mailing list problems.

- Go through postmaster mail daily and look for problems, broken .forward files, and mail alias loops. Fix the problem or tell people how to fix it.

- Answer questions outside the company.

- Truncate log files periodically.

The Mail Queue

Under high load or temporary failure conditions, sendmail puts a message into a job queue in the /var/spool/mqueue directory instead of delivering it immediately. Ordinarily, the mail queue is processed automatically. Sometimes, however, you may have to intervene manually. For example, if a major host is down for a period of time, the queue may become clogged. Although sendmail ought to recover gracefully when the host comes up, you may find performance unacceptable in the meantime.

Printing the Mail Queue

You can print the contents of the queue by specifying the -bp flag to sendmail. Type **/usr/lib/sendmail -bp | more** and press Return. A list of the queue IDs, the size of the message, the date the message entered the queue, message status, and the sender and recipients are displayed.

Format of Queue Files

The sendmail program stores temporary queue files in /var/spool/mqueue. All such queue files have the form *xfAA99999,* where *AA99999* is the ID for the file and *x* is the type. Table 3.2 shows the types of queue files.

The qf file contains a series of lines, each beginning with a code letter, as shown in Table 3.3. See Chapter 4 for more information.

The queue is automatically run at the interval specified in the sendmail.cf file. (The default is every hour.) The queue is read and sorted, and then sendmail tries to process all jobs in order. The sendmail program first checks to see if a job is locked. If locked, it ignores the job; if not locked, sendmail processes it.

Table 3.2   **Types of Queue Files**

Type	Description
d	A data file. The message body (excluding the header) is kept in this file.
l	A lock file. If this file is present, the job is currently being processed, and running the queue will not process it. For this reason, an extraneous lock file can make a job seem to disappear.
n	This separate file is created whenever an ID is created. It ensures that no mail can ever be destroyed because of a race condition. This file should not exist for more than a few milliseconds at any given time.
q	The queue control file. This file contains the information needed to process the job.
t	A temporary file. This file is an image of the qf file (see below) when it is being re-built. When the rebuild is complete, the file is renamed qf.
x	A transcript file that exists during the life of a session and shows everything that happens during that session.

Table 3.3   **Codes for the qf File**

Code	Description
P	The current message priority, which is used to order the queue. The higher the num-ber, the lower the priority. The priority increases as the message sits in the queue. The initial priority depends on the message class and the size of the message.
T	The job creation/submission time in seconds, which is used to compute when the job times out.
D	The name of the data file.
M	A message. This line is printed by using sendmail with the -bp flag and is generally used to store status information. It can contain any text.
S	The sender name.
E	Error recipient name. Error messages are sent to this user instead of to the sender. This line is optional.
H	A header definition. There may be any number of these lines. The order is impor-tant: It represents the order in the final message. The syntax is the same as header definitions in the configuration file.

Table 3.3   **Codes for the qf File (Continued)**

Code	Description
R	A recipient name. There will be one line for each recipient. The recipient name normally will be completely aliased, but is actually re-aliased when the job is processed. The recipient name must be at the end of the qf file.

If a major host goes down for several days, the queue may become prohibitively large, and sendmail will spend lots of time sorting the queue. You can fix this by moving the queue to a temporary place and creating a new queue. You can run the old queue later, when the host is returned to service.

Forcing the Queue
Follow these steps to force the queue:

1. Become superuser on the mailhost.

2. Type **ps -el | grep sendmail** and press Return. Note the PID for sendmail; you will use it in the next step.

3. Type **kill *PID*** and press Return. The old sendmail daemon is killed to keep it from trying to process the old queue directory.

4. Type **cd /var/spool** and press Return.

5. Type **mv mqueue omqueue; mkdir mqueue** and press Return. These commands move the directory mqueue and all of its contents to the directory omqueue and then create a new empty mqueue directory.

6. Type **chmod 755; chown daemon; chgrp daemon; mqueue** and press Return. These commands set the permissions of the directory to read/write/execute by others, and read/execute by group and others. They also set the owner and group to daemon.

7. Type **/usr/lib/sendmail -bd -q1h** and press Return. A new sendmail daemon is started, with a queue run time of 1 hour.

Running the Old Mail Queue
Follow these steps to run the old mail queue:

1. Type **/usr/lib/sendmail -oQ/var/spool/omqueue -q** and press Return. The -oQ flag specifies an alternate queue directory and the -q flag says to run every job in the queue. Use the -v flag if you want to see the verbose output displayed on the screen.

2. When the queue is finally emptied, type **rmdir /var/spool/omqueue** and press Return. The empty directory is removed.

You can run a subset of the queue at any time with the *-rstring* option (run queue where any recipient name matches *string*) or with the *-Mnnnnn* option to sendmail. (Run just one message with queue ID *nnnnn*.)

To run a subset of the mail queue, type **/usr/lib/sendmail -R***string* and press Return. In this example, everything in the queue for recipient wnj is processed:

```
oak% /usr/lib/sendmail -Rwnj
```

The System Log

The mail services log most errors using the syslogd program. The default is for syslogd to send messages to a system identified as the loghost.

Just as you define a system called mailhost to handle mail relaying, you can define a system called loghost in the /etc/hosts file to hold all logs for an entire NIS domain. The system log is supported by the syslogd program. You specify a loghost in the Hosts database. If no loghost is specified, then error messages from syslogd are not reported.

Here is the default /etc/syslog.conf file:

```
#ident  "@(#)syslog.conf      1.1     91/05/22 SMI"   /* SunOS 5.0 */
#
# Copyright (c) 1991 by Sun Microsystems, Inc.
#
# syslog configuration file.
#
# This file is processed by m4 so be careful to quote ('') names
# that match m4 reserved words. Also, within ifdef's, arguments
# containing commas must be quoted.
#
# Note: Have to exclude user from most lines so that user.alert
#       and user.emerg are not included, because old sendmails
#       will generate them for debugging information. If you
#       have no 4.2BSD based systems doing network logging, you
#       can remove all the special cases for "user" logging.
#
*.err;kern.debug;auth.notice;user.none          /dev/console
*.err;kern.debug;daemon,auth.notice;mail.crit;user.none /var/adm/messages

*.alert;kern.err;daemon.err;user.none           operator
*.alert;user.none                               root

*.emerg;user.none                               *

# if a non-loghost machine chooses to have authentication messages
# sent to the loghost machine, un-comment out the following line:
```

```
#auth.notice                          ifdef('LOGHOST', /var/log/authlog, @loghost)

mail.debug                            ifdef('LOGHOST', /var/log/syslog, @loghost)

#
# non-loghost machines will use the following lines to cause "user"
# log messages to be logged locally.
#
ifdef('LOGHOST', ,
user.err                                              /dev/console
user.err                                              /var/adm/messages
user.alert                                            'root, operator'
user.emerg                                            *
)
```

You can change the default configuration by editing the /etc/syslog.conf file.

When the syslogd daemon starts up, it creates the file /etc/syslog.pid, which contains its process ID number. Here is an example of a syslog.pid file:

```
oak% more /etc/syslog.pid
166
oak%
```

Here is an example of a system log file:

```
oak% tail /var/log/mailog
Apr  4 09:47:41 oak sendmail[14192]: AA14190: to=<uucp>,
delay=00:00:01, stat=Sent

Apr  4 09:47:50 oak sendmail[14195]: AA14195: message-
id=<9304041647 .AA195@oak.Eng.Sun.COM>

Apr  4 09:47:50 oak sendmail[14195]: AA14195: from=<uucp>,
size=378, class=0, received from ignatz (129.144.52.69)

Apr  4 09:47:51 oak sendmail[14197]: AA14195: to=<uucp>,
delay=00:00:01, stat=Sent

Apr  4 10:44:27 oak sendmail[14280]: AA14280: message-
id=<93040401748.AA06975@castle.Eng.Sun.COM>

Apr  4 10:44:27 oak sendmail[14280]: AA14280:
from=<winsor@castle>, size=892, class=0, received from zigzag
(129.144.1.38)

Apr  4 10:44:27 oak sendmail[14282]:AA14280: to=lautner@oak,
delay=00:00:01, stat=Sent

Apr  4 10:52:43 oak sendmail[14307]: AA14307: message-
```

```
id=<9304041753.AA05638@pigglet.Eng.Sun.COM>

Apr  4 10:52:43 oak sendmail[14307]: AA14307:
from=<nixed@pigglet>, size=918,class=0, received from
piglet (129.144.154.7)

Apr  4 10:52:44 oak sendmail[14309]: AA14307: to=lautner@ oak,
delay=00:00:01, stat=Sent
oak%
```

NOTE   *Because of the length of each entry, space has been added be-*
tween entries in this example to improve readability.

Each line in the system log contains a timestamp, the name of the system
that generated it, and a message. A large amount of information can be
logged by syslog. The log is arranged as a succession of levels. At the lowest
level, only unusual occurrences are logged. At the highest level, even the
most mundane and uninteresting events are recorded. As a convention, log
levels under 10 are considered useful. Log levels higher than 10 are usually
used for debugging.

Troubleshooting Your Mail Configuration

The following sections provide some tips and tools that you can use for troubleshooting the mail.

Checking Aliases

To verify aliases and determine whether mail can be delivered to a given recipient, type **/usr/lib/sendmail -v -bv** *recipient* and press Return. The command displays the aliases and identifies the final address as deliverable or not.
Here is an example of the output:

```
% /usr/lib/sendmail -v -bv shamira@raks
shamira... aliased to    mwong
mwong... aliased to            shamira@raks
shamira@raks... deliverable
%
```

Take extra care to avoid loops and inconsistent databases when both
local and domain-wide aliases are used. Be especially careful when you move
a user from one system to another to avoid creating alias loops.

Testing sendmail

Follow these steps to run sendmail in test mode:

1. Type **/usr/lib/sendmail -bt** and press Return. Information is displayed.

2. At the last prompt (>), type **0 *e-mail-address*** and press Return. See Chapter 4 for a complete description of the diagnostic information.

Verifying Connections to Other Systems

To verify connections to other systems, you can use the mconnect program to open connections to other sendmail systems over the network. The mconnect program runs interactively. You can issue various diagnostic commands. See the mconnect(1) manual page for a complete description.

If you cannot use mconncct to connect to an SMTP port, check these conditions:

- Is the system load too high?

- Is the sendmail daemon running?

- Docs the system have the appropriate /etc/mail/sendmail.cf file?

- Is TCP port 25 (the port that sendmail uses) active?

Other Diagnostic Information

For other diagnostic information, check the following sources:

- Look at the received lines in the header of the message. These lines trace the route the message took as it was relayed. Note that in the uucp network many sites do not update these lines, and in the Internet the lines often get rearranged. To straighten them out, look at the date and time in each line. Do not forget to account for time zone differences, and beware of clocks that have been set incorrectly.

- Look at messages from MAILER-DAEMON. These messages typically report delivery problems.

- Check the system log that records delivery problems for your group of workstations. The sendmail program always records what it is doing in the system log. You may want to modify the crontab file to run a shell script nightly that searches the log for SYSERR messages and mails any that it finds to the postmaster.

- Use the mailstats program to test mail types and determine the number of messages coming in and going out.

Customizing sendmail
Configuration Files

THE SENDMAIL PROGRAM IS A MAIL-TRANSPORT AGENT THAT USES A CON-figuration file to provide aliasing and forwarding, automatic routing to network gateways, and flexible configuration. The Solaris environment supplies the standard configuration files that most sites can use. Chapter 3 explains how to set up an electronic mail system using the standard configuration files. This chapter explains how to customize sendmail configuration files if you need to tailor them to fit your site's needs.

Sections in this chapter describe the following subjects:

- Command-line arguments to sendmail.

- sendmail parameters that you can alter.

- In-depth information on the configuration file. This section provides information for those sites that need to write their own configuration file.

- Brief but detailed explanations of several lesser-used features of sendmail.

The sendmail program can accept domain-based naming, as well as arbitrary (older) name syntaxes—resolving ambiguities using heuristics that you specify. The sendmail program can also convert messages between a pair of disparate naming schemes.

Certain special cases can be handled by ad hoc techniques, such as providing network names that appear local to hosts on other networks. For example, user@host is left-to-right syntax, and host!user is right-to-left syntax.

Overview of sendmail Functions

The sendmail program is a message router that calls administrator-selected mailer programs to deliver messages. It collects a message from a program such as mail, edits the header of the message as required by the destination mailer, and calls appropriate mailers to do delivery or queueing for network transmission. When mailing to a file, however, sendmail delivers directly. New mailers to increase heterogeneity and convenience can be added at minimal cost.

Interfaces to the Outside World

The sendmail program can communicate with the outside world in three ways:

- Using the conventional argument vector/exit status

- Using pairs of pipes

- Using SMTP over a TCP connection

Argument Vector/Exit Status

The standard way to communicate with a process is using the argument vector (command name and arguments). The argument vector sends a list of recipients, and the message body is sent on the standard input. If problems occur, anything that the mailer prints is collected and returned to the sender. After the message is sent, the exit status from the mailer is collected, and a diagnostic is printed, if appropriate.

SMTP over Pipes

The SMTP protocol can be used to run an interactive lock-step interface with the mailer. A subprocess is still created, but no recipient names are passed to the mailer from the argument list. Instead, the names are passed one at a time in commands sent to the standard input of the processes. Anything appearing on the standard output must be a standard SMTP reply code.

SMTP over a TCP Connection

This technique is similar to SMTP over pipes, except that it uses a TCP connection. SMTP over a TCP connection is normally used to connect to a sendmail process on another system. This method is exceptionally flexible because the mailer need not reside on the same machine.

How the sendmail Program Works

The following sections describe in detail how the sendmail program works. When a sender wants to send a message, the program issues a request to sendmail using one of the three methods just described. The sendmail program then goes through these steps, which are described in detail in the following paragraphs:

1. Arguments are processed and the address is parsed.

2. The message is collected.

3. The message is delivered.

4. If instructions are received from the mailer, the message is queued for retransmission.

5. If errors occur during processing, the message is returned to the sender.

Argument Processing and Address Parsing

If sendmail is called by using the argument vector or is connected to via a pipe, the arguments are first scanned and option specifications are processed. Recipient names are then collected, either from the command line or from the SMTP command, and a list of recipients is created. Aliases are expanded at this step, including mailing lists. As much validation as possible of the remote recipient is done at this step: Syntax is checked and local recipients are verified, but detailed checking of host names is deferred until delivery. Forwarding is also performed as the local recipients are verified.

The sendmail program appends each name to the recipient list after parsing. When a name is aliased or forwarded, the old name is retained in the list and a flag is set that tells the delivery phase to ignore this recipient. This list is kept free from duplicates, thus preventing alias loops and duplicate messages from being delivered to the same recipient, as might occur if a person is in two groups.

NOTE. *Users may receive duplicate copies of the same message when alias lists contain e-mail addresses for the same person using different syntaxes. The sendmail program cannot always identify the e-mail addresses as duplicates of one another.*

Message Collection

The sendmail program then collects the message, which must have a header at the beginning. The message body does not need to be formatted in any special way except that it must be composed of lines of text. (In other words, binary data is not allowed.) The header is stored in memory, and the body of the message is saved in a temporary file.

To simplify the program interface, the message is collected even if no names were valid. The message subsequently will be returned with an error.

Message Delivery

For each unique mailer and host in the recipient list, sendmail calls the appropriate mailer. Each mailer invocation sends to all users receiving the message on one host. Mailers that accept only one recipient at a time are handled properly.

The message is sent to the mailer using one of the same three interfaces used to submit a message to sendmail. Each copy of the message has a customized header added to the beginning of the message. The mailer status code is caught and checked and a suitable error message is given as appropriate. The exit code must conform to a system standard or the generic message "Service unavailable" is given.

Retransmission Queueing

When the mailer returns a status indicating that it might be able to handle the mail later, sendmail queues the mail and tries again later.

Return to Sender

When errors occur during processing, sendmail returns the message to the sender for retransmission. The letter can be mailed back (when the mail comes from a different site) or written in the dead.letter file in the sender's home directory.

Message-Header Editing

The sendmail program does some editing of the message header automatically. Header lines can be inserted under control of the configuration file. Some lines may be merged; for example, a From: and a Full-name: line may be merged under certain circumstances.

Configuration File

Almost all configuration information is read at run time from a text file:

- Macro definitions (defining the value of macros used internally) are encoded.

- Header declarations (the format of header lines that are specially processed, and lines that are added or reformatted) are embedded.

- Mailer definitions (giving information such as the location and characteristics of each mailer) are included.

- Name rewriting rules (a limited pattern-matching system used to rewrite names) are defined.

How sendmail Is Implemented

The following sections provide an overview of the syntax used in sendmail and describe some implementation details.

You can follow flag arguments with recipient name arguments unless you run in SMTP mode. In brief, the format of recipient names is

- Anything in parentheses is thrown away (as a comment).

- Anything in angle brackets (< >) is preferred over anything else. This rule implements the Internet standard that writes names in the form of *username <system-name>* and sends to the electronic *system-name* rather than to the human *username*.

- Double quotes (") demarcate phrases; backslashes (\) demarcate characters. Backslashes cause otherwise equivalent phrases to compare differently—for example, *user* and *"user"* are equivalent, but *\user* is different from either of them.

Parentheses, angle brackets, and double quotes must be properly balanced (that is, used in pairs) and nested. The rewriting rules control the rest of the needed processing.

Mail to Files and Programs

Files and programs are legitimate message recipients. Files provide archival storage of messages, useful for project administration and history. Programs are useful as recipients in a variety of situations—for example, to use mailsort to sort mail, or to have the vacation program respond with an informational message when users are away.

Any name passing through the initial parsing algorithm as a local name is scanned for two special cases:

- If the prefix is a vertical bar (|), the rest of the name is processed as a shell command.

- If the user name begins with a slash (/), the name is used as a filename, instead of a login name.

Message Collection

Once all recipient names are parsed and verified, the message is collected. The message comes in two parts: a message header and a message body. The header and the body are separated by a blank line.

The header is formatted as a series of lines of the form:

```
field-name: field-value
```

For example, a sample header might be

```
From: John Smith <Smith@Podunk.edu>
```

Field-value can be split across lines by starting the subsequent lines with a space or a tab. Some header fields have special internal meaning and have appropriate special processing. Other headers are simply passed through. Some header fields, such as time stamps, may be added automatically.

The body is a series of text lines. It is completely uninterpreted and untouched, except that lines beginning with a dot have the dot doubled when transmitted over an SMTP channel. This extra dot is stripped by the receiver.

Message Delivery

The send queue is grouped by the receiving host before transmission to implement message batching. An argument list is built as the scan proceeds. Mail to files is detected during the scan of the send list. The interface to the mailer is performed using one of the techniques described in "Overview of sendmail Functions," earlier in the chapter.

After a connection is established, sendmail makes the per-mailer changes to the header and sends the result to the mailer. If any mail is rejected by the mailer, a flag is set to invoke the return-to-sender function after all delivery is complete.

Queued Messages

If the mailer returns a "Temporary failure" exit status, the message is queued. A control file is used to describe the recipients to be sent to and various other parameters. This control file is formatted as a series of lines, each describing a sender, a recipient, the time of submission, or some other parameter of the message. The header of the message is stored in the control file so that the associated data file in the queue is just the temporary file that was originally collected.

Configuration Overview

Configuration is controlled primarily by a configuration file read at startup. Adding mailers or changing the rewriting or routing information does not require recompiling sendmail. The configuration file encodes macro definitions, header declarations, mailer definitions, rewriting rules, and options.

Macros

Macros can be used in various ways. Certain macros transmit unstructured textual information into the mail system, such as the name that sendmail will use to identify itself in error messages. Other macros are unused internally and can be used as shorthand in the configuration file.

Header Declarations

Header declarations inform sendmail of the format of known header lines. Knowledge of a few header lines is built into sendmail, such as the From: and Date: lines.

Most configured headers are automatically inserted in the outgoing message if they don't exist in the incoming message. Certain headers are suppressed by some mailers.

Mailer Declarations

Mailer declarations specify the internal name of the mailer, some flags associated with the mailer, and an argument vector to be used on the call. This vector is expanded by a macro before use.

Name-Rewriting Rules

Name-rewriting rules are the heart of name parsing in sendmail. They are an ordered list of pattern-replacement rules, which are applied to each name. In particular, ruleset 0 determines which mailer to use. The name is rewritten until it is either rewritten into a special canonical form—for example, a {*mailer, host, user*} triplet, such as {ddn, isi.edu, postel}, representing the name "postel@isi.edu"—or it falls off the end. When a pattern matches, the rule is reapplied until it fails.

The configuration file also supports the editing of names into different formats. For example, a name of the form

    ucsfcgl!tef

might be mapped into

    tef@ucsfcgl.UUCP

to conform to the internal syntax. Translations can also be done in the other direction for particular mailers.

Option Setting

Several options can be set from the configuration file. These include the pathnames of various support files, timeouts, default modes, etc.

Arguments to sendmail

The complete list of arguments to sendmail is described in detail in the sections "Command-Line Arguments" and "Configuration Options" later in the chapter. Arguments used to set the queue interval, daemon mode, and debugging flags and for using an alternative configuration file are described in the following sections.

Queue Interval

The -q flag defines how often sendmail runs the queue. If you run in mode b (the default) or i, you can set a relatively long time interval, because it is only used when a host that was down comes back up. If, however, you run in mode q, you should set a relatively short time, because the q flag defines the maximum amount of time that a message may sit in the queue. Typically, queue time is set between 15 minutes (-q15m) and 1 hour (-q1h).

Daemon Mode

If you allow incoming mail over a TCP connection, you should have a daemon running. Set the -bd flag in your /etc/rc3.d/S88sendmail file.

You can combine the -bd flag and the -q flag in one call. In this example, the daemon is specified along with a queue interval of 30 minutes:

```
# /usr/lib/sendmail -bd -q30m
```

An Alternative Configuration File

You can specify an alternative configuration file by using the -C flag. For example,

```
# /usr/lib/sendmail -Ctest.cf
```

uses the configuration file test.cf instead of the default /etc/mail/sendmail.cf. If you do not define a value for the -C flag, it uses the sendmail.cf file in the current directory.

Tuning

You can tune several configuration parameters, depending on the requirements of your site. Most of these parameters are set using an option in the configuration file. For example, the line OT3d sets option T to the value 3d (three days).

Time Values

All time intervals use a syntax of numbers and letters. For example, 10m is ten minutes, and 2h30m is two and a half hours. The full set of time symbols is shown in Table 4.1.

Table 4.1 **Time Syntax Options**

Code	Description
s	seconds
m	minutes
h	hours
d	days
w	weeks

Queue Interval

The argument to the -q flag specifies how often sendmail runs the queue. It is usually set between 15 minutes (-q15m) and 1 hour (-q1h).

Read Timeouts

The Or option in the configuration file sets the read timeout. The default read timeout is Or15m. The sendmail program may time out when reading the standard input or when reading from a remote SMTP server. If your site has problems with read timeouts, set the read timeout to a larger value, such as 1 hour (Or1h), to reduce the chance of several idle daemons piling up on your system.

Message Timeouts

The OT option in the configuration file sets the message timeout. The default message timeout is 3 days (OT3d). To inform the sender that a message could not be delivered, it should be returned after sitting in the queue for a few days.

You can flush messages that have been hanging for a short period by running the queue with a short message timeout. For example,

```
# /usr/lib/sendmail -oT1d -q
```

runs the queue and flushes anything that is 1 day old or older.

Delivery Mode

The Od option in the configuration file sets the delivery mode. The default delivery mode is Odbackground. Delivery modes, shown in Table 4.2, specify how quickly mail is delivered.

Table 4.2   **Delivery Mode Options**

Code	Description
i	Deliver interactively (synchronously)
b	Deliver in background (asynchronously)
q	Queue only (do not deliver)

There are trade-offs. Mode i passes the maximum amount of information to the sender, but is hardly ever necessary. Mode q puts the minimum load on your machine, but means that delivery may be delayed for up to the queue interval. Mode b, the default, is probably a good compromise.

Load Limiting

The goal of load limiting is to prevent wasted time during loaded periods by attempting to deliver large messages, messages to many recipients, or messages to sites that have been down for a long time.

Central mail machines often can be overloaded. Of course, the best solution is to dedicate a more powerful machine to handling mail, but the load almost always expands to consume whatever resources are allocated.

Use the Ox and OX options to limit the load caused by sendmail. The default sets no load limits if no options are used. Both of these configuration options take an argument that is an integer-load average. For example, if you specify Ox4 and OX8, then the x load limiting will be used when the load is above four, and the X load limiting will be used when the load is above eight. When the load is above the value specified in the X option, the SMTP server does not accept connections from the network. (Locally originated mail and other mail such as uucp are not affected.) The x option has a more subtle effect, controlling whether messages are queued for later delivery or are delivered immediately. The general idea is to always deliver small messages immediately, and defer large messages for delivery during off-peak periods.

The Oq option specifies the maximum size of message that is delivered immediately. The size of the message includes not only the number of bytes in the message, but also assigns penalties for a large number of recipients and for delivery attempts that were unsuccessful. The penalty per recipient is option value y, by default set to 1000. The penalty per delivery attempt is the option value z, by default set to 9000. The size limit also depends on current load, so that more and more messages are queued as the load goes higher. If the load is one above the x threshold, then the limit is halved; if the load is two above the threshold, the limit is divided by three, and so forth. Note that this limit also applies to messages that are delivered when running the queue, in contrast to earlier versions of sendmail.

Log Level

You can adjust the level of logging for sendmail. The default log level is 9. The levels are shown in Table 4.3.

Table 4.3   **Log Level Codes**

Code	Description
0	No logging
1	Major problems only

Table 4.3   **Log Level Codes (Continued)**

2	Message collections and failed deliveries
3	Successful deliveries
4	Messages being deferred (due to a host being down, and so forth)
5	Normal message queue ups
6	Unusual but benign incidents (for example, trying to process a locked queue file)
9	Log internal queue ID to external message ID mappings, which can be useful for tracing a message as it travels between several hosts
12	Several messages that are basically only of interest when debugging
16	Verbose information regarding the queue
22	All of the above

File Modes

Certain files may have a number of modes. The following sections describe the modes that you can control from the sendmail.cf file. The modes you use depend on what functionality you want and the level of security you require.

setuid

By default, sendmail is executed with the user ID set to 0 (setuid to root) so that it can deliver to programs which might write in a user's home directory. When sendmail is ready to execute a mailer program, sendmail checks to see if the user ID is 0; if so, it resets the user ID and group ID to the values set by the u and g options in the configuration file. By default, these values are Ou1 and Og1, which set both the user ID and the group ID to 1, which is daemon. You can override these values by setting the S flag to the mailer for mailers that are trusted and must be called as root. In this case, mail processing will be accounted to root rather than to the user sending the mail.

Temporary File Modes

The OF option sets the mode of all temporary files that sendmail uses. The default is OF0600. The numbers stand for the usual octal values for file permissions. Thus, 0600 is for secure mail (-rw-------) and 0644 for permissive (-rw-r--r--). If you use the more permissive mode, you do not need to run sendmail as root at all (even when running the queue). Users will be able to read mail in the queue.

Should My Aliases Database Be Writable?

You can control access to the Aliases database. Many sites permit only accredited users to make modifications to the Aliases database or to create new ones. If your site is running NIS+ and you want users to be able to use Administration Tool's Database Manager to modify existing aliases, those users must be members of the sysadmin group (GID 14) and must be accredited to make changes to the Aliases table. See Chapter 5 for more information about NIS+ security.

If you use the local /etc/mail/aliases file to control mail aliases, use UNIX file permissions to restrict or permit write access. With /etc/mail/aliases set to mode 666, any user can modify any list in the /etc/mail/aliases file.

The Configuration File

The following sections describe the configuration file in detail, including hints for writing your own file.

The syntax of the configuration file is parsed every time sendmail starts up. This syntax is optimized for speed of processing, but can be mastered with the information below.

The sendmail file uses single letters for several different functions:

- Command-line flags

- Configuration options

- Queue file line types

- Configuration file line types

- Mailer field names

- Mailer flags

- Macro names

- Class names

The following sections provide an overview of the configuration file and details of its semantics.

Parts of the sendmail Configuration File

The sendmail configuration file has three parts:

- Definition of symbols, classes, options, and parameters

- Definitions of mailers and delivery programs

■ Rulesets that determine the rules for rewriting addresses

You define symbols, classes, options, and parameters to set up the environment for sendmail.

You define your mailers and delivery programs so that sendmail knows the protocols to use and the delivery programs with which to interact.

You define rewriting rules, grouped into rulesets, to transform addresses from one form to another. In general, each rule in a ruleset is applied to a particular address. An address might be rewritten several times within a ruleset.

There are eight standard rulesets; these are applied in the order shown in Table 4.4.

Table 4.4 **Order of Application of Rulesets**

Ruleset	Description
Ruleset 3	The first ruleset applied; tries to put the address into the canonical form local-address@host-domain.
Ruleset 0	Determines what the destination is, and which mailer program to use to send mail. It resolves the destination into a triplet (*mailer, host, user*).
Ruleset D	Appends sender domain information to addresses that have no domain specified.
Ruleset 1	Rewrites the sender address.
Ruleset S	Each mailer can specify additional rulesets for the sender addresses to do final mailer-specific cleanup. These rulesets have different names for each mailer. In this example, *S* stands for a generic "sender."
Ruleset 2	Rewrites the recipient address.
Ruleset R	Each mailer can specify additional rulesets for the recipient addresses to do final mailer-specific cleanup. These rulesets have different names for each mailer. In this example, *R* stands for a generic "recipient."
Ruleset 4	Rewrites all addresses for the final time, usually from internal to external form.

NOTE. *Rulesets D, S, and R stand for rulesets that are specified in one of the mailer configuration statements. For example, R and S might be ruleset 22.*

Ruleset 0 must resolve to the internal form, which in turn is used as a pointer to a mailer descriptor. The mailer descriptor describes the interface requirements of the mailer.

Rewriting names in the message typically is done in two phases. The first phase uses ruleset 3 to map names in any format into a canonical form. The second phase maps the canonical form into the syntax appropriate for the receiving mailer. Names are rewritten by sendmail in three subphases. Rulesets 1 and 2 are applied to all sender and recipient names, respectively. You may specify mailer-specific rulesets in ruleset 3 for both sender and recipient names. Finally, ruleset 4 is applied to do any conversion to external form.

RFC 822 describes the format of the mail message itself. The sendmail program follows this RFC closely, to the extent that many of the standards described in this document cannot be changed without changing the code. In particular, the following characters have special interpretations:

< > ( ) " \

CAUTION! *Use the RFC 822 special characters < > ( ) " \ only for their designated purposes. Information between parentheses, ( ), is reserved for comments and personal names. Information between angle brackets, < >, is reserved for canonical addresses. The " sign is used to quote strings in an address or identifier. For example, ":sysmail"@somewhere.domain.com. The string is treated literally so that nothing inside it is considered an address until it reaches the system in somewhere.domain.com. The \ is used to escape a single character.*

A Sample sendmail Configuration File

Following is an example of the default main.cf file. Subsequent sections describe the syntax and semantics used in this file.

```
##################################################################
#
#       Sendmail configuration file for "MAIN MACHINES"
#
#       You should install this file as /etc/sendmail.cf
#       if your machine is the main (or only) mail-relaying
#       machine in your domain. Then edit the file to
#       customize it for your network configuration.
#
#       See the manual "System and Network Administration for the Sun
#       Workstation". Look at "Setting Up The Mail Routing System" in
#       the chapter on Communications. The Sendmail reference in the
#       back of the manual is also useful.
#
#       @(#)main.mc 1.17 90/01/04 SMI
#

###     local info

# delete the following if you do not use the sendmailvars table
Lmmaildomain

# my official hostname
# You have two choices here. If you want the gateway machine to identify
```

```
# itself as the DOMAIN, use this line:
Dj$m
# If you want the gateway machine to appear to be INSIDE the domain, use:
#Dj$w.$m
# if you are using sendmail.mx (or have a fully-qualified hostname), use:
#Dj$w

# major relay mailer - typical choice is "ddn" if you are on the
# Defense Data Network (e.g. Arpanet or Milnet)
DMsmartuucp

# major relay host: use the $M mailer to send mail to other domains
DR ddn-gateway
CR ddn-gateway

# If you want to pre-load the "mailhosts" then use a line like
# FS /usr/lib/mailhosts
# and then change all the occurences of $%y to be $=S instead.
# Otherwise, the default is to use the hosts.byname map if NIS
# is running (or else the /etc/hosts file if no NIS).

# valid top-level domains (default passes ALL unknown domains up)
CT arpa com edu gov mil net org
CT us de fr jp kr nz il uk no au fi nl se ca ch my dk ar

# options that you probably want on a mailhost:

# checkpoint the queue after this many receipients
OC10

# refuse to send tiny messages to more than these recipients
Ob10

##################################################
#
#           General configuration information

# local domain names
#
# These can now be determined from the domainname system call.
# The first component of the NIS domain name is stripped off unless
# it begins with a dot or a plus sign.
# If your NIS domain is not inside the domain name you would like to have
# appear in your mail headers, add a "Dm" line to define your domain name.
# The Dm value is what is used in outgoing mail. The Cm values are
# accepted in incoming mail. By default Cm is set from Dm, but you might
# want to have more than one Cm line to recognize more than one domain
# name on incoming mail during a transition.
# Example:
# DmCS.Podunk.EDU
# Cm cs cs.Podunk.EDU
#
```

```
# known hosts in this domain are obtained from gethostbyname() call

# Version number of configuration file
#ident  "@(#)version.m4 1.17    92/07/14 SMI"   /* SunOS 4.1    */
#
#
#               Copyright Notice
#
#Notice of copyright on this source code product does not indicate
#publication.
#
#       (c) 1986,1987,1988,1989 Sun Microsystems, Inc
#                 All rights reserved.

DVSMI-SVR4


###      Standard macros

# name used for error messages
DnMailer-Daemon
# UNIX header format
DlFrom $g $d
# delimiter (operator) characters
Do.:%@!^=/[]
# format of a total name
Dq$g$?x ($x)$.
# SMTP login message
De$j Sendmail $v/$V ready at $b

### Options

# Remote mode - send through server if mailbox directory is mounted
OR
# location of alias file
OA/etc/mail/aliases
# default delivery mode (deliver in background)
Odbackground
# rebuild the alias file automagically
OD
# temporary file mode -- 0600 for secure mail, 0644 for permissive
OF0600
# default GID
Og1
# location of help file
OH/var/lib/sendmail.hf
# log level
OL9
# default messages to old style
Oo
# Cc my postmaster on error replies I generate
OPPostmaster
```

```
# queue directory
OQ/var/spool/mqueue
# read timeout for SMTP protocols
Or15m
# status file -- none
OS/etc/mail/sendmail.st
# queue up everything before starting transmission, for safety
Os
# return queued mail after this long
OT3d
# default UID
Ou1

### Message precedences
Pfirst-class=0
Pspecial-delivery=100
Pjunk=-100

### Trusted users
T root daemon uucp

### Format of headers
H?P?Return-Path: <$g>
HReceived: $?sfrom $s $.by $j ($v/$V)
        id $i: $b
H?D?Resent-Date: $a
H?D?Date: $a
H?F?Resent-From: $q
H?F?From: $q
H?x?Full-Name: $x
HSubject:
H?M?Resent-Message-Id: <$t.$i@$j>
H?M?Message-Id: <$t.$i@$j>
HErrors-To:


############################
### Rewriting rules ###
############################


# Sender Field Pre-rewriting
S1
# None needed.

# Recipient Field Pre-rewriting
S2
# None needed.

# Name Canonicalization

# Internal format of names within the rewriting rules is:
#       anything<@host.domain.domain...>anything
```

```
# We try to get every kind of name into this format, except for local
# names, which have no host part. The reason for the "<>" stuff is
# that the relevant host name could be on the front of the name (for
# source routing), or on the back (normal form). We enclose the one that
# we want to route on in the <>'s to make it easy to find.
#
S3

# handle "from:<>" special case
R$*<>$*                    $@@                              turn into magic token

# basic textual canonicalization
R$*<$+>$*                  $2                               basic RFC822 parsing

# make sure <@a,@b,@c:user@d> syntax is easy to parse -- undone later
R@$+,$+:$+                 @$1:$2:$3                        change all "," to ":"
R@$+:$+                    $@$>6<@$1>:$2                    src route canonical

R$+:$*;@$+                 $@$1:$2;@$3                      list syntax
R$+@$+                     $:$1<@$2>                        focus on domain
R$+<$+@$+>                 $1$2<@$3>                        move gaze right
R$+<@$+>                   $@$>6$1<@$2>                     already canonical

# convert old-style names to domain-based names
# All old-style names parse from left to right, without precedence.
R$-!$+                     $@$>6$2<@$1.uucp>                uucphost!user
R$-.$+!$+                  $@$>6$3<@$1.$2>                  host.domain!user
R$+%$+                     $@$>3$1@$2                       user%host

# Final Output Post-rewriting
S4
R$+<@$+.uucp>              $2!$1                            u@h.uucp => h!u
R$+                        $: $>9 $1                        Clean up addr
R$*<$+>$*                  $1$2$3                           defocus


# Clean up an name for passing to a mailer
# (but leave it focused)
S9
R$=w!@                     $@$w!$n
R@                         $@$n                             handle <> error addr
R$*<$*LOCAL>$*             $1<$2m>$3                        change local info
R<@$+>$*:$+:$+             <@$1>$2,$3:$4                    <route-addr> canonical


#####################
# Rewriting rules

# special local conversions
S6
R$*<@$*$=m>$*              $1<@$2LOCAL>$4                   convert local domain
```

```
# Local and Program Mailer specification

Mlocal, P=/bin/mail, F=flsSDFMmnP, S=10, R=20, A=mail -d $u
Mprog,  P=/bin/sh, F=lsDFMeuP, S=10, R=20, A=sh -c $u


S10
# None needed.


S20
# None needed.

#ident  "@(#)etherm.m4  1.14    92/07/14 SMI"    /* SunOS 4.1    */
#
#               Copyright Notice
#
#Notice of copyright on this source code product does not indicate
#publication.
#
#       (c) 1986,1987,1988,1989 Sun Microsystems, Inc
#                   All rights reserved.


###############################################################
#####
#####           Ethernet Mailer specification
#####
#####   Messages processed by this configuration are assumed to remain
#####   in the same domain. This really has nothing particular to do
#####   with Ethernet - the name is historical.

Mether, P=[ICP], F=msDFMuCX, S=11, R=21, A=TCP $h
S11
R$*<@$+>$*              $@$1<@$2>$3             already ok
R$+                     $@$1<@$w>               tack on our hostname

S21
# None needed.




###############################################################
# General code to convert back to old style UUCP names
S5
R$+<@LOCAL>             $@ $w!$1                name@LOCAL => sun!name
R$+<@$-.LOCAL>          $@ $2!$1                u@h.LOCAL => h!u
R$+<@$+.uucp>           $@ $2!$1                u@h.uucp => h!u
R$+<@$*>                $@ $2!$1                u@h => h!u
# Route-addrs do not work here. Punt til uucp-mail comes up with something.
R<@$+>$*                $@ @$1$2                just defocus and punt
R$*<$*>$*               $@ $1$2$3               Defocus strange stuff


#       UUCP Mailer specification
```

```
Muucp,  P=/usr/bin/uux, F=msDFMhuU, S=13, R=23,
        A=uux - -r -a$f $h!rmail ($u)

# Convert uucp sender (From) field
S13
R$+                       $:$>5$1                     convert to old style
R$=w!$+                   $2                          strip local name
R$+                       $:$w!$1                     stick on real host name

# Convert uucp recipient (To, Cc) fields
S23
R$+                       $:$>5$1                     convert to old style


#ident   "@(#)ddnm.m4   1.7    92/07/14 SMI"    /* SunOS 4.1    */
#
#
#                 Copyright Notice
#
#Notice of copyright on this source code product does not indicate
#publication.
#
#      (c) 1986,1987,1988,1989 Sun Microsystems, Inc
#                 All rights reserved.

#############################################################
#
#                 DDN Mailer specification
#
#        Send mail on the Defense Data Network
#           (such as Arpanet or Milnet)

Mddn,   P=[TCP], F=msDFMuCX, S=22, R=22, A=TCP $h, E=\r\n

# map containing the inverse of mail.aliases
# Note that there is a special case mail.byaddr will cause reverse
# lookups in both Nis+ and NIS.
# If you want to use ONLY Nis+ for alias inversion comment out the next line
# and uncomment the line after that
DZmail.byaddr
#DZREVERSE.mail_aliases.org_dir

S22
R$*<@LOCAL>$*          $:$1
R$-<@$-)              $:$>3${Z$1@$2$}             invert aliases
R$*<@$+.$*>$*          $@$1<@$2.$3>$4             already ok
R$+<@$+>$*             $@$1<@$2.$m>$3             tack on our domain
R$+                   $@$1<@$m>                  tack on our domain


# "Smart" UUCP mailer: Uses UUCP transport but domain-style naming
Msmartuucp, P=/usr/bin/uux, F=CmsDFMhuU, S=22, R=22,
```

```
        A=uux - -r $h!rmail ($u)


###############################################################
#
#                    RULESET ZERO
#
#              This is the ruleset that determines which mailer a name goes to.

# Ruleset 30 just calls rulesets 3 then 0.
S30
R$*                        $: $>3 $1                          First canonicalize
R$*                        $@ $>0 $1                          Then rerun ruleset 0

S0
# On entry, the address has been canonicalized and focused by ruleset 3.
# Handle special cases.....
R@                         $#local $:$n                       handle <> form

# resolve the local hostname to "LOCAL".
R$*<$*$=w.LOCAL>$*         $1<$2LOCAL>$4                      thishost.LOCAL
R$*<$*$=w.uucp>$*          $1<$2LOCAL>$4                      thishost.uucp
R$*<$*$=w>$*               $1<$2LOCAL>$4                      thishost

# Mail addressed explicitly to the domain gateway (us)
R$*<@LOCAL>                $@$>30$1                            strip our name, retry
R<@LOCAL>:$+               $@$>30$1                            retry after route strip

# For numeric spec, you can't pass spec on to receiver, since old rcvr's
# are not smart enough to know that [x.y.z.a] is their own name.
R<@[$+]>:$*                $:$>9 <@[$1]>:$2                    Clean it up, then...
R<@[$+]>:$*                $#ether $@[$1] $:$2                 numeric internet spec
R<@[$+]>,$*                $#ether $@[$1] $:$2                 numeric internet spec
R$*<@[$+]>                 $#ether $@[$2] $:$1                 numeric internet spec

# deliver to known ethernet hosts explicitly specified in our domain
R$*<@$%y.LOCAL>$*          $#ether $@$2 $:$1<@$2>$3  user@host.sun.com

# etherhost.uucp is treated as etherhost.$m for now.
# This allows them to be addressed from uucp as foo!sun!etherhost!user.
R$*<@$%y.uucp>$*           $#ether $@$2 $:$1<@$2>$3  user@etherhost.uucp

# Explicitly specified names in our domain -- that we've never heard of
R$*<@$*.LOCAL>$*           $#error $:Never heard of host $2 in domain $m

# Clean up addresses for external use -- kills LOCAL, route-addr ,=>:
R$*                        $:$>9 $1                            Then continue...

# resolve UUCP-style names
R<@$-.uucp>:$+             $#uucp $@$1 $:$2                    @host.uucp:...
R$+<@$-.uucp>              $#uucp $@$2 $:$1                    user@host.uucp
```

```
# Pass other valid names up the ladder to our forwarder
#R$*<@$*.$=T>$*          $#$M $@$R $:$1<@$2.$3>$4  user@domain.known

# Replace following with above to only forward "known" top-level domains
R$*<@$*.$+>$*            $#$M $@$R $:$1<@$2.$3>$4  user@any.domain

# if you are on the DDN, then comment-out both of the lines above
# and use the following instead:
#R$*<@$*.$+>$*           $#ddn $@ $2.$3 $:$1<@$2.$3>$4  user@any.domain

# All addresses in the rules ABOVE are absolute (fully qualified domains).
# Addresses BELOW can be partially qualified.

# deliver to known ethernet hosts
R$*<@$%y>$*              $#ether $@$2 $:$1<@$2>$3  user@etherhost

# other non-local names have nowhere to go; return them to sender.
R$*<@$+.$->$*            $#error $:Unknown domain $3
R$*<@$+>$*               $#error $:Never heard of $2 in domain $m
R$*@$*                   $#error $:I don't understand $1@$2

# Local names with % are really not local!
R$+%$+                   $@$>30$1@$2                          turn % => @, retry

# everything else is a local name
R$+                      $#local $:$1                         local names
```

Configuration File Syntax

The configuration file is organized as a series of lines, each of which begins with a single character defining the semantics for the rest of the line. Lines beginning with a space or a tab are continuation lines (although in many places the semantics are not well defined). Blank lines and lines beginning with a pound sign (#) are comments.

D and L (Define Macro)

Macros are named with a single character. Although a macro can be defined with any character from the complete ASCII set, use only uppercase letters for macros that you define. However, do not use characters such as M, R, L, G, and V which are already used in the default sendmail.cf file. Lowercase letters and special symbols are used internally.

You can define macros in two ways:

■ D assigns the value directly specified.

■ L assigns the value looked up in the sendmailvars database (either the NIS+ table or the /etc/mail/sendmailvars file).

The L command is classified as an uncommitted interface.

The syntax for D macro definitions is

```
DXval
```

where *X* is the name of the macro and val is the value it should have. Spaces are not allowed. Macros can be inserted in most places using the escape sequence $X.

Here is an example of D macro definitions from the configuration file:

```
DRmailhost
DmEng.Sun.COM
```

The variable *R* is set to contain the value mailhost and the internal variable *m* is set to contain the value Eng.Sun.COM.

The m macro defines the mail domain. If it is not defined, the name service domain name is used with the first component stripped off. For example, Ecd.East.Sun.COM becomes East.Sun.COM.

The syntax for an L macro definition, which is an even more flexible way to define the mail domain name, is

```
LXsearch_key
```

where *X* is the name of the macro and *search_key* is looked up in the sendmailvars database. The value found in the entry located by the search key is assigned to *X*.

Here is an example of an internal L macro definition from the configuration file:

```
Lmmaildomain
```

The variable *m* is set to the value found in the sendmailvars database using maildomain as the search key. If the entry in the sendmailvars database looks like this example:

```
maildomain        Eng.Sun.COM
```

the value of *m* becomes Eng.Sun.COM.

New with SVR4.

NOTE.   *The sendmail program uses the sendmailvars entry in the /etc/nsswitch.conf file to determine the order in which it searches the NIS+ database and the /etc/mail/sendmailvars database.*

C, F, and G (Define Classes)
You can define classes of words to match on the left-hand side of rewriting rules. For example, you might create a class of all local names for this site so that you can eliminate attempts to send to yourself.

Classes may be named from the set of uppercase letters. Lowercase letters and special characters are reserved for system use.

You can define classes in three ways:

- C assigns the value(s) specified directly.

- F reads in the value(s) from another file or from another command.

- G assigns the value(s) looked up in the sendmailvars database (either the NIS+ database or the /etc/mail/sendmailvars file). The G command is classified as an uncommitted interface.

The syntax of the different forms of class definition is

```
CC word1 word2
FC file
FC | command
GCsearch_key
```

The first form defines the class C to match any of the named words. The second form reads words from the file into the class C, for example, FC /.rhosts. The format is used with scanf to read from the file; otherwise, the first word from each line is used. The third form executes the given command and reads the elements of the class from standard output of the command. For example,

```
FC | awk '{print $2}' /etc/hosts
```

The fourth form reads the elements of the class from the entry in the sendmailvars database pointed to by the search key. For example,

```
GVuucp-list
```

gets the definition of class V from the uucp-list entry in the sendmailvars database.

If the entry in the sendmailvars database looks like this:

```
uucp-list               castle oak cinderella
```

the value of *V* becomes castle oak cinderella.

NOTE. *The sendmail program uses the sendmailvars entry in the /etc/nsswitch.conf file to determine the order in which it searches the NIS+ database and the /etc/mail/sendmailvars database.*

You could split class definitions among multiple lines. For example,

```
CHmonet ucbmonet
```

is equivalent to

```
CHmonet
CHucbmonet
```

O (Set Option)

You can set several options (not to be confused with mailer flags or command-line arguments) from a configuration file. Options arc also represented by single characters. The syntax of this line is

```
OC ovalue
```

Option C is set to *value*. Depending on the option, *value* may be a string, an integer, a boolean (with legal values t, T, f, or F—the default is true), or a time interval. See the section "Configuration Options" later in this chapter for the list of options.

P (Precedence Definitions)

You can define values for the Precedence: field using the P control line. The syntax of this field is

```
Pname=num
```

When the *name* is found in a Precedence: field, the message class is set to *num*. Higher numbers mean higher precedence. Numbers less than zero have the special property that error messages are not returned. The default precedence is zero. For example,

```
Pfirst-class=0
Pspecial-delivery=100
Pjunk=-100
```

T (Define Trusted Users)

Trusted users are those users who are permitted to override the sender name using the -f flag. These users typically are root, uucp, daemon, and network. For some sites, it may be convenient to extend this list to include other users, perhaps to support a separate uucp login for each host. The syntax of this line is

```
T user . . .
```

You can use more than one line to define trusted users.

H (Define Header)

The format of the header lines is defined by the H line. The syntax of this line is

```
H[c ?c mflagsc ?]c hnamec :c htemplate
```

Continuation lines in this specification are inserted directly into the outgoing message. The htemplate is macro-cxpanded before it is inserted into the message. If the expansion is empty, the header line is not included. If the *mflags* (surrounded by question marks) are specified, at least one of the specified flags must be stated in the mailer definition for this header to be automatically output. If one of these headers is in the input, it is directed to the output regardless of these flags.

Special Header Lines

Several header lines have special interpretations defined by the configuration file. Others have interpretations built into sendmail that cannot be changed without changing the code. The built-in features are described in the following list:

- Return-Receipt-To: If this header is sent, a message will be sent to any specified names when the final delivery is complete. The mailer must have the l flag (local delivery) set in the mailer descriptor.

- Errors-To: If errors occur anywhere during processing, this header sends error messages to the listed names rather than to the sender. Use this header line for mailing lists so that errors are returned to the list administrator.

- To: If a message comes in with no recipients listed in the message (in a To:, CC:, or BCC: line), then sendmail adds an Apparently To: header line for each recipient specified on the sendmail command line.

S and R (Rewriting Rules)

Address parsing is done using the rewriting rules, which are a simple pattern-matching system. Scanning through the set of rewriting rules, sendmail looks for a match on the left-hand side (LHS) of the rule. When a rule matches, the name is replaced by the right-hand side (RHS) of the rule.

There are several sets of rewriting rules. Some of the rewriting sets are used internally and must have specific semantics. Other rewriting sets do not have specifically assigned semantics and may be referenced by the mailer definitions or by other rewriting sets. For example,

```
S n
```

sets the current ruleset being collected to *n*. If you begin a ruleset more than once, it deletes the old definition.

R is used to define a rule in the ruleset. The syntax of the R line is

```
Rlhs            rhs                comments
```

Here is an example of how a rule definition might look:

```
# handle "from:<>" special case
R<>                 $@@              turn into magic token
```

The fields must be separated by at least one tab character; you may use embedded spaces in the fields. The *lhs* is a pattern that is applied to the input. If it matches, the input is rewritten to the rhs. The *comments* are ignored.

M (Define Mailer)

Programs and interfaces to mailers are defined on this line. The format is

```
Mname, P=, F=, S=, R=, A=, etc.
{c field=c value}*
```

where *name* is the name of the mailer (used in error messages) and the *field=value* pairs define attributes of the mailer. The fields are shown in Table 4.5.

(Only the first character of the field name is checked.)

Table 4.5 **Mailer Definition Fields**

Field	Description
P[ath]	The path name of the mailer
F[lags]	Special flags for this mailer
S[ender]	A rewriting set for sender names
R[ecipient]	A rewriting ruleset for recipient names
A[rgv]	An argument vector to pass to this mailer
E[ol]	The end-of-line string for this mailer
M[axsize]	The maximum message length to this mailer
L[ength]	The maximum length of the argv for this mailer

Address Rewriting Rules

The following sections describe the details of rewriting rules and mailer descriptions.

Special Macros, Conditionals

Macros are referenced using the format $c *x*, where *x* is the name of the macro to be matched (LHS) or inserted (RHS). Lowercase letters are reserved for special semantics, and some special characters are reserved to provide conditionals.

The macros shown in Table 4.6 *must* be defined to transmit information into sendmail.

Table 4.6   **Required sendmail Macros**

Macro	Description
e	The SMTP entry message
j	The official domain name for this site
l	The format of the UNIX From line
n	The name of the daemon (for error messages)
o	The set of "separators" in names
q	The default format of sender names

The $e macro is printed out when SMTP starts. The first word of $e should be the $j macro. The $j macro should be in domain-name format. The $o macro is a list of characters that are considered tokens and that separate tokens when scanning. For example, if y is in the $o macro, then the input xyzzy would be scanned as four tokens: x, y, and zz and y. Finally, the $q macro specifies how a sender name should appear in a message when it is created. For example, here are the SunOS 5.*x* default special macros:

```
De$j Sendmail $v ready at $b*
DnMAILER-DAEMON
DlFrom $g $d
Do.:%@!^=/
Dq$g$?x ($x)$.|
Dj$H.$D
```

You should not need to change any of these macros except under unusual circumstances. For example, you might want to change the banner (*) for security. You might want to change | or to make several hosts look like one host.

An acceptable alternative for the $q macro is

```
$?x$x $.<$g>
```

These correspond to the following two formats:

```
nowicki@sun.COM (Bill Nowicki)
Bill Nowicki <nowicki@sun.COM>
```

Some macros are defined by sendmail for use in mailer arguments or for other contexts. These macros are shown in Table 4.7.

Table 4.7   **Additional sendmail Macro Definitions**

Macro	Description
a	The origination date in ARPANET format
b	The current date in ARPANET format
c	The hop count
d	The date in UNIX (ctime) format
f	The sender (from) name
g	The sender name relative to the recipient
h	The recipient host
i	The queue ID
m	The domain name
p	Sendmail's process ID
r	Protocol used
s	Sender's host name
t	A numeric representation of the current time
u	The recipient user
v	The version number of sendmail
w	The hostname of this site

Table 4.7 **Additional sendmail Macro Definitions (Continued)**

Macro	Description
x	The full name of the sender
z	The home directory of the recipient

You can use three types of dates. The $a and $b macros are in ARPANET format; $a is the time as extracted from the Date: line of the message (if there was one), and $b is the current date and time (used for postmarks). If no Date: line is found in the incoming message, $a is set to the current time also. The $d macro is equivalent to the $a macro in UNIX (ctime) format.

The $f macro is the ID of the sender as originally determined; when mailing to a specific host, the $g macro is set to the name of the sender relative to the recipient. For example, supposing the sender eric sends to bollard@matisse from the machine ucbarpa, the $f macro will be eric and the $g macro will be eric@ucbarpa.

The $x macro is set to the full name of the sender, which can be determined in several ways. It can be passed as a flag to sendmail; can use the value of the Full-name: line in the header if it exists; or can use the comment field of a From: line. If all of these fail—and if the message is being originated locally—the full name is looked up in the /etc/passwd file. It can also be read from the name environment variable.

When sending, the $h, $u, and $z macros get set to the host, user, and home directory (if local) of the recipient. The first two are set from the $@ and $: part of the rewriting rules, respectively.

The $p and $t macros are used to create unique strings (for example, for the Message-Id: field). The $i macro is set to the queue ID on this host; if put into the timestamp line, it can be useful for tracking messages. The $v macro is set to be the version number of sendmail; this normally is put in timestamps and has been proven extremely useful for debugging. Some people feel, however, that it is a security risk, as it may provide outsiders with information about your network setup. The $w macro is set to the primary name of this host as given by the Host table for NIS+, or gethostname(1) and gethostbyname(3) for NIS. The $c field is set to the hop count—that is, the number of times this message has been processed—which can be determined by the -h flag on the command line or by counting the timestamps in the message.

The $r and $s fields are set to the protocol used to communicate with sendmail and the sending hostname.

You can specify conditionals by using the syntax:

```
$?x text1 $| text2 $
```

This inserts *text1* if the macro $x is set, and *text2* otherwise. The else (c $|) clause may be omitted.

Special Classes
The class $=w is the set of all names by which this host is known. It can be used to delete local hostnames. The class $=m is set to the list of domain names to which this host belongs.

The Left-hand Side
The left-hand side of rewriting rules contains a pattern. Normal words are simply matched directly. Dollar signs introduce metasymbols, which match units other than simple words, such as macros or classes. The metasymbols are shown in Table 4.8.

Table 4.8   **Left-Side Metasymbols for sendmail**

Symbol	Description
$*	Match zero or more tokens
$+	Match one or more tokens
$-	Match exactly one token
$=x	Match any string in class x
$~x	Match any token not in class x
$%x	Match any token in NIS map or NIS+ table $x
$!x	Match any token not in NIS map or NIS+ table $x
$x	Match macro x

If any of the patterns match, the match is assigned to the symbol $c n for replacement on the right-hand side, where n is the index in the LHS. For example, if the LHS

```
$-:$+
```

is applied to the input

```
UCBARPA:eric
```

the rule will match, and the values passed to the RHS will be

```
$1 UCBARPA
$2 eric
```

The $%x uses the macro x to specify the name of an NIS map or NIS+ table. The special form $%y matches any hostname in the Hosts database for NIS+, in hosts.byname map for NIS, or in /etc/hosts if NIS or NIS+ is not running.

Right-hand Side Address Rewriting Rules

When the left-hand side of a rewriting rule matches, the input is replaced by the right-hand side. Tokens are copied directly from the right-hand side unless they begin with a dollar sign.

Metasymbols for more complicated substitutions are shown in Table 4.9.

Table 4.9   **Right-Side Metasymbols for sendmail**

Symbol	Description
$x	Expand macro x
$n	Substitute indefinite token n from LHS
$>n	Call ruleset n
$#mailer	Resolve to mailer
$@host	Specify host (+ prefix? ruleset return)
$:user	Specify user (+ prefix rule limit)
$[host$]	Map to primary hostname
${x name$}	Map name through NIS map or NIS+ table $x. If the map name begins with RE-VERSE, it will look things up in reverse to invert aliases.

The $c n (n being a digit) syntax substitutes the corresponding value from a $+, $-, $*, $=, or $(ap match on the LHS. It may be used anywhere.

The $>c n syntax substitutes the remainder of the line as usual and then passes it to ruleset n. The final value of ruleset n then becomes the substitution for this rule (like a procedure or function call).

Only use the $# syntax in ruleset 0. Evaluation of the ruleset stops immediately and signals to sendmail that the name has completely resolved. The complete syntax is

```
$#mailer$@host$:user
```

This specifies the {*mailer, host, user*} triplet necessary to direct the mailer. More processing may then take place depending on the mailer. For example, local names are aliased.

A right-hand side may also be preceded by a $@ or a $: to control evaluation. A $@ prefix returns the remainder of the right-hand side as the value. A $: prefix terminates the rule immediately, but the ruleset continues; thus, it can be used to limit a rule to one application. Neither prefix affects the result of the right-hand side expansion.

The $@ and $: prefixes can precede a $> spec. For example,

```
R$+                     $:$>7$1
```

matches anything, passes that to ruleset 7, and continues; the $: is necessary to avoid an infinite loop. The $[*host*]$ syntax replaces the hostname with the "official" or primary hostname—the one listed first in the *hosts.byname* NIS map, NIS+ table, DNS, or local /etc/hosts file. It is used to eliminate nicknames for hosts. The ${x *name* $} syntax replaces the string by the result of the nis_map_name indicated in macro $x.

Semantics of Rewriting Rulesets

Five rewriting sets have specific semantics, as shown in Figure 4.1.

Figure 4.1

Semantics of rewriting rulesets

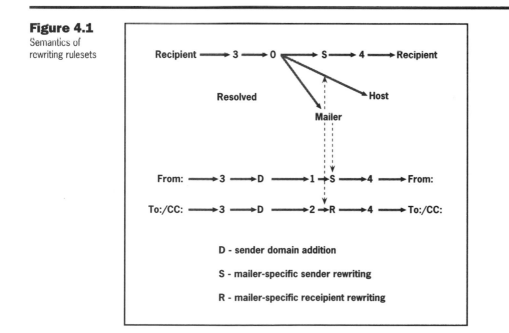

D - sender domain addition

S - mailer-specific sender rewriting

R - mailer-specific receipient rewriting

Ruleset 3 is applied by sendmail before it does anything with any name. That ruleset should turn the name into canonical form, with the basic syntax

```
local-part@host-domain-spec
```

If no @ sign is specified, then the *host-domain-spec* may be appended from the sender name (if the C flag is set in the mailer definition corresponding to the sending mailer).

Ruleset 0 is applied after ruleset 3 to names that are going to actually specify recipients. It must resolve to a {*mailer, host, user*} triplet. The mailer must be defined in the mailer definitions from the configuration file. The host is defined into the $h macro for use in the argument expansion of the specified mailer; the user is defined into $u.

Rulesets 1 and 2 are applied to all From:, To:, and CC: recipient names, respectively. Then the rulesets specified in the mailer definition line (and R=) are applied. Note that this process is done many times for one message, depending on how many mailers the message is routed to by ruleset 0.

Ruleset 4 is applied last to all names in the message. It is typically used to translate internal to external form.

The error Mailer

You can use this mailer with the special name error in ruleset 0 to generate a user error message. The user field is a message to be printed. For example, the entry

```
$#error$:Host unknown in this domain
```

on the RHS of a rule generates the specified error if the LHS matches.

Semantics of Mailer Descriptions

Each mailer has an internal name. It can be arbitrary, except that the names *local* and *prog* must be defined first and second, respectively. Ruleset 0 resolves names to this mailer name (and a host and a user name).

Give the pathname of the mailer in the P field. If this mailer will be accessed via a TCP connection, use the string [TCP] instead.

Define the mailer flags in the F field. Specify an f or an r flag to pass the name of the sender as -f or -r flags, respectively. These flags are passed only if they were passed to sendmail, so that mailers that give errors under some circumstances can be placated. If the mailer is not picky, you can just specify -f$g in the argv template. If the mailer must be called as root and if sendmail is running setuid to root, use the S flag; it will not reset the user ID before calling the mailer. If this mailer is local (that is, will perform final delivery rather than another network hop), use the flag. Quote characters (backslashes and double quotes) can be stripped from names if the s flag is specified; if it is not specified, they are passed through. If the mailer is capable of sending to more than one user on the same host in a single transaction, the m flag should be used. If this flag is on, then the argv template containing $u is repeated for each unique user on a given host. The e flag marks the mailer as being "expensive," and sendmail defers connection until a queue run. Note that the c configuration option must also be set.

The C flag is an unusual case. It applies to the mailer that the message is received from, rather than the mailer being sent to; if this flag is set, the domain specification of the sender (that is, the @host.domain part) is saved and is appended to any names in the message that do not already contain a domain specification. For example, a message of the form

```
From: eric@ucbarpa
To: wnj@monel, mckusick
```

is modified to

```
From: eric@ucbarpa
To: wnj@monet, mckusick@ucbarpa
```

if and only if the C flag is defined in the mailer corresponding to eric@ucbarpa.

The S and R fields in the mailer description are rewriting sets specific to a mailer and are to be applied to sender and recipient names, respectively. These are applied after the sending domain is appended and the general rewriting set (ruleset 1 or 2) is applied, but before the output rewrite (ruleset 4) is applied. A typical use is to append the current domain to names that do not already have a domain. For example, a header of the form

```
From: eric@host
```

might be changed to be

```
From: eric@host.Podunk.EDU
```

or

```
From: ucbvax!eric
```

depending on the domain it is being shipped into. These sets can also be used to do special-purpose output rewriting in cooperation with ruleset 4.

The E field defines the string to use as an end-of-line indication. A string containing return and newline is the default if using TCP; otherwise just a newline indicates end of line. You can use the printf backslash escapes (\r, \n, \f, \b).

Use the A field to specify an argument vector template. It may have embedded spaces. The template is expanded by a macro before being passed to the mailer. Useful macros include $h (the hostname resolved by ruleset 0) and $u (the user name or names resolved). If there is no argument with a $u macro in it, sendmail uses SMTP to communicate with the mailer. If the pathname for this mailer is [TCP], use the argument vector:

```
TCP $h [ port ]
```

where *port* is the optional port number to connect to.

If an L field exists, it specifies the maximum length of the $u macro passed to the mailer. To make UUCP mail more efficient, the L field can be used with the m flag to send multiple recipients with one call to the mailer, while avoiding mailer limitations on argument length. Even if that recipient exceeds the L= limit, $u always expands to at least one recipient.

For example, the specification

```
Mlocal, P=/bin/mail, F=flsSDFMmnP, S=10, R=20, A=mail -d $u
Mether,  P=[TCP],   F=msDFMuCX,  S=11, R=21, A=TCP $h
```

names a mailer to do local delivery and a mailer for Ethernet delivery. The first mailer is called local and is located in the file /bin/mail. It takes the -f flag, does local delivery, strips quotes from names, and delivers multiple users at once. It applies ruleset 10 to sender names in the message and applies ruleset 20 to recipient names. The argument vector to send to a message is the word *mail*, the letter *-d*, and words containing the name of the receiving user. If the -r or -f flag is inserted, it is between *mail* and *-d*.

The second mailer is called ether. It is connected via TCP and can handle multiple users at once. It defers connections and appends any domain from the sender name to any receiver name without a domain. Sender names are processed by ruleset 11 and recipient names by ruleset 21. Messages passed through this mailer have a 100,000-byte limit.

Building a New Configuration File

Building a configuration file from scratch is a complex task. Fortunately, you can accommodate almost every situation by changing an existing file. In any case, it is critical that you understand what it is that you are trying to do and come up with a policy statement for the delivery of mail. The following sections explain the purpose of a configuration file and provide some ideas for what your policy might be.

Domains and Policies

RFC 1006 describes domain-based naming. RFC 822 touches on this issue as well. Essentially, each host is given a name that is a right-to-left dot-qualified pseudopath from a distinguished root. The elements of the path are organizational entities, not physical networks.

RFC 822 and 976 specify how certain sorts of addresses should be parsed. You can configure sendmail to either follow or ignore these rules.

How to Proceed

Once you have established a policy, it is worth examining the available configuration files to decide if any of them are close enough so that you can use major parts of them. Almost always, a fair amount of boilerplate can be reused.

Always keep a backup copy of your configuration files, to protect against accidental deletion.

The next step is to build ruleset 3, which specifies a ruleset for your individual mailers. Building ruleset 3 is the hardest part of the job. Here are some guidelines:

- Beware of doing too much to the name in this ruleset, since anything you do will reflect through to the message.

- Do not strip local domains in this ruleset. This can leave you with names with no domain spec at all. Because sendmail likes to append the sending domain to names with no domain, the semantics of names can change.

- Do not provide fully qualified domains in this ruleset. Although technically legal, fully qualified domain names can lead to unpleasantly and unnecessarily long names reflected into messages. The SunOS configuration files define ruleset 9 to qualify domain names and strip local domains. Ruleset 9 is called from ruleset 0 to get all names into a cleaner form.

Once you have ruleset 3 finished, the other rulesets should be relatively simple. If you need hints, examine the supplied configuration files.

To turn on fully qualified domain names, use the sendmail.mx file and replace *Mether* with *Mddn*. Another way to turn on fully qualified domain names is to duplicate the Mddn mailer and change its name to Mether.

Testing the Rewriting Rules—the -bt Flag

When you build a configuration file, you can do a certain amount of testing using the test mode of sendmail. For example, you could invoke sendmail as

```
% sendmail -bt -Ctest.cf
```

which would read the configuration file test.cf and enter test mode. For example,

```
ADDRESS TEST MODE
Enter <ruleset> <name>
>
```

In this mode, you enter lines of the form

```
ADDRESS TEST MODE
Enter <ruleset> <name>
> rwset name
```

where *rwset* is the rewriting set you want to use and *name* is a name to which the set is applied. Test mode shows you the steps it takes as it proceeds, finally showing you the name it ends up with. You may use a comma-separated list of *rwsets* for sequential application of rules to an input; ruleset 3 is always applied first. For example,

```
ADDRESS TEST MODE
Enter <ruleset> <name>
> 1,21,4 monet:bollard
```

first applies ruleset 3 to the input monet:bollard. Ruleset 1 is then applied to the output of ruleset 3, followed similarly by rulesets 21 and 4.

If you need more detail, you can also use the -d21 flag to turn on more debugging. For example,

```
% sendmail -bt -d21.99
```

turns on an incredible amount of information; a single word name may result in several pages of information.

Command-Line Arguments

The following sections describe the arguments to sendmail that you can use on the command line. The arguments are briefly described in Table 4.10.

Table 4.10   **Command-Line Arguments for sendmail**

Argument	Description
-r *name*	The sender's name is *name*. This flag is ignored unless the real user is listed as a "trusted user" or if *name* contains an exclamation point (because of certain restrictions in UUCP).
-f *name*	An obsolete form of -r.
-h *cnt*	Sets the "hop count" to *cnt*. It shows the number of times this message has been processed by sendmail (to the extent that it is supported by the underlying networks). During processing, *cnt* is incremented; if it reaches the value of configuration option h, sendmail returns the message with an error.

Table 4.10 **Command-Line Arguments for sendmail (Continued)**

Argument	Description
-F*name*	Sets the full name of this user to *name*.
-n	Do not do aliasing or forwarding.
-t	Read the header for To:, CC:, and BCC: lines, and send to everyone listed in those lists. The BCC: line is deleted before sending. Any names in the argument vector are deleted from the send list.
-b*x*	Set operation mode to *x*. Operation modes are:
	m Deliver mail (default).
	a Run in ARPANET mode.
	s Speak SMTP on input side.
	d Run as a daemon.
	t Run in test mode.
	v Just verify recipients.
	I Initialize the Aliases database.
	p Print the mail queue.
	z Freeze the configuration file.
-q*time*	Try to process the queued-up mail. If the time is given, sendmail repeatedly runs through the queue at the specified interval to deliver queued mail; otherwise, it runs only once.
-C*file*	Use a different configuration file.
-d*level*	Set debugging level.
-o*xvalue*	Set configuration option *x* to the specified *value*.
-M *msgid*	Run given message ID from the queue.
-R *recipient*	Run messages for given recipient only from the queue.

These arguments are described in the next section, "Configuration Options."

You can specify several configuration options as primitive flags. These are the c, e, i, m, T, and v arguments. Also, you can specify the f configuration option as the -s argument.

Configuration Options

You can set the options shown in Table 4.11 using either the -o flag on the command line or the O line in the configuration file.

Table 4.11   **Configuration Options for sendmail**

Option	Description
A*file*	Use the named *file* as the alias file instead of /etc/mail/aliases. If no file is specified, use aliases in the current directory.
A*time*	If set, time to wait for an @:@ entry to exist in the Aliases database before starting up. If it does not appear after that time, rebuild the database.
B*value*	Blank substitute. Default is the dot (.) character.
b*n*	Disallow empty messages to more than *n* recipients.
c	If an outgoing mailer is marked as being expensive, do not connect immediately. A queue process must be run to actually send the mail.
c*n*	Checkpoint after *n* recipients.
D	If set, rebuild the Aliases database if necessary and possible. If this option is not set, sendmail never rebuilds the Aliases database unless explicitly requested using -bi.
d*x*	Deliver in mode *x*. Legal modes are:
	i Deliver interactively (synchronously).
	b Deliver in background (asynchronously).
	q Just queue the message (deliver during queue run).
e*x*	Dispose of errors using mode *x*. The values for *x* are:
	p Print error messages (default).
	q No messages, just give exit status.
	m Mail back errors to sender.
	w Write back errors (mail if user is not logged in).
	e Mail back errors and give zero exit status always.
f	Save UNIX-style From lines at the front of headers. Normally they are assumed redundant and are discarded.
F*n*	The temporary queue file mode, in Octal. Good choices are 644 and 600.

Table 4.11 **Configuration Options for sendmail (Continued)**

Option	Description
g*n*	Set the default group ID for mailers to run in to *n*.
H*file*	Specify the help file for SMTP [Postel82].
h *n*	Set maximum hop count to *n*.
i	Ignore dots in Incoming messages.
L*n*	Set the default log level to *n*.
m	Send to me too, even if I am in an alias expansion.
M*xvalue*	Set the macro *x* to *value*. This is intended for use only from the command line.
o	Assume that the headers may be in old format; that is, spaces delimit names. This flag actually turns on an adaptive algorithm. If any recipient name contains a comma, parentheses, or angle brackets, it is assumed that commas already exist. If this flag is not on, only commas delimit names. Headers are always output with commas between the names.
P*name*	The name of the local postmaster. If defined, error messages from the MAILER-DAEMON send the header to this name.
Q*dir*	Use the directory named in the *dir* variable as the queue directory.
q*limit*	Size limit of messages to be queued under heavy load. Default is 10,000 bytes.
R*server*	Remote mode. Deliver through remote SMTP server. Default is location of /var/mail.
r*time*	Timeout reads after *time* interval.
s	Be super-safe when running things; that is, always create the queue file, even if you are going to try immediate delivery. The sendmail program always creates the queue file before returning control to the client under any circumstances.
S*file*	Save statistics in the named file.
T*time*	Set the queue timeout to *time*. After this interval, messages that have not been successfully sent are returned to the sender.
u*n*	Set the default user ID for mailers to *n*. Mailers without the S flag in the mailer definition are run as this user.
v	Run in verbose mode.
X*n*	Set the load average value so that the sendmail daemon refuses incoming SMTP connections to reduce system load. Default is zero, which disables this feature.
x*n*	Set the load average value so that sendmail simply queues mail (regardless of the d*x* option) to reduce system load. Default is zero, which disables this feature.

Table 4.11   **Configuration Options for sendmail (Continued)**

Option	Description
y*n*	Recipient factor. Lower the delivery priority of messages with this many bytes per recipient.
Y*name*	NIS map name to be used for aliases. Default is mail.aliases.
Z*n*	Time factor. Lower the delivery priority of messages with this many bytes per delivery attempts.
z*n*	Message class factor. Lower the delivery priority of messages with this many bytes per class.

Mailer Flags

The flags you can set in the mailer description are described in Table 4.12.

Table 4.12   **Flags You Can Set in the Mailer Description for sendmail**

Flag	Description
C	If mail is received from a mailer with this flag set, any names in the header that do not have an at sign (@) after being rewritten by ruleset 3 have the @domain clause from the sender tacked on. This flag allows mail with headers of the form:

```
From: usera@local
To: userb, userc@remote
```

to be automatically rewritten as:

```
From: usera@local
To: userb@local, userc@remote
```

Flag	Description
D	This mailer wants a Date: header line.
E	Escape From lines to be >From (usually specified with U).
e	This mailer is expensive to connect to, so try to avoid connecting normally; any necessary connection occurs during a queue run.
F	This mailer wants a From: header line.
f	This mailer wants the -f *from* flag, but only if this is a network forward operation. (That is, the mailer gives an error if the executing user does not have special permissions.)
h	Preserve uppercase in hostnames for this mailer.

Table 4.12   **Flags You Can Set in the Mailer Description for sendmail (Continued)**

Flag	Description
L	Limit the line lengths as specified in RFC 821.
l	This mailer is local (that is, final delivery will be performed).
M	This mailer expects a Message-Id: header line.
m	This mailer can send to multiple users on the same host in one transaction. When a $u macro occurs in the argv part of the mailer definition, that field is repeated as necessary for all qualifying users. The L= field of the mailer description can be used to limit the total length of the $u expansion.
n	Do not insert a UNIX-style From line on the front of the message.
P	This mailer expects a Return-Path: line.
p	Always add local hostname to the MAIL From: line of SMTP, even if there already is one.
r	Same as f, but sends the -r flag.
S	Do not reset the user ID before calling the mailer. This flag would be used in a secure environment where sendmail ran as root. This flag can be used to avoid forged names.
s	Strip quote characters from the name before calling the mailer.
U	This mailer wants UNIX-style From lines with the UUCP style remote from <*host*> on the end.
u	Preserve uppercase in user names for this mailer.
X	This mailer uses the hidden dot algorithm as specified in RFC 821; basically, any line beginning with a dot will have an extra dot inserted at the front (to be stripped at the other end). This flag ensures that lines in the message containing a dot do not terminate the message prematurely.
x	This mailer expects a Full-Name: header line.

This part introduces the NIS+ naming service environment. Chapter 5 provides an overview of NIS+, explains how NIS+ differs from the Solaris 1.*x* NIS naming service, and introduces the NIS+ commands. Chapter 6 describes how to add a system as an NIS+ client in an existing NIS+ environment.

Refer to the chapters in this part if you want to familiarize yourself with the basics of the NIS+ naming service and its administrative commands, and for instructions on how to set up an NIS+ client. This part does not provide in-depth information for a system administrator who must set up and support an NIS+ environment. Refer to *All About Administering NIS+* by Rick Ramsey for the complete NIS+ story.

PART

2

NIS+

Introducing the NIS+ Environment

New with SVR4.

NIS+ IS A NETWORK INFORMATION SERVICE THAT IS NEW WITH SOLARIS 2.*x*. NIS+ is a repository of administrative information, the foundation for the Solaris 2.*x* Administration Tool applications, and a place to store network resource information that users can access without knowing the specific location of the resource. NIS+ is a component of ONC+™. ONC+ consists of a set of new and enhanced core services for enterprise-wide distributed computing. ONC+ services—including NIS+, TI-RCP, and enhanced NFS—are completely compatible and will interoperate with the installed base of ONC services, including NFS, NIS, and RPC services. NIS+ replaces Solaris 1.*x* NIS and is compatible with it. When run in compatibility mode, NIS+ serves NIS requests as well as NIS+ requests. NIS+ is designed to manage resources for distributed systems, be easier to administer in complex organizations, and provide more security than was possible with NIS.

The main function of NIS+ is to simplify system and network administration, including tasks such as adding and relocating systems and users. A second function is to act as directory assistance for the network by allowing users and applications to find other network entities easily. For example, using NIS+, you can easily locate other users and resources in the corporate network, regardless of the actual physical location of the entity.

One important benefit of NIS+ is scalability: NIS+ simplifies administration of both small and large networks. As organizations grow and decentralize, NIS+ continues to provide administrative efficiency. Another key enhancement in NIS+ is update performance. Changes made to the NIS+ information base are automatically and instantaneously propagated to replica servers across the network. You can implement tasks such as adding new systems and users much more rapidly than with NIS. NIS+ provides improved security over NIS. NIS+ lets you flexibly control access to network resources by preventing unauthorized sources from reading, changing, or destroying naming service information.

This chapter describes the differences between NIS and NIS+; how NIS+ information is organized, stored, and distributed; how NIS+ security mechanisms work; and how NIS+ information is updated. It also describes a new feature of Solaris 2.*x* system software (the name service switch file) and introduces the NIS+ commands. Chapter 6 describes how to set up an NIS+ client system on a network where NIS+ is already installed and configured. Describing NIS+ completely and providing installation and setup instructions for master and replica servers are beyond the scope of this book.

Comparison of NIS and NIS+

To help you understand the differences between NIS and NIS+, Table 5.1 compares the features of both.

Table 5.1   **Comparison of NIS and NIS+ Features**

Capability	NIS Features	NIS+ Features
Namespace	Flat.	Hierarchical.
Database	Centralized for each independent network domain.	Partitioned into directories to support each network subset or autonomous domain.
Data storage	Multiple bi-column maps with key-value pairs.	Multicolumn tables with multiple searchable columns.
Replication	Minimum of one replica server per IP subnetwork.	Each replica server can serve clients on multiple IP subnets.
Update privileges	Requires superuser privileges on master server.	Performed remotely by authorized administrators; no superuser privileges required.
Update propagation	Initiated by administrator; whole maps transferred.	Automatic and high performance updating using only updated information.
Authorization	Anyone can read all information stored in NIS database.	Fine-grained access control to NIS+ directories, tables, columns, and entries.
Resource access across domains	Not supported.	Permitted for authorized users.

The NIS+ Namespace

The NIS+ namespace is the arrangement of information stored by NIS+. You can arrange the information in the namespace in a variety of ways to suit the needs of your organization. The hierarchical namespace of NIS+ is similar to that used by DNS and by the UNIX file system. With a hierarchical namespace, you can decentralize administration and improve security. When Solaris 1.*x* NIS was developed, the basic assumption was that the network and organization-wide namespace would be small enough for one person to administer. The growth of networked computing has dictated a need to change this assumption.

NIS+ is designed to work best when the information in the NIS+ namespace is arranged into configurations called *domains*. An NIS+ domain is a collection of information about the systems, users, and network services in a portion of an organization. In the sample network shown in Figure 5.1, the domains for a fictitious company, Starlight Corporation, are organized by division.

As Starlight Corporation grows beyond a few hundred systems, the corresponding growth in size of its NIS+ directory begins to affect manageability and performance. Functional groups such as Engineering and Sales/Marketing may choose to create local subdomains and appoint (or hire) autonomous system administrators for these subdomains. These local administrators take responsibility for administering their own subdomains, thus relieving the central administration group of some of its workload.

Figure 5.1
Creation of administrative domains

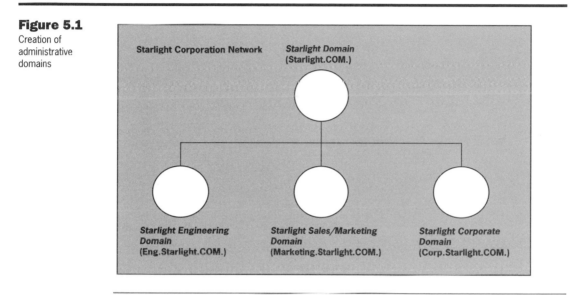

As Starlight Corporation continues to grow, further decentralized administration requirements may emerge. Administrators can continue to subdivide the domains along functional groups or other natural administrative lines, such as by location or by building. Figure 5.2 shows how the Starlight network has decentralized the Sales domain.

Each domain can be administered either locally or centrally. Alternatively, some portions of domain administration can be performed locally while others remain under the control of a central administrator. A domain can even be administered from within another domain. As more domains are created, NIS+ clients continue to have the same access to the information in other NIS+ domains of the company.

Administration Tool's Database Manager and the NIS+ commands let authorized administrators interactively administer and add, delete, or change information in NIS+ servers from systems across the domain or enterprise network. Administrators do not need to remotely log into or have superuser privileges on these servers to be able to perform administrative functions. The following sections describe the components of the NIS+ namespace. NIS+ security is discussed later in this chapter.

Figure 5.2

Hierarchical domains

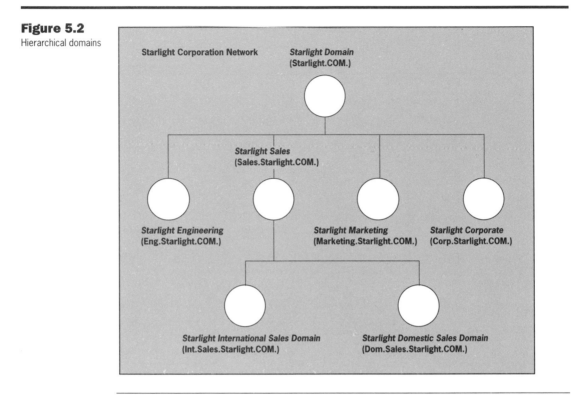

Components of the NIS+ Namespace

The NIS+ namespace contains the following components:

- Directory objects
- Table objects
- Group objects
- Entry objects
- Link objects

Directory, table, and group objects are organized into NIS+ domains. Entry objects are contained in tables. Link objects provide connections between different objects. Directory and table objects are described in detail in the following sections.

Directory Objects

Directory objects are the framework of the namespace, and divide it up into separate parts. Each domain consists of a directory object; its two administrative directories, org_dir and groups_dir; and a set of NIS+ tables, as shown in Figure 5.3.

Figure 5.3

The org_dir and groups_dir directories

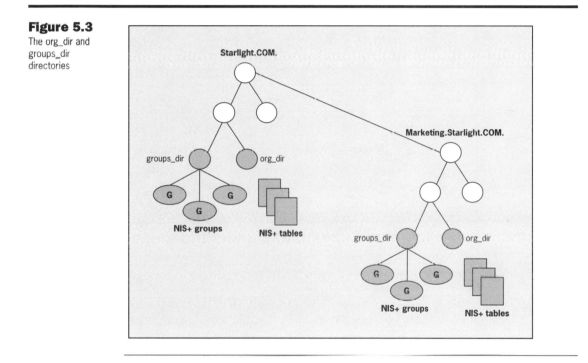

The org_dir directory contains NIS+ tables that are used for storing information about users and systems on your network. The tables are described later in this chapter. The groups_dir directory stores information about the NIS+ groups for the domain. A directory object is considered a domain only if it contains its own administrative tables in the org_dir and groups_dir subdirectories. The NIS+ scripts that are run when NIS+ is set up create these two default directories. Figure 5.4 shows the contents of the org_dir directory for the Starlight Corporation top-level domain and two subdomains.

The top-level domain in an NIS+ hierarchy is called the root domain. The root domain is the first NIS+ domain installed. Each directory contains administrative information on resources local to that domain.

Figure 5.4

An example of domains, directories, and tables in an NIS+ namespace

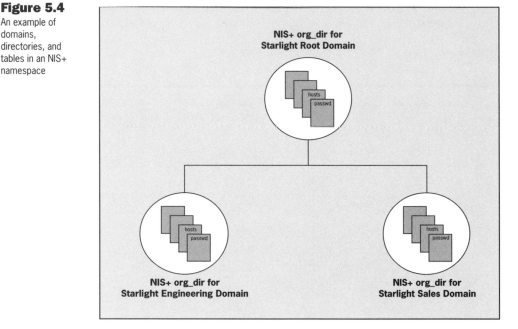

Domain Name Syntax

NIS+ domain names consist of a string of ASCII characters separated by a dot (.). These character sequences that identify the directories in an NIS+ domain are called *labels.* The order of labels is hierarchical. The directory at the left of the sequence is the one that is the most local, and the directories identifying the parts of the domain become more global the closer they are to the right, as is the convention for most e-mail domain addresses. Unlike e-mail domain addresses, you must use a dot at the end of a fully qualified NIS+ domain name. The dot identifies the global root of the namespace. NIS+ names are fully qualified when the name includes all of the labels identifying all of the directories. Figure 5.5 shows examples of some fully qualified names in an NIS+ namespace. Note that an NIS+ principal is a user or system whose credentials have been stored in the NIS+ namespace. See "NIS+ Security" later in this chapter for more information.

NOTE. *If an NIS+ command requires a fully qualified domain name and you omit the global root dot from the end of the name, a syntax error message is displayed.*

Figure 5.5

Fully qualified names
of components of
the NIS+ namespace

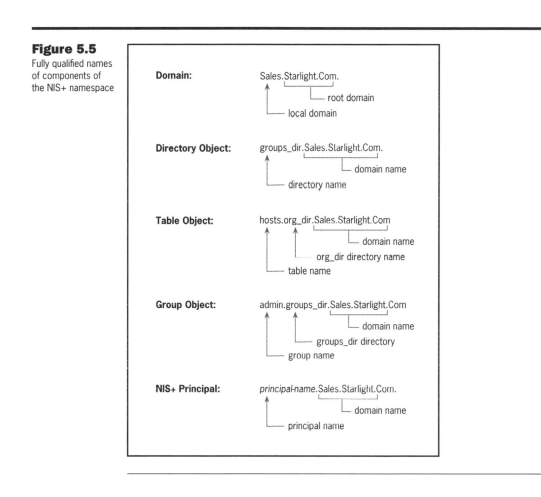

Names without a trailing dot are called *partially qualified*. For example, hosts.org_dir is a partially qualified domain name which specifies the hosts table in the org_dir directory of the default domain.

Figure 5.6 shows a more detailed example of a hierarchical namespace. In Figure 5.6, Starlight.COM is the root domain, Sales and Corp are subdomains of the root domain, Int is a subdomain of Sales, and hostname.int.sales.starlight.com is a client system in the int.sales.starlight.com. domain. The system hostname.corp.starlight.com. is a client of the Corp domain.

NOTE. *Domain names for NIS+ are not case-sensitive. You do not need to type the names with exact capitalization. The names esg.eng.starlight.com. and ESG.Eng.Starlight.COM. are identical for NIS+.*

Figure 5.6

An example of directories and domains in an NIS+ namespace

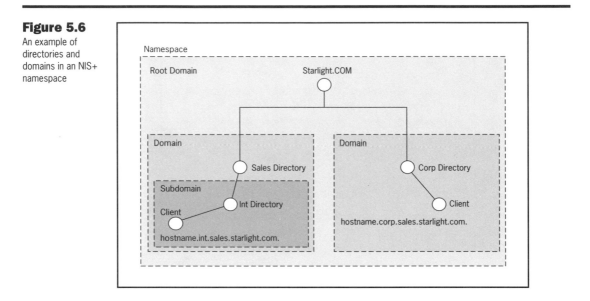

Table Objects

NIS+ table objects use columns and entries (rows) to store information for NIS+ domains. NIS+ tables provide two major improvements over the maps used by NIS. First, you can access any searchable column in an NIS+ table; with NIS maps you could search in the first column only. Duplicate maps (which were used by NIS) are unnecessary. Instead of providing NIS hosts.byname and hosts.byaddr as separate maps, NIS+ commands can search any column (name or address) marked searchable in the hosts.org_dir table. Second, an NIS+ principal's access to NIS+ tables can be controlled at three levels: at the object level of the table itself, at the column level, and at the row or entry level. If access is given at the table level, it cannot be restricted at the column or entry level. Any access granted at the column level cannot be taken away at the entry level.

In addition, you can specify a search path for each table, and you can create symbolic links between table objects and entries using the nisln command. See the nisln(1) manual page for more information about creating links.

Each table object has its own access security information that controls whether a principal has access to the table object itself. Table security is similar to UNIX file security. See "NIS+ Security" later in this chapter for more information.

NIS+ org_dir Tables

The tables in org_dir provide much of the functionality that you need to administer your network. Although you can create your own tables, you will do most of the standard NIS+ table administration using the tables in the org_dir.

Table 5.2 lists the tables in the org_dir directory in alphabetical order and briefly describes the contents of each table.

Table 5.2   **NIS+ org_dir tables**

Table	Description
aliases	Information about the e-mail aliases in the domain.
auto_home	The location of automounted home directories in the domain.
auto_master	The master automount map.
bootparams	Location of the root, swap, and dump partitions of every diskless client in the domain.
cred	NIS+ credentials for principals who have permission to access the information or objects in the domain.
ethers	The ethernet address for systems in the domain.
group	Group password, group ID, and list of members for every UNIX group in the domain. Note that the group table is for UNIX groups and should not be confused with the NIS+ groups in the groups_dir directory.
hosts	Network address and hostname of every system in the domain.
netgroup	The netgroups to which systems and users in the domain may belong.
netmasks	The networks in the domain and their associated netmasks.
networks	The networks in the domain and their canonical names.
passwd	Password information about every user in the domain.
protocols	The list of IP protocols used in the domain.
RPC	The RPC program numbers for RPC services available in the domain.
services	The names of IP services used in the domain and their port numbers.
timezone	The timezone of the domain.

See the section "Table Information Display" at the end of this chapter for a brief explanation of how to display information about these tables.

The following paragraphs briefly describe how the org_dir tables are created and populated. Creating and populating these tables is part of the procedure for setting up NIS+.

As part of setting up NIS+, a set of empty tables is created in the org_dir directory. Once the tables are created, authorized principals can add information from existing NIS maps or text files by using the nisaddent command or the nistbladm command, or by using Administration Tool's Database Manager to edit the contents of NIS+ databases. Consult *Solaris System Administrator's Guide* (see the bibliography at the back of this book) for information about how to use the Administration Tool Database Manager. If NIS+ entries already exist in the table, authorized principals can use the nisaddent command to merge NIS map information with existing NIS+ information. See the nisaddent(1) manual page for more information.

NIS+ Security

NIS+ is designed to protect the information in its directories and tables from unauthorized access. For example, an authorized user can create a table listing the home telephone number and address of members of the Starlight Engineering domain as part of the domain's NIS+ directory. Access to this table can be limited to all or part of the Engineering organization. In another example, a desktop application can create NIS+ tables of application-specific information that must be available to the entire network. In a third example, confidential personnel information, such as the company identification number and job category for employees, can be stored in an NIS+ table with access authorized on only a very selective basis.

NIS+ controls access to servers, directories, and tables in two ways:

- Authentication verifies the identity of a system or a user of NIS+.

- Authorization controls access to information stored in NIS+.

In addition to authentication and authorization of access rights, you can run the NIS+ daemon, rpc.nisd, at three different levels of security, as described in Table 5.3.

Table 5.3   **Levels of NIS+ Security**

Security Level	Description
0	Does not check the principal's credentials at all. Any client is allowed to perform any operation. Level 0 is designed for testing and setting up the initial NIS+ root domain.

Table 5.3   **Levels of NIS+ Security (Continued)**

Security Level	Description
1	Checks the principal's credentials and accepts any authentication. Because some credentials are easily forged, do not use this level on networks to which untrusted servers may have access. Level 1 is recommended for testing only.
2	Checks the principal's credentials and accepts only DES authentication (described in the next section). Level 2 is the highest level of security currently provided and is the default level assigned to an NIS+ server.

You control the level of security using the -S option when you start the rpc.nisd daemon. If a system is configured as an NIS+ server, the rpc.nisd daemon is automatically started when a system boots. When rpc.nisd is started with no arguments, the default security level is 2. To start the daemon with security level 0, use rpc.nisd-S 0. To start the daemon with security level 1, use rpc.nisd -S 1.

NIS+ Authentication

Every request to an NIS+ server is made by an NIS+ principal. An NIS+ principal can be a user or a workstation. Authentication is the process of identifying the principal who made a request to the NIS+ server by checking the principal's credentials. These credentials are based on encrypted verification information stored in the NIS+ cred table.

The purpose of authentication is to obtain the principal's name so that access rights to information in the name server can be looked up and verified. All interactions that an NIS+ principal has with an NIS+ server are authenticated.

The benefit of authentication is protection of NIS+ information from access by untrusted clients, which provides more flexible and secure administration of NIS+ servers.

Principals can have two types of credentials: LOCAL and DES. A LOCAL credential consists of the UID of an NIS+ principal. An NIS+ server uses the LOCAL UID credential to look up the identity of the principal who sent the request so that the NIS+ server can determine the principal's rights to access the requested object.

A DES credential is more complicated, and both users and systems can have such credentials. The DES credential consists of the principal's secure RPC netname and a verification field.

Table 5.4 shows the columns in the cred table and describes the type of information stored for LOCAL and DES authentication.

The first column, cname, contains the fully qualified credential name of an NIS+ principal. When the authentication type is LOCAL, the first column can contain user names only, because client systems cannot have LOCAL credentials. When the authentication type is DES, the principal name can be either a user name or a system name.

Table 5.4　　**Columns in the cred Table**

cname	auth_type	auth_name	public_data	private_data
NIS+ principal name of a client user	LOCAL	UID	GID list	None
NIS+ principal name of a client user or client system	DES	Secure RPC netname	Public key	Encrypted Private key

---

The following example shows the contents of the cred table on the system named oak. The fields are separated by colons.

```
oak% niscat -h cred.org_dir
# cname:auth_type:auth_name:public_data:private_data
oak.ESG.Eng.sun.COM.:DES:unix.oak@ESG.Eng.sun.COM:5c8349c1e0eb851a17170efb5a8dd6
3e447210341e565eaf::f8f133ebb68679c958ea4c5e43d61aad5b76c17bba4ffdefad27edc2fcd8
9cc0
winsor.ESG.Eng.sun.COM.:LOCAL:6693:1,14:
winsor.ssi.eng.sun.com.:DES:unix.6693@esg.eng.sun.com:aacf4fcdc47811b2550f443bca
4d28c1a8fcf287e81dec24::b11a448a04877fd3dfc48c599fa18cad3d7e7431ebaac7492d731dc2
f6051761
ignatz.DGDO.Eng.sun.COM.:LOCAL:6694:1:
oak%
```

The first entry shows the names of the columns in the cred table. The second entry is the DES authentication for the system oak. The third and fourth entries are LOCAL and DES authentication entries for the user winsor. The fifth entry is LOCAL authentication for user ignatz who has an account on the system. User ignatz does not have DES authentication credentials in the local domain. Only a LOCAL cred entry is needed if the user's home domain is not the local one.

NIS+ security privileges are assigned in two stages: The principal is authenticated (identified) as an authorized user, and the access rights are checked.

Figure 5.7 shows a simplified view of how NIS+ security works.

NIS+ classifies NIS+ principals into four authorization categories, as shown in Table 5.5.

Figure 5.7

How NIS+ security works

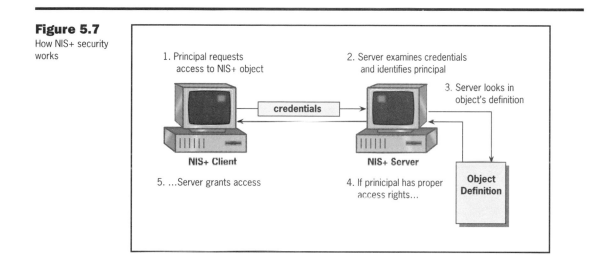

1. Principal requests access to NIS+ object

2. Server examines credentials and identifies principal

3. Server looks in object's definition

credentials

NIS+ Client

NIS+ Server

5. ...Server grants access

4. If prinicipal has proper access rights...

Object Definition

Table 5.5 **NIS+ Authorization Categories**

Abbreviation	Authorization	Description
n	Nobody	A category reserved for unauthenticated requests.
o	Owner	A single NIS+ principal who was the creator of the object. You can change the ownership of existing objects using the nischown command.
g	Group	A collection of NIS+ principals, grouped together as a convenient way to provide access to the namespace. When an object is created, it is by default assigned to the NIS+ principal's default group. NIS+ group information is stored in the NIS+ group object in the groups_dir subdirectory of every NIS+ domain.
w	World	All NIS+ principals that are authenticated by NIS+.

Access Rights

Access rights are granted not to specific NIS+ principals, but to four categories of NIS+ principals: Nobody, Owner, Group, and World, as previously described. The four types of NIS+ access rights are Read, Modify, Create, and Destroy, as shown in Table 5.6.

Each object grants access rights to the four categories of NIS+ principals: Nobody, Owner, Group, and World. Access rights for each object consist of a string of 16 characters, 4 for each principal category. In the example shown in Figure 5.8, all access rights are permitted for each authentication category.

Figure 5.8

NIS+ authentication categories and access rights

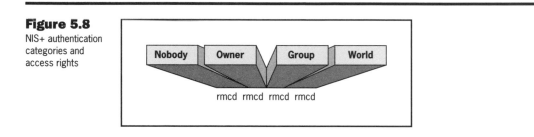

Table 5.6   **NIS+ Access Rights**

Abbreviation	Access Right	Description
r	Read	Principal can read the contents of the object.
m	Modify	Principal can modify the contents of the object.
c	Create	Principal can create new objects in a table or directory.
d	Destroy	Principal can destroy objects in a table or directory.
–	No access	Principal cannot access the object.

In the following example, Nobody has read permission; Owner has read, modify, create, and destroy permissions; Group has read and modify permissions, and World has read permission.

```
r---rmcdrm--r---
```

An NIS+ table or directory can grant one or more access rights to one or more categories of clients. For example, a directory could grant Read access to the World category, but only Modify access to the Group and Owner. NIS+ authorization supports flexible and secure administration. For example, the Group access right allows finer control for NIS+ administration. It can be used to maintain security and control as administrative authority becomes more decentralized. When NIS+ domains are first created, a group consisting of central administrative personnel could have only Modify and Create access rights to directories across the network. As the domain evolves and decentralizes, directories could grant these access rights to new groups that contain both local and central administrative personnel. Expanding access rights while maintaining access to existing administrators permits the smooth transition of control.

When you create an object, NIS+ assigns the object a default owner, group, and set of access rights. The default owner is the NIS+ principal who creates the object (in this case, you). The default group is the group named in the NIS_GROUP environment variable. The default set of access rights is:

```
----rmcdr---r---
```

You can change these default values in several different ways. One way to change the access rights of an NIS+ object or table entry is to use the nischmod command. To use the nischmod command, you must already have Modify rights to the object or entry. The nischmod command syntax is much like the syntax for the chmod command. You add access rights using the + operator and remove access rights using the - operator. For example, you would use the following syntax to add Read and Modify rights to the Group of the esg.eng.starlight.com. directory:

```
oak% nischmod g+rm esg.eng.starlight.com.
```

See the manual page for nischmod(1) for more information. See "NIS+ Commands" later in this chapter for a list of the NIS+ commands.

Once the access rights for a table object are set, they define the level of security for that table object. The only way to make entries or columns in a table more secure is to change the access rights for the table object itself. You can, however, provide additional access to the information stored in a table object by extending the rights to additional principals or by providing additional access rights to existing principals.

For example, your company may have a policy that permits anybody in the company to create, modify, or delete entries for one particular e-mail alias. Access to all other aliases is restricted to the owner of the aliases table. To implement this policy, you would create the most restrictive rights for the aliases table object itself (----rmcdr---r---), and grant free access to the entry that contains the particular alias (rmcdrmcdrmcdrmcd).

You can use the nistbladm command to set access rights to a table when it is created, to set access rights to an entry and a column when you create the entry, or to modify the access rights of an existing table. See the nistbladm(1) manual page for more information.

The NIS+ Updating Model

The NIS+ updating model is more reliable and efficient than the NIS updating model. NIS+ stores a primary copy of a directory on a master server. Zero or more replica servers store replicas of the primary copy. When you use Administration Tool or the NIS+ commands to administer NIS+, changes are made to only the directory on the master server. When a master server receives an update to an object—whether a directory, group, link, or table—the server waits about 2 minutes for other updates so that it can batch the updates. When the waiting period is complete, the server stores the updates on disk and in a transaction log, along with a timestamp, and propagates the changes to its replica servers. In contrast to NIS updates, which usually take a day or more to propagate in large organizations, NIS+ incremental updates are automatically and quickly propagated to the replicas.

The NIS+ updating model allows for more efficient use of network bandwidth, because only the changes are transmitted from master to replica servers. In addition, replica servers are contacted only once with an aggregate update to all tables occurring within a short time. If replicas are out of date, they ask for updated information since their last updating.

The NIS+ transaction log model provides rollback recovery and consistency of NIS+ databases, even in case a server fails during an update. NIS+ master and replica servers can use the transaction log to automatically repair databases to their state before a failure occurs.

NIS and NIS+ Compatibility

NIS+ provides an NIS compatibility mode. This mode lets an NIS+ server running Solaris 2.x system software answer requests from NIS as well as NIS+ clients. When the NIS+ server is set up, the NIS compatibility mode can be selected. You do not need to do any additional setup or changes for the NIS client. The NIS+ compatibility mode is one way that you can gradually make the transition from NIS to NIS+.

Another way that you can ease the transition is to set up a Solaris 1.x server to act as an NIS+ server. To accomplish this task, you must install the NIS+ SunOS 4.1 distribution on the Solaris 1.x server. The NIS+ SunOS 4.1 distribution permits Solaris 1.x servers to act as NIS+ servers without needing to upgrade to Solaris 2.x. The Solaris 2.x CD-ROM contains a complete set of SunOS 4.1.x NIS+ executables that you can install on a SunOS 4.1.x system. The executables are in a separate tar file in the root directory of the Solaris 2.x CD-ROM. You must manually install the NIS+ files following the instructions in the readme file provided on the CD-ROM. You cannot install the NIS+ files on a SunOS 4.1.x system using SunInstall.

Table 5.7 shows a matrix of possible configurations between clients and servers. The additional rows and columns for ONC NIS systems are included because many customers have ONC NIS name servers from vendors other than SunSoft.

Table 5.7   **NIS/NIS+ Compatibility**

Server Client	NIS+ SunOS 5.*x*	NIS+ SunOS 4.*x*	NIS Any ONC NIS
SunOS 5.*x*	Supported	Supported	Supported[*]
SunOS 4.*x*	Supported[**]	Supported[**]	Supported
Any ONC NIS	Supported[**]	Supported[**]	Supported

[*]   client must specify "nis" in the /etc/nsswitch.conf file. The SunOS client system can run ypbind and access the ONC nis system.

[**]   NIS+ server must run in NIS compatibility mode (-Y option).

The comparison between master servers and slave servers is as follows: NIS master servers know about NIS slave servers only; NIS does not know about NIS+. NIS+ master servers interact with NIS+ replica servers only. NIS+ does not convert NIS+ tables into maps and push them to NIS slave servers.

The Name Service Switch

New with SVR4.

Solaris 2.*x* provides a new name service switch file, /etc/nsswitch.conf, that you can use to tailor the name service policy of individual systems to use multiple name services in the Solaris 2.*x* environment. With the /etc/nsswitch.conf file you can specify:

- Which name service(s) is used for each type of configuration information such as password or host IP address

- The order in which the different name services are used for each type of information

- The criteria for search continuation if information is not found or if a name service is not available

You can use the /etc/nsswitch.conf file to set flexible policies for name service use and to describe and change these policies once site requirements change. For example, a system running the Solaris 2.*x* environment could obtain its hosts information from an NIS+ table, its group information from NIS maps, and its password information from a local /etc file.

The /etc/nsswitch.conf file also simplifies migration from NIS to NIS+, as both Solaris 1.*x* and Solaris 2.*x* systems can be clients of Solaris 1.*x* NIS servers. In addition, Solaris 2.*x* systems can be clients of both NIS and NIS+, allowing the two name services to coexist during the transition. If you combine NIS and NIS+ domains, be sure they both use the same domain name.

When you install Solaris 2.*x* system software, the /etc directory contains a default nsswitch.conf file and the files nsswitch.files, nsswitch.nis, and nsswitch.nisplus, which provide default settings for each of these possible sources of name service information: files, NIS, and NIS+, respectively. An example of the default nsswitch.nisplus file is included in Chapter 6.

When you set up an NIS+ server or client system, you must copy the /etc/nsswitch.nisplus file to /etc/nsswitch.conf. After you have copied the file, you can either use the default file or customize it to suit the needs of your site. SunSoft suggests that you start by using the default file and customize it only if you determine that you need to do so.

Table 5.8 lists the locations that the /etc/nsswitch.conf file can search for information:

Table 5.8   **Location of Name Service Information**

Location	Description
files	File on the client's local system
nisplus	An NIS+ table
nis	An NIS map
compat	Supports old-style "+" syntax for passwd and group
dns	Applies only to the hosts entry

When NIS+ searches one or more of these locations, it returns one of the four status messages listed in Table 5.9.

In the /etc/nsswitch.conf file, you can specify what action NIS+ should take when it returns one of these status messages. The actions you can specify are:

- continue—try the next source

- return—stop trying, and return this result

If no action is specified in the /etc/nsswitch.conf file, NIS+ uses the default value [NOTFOUND=continue].

Table 5.9	**Name Service Switch Status Messages**
SUCCESS	Found a valid result
UNAVAIL	Could not use the source
NOTFOUND	Information not in the source
TRYAGAIN	Source returned an "I'm busy, try later" code

The entries in the /etc/nsswitch.conf file use the following syntax:

```
table: location [location...] [status=action] [location]
```

The *table* variable contains the name of the NIS map, the NIS+ table, or the /etc file. The *location* variable specifies the first place for the system to search, using any of the locations shown in Table 5.8. If you want, you can specify additional locations to search. You can also specify an *action* (continue or return) if one of the status messages shown in Table 5.9 is encountered. An example of the default /etc/nsswitch.nisplus file is shown in Chapter 6.

In the default NIS+ file, local /etc files are not consulted for hosts, services, networks, protocols, rpc, ethers, netmasks, and bootparams unless NIS+ is down. If the entry is not found, the [NOTFOUND=return] entry prevents NIS+ from consulting the /etc files. If you want NIS+ to consult the appropriate /etc file on the local system when an entry is not found in the NIS+ table, edit the default file and remove the [NOTFOUND=return] entries.

NIS+ Administration

When NIS+ is configured on the network, you can use either Administration Tool's Database Manager or the NIS+ commands to administer NIS+. SunSoft recommends that at least one administrator be familiar with all of the NIS+ commands.

Administration Tool

You can use the Database Manager of Administration Tool (admintool) to administer most of the tables in the org_dir directory. To administer tables using the Database Manager, in addition to having the proper NIS+ credentials and access rights, you must be a member of the UNIX sysadmin group (GID 14). Consult the *Solaris System Administrator's Guide* (see the bibliography at the back of this book) for more information about using Administration Tool and setting up Administration Tool security.

NOTE. *If you have a large site, you may want to use the NIS+ commands instead of Administration Tool; displaying large databases can be time-consuming.*

NIS+ Commands

A major advantage of NIS+ over NIS is that you have direct read-write access to information served by NIS+ through the command-line and programmatic interface. You can further fine-tune control of this access using the NIS+ security authentication and access mechanisms.

The command-line interface lets you change NIS+ tables and directories on servers significantly more easily and quickly and without first creating text files and converting them into databases.

Tasks such as adding users and systems to a domain require changing information only in that domain's NIS+ directory. You can also perform these operations remotely, from systems around the domain, without needing superuser privileges or rlogin access to the NIS+ master servers.

Because you have read-write programmatic access to NIS+ information, you can develop interactive and innovative system administration applications on top of NIS+. NIS+ is used by all Solaris distributed system management application as the storage facility for administration data.

Figure 5.9 introduces the NIS+ commands. It also shows which NIS commands are available for compatibility with NIS+ and which NIS commands are not available with Solaris 2.*x* system software.

Table 5.10 alphabetically lists the NIS+ commands, shows the NIS equivalent command (if appropriate) and where the command can be used, and describes how the command is used. See the appropriate manual pages for more information about these commands.

Because NIS+ uses a completely different way to propagate new information, there are no NIS+ equivalents to the ypbind, ypwhich, ypxfr, and ypset NIS commands.

Refer to Chapter 6 for examples of how to use NIS+ commands to set up an NIS+ client. Refer to Chapter 8 for examples of how to use NIS+ commands to administer automount maps.

For some NIS+ commands, such as nistbladm -m (used to modify a specific entry in an existing entry), you must identify information in the table by using a format called an indexed name. An indexed name uses this syntax:

```
'[column=value,column=value]' table-name.directory-name
```

You must include the indexed name in single quotes (') to prevent the shell from interpreting the information between the square brackets as wildcard characters for expansion.

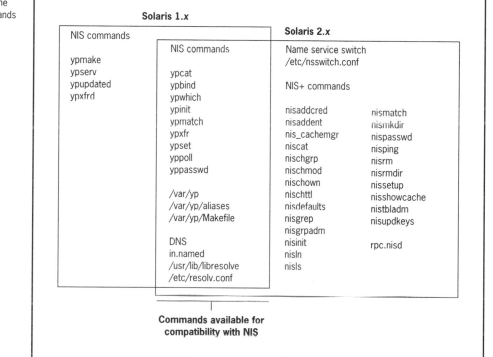

Figure 5.9
Overview of name
services commands

NOTE. *The old NIS+ manual pages incorrectly show a comma after the final bracket and before the table name.*

For example, if you want to change only one column for an existing entry, you can use the nistbladm -m command. To change just the IP address for a system in the hosts table, first you specify the new IP address you want, then you provide an indexed name for the current entry. In the following example, the IP address for cinderella is changed from 129.144.52.75 to 129.144.52.80.

```
oak% nistbladm -m addr=129.144.52.80 '[addr=129.144.52.75]'hosts.org_dir
oak%
```

Table Information Display

This section describes several ways that you can display information about table objects and can view the contents of the tables using NIS+ commands.

Table 5.10   **NIS and NIS+ Commands**

NIS+ Command	NIS Command	Used For	Description
nisaddcred*	N/A	Authentication	Maintain credentials for NIS+ principals and store them in the Cred table.
nisaddent	N/A	Tables	Put information from ASCII files or NIS maps into NIS+ tables.
nis_cachemgr	N/A	NIS+ directories	Start the NIS+ cache manager on an NIS+ client.
niscat*	ypcat	Tables	Display the format or the content of NIS+ tables and directory objects.
nischgrp	N/A	Objects	Change the NIS+ group owner of an NIS+ object.
nischmod	N/A	Objects	Change the access rights that an NIS+ object grants. Access can be changed for four categories of NIS+ principal: nobody, owner, group, and world.
nischown	N/A	Objects	Change the owner of an NIS+ object.
nischttl	N/A	Objects	Change the time-to-live value for an NIS+ object.
nisdefaults	N/A	Objects	Show the default values for an NIS+ principal: domain name, group name, system name, NIS+ principal name, access rights, directory search path, and time to live.
nisgrep*	ypmatch	Tables	Search for entries in an NIS+ table.
nisgrpadm	N/A	Administration	Use to display information for, create, or destroy an NIS+ group; also to add, remove, or test for members of existing groups.
nisinit	ypinit	Administration	Initialize an NIS+ client or server.
nisln	N/A	Objects	Create a symbolic link between two NIS+ objects.
nisls*	N/A	NIS+ directories	List the contents of an NIS+ directory.
nismatch*	ypmatch	Tables	Search for entries in an NIS+ table.
nismkdir	N/A	NIS+ directories	Create an NIS+ directory and specify its master and replica servers.

Table 5.10   **NIS and NIS+ Commands (Continued)**

NIS+ Command	NIS Command	Used For	Description
nispasswd*	yppasswd	Authentication	Change NIS+ password information.
nisping*	yppush yppoll	NIS+ directories	Update or checkpoint updates to domain replicas.
nisrm	N/A	Objects	Remove NIS+ objects from the namespace.
nisrmdir	N/A	NIS+ directories	Remove NIS+ directories from the namespace.
nissetup	N/A	Domains	Create org_dir and groups_dir directories and a complete set of standard, unpopulated NIS+ tables for an NIS+ domain.
nisshowcache	N/A	Administration	List the contents of the NIS+ shared cache that the NIS+ cache manager maintains
nistbladm†	N/A	Tables	Create or delete NIS+ tables and modify or delete entries in an existing NIS+ table.
nisupdkeys	N/A	Directories	Update the public keys stored in an NIS+ directory object.

*   an asterisk means that the NIS+ command is one that you are likely to use frequently.

The NIS+ commands require either a directory name or a fully qualified name following the name of the table in the argument. The fully qualified name is the name of the table followed by the directory where the NIS+ tables are stored and then the domain name. Note that with NIS+ commands, a fully qualified name has a period at the end of the domain name. For example, auto_master.org_dir.Sun.COM. is the fully qualified name for the auto_master table, which is in the directory org_dir in the domain Sun.COM. If you use the name of the table only, the NIS+ commands use the information from the NIS+ NIS_PATH environment variable to complete the name. You set the NIS_PATH environment variable just as you set any other shell environment variable—from a shell for the current session, or in the user's .cshrc file (C shell) or .profile file (Bourne or Korn shell). For example, to set the NIS_PATH environment variable to org_dir.ESG.Eng.Sun.COM for the C shell, type

setenv NIS_PATH org_dir.ESG.Eng.Sun.COM and press Return. The examples in this chapter assume that the NIS_PATH environment variable is set; only the directory name for each command is used.

You can display the contents of the org_dir directory using the nisls command. When you type **nisls** *directory-name*, the directory and domain name are displayed followed by a list of the contents of the directory. In the following example, the client is in the domain esg.eng.sun.com.:

```
oak% nisls org_dir
org_dir.esg.eng.sun.com.:
auto_home
auto_master
bootparams
cred
ethers
group
hosts
mail_aliases
sendmailvars
netgroup
netmasks
networks
passwd
protocols
rpc
services
timezone
oak%
```

The nisls -l command displays a long listing of the contents of the directory. In the next example, the client is in the domain esg.eng.sun.com. The *T* in the left column identifies each entry as a table object. The second column displays the access rights for the table; the third column displays the owner of the table; the fourth through eighth columns display the date the tables were created; and the ninth column displays the name of the table.

```
oak% nisls -l org_dir
org_dir.esg.eng.sun.com.:
T ----rmcdrmcdr--- oak.ESG.Eng.sun.COM. Sun Feb 28 21:24:46 1993 auto_master
T ----rmcdrmcdr--- oak.ESG.Eng.sun.COM. Sun Feb 28 21:24:48 1993 auto_home
T ----rmcdrmcdr--- oak.ESG.Eng.sun.COM. Sun Feb 28 21:24:49 1993 bootparams
T r---rmcdrmcdr--- oak.ESG.Eng.sun.COM. Sun Feb 28 21:24:51 1993 cred
T ----rmcdrmcdr--- oak.ESG.Eng.sun.COM. Sun Feb 28 21:24:53 1993 ethers
T ----rmcdrmcdr--- oak.ESG.Eng.sun.COM. Sun Feb 28 21:24:55 1993 group
T ----rmcdrmcdr--- oak.ESG.Eng.sun.COM. Sun Feb 28 21:24:56 1993 hosts
T ----rmcdrmcdr--- oak.ESG.Eng.sun.COM. Sun Feb 28 21:24:58 1993 mail_aliases
```

```
T ----rmcdrmcdr--- oak.ESG.Eng.sun.COM. Sun Feb 28 21:25:00 1993 sendmailvars
T ----rmcdrmcdr--- oak.ESG.Eng.sun.COM. Sun Feb 28 21:25:01 1993 netmasks
T ----rmcdrmcdr--- oak.ESG.Eng.sun.COM. Sun Feb 28 21:25:03 1993 netgroup
T ----rmcdrmcdr--- oak.ESG.Eng.sun.COM. Sun Feb 28 21:25:05 1993 networks
T ----rmcdrmcdr--- oak.ESG.Eng.sun.COM. Sun Feb 28 21:25:07 1993 passwd
T ----rmcdrmcdr--- oak.ESG.Eng.sun.COM. Sun Feb 28 21:25:08 1993 protocols
T ----rmcdrmcdr--- oak.ESG.Eng.sun.COM. Sun Feb 28 21:25:10 1993 rpc
T ----rmcdrmcdr--- oak.ESG.Eng.sun.COM. Sun Feb 28 21:25:12 1993 services
T ----rmcdrmcdr--- oak.ESG.Eng.sun.COM. Sun Feb 28 21:25:13 1993 timezone
oak%
```

You can display information about each table object using the niscat -o *table-name.directory-name* command. In the following example, information about the hosts table object is displayed:

```
oak% niscat -o hosts.org_dir
Object Name    : hosts
Owner          : oak.ESG.Eng.sun.COM.
Group          :
Domain         : org_dir.ESG.Eng.sun.COM.
Access Rights  : ----rmcdrmcdr---
Time to Live   : 12:0:0
Object Type    : TABLE
Table Type          : hosts_tbl
Number of Columns   : 4
Character Separator :
Search Path         :
Columns             :
        [0]     Name        : cname
                Attributes  : (SEARCHABLE, TEXTUAL DATA, CASE INSENSITIVE)
                Access Rights : ----------------
        [1]     Name        : name
                Attributes  : (SEARCHABLE, TEXTUAL DATA, CASE INSENSITIVE)
                Access Rights : ----------------
        [2]     Name        : addr
                Attributes  : (SEARCHABLE, TEXTUAL DATA, CASE INSENSITIVE)
                Access Rights : ----------------
        [3]     Name        : comment
                Attributes  : (TEXTUAL DATA)
                Access Rights : ----------------
oak%
```

The access rights for the table object are displayed on the fifth line. This table has four columns named: cname, name, addr, and comment. Each column has its own access rights, which are displayed following the name and attributes of the column. In this example, no additional access to the columns has been granted, and owner and group have read, modify, create, and delete permissions for the table object.

If you have read permission, you can display the values for a table using the niscat *table-name.directory-name* command. In the next example, the auto_master.org_dir map has two entries:

```
oak% niscat auto_master.org_dir
/bin   auto_local
/-     auto_direct
oak%
```

You can display the names of the columns and the contents using the niscat -h *table-name.directory-name* command. In the following example, the auto_master table has two columns, named "key" and "value," and the separator is a space. The auto_master.org_dir map has two entries:

```
oak% niscat -h auto_master.org_dir
# key value
/bin   auto_local
/-     auto_direct
oak%
```

NOTE. *When an NIS+ table has many entries, the output of the niscat command can be quite long. If you're searching for specific entries, you may want to use nismatch or nisgrep instead.*

You can create or delete tables using the nistbladm command. You can also use the nistbladm command to create and modify entries. See the nistbladm(1) manual page for more information. You can also look in Chapter 8 for examples of how to use the nistbladm command to create and edit automount maps.

Remember that if your login name is a member of the sysadmin group (GID 14) and you have the proper NIS+ credentials and access rights, you can use the Administration Tool's Database Manager to manage the NIS+ tables.

Setting Up NIS+ Clients

THIS CHAPTER DESCRIBES HOW TO SET UP A SUNOS 5.X SYSTEM AS AN NIS+ client when NIS+ servers are set up and running. To set up an NIS+ client, you first must create DES credentials for the client in the domain. Then, on the client system, you perform these tasks as superuser:

1. Assign the client its new domain name.

2. Set up the nsswitch.conf file.

3. Install /etc/resolv.conf, if using DNS.

4. Check the /var/nis directory to make sure it's empty.

5. Run the nisinit script to initialize the client.

6. Kill and restart the keyserv daemon.

7. Run keylogin -r to load root private key into /etc/.rootkey.

8. Reboot the client.

These tasks are described in detail later in this chapter.

Security Considerations

Both the administrator and the client must have the proper credentials and access rights. The administrator can have either (1) DES credentials in the client's home domain or (2) a combination of DES credentials in the administrator's home domain and LOCAL credentials in the client's domain. See Chapter 5 for more information about DES and LOCAL credentials.

After you create the client's credentials in the NIS+ domain, you can complete the setup process on the client system. The directory object for its home domain must have Read access for the World and Nobody categories. If you are adding a client to an NIS+ domain that already has existing clients, the directory object probably already has the proper access permissions.

You can check the access rights for the directory object with the niscat -o command. The access rights are displayed on the fifth line of the output. In this example, the World category has Read access, as shown by the r--- at the end of the access rights string:

```
rootmaster# niscat -o ESG.Eng.sun.COM.
Object Name   : ESG
Owner         : oak.ESG.Eng.sun.COM.
Group         : admin.ESG.Eng.sun.COM.
Domain        : Eng.sun.COM.
Access Rights : r---rmcdrmcdr---
```

```
Time to Live  : 12:0:0
Object Type   : DIRECTORY
Name : 'ESG.Eng.sun.COM.'
Type : NIS
Master Server :
        Name         : oak.ESG.Eng.sun.COM.
        Public Key : None.
        Universal addresses (6)
        [1] - udp, inet, 127.0.0.1.0.111
        [2] - tcp, inet, 127.0.0.1.0.111
        [3] - -, inet, 127.0.0.1.0.111
        [4] - -, loopback, oak.rpc
        [5] - -, loopback, oak.rpc
        [6] - -, loopback, oak.rpc
Time to live : 12:0:0
Default Access rights :
```

If you have Modify rights, you can change the access rights for the directory object using the nischmod command. See the nischmod(1) manual page for more information.

Prerequisites

Before you set up a SunOS 5.*x* system as an NIS+ client, the client's domain must be set up and running NIS+. If you need help setting up NIS+, refer to *All About Administering NIS+* by Rick Ramsey.

Before you start the setup procedure, check the items on the following list:

■ You must have valid DES credentials and Modify rights to the Cred table in the client's home domain. Use either the nisls -l cred.org_dir or the niscat -o cred.org_dir command to check the access rights for the Cred table.

■ The client must have Read rights to the directory object of its home domain. Use either the nisls -l *domain-name* or the niscat -o *domain-name* command to check the access rights for the domain.

■ The master server for the domain must recognize the IP address for the client system. To recognize the client's IP address, you must have an entry for the client in either the /etc/hosts file or the Hosts table for the domain. Use Administration Tool's Database Manager to display the contents of the Hosts database and, if needed, add the client name and IP address to the Hosts table.

- The client must be able to resolve the IP address of the domain master or local NIS+ replica. One or both of these host names and IP addresses must be in the client's /etc/hosts file.

Steps for Setting Up NIS+ Client Credentials

This section provides steps for setting up NIS+ client credentials from the master server. You need the name of the master server for the client's domain, the name of the client system, valid DES credentials, and Modify rights to the Cred table to perform the steps in this section.

Follow these steps to set up the credentials for an NIS+ client on the master server:

1. Log on to the master server.

2. Type

   nisaddcred -p unix.*client-name@net-name* -P *client-name.domain-name*. des *domain-name*

   and press Return. The first argument is the secure RPC name of the principal. Note that you do not type a dot (.) following the RPC net-name. The second argument associates the NIS+ principal name with the client system.

3. When prompted, type the root login password for the client.

4. Retype the root login password for the client. In this example, credentials are added to the master server named oak for a client named seachild in the domain ESG.Eng.sun.COM.

   ```
   oak% nisaddcred -p unix.seachild@esg.eng.sun.com -P
   seachild.esg.eng.sun.com. des esg.eng.sun.com.
   Adding key pair for unix.seachild@esg.eng.sun.com
   (seachild.esg.eng.sun.com.).
   ```

   Enter seachild.esg.eng.sun.com.'s root login password:

   ```
   Enter login password: <enter-root-password>
   Retype password: <enter-root-password>
   ```

Steps for Setting Up an NIS+ Client

This section provides steps for setting up an NIS+ client once the client credentials have been created on the master server. You need the name of the master server, the domain name, and the superuser password for the client system to perform the steps in this section.

Follow these steps to set up an NIS+ client:

1. Make sure that credentials for the client system have been added to the master server. To verify the values in the Cred table, type **nisgrep** *hostname* **cred.org_dir** and press Return.

2. Become superuser on the client system.

3. Follow these steps if you need to assign a new domain name to the client system. If the domain name for the client system is correct, skip to step 4.

   a. Type **domainname** *domainname* and press Return. You have changed the name of the domain for the client system. Note that you do not include a dot (.) at the end of the domain name. In this example, the domain name is changed to esg.eng.sun.com.

   ```
   # domainname esg.eng.sun.com
   #
   ```

   b. Type **domainname** and press Return. The current domain name is displayed. Check to make sure you entered it correctly. If you need to make any changes, redo step a.

   ```
   # domainname
   esg.eng.sun.com
   ```

   c. Type **domainname > /etc/defaultdomain** and press Return. You have redirected the domain name into the /etc/defaultdomain file so that the proper domain name is used when the system is rebooted. To ensure that all processes use the new domain name, you must at some point reboot the system. We suggest rebooting as the last step in this procedure.

4. Type **more /etc/nsswitch.conf** and press Return. The contents of the default /etc/nsswitch.conf file are displayed. You want to use the NIS+ version of the nsswitch.conf file. If the /etc/nsswitch.conf file on the client system looks like the following example, skip to step 7.

   ```
   # more /etc/nsswitch.conf
   #
   # /etc/nsswitch.nisplus:
   #
   # An example file that could be copied over to
   /etc/nsswitch.conf; it
   # uses NIS+ (NIS Version 3) in conjunction with files.
   #
   # "hosts:" and "services:" in this file are used only
   ```

```
if the /etc/netconfig
# file contains "switch.so" as a nametoaddr library for
"inet" transports.

# the following two lines obviate the "+" entry in
/etc/passwd and /etc/group.
passwd:     files nisplus
group:      files nisplus

# consult /etc "files" only if nisplus is down.
hosts:      nisplus [NOTFOUND=return] files
#Uncomment the following line, and comment out the
above, to use both DNS and NIS+
#hosts:        nisplus dns [NOTFOUND=return] files

services:   nisplus [NOTFOUND=return] files
networks:   nisplus [NOTFOUND=return] files
protocols:  nisplus [NOTFOUND=return] files
rpc:        nisplus [NOTFOUND=return] files
ethers:     nisplus [NOTFOUND=return] files
netmasks:   nisplus [NOTFOUND=return] files
bootparams: nisplus [NOTFOUND=return] files

publickey:  nisplus

netgroup:   nisplus

automount:  files nisplus
aliases:    files nisplus
```

5. If you need to change to the NIS+ /etc/nsswitch.conf file, type **cp /etc/nss-witch.nisplus /etc/nsswitch.conf** and press Return.

6. If the system was configured as an NIS+ server or client, you will need to remove any files in the /var/nis directory and kill the cache manager.

   a. Type **ls /var/nis** and press Return.

   b. If any files exist, type **rm -rf /var/nis/*** and press Return.

   c. Type **ps -ef | grep nis_cachemgr** and press Return. Note the PID for nis_cachemgr. You will use it in the next step.

d. Type **kill *PID*** and press Return. In this example, the client system already has a coldstart file and a directory cache file:

```
# ls /var/nis
NIS_COLD_START        NIS_SHARED_CACHE
# rm -rf /var/nis/*
# ps -ef | grep nis_cachemgr
   root  295    260 10 15:26:58 pts/0  0:00 grep nis_cachemgr
   root  286      1 57 15:21:55 ?       0:01 /usr/sbin/nis_cachemgr
# kill 286
#
```

7. Edit the /etc/hosts file of the client and add the name and IP address of the master server.

8. Type **nisinit -cH *master-server*** and press Return. The initialization should take only a few seconds. In the following example, oak is the master server. If this step does not work, check to make sure that the master server name and IP address are in the /etc/hosts file.

```
# nisinit -cH oak
This machine is in the ESG.Eng.sun.COM. NIS+ domain.
Setting up NIS+ client ...
All done.
```

9. Type **ps -ef | grep keyserv** and press Return. Note the process ID of the keyserv daemon. You will use it in the next step.

10. Type **kill *PID*** and press Return. You have killed the keyserv daemon.

11. Type **keyserv** and press Return. You have restarted the keyserv daemon so that it will re-read the public key entry in the /etc/nsswitch.conf file, as shown in the following example:

```
# ps -ef | grep keyserv
root  145    1 67 16:34:44   ?   keyserv
  # kill 145
# keyserv
#
```

12. Type **keylogin -r** and press Return.

13. When prompted, type the root password for the client system. This password must be the same password that was used to create the client's DES credentials. The password is used to decrypt the client's private key and is stored in the /etc/.rootkey file.

```
client1# keylogin -r
Password: <enter-root-password>
Wrote secret key into /etc/.rootkey
```

14. Type **init 6** and press Return. The system is rebooted and the NIS+ configuration is complete.

Verification of the Setup

The following sections describe some ways that you can verify that the system has been properly configured as an NIS+ client.

Verify That the Cache Manager Is Running

Check to see if nis_cachemgr is running. Type **ps -ef | grep nis_cachemgr** and press Return. In this example, the cache manager is running:

```
seachild% ps -ef | grep nis_cachemgr
    root   105     1 51 16:52:17 ?        0:01 /usr/sbin/nis_cachemgr
  winsor   251   240 15 20:11:07 pts/1    0:00 grep nis_cachemgr
seachild%
```

Check the Contents of the /var/nis Directory

When an NIS+ client is set up properly, the /var/nis directory has one or more files. Type **ls /var/nis** and press Return. The contents of /var/nis should look like this example:

```
seachild% ls /var/nis
NIS_COLD_START
NIS_SHARED_DIRCACHE
seachild%
```

Verify That the NIS+ Commands Succeed

When an NIS+ client is set up properly, you should be able to use the NIS+ commands. For example, type **nisls org_dir** and press Return. When the command is successful, a list of the tables in the org_dir directory is displayed, as shown in this example:

```
seachild% nisls org_dir
org_dir.ESG.Eng.sun.COM.:
auto_master
auto_home
bootparams
```

```
cred
ethers
group
hosts
mail_aliases
sendmailvars
netmasks
netgroup
networks
passwd
protocols
rpc
services
timezone
seachild%
```

This part describes the Solaris 2.*x* automounter services in two chapters.

Chapter 7 describes automount terminology and the components of automounting, explains how the automounter works, recommmends automounting policies, and tells you how to plan your automounter services.

Chapter 8 describes how to set up and administer automounter maps.

Refer to the chapters in this part if you need to set up a new automount service or modify an existing one.

3

Automounter Services

7

Understanding the Automounter

T HE AUTOMOUNTER WORKS WITH THE NFS (NETWORK FILE SYSTEM) TO mount and unmount directories from other systems on the network, as they are needed. The automounter supplements the virtual file system table (/etc/vfstab) and manual mount and unmount activities with an automatic, on-demand facility. When the user types a command that accesses a remote file or directory, the automounter consults a series of maps—described in detail later in this chapter—to determine which directories to mount, which system to mount them from, and where to mount them on the user's local system. The directory remains mounted as long as it is in use. When the user exits from the file or directory, the resource is automatically unmounted if it has not been accessed for 5 minutes.

Although you could administer the automounter by editing local automount maps in the /etc directory, Sunsoft recommends that you use the NIS+ naming service with the automounter. Using NIS+ will create a consistent global name space for your users and a centralized control model for your administrators. The instructions in this chapter and in Chapter 8 are for the recommended configuration, which is using the automounter with NIS+. (*All About Administering NIS+,* by Rick Ramsey, offers complete instructions for setting up and administering NIS+; see the bibliography at the back of this book for the complete reference.)

SunOS 5.*x* system software uses the SunOS 4.*x* automount program with some minor modifications. If you are familiar with SunOS 4.*x* automount services, you will be able to easily set up and administer the automounter for SunOS 5.*x* systems. You will also find that it is easy to administer automounting on a network where some systems run SunOS 4.*x* and others run SunOS 5.*x* system software. To help you find the modifications, in this book information that is new to the SunOS 5.*x* automounter has an icon in the margin that reads "New with SVR4."

This chapter describes some automount terminology, the automount maps and mount points, and how automounting works. It also provides some example maps and suggests recommended policies for planning how to use automounting in your network environment. (How to create and edit automount maps will be discussed in the next chapter.)

NFS Terminology

NFS, which is the SunOS 5.*x* distributed file system, is the industry's most widely available file-sharing system, adopted and shipped by more than 300 vendors. The terms in this discussion are commonly used to describe how resources are shared using NFS and how these terms relate to the automounter.

Server and Client Systems

The terms *server* and *client* are used to describe the roles that systems perform when they interact to share resources. These terms are part of general distributed computing terminology and are not specific to either NFS or the automounter. A *server* is a system that shares (exports) file systems so that they are accessible to other systems on the network. A *client* is a system that accesses some or all of its files from one or more servers.

You do not need to set up server file systems in a special way for access by the automounter. As long as the file systems are shared for NFS access, the automounter software can mount and unmount them.

Mount Points

Mount points are directories on a client system that are used as a place to attach (or mount) another file system. When you mount or automount a file system on a mount point, any files or directories that might be stored locally in the mount point directory are masked as long as the file system is mounted. These files are not permanently affected by the mounting process, and they become available again when the file system is unmounted. However, mount directories are usually empty so existing files will not be obscured.

The Virtual File System Table

Each system has a virtual file system table (/etc/vfstab) that specifies which file systems are mounted by default. Local ufs (UNIX file system) file systems and NFS file systems that are mounted automatically when a system boots are specified in this file. The /etc/vfstab file has additional entries for file systems, such as swap and proc, that are used by the system. In addition, the /etc/vfstab file may have entries for pcfs (personal computer file system) and cdrom file systems.

The automounter does not use the /etc/vfstab file to specify which file systems to mount and unmount. It uses maps instead, because they are more flexible and enable a consistent network-wide view of all file names.

You can mount some file systems using the /etc/vfstab file and others, using the automounter without any conflict. In fact, some file systems—such as local file systems and file systems shared from a server—must not be automounted.

CAUTION! *Do not create entries in the /etc/vfstab file for file systems that will be automounted. Conversely, do not put file systems that are included in the /etc/vfstab file into any of the automount direct maps. These redundant entries can seriously degrade system performance and generate a lot of unnecessary network traffic.*

Mount and Unmount

Most user file systems are automatically mounted when the system boots, using entries in the /etc/vfstab file. If users need to mount any additional file systems or unmount a mounted file system, they must have superuser privileges to do so and must use the mount and unmount commands. When file systems are automounted, users do not need to have superuser privileges to mount and unmount them.

For a description of the types of file systems and for information on how to share, mount, and unmount files, refer to *The Solaris System Administrator's Guide*, by Janice Winsor. (See the bibliography at the back of this book.)

The Mount Table (/etc/mnttab)

The SunOS 5.*x* system software uses a mount table, maintained in the /etc/mnttab file, to keep track of currently mounted file systems. Whenever users mount or unmount a file system, using either the mount/unmount commands or the automounter, /etc/mnttab is modified to show the list of currently mounted file systems.

NIS+ Terminology

NIS+ is the SunOS 5.*x* enterprise naming service. Information used by NIS+ is stored in tables, also called databases, which can be administered using the nistbladm (NIS+ table administration) command. You can administer some of the NIS+ tables using Administration Tool's Database Manager. NIS+ implementations of automount maps also are called databases or tables. For example, you administer the NIS+ Auto_home database using the Database Manager. You administer the NIS+ auto_master table, and any other NIS+ auto_*variable* tables you create, using the nistbladm command.

Automount Terminology

This section describes terms that are specific to the automounter.

Automounter

The automounter (also referred to as the automount program) is a daemon that is started at boot time by the rc2 script and runs in the background. It automatically mounts and unmounts NFS file systems as needed. Information provided in maps in the /etc directory that have the prefix auto_ is used to mount and unmount directories and subdirectories that are listed in the automount maps. The term *automounter* here refers to the automount program and the functionality that it provides, and the term *automounting* describes the activities of the automount program.

With Solaris 2.3 system software, the automount program splits into two programs: an automount daemon and a separate automount program. Both are run when the system is booted. See "How the Automounter Works" later in this chapter for more information.

Automount Maps

The automounter uses maps to determine which file systems to mount and where to mount them. There are three kinds of automount maps: master, indirect, and direct. Map names must always have auto_ as a prefix.

NOTE. *SunOS 4.x automount maps used the "auto." prefix naming convention. You do not need to rename your SunOS 4.x automount maps for them to be compatible with the SunOS 5.x automounter. The SunOS 5.x automounter looks first for files with an auto_ prefix. If none are found, it looks for files with an auto. prefix.*

The Master Map

The master map, named auto_master, is the master file consulted by the automounter when the system starts up. It contains the default mount points /net and /home and the names of the direct or indirect maps that the automounter consults.

Indirect and Direct Maps

The indirect and direct maps contain detailed information that the automounter uses to mount and unmount the file systems. You specify indirect maps using a simple path name; you specify direct maps using an absolute path name. See "Indirect Maps" and "Direct Maps" later in this chapter for more information.

The most commonly used indirect map is the home directory map, which contains the mount point and the names of the home directories to be automatically mounted. You can use the Administration Tool's Database Manager to administer the automounter's home directory database.

Automount Maps and Mount Points

The following sections describe the syntax of automount maps, the auto_master default mount points, and the mount point required for direct maps.

The Default Automount Maps

SunOS 5.*x* system software provides you with two default automounter maps: auto_master and auto_home.

The Master Map

New with SVR4.

The master map is located in the /etc directory. As indicated earlier, this map contains the default mount points /net and /home. These default mount points are new with SVR4. We suggest that you use them as a convenient way to maintain a consistent name space.

The syntax of entries in the auto_master map is:

```
mount-point      map-name      [mount-options]
```

The full pathname of a directory is *mount-point*. If the directory does not exist, the automounter creates it, if possible. The map used by the automounter to find the mount points and locations of the file systems is named *map-name*. Finally, *mount-options* is an optional list of comma-separated options that control the mounting of the entries specified by *map-name*. Options specified in the *map-name* map take precedence over options specified in the auto_master map. The *mount-options* used by the automounter are the same mount-options used in the /etc/vfstab file. Table 7.1 shows the most common mount options. See the mount_nfs(1M) manual page for a complete list of NFS mount options.

Table 7.1 **Mount Options**

Option	Description
rw	Resource is mounted read-write. If no option is specified, the resource is mounted rw.
ro	Resource is mounted read-only.
suid	Set user ID execution is allowed. If no option is specified, the resource is mounted suid.
nosuid	Set user ID is not allowed.
soft	Return an error if the server does not respond.
hard	Continue retrying the mount request until the server responds.
intr	Allow keyboard interrupts to kill a process that is hung while waiting for a response on a hard-mounted file system. The default is intr.

Table 7.1	Mount Options (Continued)	
Option	**Description**
nointr	Do not allow keyboard interrupts to kill a process that is hung while waiting for a response on a hard-mounted file system.

Here is the default auto_master map:

```
# Master map for automounter
#
+auto_master
/net        -hosts          -nosuid
/home       auto_home
```

Each system has a copy of the default /etc/auto_master map. The +auto_master entry provides a link to the NIS or NIS+ auto_master map. This entry is the first entry in the file, to ensure that the NIS or NIS+ auto_master map overrides information that is specified locally.

NOTE. *NIS+ provides backward compatibility with SunOS 4.x auto.master and other auto. files. If the automounter does not find any maps with an auto_ prefix, it searches for maps with an auto. prefix.*

New with SVR4.

The default auto_master map contains a /net mount point as part of an entry that automatically includes all systems under the special map -hosts. This built-in map uses the NIS+ hosts.org_dir map to locate exported file systems on a remote host system when the user specifies a system by name. What this means to users is that they can gain access to any files on systems that are listed in the NIS+ Hosts database by using the usual SunOS commands. For example, suppose that Fred sends e-mail telling you that a document is available on his system for review. Fred includes the system name—oak—and the path to the document—/export/home/fred/Newprojects/review.doc—in the e-mail message. He may even show the path as /net/oak/export/home/fred/Newprojects/review.doc. To print the file without copying it to your local system, you would type:

```
castle% lp /net/oak/export/home/fred/Newprojects/review.doc
castle%
```

To copy the file to your current working directory on your local system, you would type:

```
castle% cp /net/oak/export/home/fred/Newprojects/review.doc .
castle%
```

If you know the file is somewhere on the system named oak, but you are not sure of the complete path name, you can work your way down through the file system, as shown in this example:

```
castle% cd /net/oak
castle% ls
export
castle% cd export;ls
home
castle% cd home;ls
fred ignatz newton magic
castle% cd fred;ls
Newprojects Status Oldprojects
castle% cd Newprojects;ls
review.doc
castle% pwd
/tmp_mnt/net/oak/export/home/fred/Newprojects
castle%
```

If NIS+ is not running, the -hosts map consults the /etc/hosts file. For example, if a user types **cd /net/castle** and the system named castle is in the Hosts database, castle is mounted on /net as /tmp_mnt/net/castle. The -nosuid option prevents users from mounting setuid programs that are a security threat on the /net mount point.

New with SVR4.

The default auto_master map also contains a /home mount point and the auto_home map name so that you do not need to make a special entry in the auto_master map for auto_home. Sunsoft recommends that you use /home/*user-name* as your naming convention instead of the SunOS 4.*x* naming convention of /home/*system-name*/*user-name*.

The auto_master map is parsed from top to bottom. The top entry takes precedence. Consequently, when you use NIS+ maps to set up a global name space, the local /etc/auto_master maps should always have the +auto_master entry at the top of the file.

You can add new entries to the NIS+ auto_master map and take them away, although you should be careful about deleting entries from the NIS+ auto_master map. If you want to change the default mount point, change the /net -hosts entry to /net -null and define your new mount point. For example, to change the mount point to /foo, you would add the entry:

```
/foo    -hosts    -setuid
```

NOTE. *Although you can change the default /net mount point, Sunsoft recommends that you use the /net mount point to make the automounter easier to administer, to provide a consistent name space for your users, and to ensure compatibility* *with future automounter releases. If you have a different default mount point, consider gradually making the transition toward the recommended default.*

When you create new indirect or direct maps, you must add the mount points and map names to the NIS+ auto_master table so that the automounter knows to look for them. If you create a direct map, use /- as the mount point. The automounter recognizes this mount point as an instruction to not associate the entries in the auto_direct map with any directory. See Chapter 8 for step-by-step instructions for creating indirect and direct maps and updating the auto_master map.

The Home Directory Map

New with SVR4.

The home directory map, located in the /etc directory, is named auto_home. The default map contains a +auto_home link to the NIS+ auto_home database.

The syntax of entries in the auto_home map is:

```
user-name      [mount-options]      server:pathname
```

The user's login name is *user-name*, which is used as the mount point for the home directory. An optional, comma-separated list of options, [*mount-options*], controls the mounting of the user's home directory. If no options are specified, the home directory is mounted read-write. The *server:pathname* variable specifies the name of the server and the path to the user's home directory.

Here is the default auto_home map:

```
# Home directory map for automounter
#
+auto_home
```

Each system has a copy of the default /etc/auto_home map. The +auto_-home entry provides a link to the NIS or NIS+ Auto_home database. Sunsoft recommends that you use the Administration Tool's Database Manager to administer the NIS+ Auto_home database.

The Database Manager's Auto_home Database window, shown in Figure 7.1, displays the user name and the path from the NIS+ auto_home table.

To add an entry, choose Add Entry from the Edit menu. The Add Entry window is displayed. Type the user's name in the User Name text field and the server name, a colon, and the path to the user's home directory in the Path text field. Figure 7.2 shows an example of an entry.

In this example, the home directory for the user named winsor would be mounted from oak:/export/home/winsor on /home/winsor on the user's local system. When the user types *pwd* in the home directory, the local path is displayed as /tmp_mnt/home/winsor. With Solaris 2.3 system software, the /tmp_mnt mount point will not be displayed as part of the path name, and the local path will be displayed as /home/*username*.

Figure 7.1

The Auto_home Database window

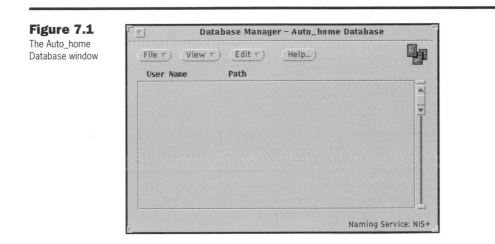

Figure 7.2

Example of an Auto_home database entry

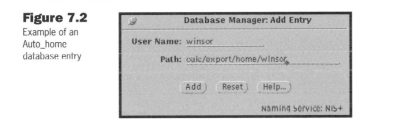

Indirect Maps

In an indirect map, you specify a simple name as the mount point (no slashes). The auto_home map is a good example of an indirect map that mounts a resource from a single server. You can create as many other indirect maps as you like so that you can provide users access to files exported from one or more servers.

The simple syntax for indirect maps is the same as for the auto_home map:

```
key     [mount-options]     server:pathname
```

The simple path name is *key*, which is used as the mount point for the re-source. An optional, comma-separated list of options, [*mount-options*], con-trols the mounting of the resource. If no options are specified, the resource is mounted read-write. The name of the server and the path to the resource is *server:pathname*.

Map entries can describe any number of resources, from different locations and with different mount options. For example, in this auto_local file, FrameMaker and OpenWindows are made available from different servers:

```
# Indirect map for executables: auto_local
#
openwin     -ro  oak:/usr/openwin
frame-3.1   ash:/usr/local/frame.3.1
```

You can specify more than one server location, use shortcuts and wildcard characters to shorten entries with similar characteristics, and set weighting factors for each server named by including an integer in parentheses. The most likely to be selected is (0); progressively higher values decrease the chance of being selected. For more information, see "Syntax and Shortcuts for Map Entries" following soon in this chapter.

Direct Maps

In direct maps, you specify an absolute path name as the mount point. Use a direct map only if you cannot create the map indirectly.

The simple syntax for a direct map is:

```
key      [mount-options]     server:pathname
```

The absolute path name is *key* and it is to be used as the mount point. An optional, comma-separated list of options, [*mount-options*], controls the mounting of the resource. If no options are specified, the resource is mounted read-write. The name of the server and the path to the resource are *server:pathname*.

By convention, create only one direct map, named auto_direct, and use it for all file systems you want to mount using an absolute path name.

Manual pages are a good example of an entry you might want to automount in a direct map. To show you the difference between indirect and direct maps for manual pages, let's first see how an indirect map would look. If you created an indirect map named auto_man to automount man pages from a server named oak on mount point /usr/man, it would look like this:

```
# Indirect map for man pages: auto_man
#
man1     oak:/usr/share/man/man1
man1b    oak:/usr/share/man/man1b
man1c    oak:/usr/share/man/man1c
man1f    oak:/usr/share/man/man1f
man1m    oak:/usr/share/man/man1m
man1s    oak:/usr/share/man/man1s
man2     oak:/usr/share/man/man2
```

```
man3      oak:/usr/share/man/man3
man3b     oak:/usr/share/man/man3b
man3c     oak:/usr/share/man/man3c
man3e     oak:/usr/share/man/man3e
man3g     oak:/usr/share/man/man3g
man3i     oak:/usr/share/man/man3i
man3k     oak:/usr/share/man/man3k
man3m     oak:/usr/share/man/man3m
man3n     oak:/usr/share/man/man3n
man3r     oak:/usr/share/man/man3r
man3s     oak:/usr/share/man/man3s
man3x     oak:/usr/share/man/man3x
man4      oak:/usr/share/man/man4
man4b     oak:/usr/share/man/man4b
man5      oak:/usr/share/man/man5
man6      oak:/usr/share/man/man6
man7      oak:/usr/share/man/man7
man9      oak:/usr/share/man/man9
man9e     oak:/usr/share/man/man9e
man9f     oak:/usr/share/man/man9f
man9s     oak:/usr/share/man/man9s
man1      oak:/usr/share/man/man1
mann      oak:/usr/share/man/mann
```

You must also create a corresponding entry named auto_man in the NIS+ auto_master map so that the automounter knows to look for the auto_man map.

If you do not want to create directories for each manual group, you can instead create a direct map with a single entry to automount manual pages. The manual page direct map entry might look like this:

```
# Direct map: auto_direct
#
# Entry for automounting manual pages
#
/usr/man     oak:/usr/share/man
```

This map creates a direct association between the shared directory and the mount point.

You must also create a corresponding entry with the mount point /- and the auto_man map name in the NIS+ auto_master map so that the auto-mounter knows to look for the auto_man map and to use the absolute path name from the direct map as the mount point. In this case, you can clearly see the benefits of using a direct map. Be sparing, however, in your use of direct maps. Using direct maps can generate a lot of network traffic because of unnecessary mounting.

Syntax and Shortcuts for Map Entries

These sections describe the syntax and shortcuts you can use for map entries. The examples show indirect maps, but you can also use these same shortcuts for the *mount-options* and *server:pathname* fields of direct maps.

Specifying Multiple Servers

You can specify more than one server as the resource for one mount point. If you specify more than one server in the *server:pathname* field, the automounter mounts the file system from the first server that replies to the mount request from the local net or subnet. If no server responds, all servers on the list are retried.

Here is the syntax for multiple locations for the same mount point. Note that the last entry does not have a backslash.

```
key        [mount-options]        server:pathname \
           [mount-options]        server:pathname \
           [mount-options]        server:pathname
```

The backslash at the end of each line tells the automounter to consider the entire entry as one line, and it makes the entry easier for administrators to read. For example, to mount the OpenWindows executable from three servers, the map entry could look like this:

```
openwin      -ro     oak:/usr/openwin \
             -ro     ash:/usr/openwin \
             -ro     elm:/usr/openwin
```

In this entry, each server specifies the same mount-options. You can combine them following the key by using this syntax:

```
key        [mount-options]\
               server:pathname \
               server:pathname \
               server:pathname
```

Using the syntax that combines mount-options for all servers, the entry looks like this:

```
openwin        -ro\
                   oak:/usr/openwin\
```

```
ash:/usr/openwin\
elm:/usr/openwin
```

This example works in exactly the same way as the preceding openwin example.

Specifying Multiple Servers with the Same Path

You can shorten the previous example because each of the locations uses the same path. Combine the server names on one line and separate them with commas, using this syntax:

```
key  [mount options] server1,server2,server3:pathname
```

Using the syntax that combines *mount-options* for all servers, and the names of the servers, the entry looks like this:

```
openwin    -ro   oak,ash,elm:/usr/openwin
```

This example works in exactly the same way as the previous two examples.

Specifying Weighting Factors for Each Server

You can specify weighting factors for each server in the list by putting a number in parentheses after the name of the server. Server(0) is most likely to be selected, with progressively higher values decreasing the chance of being selected. If you do not specify a number, the automounter assumes the server to have a (0) weighting, and thus the highest priority.

NOTE. *Some older versions of the automounter do not recognize the server-weighting values. When the automounter does not recognize the weighting values, servers with such values are ignored. Consequently, if you want to share automount maps among systems of various release levels, do not use the weighting factors.*

Here is the syntax for weighting factors:

```
key     [mount-options]\
            server1(n),server2(n),server3(n):pathname
```

Using the syntax that combines *mount-options* for all servers and combines the names of the servers with weighting factors, the entry looks like this:

```
openwin    -ro\
            oak,ash(1),elm(2):/usr/openwin
```

In this example, the server oak has the highest priority, (0), the server ash has the second highest priority, and the server elm, the third.

You can use the weighting factor for any list of servers, whether they are on individual lines or are combined on the same line, by following the name of the server with a weighting factor number in parentheses.

NOTE. *Server proximity takes precedence over the weighting value. For example, a server on a local subnet is chosen even if it has a higher weighting value than a server on a different subnet. The weighting value is used to choose between servers that have the same network proximity.*

Using Map Variables

The automounter provides predefined map variables, similar to environment variables, that you can use in defining paths. In Solaris 2.0 and 2.1, the map variables are ARCH and CPU.

NOTE. *The $ARCH variable is obsolete. It uses the output of the /usr/kvm/arch command, which is provided for compatibility. Use the $CPU variable instead.*

New with SVR4.

When you include $CPU as part of the path, the map variable returns the name of the system architecture, as it would be returned by the uname -p command.

```
oak% uname -p
sparc
oak%
```

In this example, the uname -p command returns the architecture sparc.

If you have a server exporting binaries for both SPARC and Intel 486 architectures from /usr/local/bin/sparc and /usr/local/bin/i486, respectively, you can create a map entry, using the $CPU command, that mounts the binaries appropriate for each system's architecture. The entry would look like this:

```
bin     -ro     server:/usr/local/bin/$CPU
```

With this entry, the map can be used for clients running all architectures.

The Solaris 2.3 system software will provide additional predefined map variables, as described in Table 7.2.

Table 7.2   **Solaris 2.3 Predefined Map Variables**

Variable	Means	Command	Example
ARCH	architecture type	/usr/kvm/arch	sun4, i486pc
CPU	processor type	uname -p	sparc, i486

Table 7.2	Solaris 2.3 Predefined Map Variables (Continued)			
	Variable	Means	Command	Example
	HOST	hostname	uname -n	castle
	OSNAME	operating system name	uname -s	SunOS
	OSREL	operating system release	uname -r	5.2
	OSVERS	operating system version	uname -v	Generic

How the Automounter Works

These sections provide an overview of how the automounter works. When a system is booted, the automounter daemon is started from the /etc/init.d/nfs.client script. With Solaris 2.3 system software, the boot procedure is split into two programs: an automount command and an automountd daemon. The startup script for Solaris 2.3 system software is /etc/init.d/autofs.

The automounter checks for the local auto_master map. When the first entry in the local auto_master map is +auto_master, the automounter consults the NIS+ auto_master table, builds a list of the specified mount points, and consults the auto_variable maps it finds listed there. When the first entry in the local auto_master map is not +auto_master, the automounter consults the local auto_variable maps. The startup procedure for Solaris 2.0, 2.1, and 2.2 system software is shown in Figure 7.3. If no NIS+ auto_master map is found, NIS+ searches for an NIS auto.master map.

When a user changes to a directory that has a mount point controlled by the automounter, the automounter intercepts the request and mounts the remote file system in the /tmp_mnt directory if it is not already mounted.

On the other hand, when a user changes out of a directory controlled by the automounter, the automounter waits a predetermined amount of time (the default is 5 minutes) and unmounts the file system if it has not been accessed during that time. Using the automounter is illustrated in Figure 7.4.

In Figure 7.4, when the user types *cd*, the automounter looks in the table that was created at boot time from the NIS+ auto_master map and NIS+ auto_home map and mounts the user's home directory from the server named oak. When the user types *man lp*, the automounter looks in the table that was created at boot time, mounts the manual pages on /usr/man, and displays the manual page for the lp command. After 5 minutes of inactivity, the manual pages are unmounted. When the user types *maker&*, the automounter looks in the table that was created at boot time and mounts the executable for FrameMaker on /bin/frame3.1.

Figure 7.3

Starting the
automounter

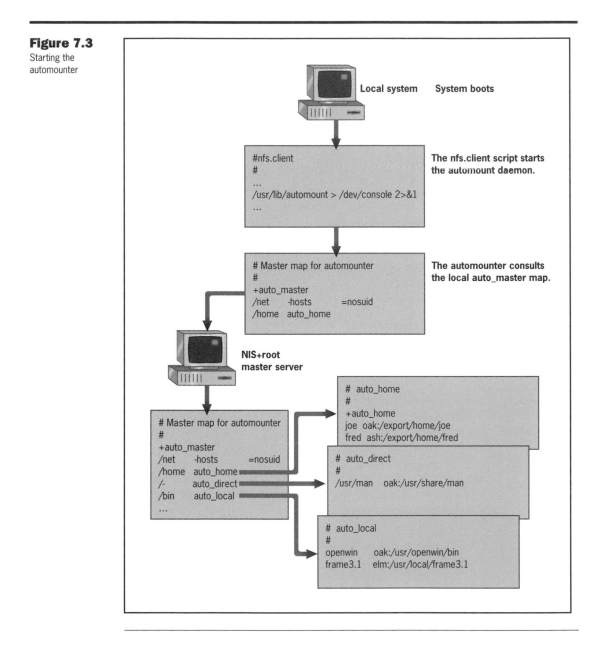

Figure 7.4

Using the
automounter

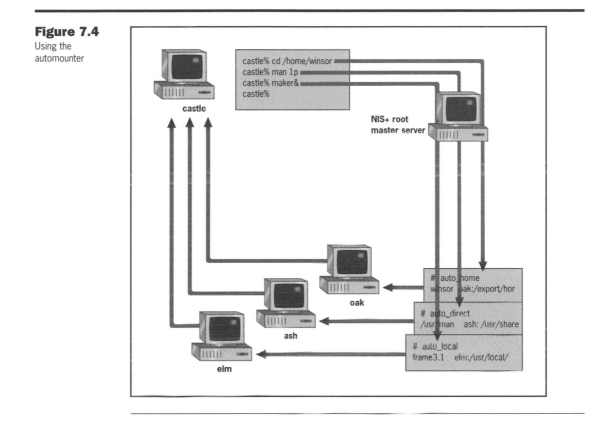

How to Plan for Automounting

In these discussions about the automounter, it is assumed that you are administering a network of systems running SunOS 4.x and SunOS 5.x system software, and that you are using NIS on the 4.x systems and NIS+ on the 5.x systems. This configuration provides you with a global name space so that you can mount file systems that are exported from any server on the network. It also creates host-independent resources so that you can specify a list of servers from which file systems can be mounted, and allows you to relocate resources from one server to another without disrupting the user environment.

NOTE.   *Although you can set up the automounter using local maps, Sunsoft strongly recommends that you do not do so. Decentralized and local maps are more complicated and expensive to maintain, and they are difficult to update consistently. Sunsoft is implementing many new automount features in future versions of Solaris system software. Some of these new features will work only with maps stored in NIS+.*

Recommended Automounting Policies

Before you begin planning your automounting, review the list of recommended policies in the following sections. They may affect how you set up your automount maps.

- Use the default mount points /net and /home. If your site uses a different mount point naming scheme, convert your site gradually to use the default mount point names to ensure compatibility with future releases.

- Always use the NIS+ (or NIS) maps. Discourage use of local maps.

- Use indirect maps as much as you can to minimize the excessive network traffic that can be generated by direct maps.

- Use direct maps only when absolutely necessary.

- Use two-level home directory names (/home/*username*) instead of the SunOS 4.*x* three-level home directory names (/home/*server*/*username*).

- Because the automounter uses the /home directory as a mount point, do not use just /home as the top-level directory name on the servers that contain users' home directories. Create user's home directories as a three-level path (/export/home/*username*). Most importantly, make sure that user disk partitions are not mounted on or under /home. Multiple partitions may require separate mount points, for example, /export/home1, /export/home2, and so on.

- Never automount local or shared file systems. Mount them from the system's local /etc/vfstab file.

- Do not put entries that are already in the /etc/vfstab file into automount direct maps.

- If your site has a mixture of systems running SunOS 4.*x* and SunOS 5.*x*, you do not need to change the names of your SunOS 4.*x* automount maps from auto.*variable* to auto_*variable*. NIS searches for auto.master if it cannot find an auto_master map. In fact, you should never change the SunOS 4.*x* auto.master map name; this name is required by the SunOS 4.*x* automounter.

Prerequisites for Using the Automounter

These sections describe the prerequisites for using the automounter. Before creating automount maps, the network should be up and running NIS+ on SunOS 5.*x* systems and NIS on SunOS 4.*x* systems.

Each system on the network should have the default auto_master and auto_home maps in its local /etc directory. These maps are automatically installed with the system software.

Servers and the Automounter

Automounter use is completely transparent to servers. A server has no way of telling whether files it shares are accessed using the mount command or using the automounter. As long as you set up your server file systems and share (export) them, you do not need to do any additional administration to plan for or set up the automounter.

When planning for automounter setup, you need a list of servers that have the file systems you want to automount, and the path to the resources.

If servers are accessible to user logins, you should set them up like clients. The automounter on a server will correctly handle references to local file systems. You must not mount local file systems at automount mount points.

Clients and the Automounter

As long as you use NIS_ to store automount maps, you do not need to do anything special to administer client systems of the automounter. If you use local /etc/auto_* maps, you must manually update them using editors or RCP.

NIS+ Maps

When you use NIS+ with the automounter, all you need to do to set up and administer the automounter is create and modify NIS+ automount maps. Chapter 8 describes how to create, modify, or delete entries in NIS+ automount maps.

The auto_master map must contain a list of mount points, optional mount options, and names of the maps. The auto_home map must contain a list of user names and the server and path to each user's home directory.

You can create additional maps, both indirect and direct, to provide access to executables, manual pages, source files, project files, or any other set of files that are made available from a server.

CHAPTER

Setting Up the Automounter

Setting Up Automount Server Systems

Setting Up Automount Client Systems

Displaying Information about NIS+ Automount Maps

Setting Up NIS+ Automount Maps

THIS CHAPTER DESCRIBES HOW TO SET UP THE AUTOMOUNTER ON A NETwork that is running NIS+ on SunOS 5.*x* systems and NIS on SunOS 4.*x* systems. If you need help setting up NIS+, refer to *All About Administering NIS+* by Rick Ramsey. (See the bibliography at the back of this book.)

Setting Up Automount Server Systems

A system becomes an NFS server by sharing some of its file systems over the network. A server keeps a list of currently exported file systems and their access restrictions (such as read-write or read-only). You share a resource by adding an entry to the /etc/dfs/dfstab (distributed file system table) on the server and then typing **shareall**. See the dfstab(4) and the share(1M) manual pages for more information.

You do not need to perform any additional steps to make the shared file systems available to the automounter.

Setting Up Automount Client Systems

Client systems that use the automounter need to have the default auto_master and auto_home maps in their local /etc directory. These default files are included as part of system software installation. You should not need to edit these default files.

If you have problems with automounting from a system, check to make sure it has the default auto_master and auto_home maps, and that they are in the /etc directory. If the maps are there, check to make sure that the auto_master map contains the +auto_master entry and that the auto_home map contains the +auto_home entry. These entries tell the automounter to use the NIS+ automounter maps. If the entries are not present, the automounter uses only the information from the local /etc automount maps.

Displaying Information about NIS+ Automount Maps

The following sections describe how to display information about the format and content of NIS+ automount maps using the -o and -v options to the niscat command. You do not need to be root or a member of the sysadmin group (GID 14) to display information using the niscat command. You do need to have, at least, read permission for the NIS+ automount tables. See Chapter 7 for more information about NIS+ and security. For complete information about how to set up and administer NIS+, refer to *All About Administering NIS+*, mentioned earlier in this chapter.

Displaying the Format of NIS+ Automount Maps

Information used by NIS+ is stored in tables on the NIS+ root master server. Copies of these tables are stored on NIS+ replica servers. The automount maps are instances of NIS+ tables. You can display the format of any existing NIS+ automount map using the niscat -o command. The format shows information about the NIS+ table, its ownership and permissions, and the names, attributes, and access rights of each column. Use the niscat -o command when you want to find out information such as permissions for the map, or names of the columns.

The syntax of the niscat -o command is:

```
niscat -o table-name.directory.domain-name.
```

For NIS+ automount tables, the more specific syntax is:

```
niscat -o auto_name.org_dir.domain-name.
```

NOTE. *NIS+ tables require a fully qualified domain name—the name of the map, the directory where the map is stored (org_dir), and the domain name followed by a dot (.). If you omit the trailing dot, a syntax error is displayed. If the NIS_PATH environment variable is set, then you do not have to specify the complete path to the org_dir directory. You can type* **table-name.directory** *(with no trailing dot) and press Return. The examples in this book use the fully qualified domain name for completeness. See Part 2 for more information about NIS+.*

In the example below, format information about the NIS+ auto_home map in the sun.COM. domain is displayed:

```
oak% niscat -o auto_home.org_dir.sun.COM.
Object Name   : auto_home
Owner         : oak.sun.COM.
Group         : admin.sun.COM
Domain        : org_dir.sun.COM.
Access Rights : ----rmcdrmcdr---
Time to Live  : 12:0:0
Object Type   : TABLE
Table Type         : automount_map
Number of Columns  : 2
Character Separator :
Search Path        :
Columns            :
       [0]     Name           : key
               Attributes     : (SEARCHABLE, TEXTUAL DATA, CASE SENSITIVE)
               Access Rights  : ---------------
       [1]     Name           : value
               Attributes     : (TEXTUAL DATA)
               Access Rights  : ---------------
oak%
```

See Part 2 for more information about NIS+ security and how to interpret this information.

Displaying the Contents of NIS+ Automount Maps

You can display the content (or value) of the columns of any existing NIS+ automount map using the niscat -v command. Use this command when you want to determine the values set for an automount map or to verify that an entry has been successfully created.

The syntax of the niscat -v command is:

```
niscat -v table-name.directory.domain-name.
```

For NIS+ automount tables, the more specific syntax is:

```
niscat -v auto_name.org_dir.domain-name.
```

In the example below, the NIS+ auto_home map for the domain sun.COM. contains only one entry; the user winsor automounts a home directory from oak:/export/home/winsor.

```
oak% niscat -v auto_home.org_dir.sun.COM.
winsor   oak:/export/home/winsor
oak%
```

Setting Up NIS+ Automount Maps

All of the setup and administration of automounting on a network—running NIS+ on SunOS 5.x systems and NIS on SunOS 4.x systems—involves creating and maintaining NIS+ automount maps. The steps in the following sections describe how to create these maps on the NIS+ root master server. See "Administering Automount NIS+ Maps" later in this chapter for information about how to modify existing maps.

Setting Up the auto_home Map

The auto_home map is created as part of setting up the NIS+ root master server. You will not need to create it separately. Use Administration Tool's Database Manager to read or edit the contents of this map and to set up home directory information for your users.

NOTE. *Before you can use Administration Tool to edit the Auto_home database on the NIS+ root master server, you must be a member of the sysadmin group (GID 14) and have create and delete permission for the Auto_home database. See Chapter 5 for information about NIS+ permissions.*

Follow these steps to set up your initial entries in the Auto_home database:

1. Make a list of each user namc, with the server and path to each user's home directory.

2. Type **admintool &** and press Return to start the Administration Tool. The Administration Tool window is displayed.

3. Click SELECT on the Database Manager icon. The Database Manager window is displayed.

4. Click SELECT on the Auto_home database entry.

5. Check to be sure the NIS+ text field shows the correct domain name. If you want to add the users to a different domain, type the name of the domain you want to use.

6. Click SELECT on Load. The Auto_home Database window is displayed, as shown in Figure 8.1. The window does not display any initial entries.

Figure 8.1

The Auto_home database window

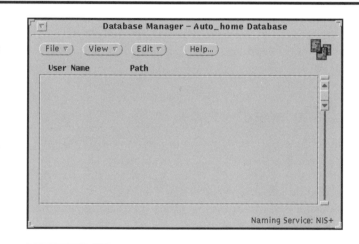

7. Choose Add Entry from the Edit menu. The Add Entry window is displayed, as shown in Figure 8.2.

8. For each user account:

   a. Type the name of the user in the User Name text field.

   b. Type *server-name:pathname* in the Path text field.

   c. Click SELECT on Add.

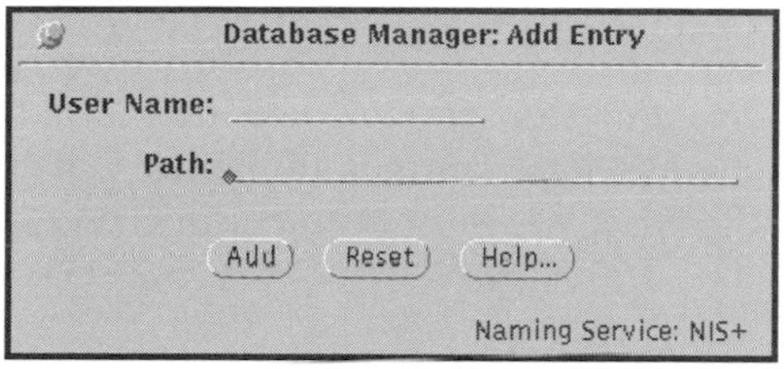

Figure 8.2

The Auto_home database Add Entry window

Database Manager: Add Entry

User Name:

Path:

Add   Reset   Help...

Naming Service: NIS+

In the example shown in Figure 8.3, user winsor has a home directory on the server oak. The path is /export/home/winsor.

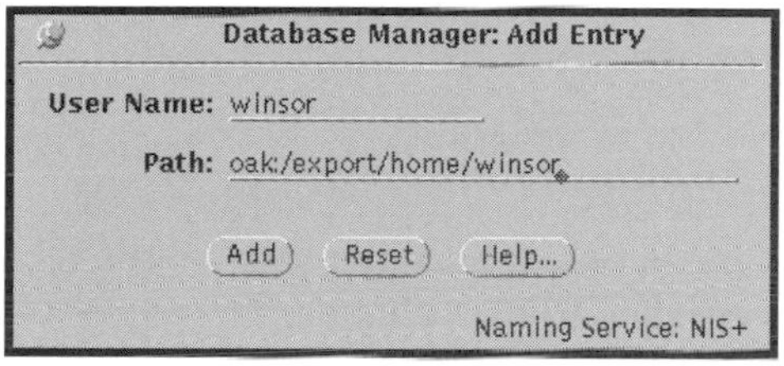

Figure 8.3

An example of adding an entry

Database Manager: Add Entry

User Name: winsor

Path: oak:/export/home/winsor

Add   Reset   Help...

Naming Service: NIS+

4. When you have completed adding the entries, click SELECT on the push pin (upper-left corner of the figure) to dismiss the Add Entry window.

NOTE. *You do not need to make an entry for the auto_home map in the NIS+ auto_master map. The entry is already included in the default auto_master map. Consult* All About Administering NIS+ *(mentioned earlier) for information about how to set up NIS+ and how to convert the contents of NIS maps into NIS+ tables.*

Setting Up Indirect Maps

Use the NIS+ command nistbladm to create and edit indirect maps on the NIS+ root master server.

NOTE. *The nistbladm command requires a fully qualified name for the table—that is, the name of the table followed by the directory where the NIS+ tables are stored and then the domain name. Note that, with NIS+ commands, a fully qualified name has a period at the end of the domain name. For example, auto_master.org_dir.Sun.COM. is the fully qualified name for the auto_master table, which is in the directory org_dir in the domain Sun.COM.*

1. Decide which indirect maps you want to create. Make a list of the mount points, servers, and path names for each indirect map.

2. Log on to the NIS+ root master server. If you are a member of the group that has permission to edit NIS+ automount tables, you can edit the tables as yourself. Otherwise, you must become superuser on the NIS+ root master.

3. For each indirect map you want to create, type

```
nistbladm -c automount_map key=S value=S auto_table-name.org_dir.domain-name.
```

and press Return. The -c option creates the table, assigns it the table type "automount," creates two columns named "key" and "value" that are searchable, and assigns the table name auto_*table-name*. Note that any mount options you specify are part of the value.

4. For each entry in the table, type

```
nistbladm -a key=mount-point value=options,pathname
auto_table-name.org_dir.domain-name.
```

and press Return. The -a option adds the entry to the table you specify, and the values are assigned to the columns.

5. To display the values in the table, type

```
niscat -v auto_table-name.org_dir.domain-name.
```

and press Return.

6. For each map you create, you must add an entry to the auto_master map.

   a. To display the names of the columns in the auto_master map, type

   ```
   niscat -o auto_master.org_dir.domain-name.
   ```

   and press Return.

   b. For each entry, type

```
nistbladm -a key=mount-point value=map-name auto_master.org_dir.domain-name.
```

   and press Return.

The auto_master map is read at boot time only, or when the automounter is started. After you have completed creating new maps and have added the mount point and map name to the auto_master map, you must stop the automounter and restart it. With Solaris 2.3, you do not need to stop and restart the automounter. Instead, just run the automount command.

NOTE. *You could restart the automounter and read the auto_master map by booting the system. To avoid interrupting services, however, we suggest that you restart the automounter from the command line.*

Follow these steps to stop the automounter and restart it.

CAUTION! *Never use the -9 option to kill the automounter.*

1. Become superuser on the system where you changed the auto_master map.

2. Type **ps -ef | grep automount** and press Return.

3. Type **kill -1 *PID*** and press Return.

4. Type **/usr/lib/nfs/automount** and press Return.

In the following example, we create an indirect automount_map named auto_local in the org_dir domain for sun.COM, enter two rows in the table, add the indirect map to the NIS+ auto_master table, and stop and then restart the automounter.

```
oak% su
Password:
oak# nistbladm -c automount_map key=S value=S auto_local.org dir.sun.COM.
oak# nistbladm -a key=openwin value=oak:/usr/openwin auto_local.org_dir.sun.COM.
oak# nistbladm -a key=frame3.1 value=ash:/usr/local/frame3.1
auto_local.org_dir.sun.COM.
oak# niscat -v auto_local.org_dir.sun.COM.
openwin  oak:/usr/openwin
frame3.1  ash:/usr/local/frame3.1
oak# niscat -o auto_master.org_dir.sun.COM.
Object Name    : auto_master
Owner          : oak.sun.COM.
Group          : admin.sun.COM
Domain         : org_dir.sun.COM.
Access Rights  : ----rmcdrmcdr---
Time to Live   : 12:0:0
Object Type    : TABLE
Table Type         : automount_map
Number of Columns  : 2
Character Separator :
Search Path        :
Columns            :
        [0]    Name          : key
               Attributes    : (SEARCHABLE, TEXTUAL DATA, CASE SENSITIVE)
               Access Rights : ----------------
        [1]    Name          : value
               Attributes    : (TEXTUAL DATA)
               Access Rights : ----------------
oak# nistbladm -a key=/bin value=auto_local auto_master.org_dir.sun.COM.
```

```
oak# niscat -v auto_master.org_dir.sun.COM.
/bin auto_local
oak# ps -ef | grep automount
 root  131    1 16  21:18:47 ?      0:00  /usr/lib/nfs/automount
 root  407  398 14  23:14:00 pts/3 0:00 grep automount
oak# kill -1 131
oak# /usr/lib/nfs/automount
oak#
```

Setting Up a Direct Map

You set up a direct map in the same way that you set up indirect maps, using the NIS+ nistbladm command. The only difference is that, by convention, the direct map is named auto_direct, and you use the complete path name in the key field. By convention, all direct mounts are included in the map named auto_direct.

See the section "Setting Up Indirect Maps" earlier in the chapter for complete instructions.

The example below sets up a direct map named auto_direct, with one entry for automounting manual pages, and adds the direct map to the auto_master map. At the end of the example, the automounter is stopped and then restarted.

```
oak% su
Password:
oak# nistbladm -c automount_map key=S value=S auto_direct.org_dir.sun.COM.
oak# nistbladm -a key=/usr/man value=-ro,oak:/usr/share/man
auto_direct.org_dir.sun.COM.
oak# niscat -v auto_local.org_dir.sun.COM.
/usr/man  -ro  oak:/usr/share/man
oak# niscat -o auto_master.org_dir
Object Name   : auto_master
Owner         : oak.sun.COM.
Group         : admin.sun.COM.
Domain        : org_dir.sun.COM.
Access Rights : ----rmcdrmcdr---
Time to Live  : 12:0:0
Object Type   : TABLE
Table Type        : automount_map
Number of Columns : 2
Character Separator :
Search Path         :
Columns             :
        [0]     Name    : key
                Attributes    : (SEARCHABLE, TEXTUAL DATA, CASE SENSITIVE)
                Access Rights : ---------------
        [1]     Name    : value
                Attributes    : (TEXTUAL DATA)
                Access Rights : ---------------
oak# nistbladm -a key=/- value=auto_direct auto_master.org_dir.sun.COM.
```

```
oak# niscat -v auto_master.org_dir.sun.COM.
/bin auto_local
/- auto_direct
oak# ps -ef | grep automount
 root  138   1 16  21:18:47 ?      0:00  /usr/lib/nfs/automount
 root  412 398 14  23:14:00 pts/3 0:00 grep automount
oak# kill -1 138
oak# /usr/lib/nfs/automount
oak#
```

Setting Up the Master Map

When the NIS+ root master server is configured, the NIS+ auto_master map is created automatically. You do not need to create it as a separate step.

You do, however, need to make sure that you provide an entry in the NIS+ auto_master map for each direct map and indirect map that you create.

The section "Setting Up Indirect Maps" contains information on how to edit the NIS+ auto_master map. That information is summarized here for your reference.

Follow these steps to add an entry to the NIS+ auto_master map.

1. Display the names of the columns in the auto_master map by typing **niscat -o auto_master.org_dir.***domain-name.* and press Return.

2. To add each entry, type **nistbladm -a key=***mount-point* **value=***map-name* **auto_master.org_dir.***domain-name.* and press Return.

3. Stop and restart the automounter. (Remember that you do not need to do this with Solaris 2.3—just run the automount command.)

Administering NIS+ Automount Maps

The following sections describe how to modify entries in existing automount maps and how to delete entries from NIS+ automount maps.

Modifying NIS+ Automount Maps

You can use the -A option for nistbladm to force an overwrite of information in an existing NIS+ automount map.

The syntax for the nistbladm -A option is shown below. You must specify a value for each of the columns in the table.

```
nistbladm -A column= ... table-name.domain-name.
```

For NIS+ automount tables, the more specific syntax is:

```
nistbladm -A key= value= auto_name.org_dir.domain-name.
```

In the next example, the administrator typed *key=bin* instead of *key=/bin* for the auto_local entry in the auto_master table. When the system booted, the automounter displayed an error message informing the administrator that the name "bin" in the auto_master table needed to be changed to "/bin".

Here's how the administrator changed the entry using the nistbladm -A command:

```
oak% nistbladm -A key=/bin value=auto_local auto_master.org_dir.sun.COM.
oak%
```

Deleting Entries from NIS+ Automount Maps

You can delete rows from NIS+ automount maps using the nistbladm -r command and specifying one of the columns.

Here's the syntax for the nistbladm -r option:

```
nistbladm -r column= table-name.domain-name.
```

For NIS+ automount tables, the more specific syntax is:

```
nistbladm -r column= auto_name.org_dir.domain-name.
```

If you create an incorrect entry, you can delete it. Our administrator who created the key=bin value=auto_local entry in the NIS+ auto_master map could have deleted the entry in this way and then created a new one:

```
oak% niscat -v auto_master.org_dir.sun.COM.
bin  auto_local
/-  auto_direct
oak% nistbladm -r key=bin auto_master.org_dir.sun.COM.
oak% niscat -v auto_master.org_dir.sun.COM.
/-  auto_direct
nistbladm -a key=/bin value=auto_local auto_master,org_dir.sun.COM.
oak%
```

This part describes the Solaris 2.*x* Service Access Facility (SAF) in three chapters.

Chapter 9 provides an overview of the SAF and describes the port monitors and services used by the SAF. Chapter 10 describes how to set up and administer the SAF for modems and terminals. Chapter 11 describes how to set up and administer the SAF for printers and how to troubleshoot printing problems.

Refer to the chapters in this part if you need to set up a new SAF service for terminals, modems, or printers or to modify an existing one.

PART

4

**Service Access
Facility**

Understanding the Service Access Facility

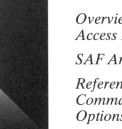

Overview of the Service Access Facility

SAF Architecture

Reference to SAF Commands, Tasks, and Options

New with SVR4.

THE SERVICE ACCESS FACILITY (SAF) IS A GROUP OF DAEMONS AND AD-ministrative commands that provide a flexible administrative framework for managing service requests in an open-systems environment. You use the SAF to set up and administer port monitors so that users can log in from a terminal or a modem and can use network printing resources. The SAF replaces the SunOS 4.*x* getty, login, and stty commands and the /etc/gettytab and /etc/ttytab files. SAF controls and configures terminals and printers using the terminfo database.

Solaris 2.3 system software offers a graphical user interface to the SAF that you can use to set up and configure modems and character terminals. See Appendix B for information about how to use the Administration Tool Serial Port Monitor. If you are running Solaris 2.3 system software, SunSoft recommends that you use the Serial Port Monitor to configure modems and character terminals.

Benefits of the SAF

The SAF is an open-systems solution that controls how users access their UNIX system through TTY devices and local area networks. The SAF offers well-defined interfaces so that customers and value-added resellers can easily add new features and configure existing ones.

Flexibility is an important requirement in an open-systems environment. Service of incoming connection requests must be available independent of the location or connection path of the requester. Both local and remote requests must be handled, as much as possible, independent of the available network transports.

Restrictions in previous System V and BSD-based versions of UNIX prevented this type of open-systems computing environment. Those restrictions included:

- Lack of selective access control.

- Inflexible getty. Only the login service was provided, because it was hard-wired in.

- Difficulty in selectively disabling/enabling login service.

- Impossibility of scaling an increasing number of ports because of the model of one getty per potential access port.

- Inaccuracy of /etc/utmp accounting for remote services.

- Mixed or no authentication for non-RPC and TCP/IP requests.

You can use the Solaris 2.*x* SAF framework if you want to create a complex application such as the banking database service shown in Figure 9.1.

Figure 9.1

A typical bank
database server

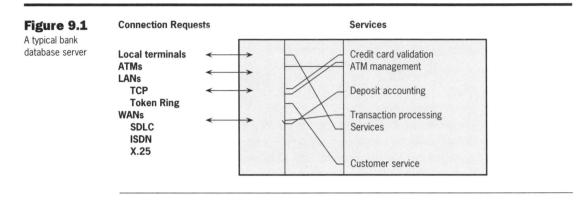

The left side of the figure shows incoming connection requests for services—some from local terminals, others from automatic teller machines (ATMs). The right side shows the service that is provided. Many requests come from local area networks running a variety of different transport protocols. Bank networks usually have wide-area network connections over a variety of datalink layers, such as X.25, SDLC, and, in the future, ISDN.

The SAF Daemons

The SAF uses the Service Access Controller daemon (sac) to oversee all the SAF port monitors. The sac daemon is started at boot time at run level 2 by init. Two port monitors watch for activity on a port.

- The ttymon port monitor handles requests for login services. Solaris 2.*x* provides a default set of ttymon services for use with a stand-alone system. You need to set up a ttymon port monitor to process login requests from modems and additional terminals (such as Wyse terminals) if you configure them for a system.

- The listen port monitor handles requests for network services such as remote printing and remote file access. You need to set up a listen port monitor to provide remote printing services.

Once the ports are configured, the port monitors are automatically started any time a system is running in multiuser mode. The ttymon and listen port monitors are described in more detail later in this chapter.

The SAF Commands

You use three SAF commands to administer modems and alphanumeric terminals—sacadm, pmadm, and ttyadm. You use also three SAF commands to administer printing—sacadm, pmadm, and nlsadmin.

Use the sacadm command to add and remove port monitors. This command is your main link with the Service Access Controller (SAC) and its administrative files /etc/saf/_sactab, /etc/saf/_safconfig, and /etc/saf/*pmtag*/_config.

NOTE. *Although these configuration files are ASCII text and can be edited if you make changes to them, the SAC may not be aware of the changes. SunSoft recommends that you do not edit these files directly. Instead, you should use the sacadm and pmadm commands to make changes to the SAF administrative files.*

Use the pmadm command to add or remove a service and to associate a service with a particular port monitor. Each port monitor has its own administrative file.

You use two additional commands, ttyadm and nlsadmin, as part of the command-line arguments to pmadm to provide input specific for a port monitor. The ttyadm command provides information for the ttymon port monitor; the nlsadmin command provides information for the listen port monitor. SAF commands use many options and arguments, and can be quite lengthy. See the section "Reference to SAF Commands, Tasks, and Options" at the end this chapter for more information.

SAF Architecture

Figure 9.2 shows the architecture of SAF. Each of the architectural elements is described in the following paragraphs.

The init Process

The init process controls the overall state of the system and creates processes using the information stored in the /etc/inittab file. The init process monitors the SAC. The /etc/inittab file has an entry that restarts the sac process if init receives a signal indicating that the sac process has died.

Service Access Controller

The sac daemon controls the overall state of arbitrary processes that are started in response to connection requests. The sac daemon receives all requests to enable, disable, start, or stop port monitors, and takes the appropriate action. If port monitor processes are terminated, sac is responsible for restarting them.

Figure 9.2

Service Access
Facility architecture

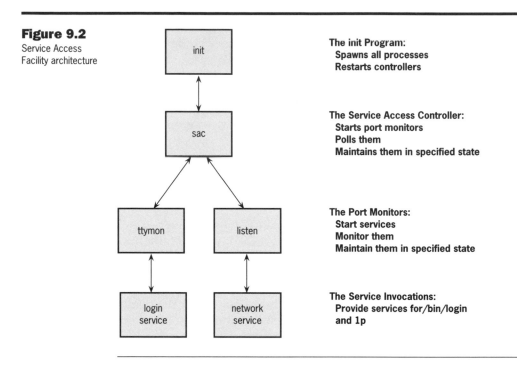

The init Program:
Spawns all processes
Restarts controllers

The Service Access Controller:
Starts port monitors
Polls them
Maintains them in specified state

The Port Monitors:
Start services
Monitor them
Maintain them in specified state

The Service Invocations:
Provide services for/bin/login
and 1p

The sac is started from this entry in the /etc/inittab file:

```
sc:234:respawn:/usr/lib/saf/sac -t 300
```

NOTE. *The rc scripts do not control the sac process.*

When sac is started, first it customizes its own environment by reading the /etc/saf/_sysconfig configuration file. Each system has one /etc/saf/_sysconfig file. When the sac process is started, this file is interpreted and used for all port monitors on the system. Modifications to the environment from this file are inherited by all of sac's children.

Then sac starts all designated port monitors using information from the /etc/saf/_sactab file. For each port monitor to be started, sac forks a port monitor child process. The ttymon port monitor reads its configuration information from the /etc/saf/*pmtag*/_pmtab port monitor table. If configured, the listen port monitor reads its configuration information from the /etc/saf/*pmtag*/_pmtab file. You set the value of the *pmtag* variable when you use the sacadm command to create the port monitor. The default name for the ttymon port monitor for serial ports is zsmon; the default name for the listen port monitor is tcp.

Once the port monitors are running, sac polls them periodically for status information. If a port monitor that should be running has stopped, sac will restart it if a non-zero restart count was specified when the port monitor was created.

Port Monitors

Port monitors monitor a set of homogeneous incoming requests on a system port, detect incoming requests, and connect them to the appropriate service process. As already mentioned, Solaris 2.x system software provides a TTY port monitor daemon named ttymon, and a network port monitor daemon named listen.

To find out which port monitors are running and to show the status, type **sacadm -l** and press Return.

```
oak% /usr/sbin/sacadm -l
PMTAG           PMTYPE        FLGS RCNT STATUS    COMMAND
zsmon           ttymon        -    Ø    ENABLED   /usr/lib/saf/ttymon #
oak%
```

In this example, only the ttymon monitor, which is identified by the default port monitor tag of zsmon, is started, and the status is ENABLED. Table 9.1 describes the fields shown in the output of the sacadm -l command.

Table 9.1   **Fields in the sacadm -l Output**

Field	Description
PMTAG	A unique tag that identifies a particular port monitor. The system administrator assigns the name of the port monitor. The *pmtag* is used by the sac to identify the port monitor for all administration. Use the default ttymon *pmtag*, zsmon, for ttymon ports A and B; use the listen *pmtag*, tcp, for listen ports in the United States. PMTAG can contain up to 14 alphanumeric characters.
	The default ttymon *pmtag*, zsmon, was chosen because SPARCstation serial port chips are made by Zilog. In practice, a server may have hundreds of serial ports. If so, SunSoft recommends creating one port monitor for each serial port device. For example, consider a server that has two built-in serial ports and two add-in serial port boards, known as asynchronous line multiplexers, or ALMs. You could set up three port monitors and name them zsmon, alm1, and alm1. The service tag, *svctag*, could be named "a" and "b" for zsmon, and 0–7 for alm1 and alm2. (An alm usually has eight ports, numbered 0 through 7.)
	The default listen *pmtag*, tcp, was chosen because the device associated with it is the network. In the United States, the network is usually tcp. In Europe, the network is usually X.25. Always create the *pmtag* listen variable so that it describes the network.

Table 9.1 **Fields in the sacadm -l Output (Continued)**

Field	Description
PMTYPE	The type of the port monitor: ttymon or listen.
FLGS	If no flag is specified, the port monitor is started and enabled. The d flag specifies that when the port monitor is started, it is not enabled. The x flag specifies that the port monitor is not to be started.
RCNT	Retry count specifies the number of times a port monitor can fail before its state is changed to FAILED. If no count is specified, the field is set to 0 and the port monitor is not restarted if it fails.
STATUS	The status of activity for the port monitor. Possible states are STARTING, ENABLED, DISABLED, STOPPING, NOTRUNNING, and FAILED. The FAILED message is displayed if the SAC cannot start the port monitor after the number of tries specified by RCNT.
COMMAND	The complete path name of the command that starts the port monitor followed by a # and any comment that was entered when the port monitor was configured.

Refer to Chapter 10 for information about how to configure, start, and enable the ttymon port monitor. Refer to Chapter 11 for information about how to configure, start, and enable the listen port monitor.

To view the contents of the port monitor administrative file, type **pmadm -l** and press Return.

```
oak% /usr/sbin/pmadm -l
PMTAG            PMTYPE          SVCTAG         FLGS ID       <PMSPECIFIC>
zsmon            ttymon          ttya           u    root     /dev/term/a I -
/usr/bin/login - 9600 ldterm,ttcompat ttya login:  - tvi925 y  #
zsmon            ttymon          ttyb           u    root     /dev/term/b I -
/usr/bin/login - 9600 ldterm,ttcompat ttyb login:  - tvi925 y  #
oak%
```

In this example, the ttymon ports /dev/term/a and /dev/term/b show the default Solaris 2.x configuration. Table 9.2 describes the fields shown in the output of the pmadm -l command.

The ttymon Port Monitor

The ttymon STREAMS-based port monitor performs the functions provided by getty in SunOS 4.x system software. In addition, ttymon initializes and monitors tty ports, sets terminal modes and line speeds, invokes service on serial ports when it receives a connection request, and idles while a service is connected.

Table 9.2	Fields in the pmadm -l Output

Field	Description
PMTAG	A unique tag that identifies a particular port monitor. The system administrator assigns the name of the port monitor. The *pmtag* is used by the SAC to identify the port monitor for all administration. Use the default *pmtag* zsmon for ttymon ports; use the *pmtag* tcp for listen ports. PMTAG can contain up to 14 alphanumeric characters.
PMTYPE	The type of the port monitor: ttymon or listen.
SVCTAG	A tag unique to the port monitor that identifies a service. The service tags for the serial ports are ttya and ttyb. A service requires both a service tag and a port monitor tag to identify it uniquely.
FLGS	If no flag is specified, the port is enabled and no utmp entry is created for the service. The x flag specifies that the port should not be enabled; the u flag specifies that a utmp entry should be created for this service. Some services, such as login, will not start unless a utmp entry has been created.
ID	The login name of the person who starts the service, typically root.
PMSPECIFIC	The address, name of a process, name of a STREAMS pipe, or baud rate and configuration for a login port.

NOTE. *In Solaris 2.x the serial ports /dev/term/a and /dev/term/b are provided with a default configuration for the ttymon port monitor with a pmtag of zsmon.*

Each instance of ttymon can monitor multiple ports, as specified in the port monitor's administrative file. You configure the administrative file using the pmadm and ttyadm commands.

When an instance of ttymon is started by the sac daemon, ttymon starts to monitor its ports. For each port, it first initializes the line disciplines, if specified, and the speed and terminal settings. The values it uses for terminal initialization are taken from the appropriate entry in the tty settings file, which is maintained by the sttydefs command. Default line disciplines on ports are set up by the autopush(1M) facility. You do not need to do anything to configure autopush.

The listen Port Monitor
The listen process "listens" for network service requests, accepts requests when they arrive, and starts services in response to the requests.

NOTE. *No listen processes are started by default in Solaris 2.x system software.*

The listen process provides services similar to those provided by the traditional Internet Services daemon, inetd. In Solaris 2.*x* system software, the inetd daemon is started with the -s option to run standalone outside the SAF.

CAUTION! *Solaris 2.x does not support running inetd under SAF. Be sure that the -s option is always present.*

Service Invocations

A service invocation is a process that provides the requested service to the incoming connection request. A service invocation can be a process such as login or lp. The ttymon port monitor works only with the login process, and the listen port monitor works only with the LP print service. The SAF architecture is structured so that programmers can write new port monitors to support other processes specified by the port monitor.

Port Monitor States

Port monitors can be in operational, transitional, or inactive states. Once added, port monitors can be in one of six states, as shown in Figure 9.3.

Figure 9.3
Port monitor state model

Once added, port monitors are in one of six states.

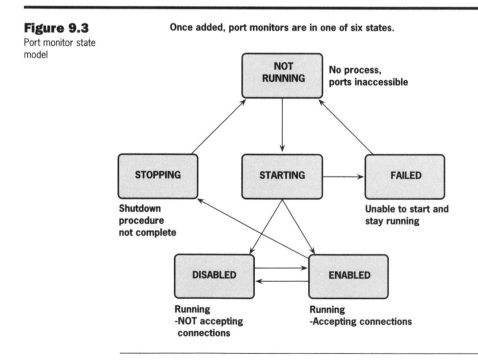

Operational States

Port monitor operational states are ENABLED and DISABLED. Port monitors are started and enabled by default when you add them. Port monitors are stopped and disabled by default when you remove them. When a port monitor is enabled, it accepts requests for service. When a port monitor is disabled, existing services continue, but new service requests are refused. When a port monitor service is killed, all services are terminated.

Transitional States

A port monitor may be STARTING or STOPPING. When a port monitor is in the process of starting, it is in an indeterminate state on the way to being either enabled or disabled. When a port monitor is stopping, it has been terminated manually but has not yet completed its shutdown procedure. Consequently, it is in an indeterminate state on the way to NOTRUNNING.

Inactive States

An inactive port monitor is either NOTRUNNING or has FAILED. A failed port monitor is unable to start and remain running. When a port monitor is not running, it has been killed. All ports it was monitoring are inaccessible. Unlike the disabled state, when a port monitor is not running, the system cannot write a message on the inaccessible port telling the user that it is disabled. If the message option is not used, an external user cannot determine whether a port is disabled or not running.

The Line Control Model

The line control model for Solaris 2.x system software is different from that of Solaris 1.x releases. The files /etc/gettytab and /etc/ttytab have been removed. Line settings are now stored in the /etc/ttydefs file and in the ttymon configuration files. Table 9.3 compares the Solaris 1.x and Solaris 2.x line control models.

Table 9.3   **Comparison of Solaris 1.x and Solaris 2.x Line Control Models**

Feature	Solaris 1.x File	Solaris 2.x File
Database descriptor	/etc/termcap /etc/terminfo	/etc/terminfo
Set terminal I/O operation	stty (BSD)	stty (SVR4)
Line settings and sequences	/etc/gettytab /etc/ttytab	/etc/ttydefs
Administer tty definitions		ttydef(1M)

Figure 9.4 shows how the terminal control and the SAF interact. The init program starts sac, which controls the ttymon port monitor. In turn, ttymon monitors serial port devices. It connects incoming requests to services, which are login processes. Port monitors monitor the device or network transport, add and delete services, and start and stop services at the appropriate time. You use the stty and tput commands to configure the terminal I/O settings to match the characteristics of the terminal. When ttymon gets a character from the terminal, it starts a login to the terminal. When the user logs out, ttymon hangs up to recycle the serial port and waits for another service request.

Figure 9.4
Terminal control architecture

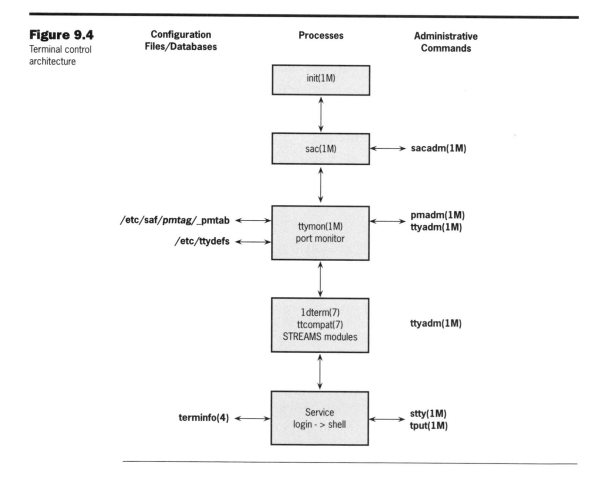

The /etc/ttydefs File

The /etc/ttydefs file defines baud rates and terminal settings for tty ports. When you set up modems, you use the ttyadm -l *ttylabel* argument as part of the pmadm command line argument to specify information about the baud rate and settings of the modem. The *ttylabel* variable specifies the first field for an entry in the /etc/ttydefs file. When ttymon initializes a port, it uses the information from the /etc/saf/*pmtag*/_pmtab file to search the /etc/ttydefs file for an entry that contains the *ttylabel* that matches the *ttylabel* for the port. Each entry in the /etc/ttydefs file has five fields separated by colons.

```
ttylabel:initial-flags:final-flags:autobaud:nextlabel
```

The *initial-flags* field contains the initial terminal input and output settings. The *final-flags* field contains the terminal input and output values set by ttymon after a connections request is made and before the port service is started. The *autobaud* field allows ttymon to determine the line speed of the TTY port by analyzing the first Return received and setting the speed accordingly. To enable autobaud, the field must contain the character *A*. If the field is empty, autobaud is disabled. The *nextlabel* field is used to specify a hunt sequence that links speeds together in a closed set. For example, 4800 may be linked to 1200, which is linked to 2400, which is finally linked to 4800. If the current ttydefs entry does not provide a compatible line speed, the next speed in the sequence is tried.

The default /etc/ttydefs file follows.

```
oak% more /etc/ttydefs
# VERSION=1
38400:38400 hupcl:38400 hupcl::19200
19200:19200 hupcl:19200 hupcl::9600
9600:9600 hupcl:9600 hupcl::4800
4800:4800 hupcl:4800 hupcl::2400
2400:2400 hupcl:2400 hupcl::1200
1200:1200 hupcl:1200 hupcl::300
300:300 hupcl:300 hupcl::38400

38400E:38400 hupcl evenp:38400 evenp::19200
19200E:19200 hupcl evenp:19200 evenp::9600
9600E:9600 hupcl evenp:9600 evenp::4800
4800E:4800 hupcl evenp:4800 evenp::2400
2400E:2400 hupcl evenp:2400 evenp::1200
1200E:1200 hupcl evenp:1200 evenp::300
300E:300 hupcl evenp:300 evenp::19200
auto:hupcl:sane hupcl:A:9600

console:9600 hupcl opost onlcr:9600::console
console1:1200 hupcl opost onlcr:1200::console2
console2:300 hupcl opost onlcr:300::console3
console3:2400 hupcl opost onlcr:2400::console4
```

```
console4:4800 hupcl opost onlcr:4800::console5
console5:19200 hupcl opost onlcr:19200::console

contty:9600 hupcl opost onlcr:9600 sane::contty1
contty1:1200 hupcl opost onlcr:1200 sane::contty2
contty2:300 hupcl opost onlcr:300 sane::contty3
contty3:2400 hupcl opost onlcr:2400 sane::contty4
contty4:4800 hupcl opost onlcr:4800 sane::contty5
contty5:19200 hupcl opost onlcr:19200 sane::contty

4800H:4800:4800 sane hupcl::9600H
9600H:9600:9600 sane hupcl::19200H
19200H:19200:19200 sane hupcl::38400H
38400H:38400:38400 sane hupcl::2400H
2400H:2400:2400 sane hupcl::1200H
1200H:1200:1200 sane hupcl::300H
300H:300:300 sane hupcl::4800H

conttyH:9600 opost onlcr:9600 hupcl sane::contty1H
contty1H:1200 opost onlcr:1200 hupcl sane::contty2H
contty2H:300 opost onlcr:300 hupcl sane::contty3H
contty3H:2400 opost onlcr:2400 hupcl sane::contty4H
contty4H:4800 opost onlcr:4800 hupcl sane::contty5H
contty5H:19200 opost onlcr:19200 hupcl sane::conttyH
```

Figure 9.5 shows how the *ttylabel* entry in the /etc/saf/zsmon/_pmtab file matches an entry in the /etc/ttydefs file. In this example, the *ttylabel* is part of the default entry provided by Solaris 2.x system software for serial port B.

The /etc/ttydefs file also contains information about speed and terminal settings for the TTY ports on a system. You can use the sttydefs(1M) administrative command to create new entries in the /etc/ttydefs file. See the sttydefs(1M) manual page for information about how to configure the /etc/ttydefs file.

The terminfo Database

The terminfo database describes the characteristics of TTY devices. The source files in terminfo specify a set of capabilities for a device by quantifying certain aspects of the device, and by specifying character sequences that control particular results. This database is often used by applications such as vi and curses, as well as the ls and more commands. Information in the terminfo database is stored in a compiled binary format. The terminfo compiler, tic(1M), translates a terminfo file from source format to the required compiled binary format.

Figure 9.5

How ttymon
identifies the *ttylabel*
in the /etc/ttydefs
file

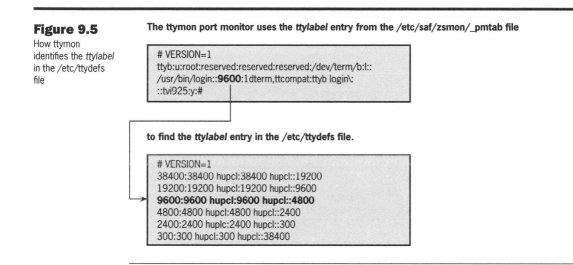

The ttymon port monitor uses the *ttylabel* entry from the /etc/saf/zsmon/_pmtab file

```
# VERSION=1
ttyb:u:root:reserved:reserved:reserved:/dev/term/b:l::
/usr/bin/login::9600:1dterm,ttcompat:ttyb login\:
::tvi925:y:#
```

to find the *ttylabel* entry in the /etc/ttydefs file.

```
# VERSION=1
38400:38400 hupcl:38400 hupcl::19200
19200:19200 hupcl:19200 hupcl::9600
9600:9600 hupcl:9600 hupcl::4800
4800:4800 hupcl:4800 hupcl::2400
2400:2400 huplc:2400 hupcl::300
300:300 hupcl:300 hupcl::38400
```

If you have site-specific termcap entries for devices, you can use the
captoinfo utility to convert those entries into terminfo source format. Then use
the tic compiler to translate the data to compiled format. See the captoinfo(1M)
and tic(1M) manual pages for more information.

The tput Utility

Use the tput(1M) utility to initialize or reset the terminal or to make terminal-
dependent capabilities and information available to the shell. The tput command sets terminal characteristics using data in the terminfo database. The
tput utility is similar to the SunOS 4.*x* tset(1B) utility, which is provided in the
SunOS/BSD Compatibility Package. The tput utility uses the following syntax:

```
tput [-Ttype] init
tput[-Ttype] reset
```

The stty Command

The /usr/bin/stty command is the SVR4 version of the command. The
/usr/ucb/stty command is available in the SunOS/BSD Compatibility Package.
Use of the options varies, depending on which version of stty you are using.
The stty command uses this syntax:

```
stty [-a] [-g] [options]
```

The -a flag lists current options using their termio names. The -g flag lists
the same information in a format that can be used as an argument to another
stty command.

The following examples show the default line settings, using first the /usr/bin/stty command and then the /usr/ucb/stty command.

```
oak% /usr/bin/stty
speed 9600 baud; evenp hupcl
rows = 66; columns = 80; ypixels = 508; xpixels = 61289;
swtch = <undef>;
brkint -inpck icrnl -ixany imaxbel onlcr
echo echoe echok echoctl echoke iexten
oak% /usr/ucb/stty
speed 9600 baud; evenp hupcl
rows = 66; columns = 80; ypixels = 508; xpixels = 61289;
swtch = <undef>;
-inpck imaxbel
crt iexten
oak%
```

Table 9.4 compares the default line settings for SunOS 4.*x* and Solaris 2.*x*. Note that the dash means not to set the value.

Table 9.4   Default Line Settings

SunOS 4.*x*	Solaris 2.*x*	Description
9600	9600	
evenp	-parity	Even parity/disable parity.
	hupcl	Hang up connection on close.
	rows=X, columns=X, ypixels=0	Set number of rows, columns, and ypixels.
xpixels=0		Set xpixels to 0.
	swtch=<undef>, dsusp=<undef>	
	brkint	Signal INTR on break.
-inpck	-inpck	Disable input parity checking.
	icrnl	Map CR to NL on input.
	-ixany	Do not allow only DC1 to restart output.
imaxbel	imaxbel	Echo BEL when the input line is too long.
	onlcr	Map NL to CR-NL on output.

Table 9.4 **Default Line Settings (Continued)**

SunOS 4.x	Solaris 2.x	Description
	tab3	Select style of delay for horizontal tabs.
	echo	Echo back every character typed.
	echoe	Echo ERASE character as a backspace-space-backspace string.
	echok	Echo NL after KILL character.
	echoctl	Echo control characters as ^char, delete as ^?.
	echoke	BS-SP-BS erase entire line.
iexten	iexten	Enable extended functions for input data.

UUCP Files

To use UUCP, tip, or cu with modems and terminals, you must use information from or add information to the /etc/uucp/Dialers and /etc/uucp/Devices files. Each of these files is described in the following sections.

The /etc/uccp/Dialers File

The /etc/uucp/Dialers file contains information that specifies the initial conversation that takes place on a line before it can be made available for transferring data. This conversation is usually a sequence of character strings that is transmitted and expected. The string often contains a telephone number that is dialed using an automatic call unit (ACU). Each entry in /etc/uucp/Dialers begins with a label identifying the type of the modem. The Solaris 2.x /etc/uucp/Dialers file contains support for many different modem types. Each type of caller included in the /etc/uucp/Devices file should be contained in the /etc/uucp/Dialers file except for built-in callers. You probably will not need to create an entry in this file. You will need to look in this file to verify that it contains an entry appropriate for your modem and to determine the *type* to use when you edit the /etc/uucp/Devices file.

Each line consists of three parts: the name of the caller, the table that translates the phone number into the code for the particular device, and a chat script to establish the connection. Comments at the beginning of the /etc/uucp/Dialers file explain the codes shown in the brief excerpt that follows.

```
penril  =W-P   "" \d > Q\c : \d- > s\p9\c )-W\p\r\ds\p9\c-) y\c : \E\TP > 9\c OK
ventel--=&-%    "" \r\p\r\c $ <K\T%%\r>\c ONLINE!
vadic   =K-K    "" \005\p *-\005\p-*-\005\p-* D\p BER? \E\T\e \r\c LINE
```

```
develcon ""        "" \pr\ps\c est:\007 \E\D\e \n\007
micom    ""        "" \s\c NAME? \D\r\c GO
direct
##########
#        The following entry is for use with direct connections
#        using ttymon with the -b and -r options on both ends,
#        or the old uugetty with the -r option.
##########
uudirect ""        "" \r\d in:--in:

#   Rixon Intelligent Modem -- modem should be set up in the Rixon
#   mode and not the Hayes mode.
#
rixon   =&-%      "" \r\r\d $ s9\c )-W\r\ds9\c-) s\c : \T\r\c $ 9\c LINE

#    Hayes Smartmodem -- modem should be set with the configuration
#    switches as follows:
#
#        S1 - UP        S2 - UP        S3 - DOWN        S4 - UP
#        S5 - UP        S6 - DOWN      S7 - ?           S8 - DOWN
#
hayes   =,-,      "" \dA\pTE1V1X1Q0S2=255S12=255\r\c OK\r \EATDT\T\r\c CONNECT
```

The /etc/uucp/Devices File

The /etc/uucp/Devices file contains information for all the devices that may be used to establish a link to remote systems. Provisions are made for several types of devices such as automatic-call units, direct links, and network connections. You will need to add an entry to the /etc/uucp/Devices file if you want to set up support for a bidirectional modem. Each entry in the Devices file has the following format:

type line line2 class dialer-token-pairs

The excerpt from the /etc/uucp/Devices file that follows contains one entry for a standard modem line and one entry for a 2400 baud Hayes-compatible modem for serial port A.

```
# ---Standard modem line
ACU contty - 1200 penril
# ---Bidirectional modem line; 2400 baud, Hayes compatible
ACU cua/a,M - 2400 hayes
```

The *type* argument you supply when editing the /etc/uccp/Devices file is the name of the modem as displayed at the end of the entry from the /etc/ uucp/Devices file. It points to an entry in /etc/uucp/Dialers.

SAF Log Files

The SAF records port monitor behavior in the /var/saf/_log file. In addition, each ttymon port monitor has its own log file, /var/saf/*pmtag*/log, where it records information such as messages that it receives from sac and services that it starts.

 An example of the end of the /var/saf/_log file follows. This information shows that the system was rebooted three times and that the ttymon port monitor zsmon was started and enabled successfully each time.

```
oak% tail /var/saf/_log
Mon Mar 15 14:23:12 1993; 199; port monitor <zsmon> changed state from STARTING
to ENABLED
Fri Mar 19 09:43:18 1993; 199; *** SAC starting ***
Fri Mar 19 09:43:19 1993; 203; starting port monitor <zsmon>
Fri Mar 19 09:43:19 1993; 199; port monitor <zsmon> changed state from STARTING
to ENABLED
Wed Mar 24 15:24:24 1993; 437; *** SAC starting ***
Wed Mar 24 15:24:25 1993; 443; starting port monitor <zsmon>
Wed Mar 24 15:24:25 1993; 437; port monitor <zsmon> changed state from STARTING
to ENABLED
Thu Mar 25 20:36:11 1993; 201; *** SAC starting ***
Thu Mar 25 20:36:12 1993; 208; starting port monitor <zsmon>
Thu Mar 25 20:36:13 1993; 201; port monitor <zsmon> changed state from STARTING
to ENABLED
oak%
```

 Following is an example of the /var/saf/_log file from another system that has a listen tcp port monitor configured.

```
seachild% tail /var/saf/_log
Wed Mar 24 12:06:19 1993; 176; *** SAC starting ***
Wed Mar 24 12:06:20 1993; 181; starting port monitor <tcp>
Wed Mar 24 12:06:20 1993; 182; starting port monitor <zsmon>
Wed Mar 24 12:06:21 1993; 176; port monitor <zsmon> changed state from STARTING
to ENABLED
Wed Mar 24 12:06:22 1993; 176; port monitor <tcp> changed state from STARTING
to ENABLED
Thu Mar 25 20:47:44 1993; 177; *** SAC starting ***
Thu Mar 25 20:47:44 1993; 183; starting port monitor <tcp>
Thu Mar 25 20:47:45 1993; 184; starting port monitor <zsmon>
Thu Mar 25 20:47:45 1993; 177; port monitor <zsmon> changed state from STARTING
to ENABLED
Thu Mar 25 20:47:46 1993; 177; port monitor <tcp> changed state from STARTING
to ENABLED
seachild%
```

An example of the end of the /var/saf/zsmon/log file is shown next. This information shows more detailed information about how the ttymon port monitor zsmon was initialized successfully.

```
oak% tail /var/saf/zsmon/log
Thu Mar 25 20:36:13 1993; 208; PMTAG: zsmon
Thu Mar 25 20:36:13 1993; 208; Starting state: enabled
Thu Mar 25 20:36:13 1993; 208; Got SC_ENABLE message
Thu Mar 25 20:36:13 1993; 208; max open files = 1024
Thu Mar 25 20:36:13 1993; 208; max ports ttymon can monitor = 1017
Thu Mar 25 20:36:13 1993; 208; *ptr == 0
Thu Mar 25 20:36:13 1993; 208; SUCCESS
Thu Mar 25 20:36:13 1993; 208; *ptr == 0
Thu Mar 25 20:36:13 1993; 208; SUCCESS
Thu Mar 25 20:36:13 1993; 208; Initialization Completed
oak%
```

An example of the end of the /var/saf/tcp/log file follows.

```
seachild% tail /var/saf/tcp/log
04/06/93 15:11:10; 183; Connect: fd 7, svctag lpd, seq 117, type passfd
04/06/93 15:11:12; 183; Connect: fd 7, svctag lpd, seq 118, type passfd
04/06/93 15:26:12; 183; Connect: fd 7, svctag lpd, seq 119, type passfd
04/06/93 15:26:13; 183; Connect: fd 7, svctag lpd, seq 120, type passfd
04/06/93 15:34:02; 183; Connect: fd 6, svctag 0, seq 41, type exec
04/06/93 15:34:03; 3391; NLPS (lp) passfd: /var/spool/lp/fifos/listenS5
04/06/93 15:50:10; 183; Connect: fd 7, svctag lpd, seq 121, type passfd
04/06/93 15:50:11; 183; Connect: fd 7, svctag lpd, seq 122, type passfd
04/06/93 16:05:12; 183; Connect: fd 7, svctag lpd, seq 123, type passfd
04/06/93 16:05:12; 183; Connect: fd 7, svctag lpd, seq 124, type passfd
seachild%
```

You should periodically clear out or truncate these log files. If you want cron to do the cleanup for you, add the appropriate entries to the /var/spool/cron/crontabs/root file.

Reference to SAF Commands, Tasks, and Options

The following sections provide a quick reference to the variables used in SAF commands; to tasks performed with the sacadm and pmadm commands; and to options for the sacadm, pmadm, ttyadm, and nlsadmin commands. Refer to Chapter 10 for step-by-step instructions on how to use the SAF commands to set up modems and terminals. Refer to Chapter 11 for step-by-step instructions on how to use the SAF commands to set up printers.

Quick Reference to SAF Variables

Table 9.5 describes the variables used with the SAF commands.

Table 9.5   **Variables Used with the SAF commands**

Variable	Example	Description
pmtag	zsmon	Name of a specific instance of a port monitor
svctag	b	The name of the port in the /dev/term directory
dev-path	/dev/term/b	The full name of the tty port device file
ttylabel	2400H	The baud rate and line discipline from the /etc/ttydefs file
type	ventel	The type of the modem, as specified in the /etc/uucp/Devices file

Quick Reference to Service Access Control (sacadm)

Table 9.6 provides a task-oriented quick reference to the tasks you perform using the sacadm command.

Table 9.6   **Quick Reference to the Service Access Controller**

Task	Command Syntax
Add a port monitor	sacadm -a -p pmtag -t ttymon -c /usr/lib/saf/ttymon -v `ttyadm -V` -y "comment"
Disable a port monitor	sacadm -d -p pmtag
Enable a port monitor	sacadm -e -p pmtag
Kill a port monitor	sacadm -k -p pmtag
List status information for a port monitor	sacadm -l -p pmtag
Remove a port monitor	sacadm -r -p pmtag
Start a port monitor	sacadm -s -p pmtag
Add a listen port monitor	sacadm -a -p pmtag -t listen -c /usr/lib/saf/listen -v `ttyadm -V` -y "comment"

Table 9.7 describes the options to the sacadm command.

Table 9.7   Options to sacadm Command

Option	Description
a	Add a port monitor.
p	Specify an identifying port monitor tag (*pmtag*) for the port monitor.
t	Specify the type of the port monitor, either ttymon or listen.
c	Specify the commands used to start a port monitor.
v	Specify the version number of the port monitor. Use ttyadm -V to find out the version number to use, or use `ttyadm -V` as an argument to the -v option.
f	Specify one or both flags. The d flag specifies that the port monitor is not enabled. The x flag specifies that the port monitor is not started.

Quick Reference to Port Monitor Administration (pmadm)

Table 9.8 provides a quick reference to the tasks you perform using the pmadm command.

Table 9.8   Quick Reference to Port Monitor Administration (pmadm)

Task	Command Syntax
Add a standard terminal service	pmadm -a -p *pmtag* -s *svctag* -i root -v `ttyadm -V` -m "`ttyadm -i 'terminal disabled.' -l contty -m ldterm,ttcompat -d *dev-path* -s /usr/bin/login`"
Disable a ttymon port monitor	pmadm -d -p *pmtag* -s *svctag*
Enable a ttymon port monitor	pmadm -e -p *pmtag* -s *svctag*
List all services	pmadm -l
List status information for one ttymon port monitor	pmadm -l -p *pmtag* -s *svctag*
Add a listen service	pmadm -a -p *pmtag* -s lp -i root -v `nlsadmin -V` -m "`nlsadmin -o /var/spool/lp/fifos/listenS5`"

Table 9.8   **Quick Reference to Port Monitor Administration (pmadm) (Continued)**

Task	Command Syntax
Disable a listen port monitor	pmadm -d -p *pmtag* -s lp
Enable a listen port monitor	pmadm -e -p *pmtag* -s lp
List status information for one ttymon port monitor	pmadm -l -p *pmtag*

Table 9.9 describes the options to the pmadm command.

Table 9.9   **Options to the pmadm Command**

Option	Description
a	Add a service.
p	Specify the port monitor tag (*pmtag*)—for example, zsmon.
s	Specify the service tag associated with a given service (*svctag*)—for example, ttya for serial port A.
i	Specify the identity assigned to the service when it is started.
f	Specify one or both flags. The x flag does not enable the specified service. The u flag creates a utmp entry for the service.
v	Specify the port monitor version number. Use ttyadm -V to find the version number, or use `ttyadm -V` as an argument to the -v option.
m	Identify port monitor-specific options to be included on the -a command line.

Table 9.10 shows the options to the ttyadm command. You usually include the ttyadm command and its options in backquotes (``) as part of the pmadm command.

Table 9.10   **Options to the ttyadm Command**

Option	Description
d	Specify the full path name of the device file for the tty port—for example, /dev/term/a for serial port A.
l	Specify the ttylabel from the /etc/ttydefs file that the port monitor uses to set the proper baud rate—for example, 9600.
s	Specify the service path name to be used when a connection request is received—for example, /usr/bin/login.
V	Display the version number of the SAF.

Table 9.11 shows only the options to the nlsadmin command that can be included as part of the command-line argument for the sacadm and pmadm commands. See the nlsadmin(1M) manual page for further information.

Table 9.11   **Options to the nlsadmin Command**

Option	Description
A	Interpret the address as private for the server. The listener monitors this address and dispatches all calls arriving on this address directly to the designated service. This option may not be used with the -D option.
c *"cmd"*	Specify the full pathname of the server and its arguments. Use double quotes around the pathname to ensure that it is interpreted as a single word by the shell.
D	Dynamically assign a private address selected by the transport provider. This option is frequently used with the -R option for RPC services. This option may not be used with the -A option.
o *streamname*	Specify the full pathname of a FIFO or named STREAM through which a server is receiving the connection.
p *modules*	If this option is specified, the modules are interpreted as a list of STREAMS modules for the listener to push before starting the service. Modules are pushed in the order they are specified. Specify the modules as a comma-separated list with no spaces.
R	Register an RPC service whose address, program number, and version number are registered with the rpcbinder for this transport provider.
V	Display the version number of the SAF.

Quick Reference to SAF Administrative Files

Table 9.12 lists the SAF configuration and log files.

Table 9.12 **Quick Reference to SAF Administrative Files**

Option	Description
/etc/saf/_sysconfig	The per-system configuration script.
/etc/saf/_sactab	The administrative file for SAC contains configuration data for the port monitors that SAC controls.
/etc/saf/*pmtag*	The home directory for port monitor *pmtag*.
/etc/saf/*pmtag*/_pmtab	The administrative file for the *pmtag* port monitor.
/var/saf_log	The log file for SAC.
/var/saf/*pmtag*	The directory for files created by the *pmtag* port monitor.
/var/saf/*pmtag*/log	The log file for the *pmtag* port monitor.

C H A P T E R

10

Setting Up Modems and Character Terminals

THIS CHAPTER DESCRIBES HOW TO USE THE TTYMON PORT MONITOR TO set up the Service Access Facility (SAF) for modems and character terminals. See Chapter 11 for information on how to use the SAF to set up printers.

You perform three basic tasks to set up a serial port device such as a modem or a character terminal:

1. Use the sacadm command to add a port monitor (if one is not already configured).

2. Use the pmadm command to designate a service to be associated with the new port monitor.

3. Edit one or more communications-related files, as needed.

Using Variables in SAF Commands

The following sections describe the variables used in the SAF commands in the rest of this chapter. When using SAF commands, you supply arguments to specify one (or more) of the variables described in Table 10.1. These variable names were chosen to match the names of the fields used to display the output of SAF commands. These variables and the files they use are described in the following sections.

Table 10.1 **Variables Used with the SAF Commands**

Variable	Example	Description
pmtag	zsmon	Name of a specific instance of a port monitor
svctag	ttyb	The name of the port
dev-path	/dev/term/b	The full name of the tty port device file
ttylabel	2400H	The baud rate and line discipline from the /etc/ttydefs file
type	hayes	The type of the modem, as specified in the /etc/uucp/Devices file

The Port Monitor Tag (*pmtag*)

You use the *pmtag* variable to specify the name you assign to a specific instance of a port monitor. You can give port monitors any name you like, provided the name is unique and contains no more than 14 alphanumeric characters. The default *pmtag* variable for Solaris 2.*x* system software is zsmon for serial ports A and B. If you install a multiplexer, serial ports are automatically configured as part of the installation process, and are given the *pmtag* variable ttymon0. SunSoft suggests that you use the system-defined *pmtag* variables.

The Service Tag (*svctag*)

Each port assigned to a port monitor has its own service tag. By convention, *svctag* is tty followed by the name of the port in the /dev/term directory. For example, for device /dev/term/b, the corresponding *svctag* is ttyb. For /dev/term/7, the *svctag* is tty7.

NOTE. *You can assign any* svctag *name that you like, as long as you use it consistently.*

To display a list of currently active services, type **pmadm -l** and press Return. You do not need to be superuser to display a list of currently active services. In the following example, the default zsmon services for serial ports A and B are displayed.

```
oak% pmadm -l
PMTAG           PMTYPE          SVCTAG          FLGS ID        <PMSPECIFIC>
zsmon           ttymon          ttya            u    root      /dev/term/a I -
/usr/bin/login  - 9600 ldterm,ttcompat ttya login:  - tvi925 y  #
zsmon           ttymon          ttyb            u    root      /dev/term/b I -
/usr/bin/login  - 9600 ldterm,ttcompat ttyb login:  - tvi925 y  #
oak%
```

In the preceding example, the *pmtag* is zsmon; the *pmtype* is ttymon; the *svctag* is ttya and ttyb; the flag is u (which creates a utmp directory for the service); the ID is root; and the port monitor-specific information includes the device path, I (initialize only), a login account, 9600 baud rate, terminal configuration information, and the "login:" prompt.

NOTE. *A single port monitor can handle multiple requests for the same service concurrently, so it is possible for the number of active login services to exceed the number of ttymon port monitors.*

The Device Path (*dev-path*)

You use the *dev-path* variable to specify the full name of the tty port device file to which the modem or character terminal is connected. For example, the pathname for a character terminal or modem connected to serial port A is /dev/term/b. A terminal attached to the first port of a serial port adapter board or multiplexer would be /dev/term/00.

NOTE. *Do not use /dev/cua/* device names to set up the SAF. The tip, cu, and uucp commands should, however, be set up to call out on /dev/cua/*, and not /dev/term/* devices. If you call out on /dev/term with the tip command, the message "link down" is displayed, and the cu command times out.*

The Baud Rate and Line Discipline (*ttylabel*)

You use the *ttylabel* variable to specify which entry in the /etc/ttydefs file is used when the SAF searches for the proper baud rate and line discipline. The following example shows the lines from the /etc/ttydefs file for the ttylabels 2400H and 1200H.

```
2400H:2400:2400 SANE HUPCL::1200H
1200H:1200:1200 sane hupcl::300H
```

Type of Modem

The type of modem you use is discussed later in this chapter, under "Modem Connection and Switch Settings" and individual modem names.

Comments

You can add comments (in double quotes) to both the pmadm and sacadm comments after the -y flag when adding a port monitor or service. Any comments you add are displayed when you use the -l option to the sacadm or pmadm command to display port monitors or services.

Use comments to specify the ports with which the various port monitors are associated.

Setting Up Modems

You can set up a modem in three ways:

- Dial-out service. You can access other systems, but other systems cannot call your system.

- Dial-in service. Other systems can call your system through the modem, but you cannot call other systems.

- Bidirectional service provides both dial-in and dial-out capabilities.

Using one of these modem services, you can tip or cu to a remote system.

Hardware Carrier Detect Setting

You must disable hardware carrier detect. On Sun systems, you can do this in two ways. One way is to:

1. Become superuser.

2. Type **eeprom ttyb-ignore-cd=false** and press Return.

Alternatively, follow these steps to disable hardware carrier detect on Sun systems:

1. Halt the system.

2. At the ok PROM prompt, type **setenv ttyb-ignore-cd=false** and press Return.

3. Type **boot** and press Return to reboot the system.

Modem Connection and Switch Settings

Connect the modem to a serial port with an RS-232-C cable that has pins 2 through 8 and pin 20 wired straight through. You may also use a full 25-pin cable to connect the modem to the system. Make sure all the connections are secure.

SunOS 5.x system software supports many popular modems. Models that work well include the Hayes Smartmodem™ 1200, the USRobotics™ Courier 2400™, and the Telebit™ TrailBlazer™. The following sections suggest switch settings for each of these three models.

The switch setting examples work with the tip and uucp commands. SunSoft suggests that you first try the default switch settings for the modem. If the default switch settings do not work, try the switch settings suggested in the following sections. Always read the manufacturer's manual before changing any settings.

NOTE. *After changing the switch settings on any model, turn off power to the modem, wait a few seconds, and then turn on power again.*

Hayes Smartmodem 1200

The proper switch settings for the Hayes Smartmodem 1200 follow. On the Hayes Smartmodem 1200 modem panel, down is On and up is Off.

- Switch 1 up for hardware data terminal ready

- Switch 2 down for numeric result codes

- Switch 3 down to send result codes

- Switch 4 down to not echo commands

- Switch 5 up to answer incoming calls

- Switch 6 up for hardware carrier detect

- Switch 7 up for connection to RJ11 modular jack

- Switch 8 down to enable command recognition

USRobotics Courier 2400

The proper switch settings for the USRobotics Courier 2400 modem follow. The USRobotics Courier 2400 modem has two switch panels: a 10-switch panel and a single "Quad" switch panel. On the USRobotics modem, down is On and up is Off.

- Switch 1 up for hardware data terminal ready

- Switch 2 down for numeric result codes

- Switch 3 down to send result codes

- Switch 4 down to not echo commands

- Switch 5 up to answer incoming calls

- Switch 6 up for hardware carrier detect

- Switch 7 up for connection to RJ11 modular jack

- Switch 8 down to enable command recognition

- Switch 9 down to not disconnect with +++

- Switch 10 up—feature not used

- "Quad" switch up

- Pins 2 and 3 wired straight through

Telebit TrailBlazer

You must set internal registers for the TrailBlazer modem to use it properly with cu and uucp. The first time the system is connected to the modem, enter the following setup sequence to use the TrailBlazer:

```
AT &F Q6 S51=254 S52=2 S53=1 S54=3 S58=0 S111=30 &W
```

NOTE. *This sequence may be slightly different from the one shown in the TrailBlazer documentation. Read the TrailBlazer documentation to make sure the sequence is right for your system.*

Other Modem Settings

Hayes-compatible modems that use the Hayes AT command set may work with cu and uucp software. Use the following configurations:

- Use hardware data terminal ready (DTR). When the system drops DTR (for example, when someone logs off), the modem should hang up.

- Use hardware carrier detect (CD). The modem raises the CD line only when there is an active carrier signal on the phone connection. When carrier drops, either because the other end of the connection is terminated or the phone connection is broken, the system is notified and acts appropriately. The CD signal is also used for coordinating dial-in *and* dial-out use on a single serial port and modem.

- Respond with numeric result codes.

- Send result codes.

- Do not echo commands.

Variables Used to Set Up Modems

To set up a dial-in or a bidirectional modem, you need information for these variables:

- *svctag*   the name of the port the modem is connected to (typically, ttya or ttyb).

- *pmtag*   the name of the port monitor service (for Sun systems, zsmon).

- *dev-path*   the name of the device for the port (typically, /dev/term/a or /dev/term/b).

- *ttylabel*   the entry in the /etc/ttydefs file that is used to set the proper baud rate and line discipline—for example, contty3H for a Hayes-compatible modem.

- *type*   the type of the modem from the /etc/uucp/Dialers file—for example, the type for a Hayes modem is hayes.

SAF Configuration for Modems

To configure the SAF for modems, you must use the pmadm and ttyadm commands. Solaris 2.3 provides a Serial Port Manager as part of the Administration Tool that you can use to configure SAF for modems. See Appendix B for more information. Follow the steps in this section to set up the SAF to use a modem for dial-in or bidirectional service.

1. Become superuser.

2. Type **pmadm -l** and press Return. A list of all available port monitors is displayed. Note the PMTAG, PMTYPE, and SVCTAG values for the modem port. Substitute these values for the appropriate variables in the next steps.

3. Type **pmadm -r -p** *pmtag* **-s** *svctag* and press Return. You must remove the existing configuration for the service tag before you can create a new one. If the message "Invalid request, pmtag: not found" comes up, then the port monitor is not configured. Continue to the next step.

4. To set up the port monitor for use with the modem, type **pmadm -a -p** *pmtag* **-s** *svctag* **-i root -fu -v `ttymon -V` -m "`ttyadm -t** *terminfo-type* **-b -d** *dev-name* **-l** *ttylabel* **-m ldterm,ttcompat -s /usr/bin/login -S n`"** and press Return. The -a option adds the service, the -p option specifies the port monitor tag, the -s option specifies the service tag, the -i option sets root as the ID of the owner, the -fu option creates a utmp directory for the service, the -v option specifies the version number, and the -m option specifies the information specific to the port monitor using input from the ttyadm command. The ttyadm -t option specifies the type of the terminal as specified by the terminfo database, the -b option specifies that the service is bidirectional, the -d option specifies the device name, the -l option specifies the tty label, the -m ldterm,ttcompat command specifies the STREAMS modules to be pushed, the -s option specifies a login service, and the -S n option sets the hardware carrier on.

5. Type **pmadm -l** and press Return. Check the output to make sure that you configured the port monitor service properly.

6. Type **grep cua***n* **/etc/remote**. This entry in the /etc/remote file sets the correct baud rate for the port. In this example, the information for cuab is correct:

```
# grep cuab /etc/remote
cuab:dv=/dev/cua/b:br#2400
#
```

If the entry is not in the /etc/remote file, edit the file and add it.

7. Edit the /etc/uucp/Devices file and add the following entry, where *n* is the name of the device in the /dev/term directory—for example, b for /dev/term/b:

```
ACU term/n,M - ttylabel type
```

NOTE. *If you are setting up service on a bidirectional port, you must enable login individually for each port. To enable logins, type **pmadm -e -p pmtag -s svctag** and press Return.*

In the following example, a Hayes-compatible 2400 baud modem is configured for bidirectional service on serial port_B. Note that the contty3H entry is an entry for a 2400 baud modem.

```
oak# pmadm -l
PMTAG           PMTYPE          SVCTAG          FLGS ID        <PMSPECIFIC>
zsmon           ttymon          ttya            u    root      /dev/term/a I -
/usr/bin/login - 9600 ldterm,ttcompat ttya login:  - tvi925 y  #
zsmon           ttymon          ttyb            u    root      /dev/term/a I -
/usr/bin/login - 9600 ldterm,ttcompat ttyb login:  - tvi925 y  #
oak# pmadm -r -p zsmon -s ttyb
oak# pmadm -a -p zsmon -s ttyb -i root -fu -v `ttyadm -V` -m "`ttyadm -t tvi925
-b -d /dev/term/b -l contty3H -m ldterm,ttcompat -s /usr/bin/login -S n`"
oak# pmadm -l
PMTAG           PMTYPE          SVCTAG          FLGS ID        <PMSPECIFIC>
zsmon           ttymon          ttya            u    root      /dev/term/a I -
/usr/bin/login - 9600 ldterm,ttcompat ttya login:  - tvi925 y  #
zsmon           ttymon          ttyb            u    root      /dev/term/b b -
/usr/bin/login - contty3H ldterm,ttcompat login:  - - n  #
oak# sacadm -l
PMTAG           PMTYPE          FLGS RCNT STATUS     COMMAND
zsmon           ttymon          -    0    ENABLED    /usr/lib/saf/ttymon #
oak# grep cuab /etc/remote
cuab:dv=/dev/cua/b:br#2400
oak# vi /etc/uucp/Devices
Add the following line to the end of the file:
ACU cua/b,M - contty3H hayes
```

Dial-Out Modem Service Configuration

If you want to dial out on the modem, you do not need to configure SAF files. Once the modem is connected to the system and its switches are properly set, follow these steps to configure dial-out service:

1. Edit the /etc/uucp/Devices file and add the following line, where *n* is the name of the device in the /dev/cua directory. Use the *type* hayes for Hayes-compatible modems.

```
ACU cua/n,M - ttylabel type
```

2. Type **pmadm -d -p** *pmtag* **-s** *svctag* and press Return. Login service is disabled. (Permitting logins for a modem that is set up to provide dial-out service only is a security hole.)

Modem Connection Troubleshooting

When troubleshooting problems with modem connections, first check the following list with the user:

- Was the correct login ID or password used?

- Is the terminal waiting for xon flow control key?

- Is the serial cable loose or unplugged?

- Is the terminal configuration correct?

- Is the terminal turned off?

Continue troubleshooting by checking the configuration of the terminal or the modem.

- Was the proper *ttylabel* used?

- Does the *ttylabel* setting of the modem match the *ttylabel* of the SAF?

- If you have changed any modem switches, turn the power to the modem off, wait a few seconds, and turn it on again.

If the problem persists, check the system software.

- Was the port monitor configured to service the modem?

- Does it have the correct *ttylabel* associated with it?

- Does the *type* definition match a setting in the /etc/ttydefs file?

- Is the port monitor enabled? (Use the sacadm -l -p *pmtag* command.)

- Is the service enabled? (Use the pmadm -l -p *pmtag* command.)

If the SAC is starting the ttymon port monitor, the service is enabled, and the configuration matches the port monitor configuration, continue to search for the problem by checking the serial connection. A serial connection consists of serial ports, cables, modems, and terminals. Test each of these parts by using it with two other parts that are known to be reliable.

To check for cable problems, a breakout box is helpful. It plugs into the RS-232-C cable. A patch panel lets you connect any pin to any other pins. A breakout box often contains light-emitting diodes that show whether a signal is present on each pin.

Continue troubleshooting by checking each of the following:

- If you cannot access a port, and the ps command shows that a process is running on it, make sure that pin 8 in the cable is connected. If that does not work, check that the device driver is configured properly to set the correct flag for the line to Off.

- If the error message "can't synchronize with hayes" is displayed when using a Hayes-compatible modem, check the /etc/remote file and make sure that you have changed at=ventel to at=hayes.

- If the message "all ports busy" is displayed, the port may actually be busy running a dial-in user. Use the ps command to see what is running. You should also check to be sure the carrier detect is set up properly. Type **pmadm -l** and press Return. If the last flag in the PMSPECIFIC field is y, delete the entry and reconfigure it making sure that you use -S n (not -S y) as the last argument for ttymon. If the port still shows as busy, check the /var/spool and /var/spool/locks directories for leftover lock files. The file will have a name like LCK.cua0.

Setting Up the SAF for Character Terminals

The Solaris 2.x system software is automatically configured to work properly with Sun graphics display monitors. You do not need to do any additional SAF configuration to use them. The word *terminal* is used here to describe a character terminal—a serial port device that displays only letters, numbers, and other characters such as those produced by a typewriter. The VT100 model, for example, is a popular type of character terminal that many other terminals can emulate.

Not all systems require character terminals. You may want to attach a character terminal to a server as an inexpensive control console or to a malfunctioning system's serial port to use for diagnostics.

If you do attach a character terminal to a system, you need to use the SAF to set it up. See Chapter 9 for background information about terminal control.

Terminal Connection

Use a null modem cable to connect a character terminal to serial ports on Sun systems. A null modem cable swaps lines 2 and 3 so that the proper transmit and receive signals are communicated between two DTE devices. Line 7 goes straight through, connecting pin 7 of the devices at each end of the null modem cable.

SAF Configuration for Character Terminals

Solaris 2.*x* systems come with a ttymon port monitor named zsmon, and with serial ports A and B already configured with default settings for terminals, as shown in the following example:

```
oak% /usr/sbin/sacadm -l
PMTAG           PMTYPE          FLGS RCNT STATUS      COMMAND
zsmon           ttymon          -    0    ENABLED     /usr/lib/saf/ttymon #
oak% /usr/sbin/pmadm -l
PMTAG           PMTYPE          SVCTAG       FLGS ID       <PMSPECIFIC>
zsmon           ttymon          ttya         u    root     /dev/term/a I -
/usr/bin/login - 9600 ldterm,ttcompat ttya login:  - tvi925 y  #
zsmon           ttymon          ttyb         u    root     /dev/term/b I -
/usr/bin/login - 9600 ldterm,ttcompat ttyb login:  - tvi925 y  #
oak%
```

The I in the second field means that the service is initialized for the hardware configuration, but connection to the service is not enabled.

You probably only need to add a login service to configure an existing port. Follow these steps to configure the SAF for a character terminal:

1. Become superuser.

2. Type **sacadm -l** and press Return. Check the output to make sure that a ttymon port monitor is configured. It is unlikely that you will need to add a new port monitor. If you do need to add one, type **sacadm -a -p** *pmtag* **-t ttymon -c /usr/lib/saf/ttymon -v `ttymon -V`** and press Return.

3. Type **pmadm -a -p** *pmtag* **-s** *svctag* **-i root -fu -v `ttymon -V` -m "`ttyadm -t** *terminfo-type* **-d** *dev-path* **-l** *ttylabel* **-s /usr/bin/login`"** and press Return. The port is configured for a login service.

4. Attach all cords and cables to the terminal and turn it on.

In this example, a ttymon port monitor called ttymon0 is created and a login is enabled for serial port /dev/term/00:

```
oak% su
Password:
# sacadm -l
PMTAG           PMTYPE          FLGS RCNT STATUS      COMMAND
zsmon           ttymon          -    0    ENABLED     /usr/lib/saf/ttymon #
# sacadm -a -p ttymon0 -t ttymon -c /usr/lib/saf/ttymon -v `ttyadm -V`
# sacadm -l
PMTAG           PMTYPE          FLGS RCNT STATUS      COMMAND
ttymonm0        ttymon          -    0    STARTING    /usr/lib/saf/ttymon #
zsmon           ttymon          -    0    ENABLED     /usr/lib/saf/ttymon #
# pmadm -a -p ttymon0 -s tty00 -i root -fu -v `ttyadm -V` -m "`ttyadm -t tvi925
```

```
-d /dev/term/00 -1 9600 -s /usr/bin/login`"
# pmadm -1
PMTAG          PMTYPE         SVCTAG         FLGS ID        <PMSPECIFIC>
zsmon          ttymon         ttya           u    root      /dev/term/a I -
/usr/bin/login - 9600 ldterm,ttcompat ttya login: - tvi925 y #
zsmon          ttymon         ttyb           u    root      /dev/term/b I -
/usr/bin/login - 9600 ldterm,ttcompat ttyb login: - tvi925 y #
ttymon0        ttymon         tty00          u    root      /dev/term/00 - - -
/usr/bin/login - 9600 login: - tvi925 - #
#
```

Terminal Connection Troubleshooting

When troubleshooting problems with terminal connections, first check the following list with the user:

- Was the correct login ID or password used?

- Is the terminal waiting for xon flow control key?

- Is the serial cable loose or unplugged?

- Is the terminal configuration correct?

- Is the terminal turned off?

    Continue troubleshooting by checking the configuration of the terminal.

- Was the proper *ttylabel* used?

- Does the *ttylabel* setting of the modem match the ttylabel of the SAF?

    If the problem persists, check the system software.

- Was the port monitor configured to enable logins?

- Does it have the correct *ttylabel* associated with it?

- Is the port monitor enabled? (Use the sacadm -l -p *pmtag* command.)

- Is the service enabled? (Use the pmadm -l -p *pmtag* command.)

    If the SAC is starting the ttymon port monitor, the service is enabled, and the configuration matches the port monitor configuration, continue to search for the problem by checking the serial connection. A serial connection consists of serial ports, cables, and terminals. Test each of these parts by using it with two other parts that are known to be reliable.

    To check for cable problems, a breakout box is helpful. It plugs into the RS-232-C cable. A patch panel lets you connect any pin to any other pins. A breakout box often contains light-emitting diodes that show whether a signal is present on each pin.

If you cannot access a port, and the ps command shows that a process is running on it, make sure that pin 8 in the cable is connected. If that does not work, check that the device driver is configured properly to set the correct flag for the line to Off.

11

Setting Up Printing Services

SUNSOFT RECOMMENDS THAT YOU USE ADMINISTRATION TOOL'S PRINTER Manager to set up printing on systems running Solaris 2.1 (or later) system software. Consult the *Solaris System Administrator's Guide* for information on how to use the Printer Manager and for information on how to use printing commands. See the bibliography at the back of this book for a complete reference.

This chapter describes how to set up printing services from a command line using SAF commands and the listen port monitor.

The network at your site may comprise many systems—some may be running Solaris 2.*x* system software, and others may be running SunOS 4.*x*. You need to decide which systems will have local printers directly cabled to them and which systems will connect to printers over the network. The system that has the printer connected to it and makes the printer available to other systems is called a *print server*. The system that has its printing needs met by a print server is called a *print client*.

You perform three basic tasks to set up printing services:

■ Setting up local printers

■ Setting up print servers

■ Setting up print clients

You can have the following client–server combinations:

■ SunOS 5.*x* print clients with a SunOS 5.*x* print server

■ SunOS 5.*x* and SunOS 4.*x* print clients with a SunOS 5.*x* print server

■ SunOS 5.*x* and SunOS 4.*x* print clients with a SunOS 4.*x* print server

This chapter describes how to set up printing services using the SunOS 5.*x* LP print service. Refer to your SunOS 4.*x* documentation for information on how to set up SunOS 4.*x* print servers and print clients.

System Requirements for a Print Server

You can attach a printer to a stand-alone system or to any system on the network. Any networked system with a printer and adequate system resources may be made into a print server.

Each print server should have the following system resources:

■ Spooling directory space of 8MB (or more)

■ Hard disk strongly recommended (not required)

■ Memory of 12MB (or more)

■ Swap space of 20 to 24MB (or more)

If the print server has a /var directory that resides in a small partition, and if a large amount of disk space is available elsewhere, you can use that space as spooling space by mounting it on the /var directory on the print server. Consult the *Solaris System Administrator's Guide* for information about mounting file systems and editing the /etc/vfstab file.

Table 11.1 provides some common disk configuration information and recommendations for the number of average users the configuration can serve.

Table 11.1   Typical Disk Configuration Information

Disk Size (MB)	/var Partition (MB)	Spooling Space (MB)	Number of Users
104	8	4	1– 3
207	16	12	1–16
424	212	206	1–32
669	335	328	1–64
991	500	490	1–64 or more
1360	335	206	1–32

Printer Configuration Information

To configure a printer on the network, you need the following configuration information:

■ The serial (or parallel) device name (required)

■ A unique name for the printer (required)

■ The printer type (required)

■ The type of file content (required)

■ The filter names for your printer (required)

■ The universal address version of the print server's Internet Protocol (IP) address required for printing between systems (required)

- The description of the printer to convey to users (recommended, optional)

- The default printer for each system (recommended, optional)

Configuration information is stored in the LP configuration files in the /etc/lp directory.

Printer Device Name

The *printer-device-name* identifies the port to which the printer is connected. When you use the -v option to identify the port, the lpadmin command uses the stty settings from the standard printer interface program to initialize the printer port.

Printer Name

Choose a *printer-name* for the printer you are adding to a system. A printer name must be unique among all printers known to the system, and can contain a maximum of 14 alphanumeric characters and underscores. When administering printers in a complex network, keep printer names unique within the bounds of the administrative domain.

You should also establish conventions when naming printers. Choose printer names that are meaningful and easy to remember. A printer name can identify the type of printer, its location, or the print server name. Establish a naming convention that works for your site. For example, if you have different types of printers on the network, including the printer type as part of the printer name can help users choose an appropriate printer. You could identify, for instance, PostScript printers with the letters *PS*. If, however, all of the printers at your site are PostScript printers, you would not need to include *PS* as part of the printer name.

You use printer names to:

- Add the printer to the LP print service

- Change the configuration of the printer

- Monitor the print queue

- Check the status of the printer

- Accept or cancel print requests for the printer

- Enable or disable the printer

- Specify a default printer

- Submit a print job to a particular printer

Printer Type

A *printer-type* is the generic name for a printer. By convention, it is often derived from the manufacturer's name. For example, the printer type for the Digital Equipment Corporation (DEC) LN03 printer is ln03. However, one common printer type—PS, for PostScript laser printer—does not follow this convention. PS is used for many different models of PostScript printers.

For a local PostScript printer, use either PS or PSR (which reverses the pages) as the printer type. PSR works reliably only with PostScript files that conform to the standards in Appendix C of the *PostScript Language Reference Manual*. Refer to the bibliography at the back of this book for a complete reference.

The printer type must match an entry in the terminfo database. The LP print service uses the printer type to extract information about the capabilities of the printer from the terminfo database, as well as the control data to use to initialize a particular printer before printing a file.

You specify the printer type with the -T option of the lpadmin command, where *printer-type* matches the name of a file in the terminfo database, which contains compiled terminal information files. These files are located in the /usr/share/lib/terminfo/* directories. For example, the terminfo file for the type name PS is /usr/share/lib/terminfo/P/PS.

If a printer can emulate more than one kind of printer, you can assign it several types. If you specify more than one printer type, the LP print service uses one of the types as appropriate for each print request.

If you don't specify a type, the default type is unknown, and the local printer does not get initialized before printing a file. When specifying the printer type on a SunOS 5.*x* print client, the default type unknown is desirable.

File Content Type

The *file-content-type* tells the LP print service what types of files can be printed directly on each printer. Print requests can ask for a type, and the LP print service uses this type to match jobs to printers. Most printers can print two types of files:

- The same type as the printer type (for example, PS for PostScript)

- The type simple (an ASCII file)

Some printers can accept and print several types of files. You can specify the names of the content types as a list. Table 11.2 lists some common file content types for local printers.

Table 11.2   **Common File Content Types for Local Printers**

Type	Description
any	Accepts any file content type
cif	Output of BSD cifplot
daisy	Daisy wheel printer
dmd	DMD
fortran	ASA carriage control format
otroff	Cat typesetter instructions generated by BSD or pre-System V troff (old troff)
plot	Plotting instructions from Tektronix displays and devices
PS	PostScript language
raster	Raster bitmap format for Varian raster devices
simple	ASCII file
tex	DVI format files
troff	Device-independent output from troff

Note. If you specify more than one printer type, you must specify simple as one of the content types.

Content type names may look like printer names, but you are free to choose content type names that are meaningful to you and the users of the printers. You specify the file content type with this command:

```
lpadmin -p printer-name -I file-content-type
```

The content types to use for a Solaris 2.*x* print client are any, simple, and PS. If you omit content type, the default is any, which filters files on the print server. The type PS filters files on the client.

Table 11.3 lists the printer type and content type for frequently used PostScript printers.

NOTE.   *The name* simple *means ASCII file, and* any *means any file content type. Be sure to use them consistently. The name* terminfo *is reserved as a reference to all types of printers.*

All printers in Table 11.3 are either PS or PSR. PS prints a banner page first, and prints the document from front to back. PSR reverses the pagination, printing the pages in reverse order, with the banner page last. File content type is PS for all these models.

Table 11.3   **Frequently Used PostScript Printers**

Manufacturer	Model
Apple	Personal LW II
Apple	LaserWriter IINT
Apple	LaserWriter IINTX
Canon	BJ-10
Canon	BJ-130e
Canon	LBP-4
Canon	LBP-8
Epson	all
GammaData	System300
Hewlett-Packard	II, IIP, IID
Hewlett-Packard	III, IIIP, IIID
Hewlett-Packard	Deskjet+
Apple	LaserWriterII
Mitsubishi Electric	G650
Mitsubishi Electric	G370
Mitsubishi Electric	S340
Pacific	Rim Data Sciences
QMS	PS 410
QMS	PS 810
Raster Graphics	ColorStation
Seiko	5504
Seiko	5514
Sharp	JX-730
Shinko	CHC-635
Shinko	CHC-645-2
Shinko	CHC-645-4

Table 11.3   Frequently Used PostScript Printers (Continued)

Manufacturer	Model
Shinko	CHC-345
Shinko	CHC-445
Shinko	CHC-445
Shinko	CHC-445-4
Shinko	CHC-745-2
Talaris/Ricoh	1590, 1590-T
Talaris/Xerox	2492-B
Talaris	2090
Talaris/Olympus	3093
Talaris/Olympus	5093
Tektronix	Phaser DXN
Tektronix	Phaser SXS
Versatec	8836
Versatec	C25xx series
Versatec	CE3000 series
Versatec	7000 series
Versatec	V-80 series
Versatec	8200 series
Versatec	8500 series
Versatec	CADMate series
Versatec	8600 series
Versatec	8900 series

Table 11.4 lists additional non-PostScript printers and shows the printer type to use for configuring each printer. The file content type is simple for all these printers.

Table 11.4 **Non-PostScript Printers**

Printer	Printer Type
Daisy	daisy
Datagraphix	datagraphix
DEC LA100	la100
DEC LN03	ln03
DECwriter	decwriter
Diablo	diablo
Diablo	diablo-m8
Epson 2500 variations	epson2500
Epson 2500 variations	epson2500-80
Epson 2500 variations	epson2500-hi
Epson 2500 variations	epson2500-hi80
IBM Proprinter	ibmproprinter
Qume Sprint 5	qume5
Texas Instruments 800	ti800

Print Filters

Print filters are programs that convert print requests from one format to another. The LP print service uses filters to:

- Convert a file from one data format to another so that it can be printed properly on a specific type of printer

- Handle the special modes of printing, such as two-sided printing, landscape printing, or draft- or letter-quality printing

- Detect printer faults and notify the LP print service of them so that the print service can alert users and system administrators

Not every print filter can perform all these tasks. Because each task is printer-specific, they can be implemented separately.

Solaris 2.*x* system software provides a default set of PostScript filters. Some of the TranScript filters used with SunOS 4.*x* have Solaris 2.*x* equivalents, and some do not. Table 11.5 lists and describes the default PostScript filters and identifies the TranScript filters, when applicable.

Table 11.5   **PostScript Filters**

Filter	Action	TranScript Equivalent
download	download fonts	
dpost	ditroff to PostScript	psdit
postdaisy	daisy to PostScript	
postdmd	dmd to PostScript	
postio	communicate with printer	pscomm
postior	communicate with printer	
postmd	matrix gray scales to PostScript	
postplot	plot to PostScript	psplot
postprint	simple to PostScript	enscript
postreverse	reverse or select pages	psrev
posttek	TEK4014 to PostScript	ps4014

Solaris 2.*x* system software does not provide the following filters:

- TEX
- oscat (NeWSprint™ opost)
- Enscript

Universal Address for the Print Server

The *universal-address* is required for setting up both print servers and print clients. As part of configuring the network listen process to listen for print requests from other systems, you must provide the universal address—the Internet Protocol address (IP address) of the print server in hexadecimal form—to the LP print service. You find the universal address with the lpsystem -A command. The universal address has four parts, as shown in Figure 11.1. The last part, RFU, means Reserved for Future Use, and could be used for other families of addresses (for example, Open Systems Interface) in the future.

Figure 11.1
Parts of the
universal address

0002	0203	81941488	0000000000000000
Internet family	TCP port	IP address	RFU

Printer Description (Optional)

You can define a *printer-description* for a printer. The description can contain any helpful information that would benefit its users. For example, the description could say where the printer is located, or whom to call when the printer has problems.

Users can display the printer's description by typing the command:

```
% lpstat -D -p printer-name
```

Default Printer (Optional)

You can specify a *default-printer* for each system, even if it is the only printer connected to the system. When you specify a default printer, users do not need to type the default printer name when they use LP print service commands. However, they can override the default by explicitly naming a printer or setting the LPDEST environment variable. Before you can designate a default printer, it must be known to the LP print service on the system.

Local PostScript Printer Setup

The first task in setting up a print server is to set the printer up as a local Solaris 2.*x* printer. You generally perform the following tasks to set up a local printer:

- Connect the printer to the system.

- Set the printer switches or configure baud rate, port, and other settings.

- Plug the printer into a power outlet.

- Define the characteristics of the printer to the LP print service (using the lpadmin command).

  You need the following information to set up a local printer:

- System's superuser password

- Device name (typically, /dev/term/a or /dev/term/b)

- Unique printer name

- Printer type

- Printer file content type

- Printer description (optional)

Refer to the section "Printer Configuration Information" earlier in this chapter if you need more information. Follow these steps to configure a local printer:

1. Connect the printer to the system and turn on the power to the printer. See the printer manual for setup information. Printer cables usually are connected to a serial port.

2. Become superuser.

3. Type **chown lp /dev/term/***address* and press Return. The lp user now owns the port device to which the printer is connected. For a serial port, *address* is usually a or b.

4. Type **chmod 600 /dev/term/***address* and press Return. Now only lp can access the printer port device.

5. Type **lpadmin -p** *printer-name* **-v /dev/term/***address* and press Return. The printer is registered with the LP print service.

6. Type **lpadmin -p** *printer-name* **-T** *printer-type* and press Return. Use PS for PostScript or PSR for PostScript reverse (to reverse the order of the pages) as the printer type for a PostScript printer. The printer type is registered with the LP print service.

NOTE. *If you specify printer type PS and pages print in reverse order, try printer type PSR.*

7. Type **lpadmin -p** *printer-name* **-I** *file-content-type* and press Return. The file content type is specified. If you specify more than one type, separate the names with commas. Alternatively, you can enclose the list in double quotes and separate the names with spaces.

8. Type **cd /etc/lp/fd** and press Return. You are in the directory that contains the print filter descriptor files.

9. Type the following script to install the PostScript filters:

```
# sh
# for f in download dpost postio postior postprint postreverse
> do
> lpfilter -f $f -F $f.fd
> done
#
```

10. Type **accept** *printer-name* and press Return. The printer is now ready to begin accepting (queuing) print requests.

11. Type **enable** *printer-name* and press Return. The printer is now ready to process print requests in the print queue.

12. (Optional) Type **lpadmin -p** *printer-name* **-D** *"comment"* and press Return. Attaching a description can give users helpful information, such as where the printer is located. The comment is displayed as part of the printer status.

13. (Recommended) Type **lpadmin -d** *printer-name* and press Return. The printer you specify is established as the default printer for the system.

14. Type **lpstat -t** and press Return. Check the messages displayed to verify that the printer is accepted and enabled.

15. Type **lp** *filename* and press Return. If you specified a default printer in step 13, you do not need to include the printer destination (-d *printer-name*). The file you choose is sent to the default printer. If the file does not print correctly or is not printed on the correct printer, see the section "Printing Problems" later in this chapter for help.

After you have set up the local printer, you can set the system up to become a print server. See "Print Server Setup" for instructions.

The following example is based on a network of five systems. You have one PostScript printer on the network. You designate pine as the print server, because it can support printing for all five systems.

The following characteristics are established for this printer:

- Printer name: pinecone

- Printer type: PS

- File content type: PS

■ Device Name: /dev/term/b (the port used to connect the printer)

```
pine% su
# lpstat -r
scheduler is running
# chown lp /dev/term/b
# chmod 600 /dev/term/b
# lpadmin -p pinecone -v /dev/term/b
# lpadmin -p pinecone -T PS
# lpadmin -p pinecone -I PS
# cd /etc/lp/fd
# lpfilter -f download -F download.fd
# lpfilter  f dpost  F dpost.fd
# lpfilter -f postio -F postio.fd
# lpfilter -f postior -F postior.fd
# lpfilter -f postprint -F postprint.fd
# lpfilter -f postreverse -F postreverse.fd
# accept pinecone
destination "pinecone" now accepting requests
# enable pinecone
printer "pinecone" now enabled
# lpadmin -p pinecone -D "PostScript Laser printer in Building 5, Room 262"
# lpadmin -d pinecone
# lpstat -t
scheduler is running
system default destination: pinecone
device for pinecone: /dev/term/b
pinecone accepting requests since Mon Mar 4 14:37:55 PST 1991
printer pinecone is idle. enabled since Mon Mar 4 14:37:59 PST 1991. available.
# lp -d pinecone /etc/passwd
request id is pinecone-1 (1 file)
#
```

Print Server Setup

After you set up a local printer, you need to perform the following tasks to set up a Solaris 2.*x* system (with its printer) to act as a print server:

■ Configure the port monitor.

■ Register the network listen service.

■ Identify the print clients.

Before you set up a system as a print server, you should first add and configure a local printer. See "Local PostScript Printer Setup" for instructions. The system should also be connected to a network.

You need the following information:

■ The superuser password for the print server system

- The name of the printer
- The name of the print server
- The names of the systems that will be print clients

Adding the listen Service

For print clients to access a print server running Solaris 2.*x* system software, you must configure the listen port monitor on the print server to accept service requests and to notify the LP print service of such requests. In addition, you must configure the listen port monitor on each Solaris 2.*x* print client.

Follow these steps to add the listen port monitor:

1. If not already done, set up the local printer.

2. Become superuser on the server system.

3. Type **sacadm -a -p tcp -t listen -c "/usr/lib/saf/listen tcp" -v `nlsadmin -V` -n 9999** and press Return. The -a option adds the port specified by the -p option. The -t option identifies the type of service. The -c option specifies which command is used to start the port monitor, the -v option specifies the version of the network listen process, and the -n option specifies the number of times SAC will restart the process if it dies. The listen port monitor is configured.

4. Type **sacadm -l** and press Return. When the network listen service is started and enabled, the following information is displayed:

```
# sacadm -1
PMTAG       PMTYPE    FLGS RCNT STATUS    COMMAND
tcp         listen    -    9999 ENABLED   /usr/lib/saf/listen tcp #
```

NOTE.   *It may take several minutes before the network listen service is enabled.*

Creating the listen Services

The LP print service uses a connection-oriented protocol to establish connections for incoming requests from remote systems. When the port monitor is configured, you register the following listen services:

- Service 0
- listenS5
- listenBSD

These services "listen" for print requests from print clients, or confirmations from the server. When a communication is detected, the service hands over the process to the lpNet daemon.

You use the universal address, or a modified version of it, to set up the listen port monitors. The first four digits identify the Internet family. The fifth through eighth digits identify the TCP port. For the modified version, replace port number 0203 with 0ACE. (The first digit is a zero.) To display the universal address, type **lpsystem -A** and press Return. The system's universal address is displayed, as shown in the following example:

```
# lpsystem -A
000202038194180e0000000000000000
#
```

Table 11.6 lists the variable input to the pmadm command used to configure the three listen port monitors.

Table 11.6   **Variable Input to the pmadm Command Options**

type Value	*nlscmd* Value
lp	nlsadmin -o /var/spool/lp/fifos/listenS5
lpd	nlsadmin -o /var/spool/lp/fifos/listenBSD -A '\xaddress'
0	nlsadmin -c /usr/lib/saf/nlps_server -A '\xmodified_address'

Note. Type **\x** at the beginning of the universal (or modified universal) address exactly as shown. In addition, the address must be enclosed in single quotation marks so that the backslash is not stripped off.

The following steps describe how to create the three listen port monitors:

1. Type **pmadm -a -p tcp -s type -i root -m `nlscmd` -v `nlsadmin -V`** and press Return. Repeat this step for each of the three service types. The listen port monitor is configured to listen to requests from the LP print service for both Solaris 2.*x* and SunOS 4.*x* print clients.

2. Type **cat /var/saf/tcp/log** and press Return. Examine the messages displayed to make sure that the services are enabled and initialized.

The following example registers all three network listen services for the print server pine:

```
# lpsystem -A
000202038194180e0000000000000000
# pmadm -a -p tcp -s lp -i root -m `nlsadmin -o /var/spool/lp/fifos/listenS5`
-v `nlsadmin -V`
# pmadm -a -p tcp -s lpd -i root -m `nlsadmin -o /var/spool/lp/fifos/listenBSD
-A '\x000202038194180e0000000000000000'` -v `nlsadmin -V`
# pmadm -a -p tcp -s 0 -i root -m `nlsadmin -c /usr/lib/saf/nlps server -A
'\x00020ACE8194180e0000000000000000'` -v `nlsadmin -V`
pine# cat /var/saf/tcp/log
10/28/91 10:22:51; 178; @(#)listen:listen.c      1.19.9.1
10/28/91 10:22:51; 178; Listener port monitor tag: tcp
10/28/91 10:22:51; 178; Starting state: ENABLED
10/28/91 10:22:51; 178; Service 0: fd 6 addr \x00020ACE8194180e0000000000000000
10/28/91 10:22:51; 178; Service lpd: fd 7 addr \x000202038194180e0000000000000000
10/28/91 10:22:52; 178; Net opened, 2 addresses bound, 56 fds free
10/28/91 10:22:52; 178; Initialization Complete
#
```

Specifying the Print Client Systems

For print client systems to access a Solaris 2.*x* print server, you must tell the print server which systems can send print requests. In effect, you have to register the names of the print clients with the LP print service on the server. This information is stored in the file /etc/lp/Systems.

To configure print client systems, type **lpsystem client-system1 client-system2...** and press Return. The print client systems that are to use the print server are identified. You can specify more than one system name, separating them with spaces. You can add print clients at any time by using the command in this step.

The following example shows how to identify the print clients oak, ash, elm, and maple.

```
# lpsystem oak ash elm maple
"oak" has been added.
"ash" has been added.
"elm" has been added.
"maple" has been added.
```

NOTE. *The Solaris 2.1 release provides a patch so that any client can print on any print server. This feature is useful for cutting down on print client administration in large corporations.*

You can perform additional optional setup steps, depending on the type of printer and the printing policies you want to set for your site. For example, you may want to create a class of printers and include the printer in that class. Or you may want to set up the printer to use a certain form.

The next task, after you have set up the print server, is usually to set up print clients. It is difficult to tell if you set up the print server correctly until you set up a print client and try to print from it.

Print Client Setup

On each Solaris 2.x print client, you need to complete the following tasks so the print client can use the printer connected to the print server:

- Start the LP print service scheduler.

- Identify the printer and server system to which the printer is connected.

- Define the characteristics of the printer.

- Configure the port monitor and register the listen services with the port monitor.

Setting up print servers and clients presumes you have a network that enables access between systems. If your network is running the Network Information Service Plus (NIS ।), you should already have enabled access between systems. If your network is not running NIS or NIS+, before setting up print servers and print clients you must add the Internet address and system name for each client system to the /etc/hosts file on the print server. You must also include the Internet address and system name for the print server in the /etc/hosts file of each print client system.

Before you set up print clients, the print server must be installed and configured and the systems must be able to access one another over the network.

You need the following information to configure print clients:

- Superuser password of the print server

- Superuser password for each print client system

- Names of printer, server, and clients

- Printer type (optional; if you do not specify a printer type, unknown is used as the default.)

- Printer file content type (optional; if you do not specify a file content type, any is used as the default.)

Follow the steps below on the Solaris 2.*x* print server.

NOTE. *If the print clients are to use a SunOS 4.1 print server, skip the next three steps.*

1. Become superuser.

2. Type **lpstat -p** *printer-name* **-l** and press Return. The type, file content, and class of the printer are displayed. Make a note of the information because you will use this information in subsequent steps.

3. If you have not already identified the print clients to the print server, type **lpsystem** *client-system1 client-system2...* and press Return.

On each Solaris 2.*x* print client:

1. Become superuser.

2. Specify the type of print server system:

   a. For Solaris 2.*x* print servers, type **lpsystem -t s5** *server-system-name* and press Return. The print server system is identified as a Solaris 2.*x* print server. The information is added to the /etc/lp/Systems file on the print client.

   b. For SunOS 4.*x* print servers, type **lpsystem -t bsd** *server-system-name* and press Return. The print server system is identified as a SunOS 4.*x* print server. The information is added to the /etc/lp/Systems file on the print client.

3. Type **lpadmin -p** *printer-name* **-s** *server-system-name* and press Return. The printer on the print server is identified.

4. (Optional) Type **lpadmin -p** *printer-name* **-T unknown** and press Return. If you omit this step, the printer type unknown is used as the default.

5. (Optional) Type **lpadmin -p** *printer-name* **-I** *file-content-type* and press Return. Specify the file content type as simple, any, or PS. If you omit this step, a file content type of any is used as the default. The name simply means ASCII file. Use any when you want files to be filtered on the print server. Use PS to indicate that the print server supports PostScript and to have the files filtered on the print client.

6. Type **cd /etc/lp/fd** and press Return. You are in the directory that contains the print filter descriptor files.

7. Type the following script to install the PostScript filters:

```
# sh
# for f in download dpost postio postior postprint postreverse
> do
> lpfilter -f $f -F $f.fd
> done
#
```

8. Type **accept** *printer-name* and press Return. The LP print system now accepts print requests.

9. Type **enable** *printer-name* and press Return. The printer is enabled and can process print requests.

10. (Optional) Type **lpadmin -p** *printer-name* **-D** "*comment*" and press Return. Attaching a description can give the user helpful information, such as where the printer is located. The comment is displayed as part of the printer status.

11. (Recommended) Type **lpadmin -d** *printer-name* and press Return. The printer you specify is configured as the default printer for the client system.

12. Type **lpstat -t** and press Return. Check the messages displayed to verify that the printer is accepted and enabled.

13. Type **lp -d** *printer-name filename* and press Return. The file you choose is sent to the printer. If the file did not print correctly or did not print on the printer you expected, see "Printing Problems" later in this chapter for help.

Follow these additional steps on Solaris 2.*x* print clients only to set up the SAF. You do not need to do any additional configuration for a SunOS 4.*x* print client.

1. Type **sacadm -a -p tcp -t listen -c "/usr/lib/saf/listen tcp" -v `nlsadmin -V` -n 9999** and press Return. The network listen service that listens for TCP/IP requests is started.

2. Type **sacadm -l** and press Return. When the network listen service is starting, the following information is displayed:

```
# sacadm -l
PMTAG      PMTYPE     FLGS RCNT STATUS    COMMAND
tcp        listen      -   9999 ENABLED   /usr/lib/saf/listen tcp #
```

NOTE. *It may take several minutes before the network listen service is enabled.*

3. Type **lpsystem -A** and press Return. The system's universal address is displayed. You use the universal address, or a modified version of it, to configure the port monitors. The first four digits identify the Internet family. The fifth through eighth digits identify the TCP port. For the modified version, replace port number 0203 with 0ACE. (The first digit is a zero.)

Table 11.7 lists the variable input to the pmadm command used to configure the three listen port monitors.

Table 11.7   **Variable Input to the pmadm Command Options**

type Value	*nlscmd* Value
lp	nlsadmin -o /var/spool/lp/fifos/listenS5
lpd	nlsadmin -o /var/spool/lp/fifos/listenBSD -A '*xaddress*'
0	nlsadmin -c /usr/lib/saf/nlps server -A '\\x*modified address*'

Note. Type **\x** at the beginning of the universal (or modified universal) address in the next step exactly as shown. In addition, the address must be enclosed in single quotation marks so the backslash is not stripped off.

4. Type **pmadm -a -p tcp -s** *type* **-i root -m `*nlscmd*` -v `nlsadmin -V`** and press Return. Repeat the command for each of the three types. The port monitor is configured to listen to requests from the LP print service.

5. Type **cat /var/saf/tcp/log** and press Return. Examine the messages displayed to make sure that the services are enabled and initialized.

The following example shows the steps for setting up a Solaris 2.*x* print client oak to print on pinecone, which is connected to the Solaris 2.*x* print server pine. Beginning with the lpsystem command, you would perform the same steps on other print clients such as ash, elm, and maple to let them become print clients of pine. You must tell each client system about the print server and the characteristics of its printer.

```
oak% rlogin pine
pine% lpstat -p pinecone -l
printer pinecone is idle. enabled since Wed Jan 2 18:20:22 PST 1991. available.
        Content types: PS
        Printer types: PS
        Description:
        Users allowed:
                (all)
        Forms allowed:
                (none)
        Banner not required
```

```
        Character sets:
                (none)
        Default pitch:
        Default page size:
pine% su
# lpsystem -t s5 oak
"oak" has been added.
pine% logout
oak% su
# lpsystem -t s5 pine
"pine" has been added.
# lpadmin -p pinecone -s pine -T PS -I PS
# cd /etc/lp/fd
# lpfilter -f download -F download.fd
# lpfilter -f dpost -F dpost.fd
# lpfilter -f postio -F postio.fd
# lpfilter -f postior -F postior.fd
# lpfilter -f postprint -F postprint.fd
# lpfilter -f postreverse -F postreverse.fd
# accept pinecone
destination "pinecone" now accepting requests
# enable pinecone
printer "pinecone" now enabled
# lpadmin -p pinecone -D "PostScript Laser printer in Building 5, Room 262"
# lpadmin -d pinecone
# lpstat -t
scheduler is running
system default destination: pinecone
system for pinecone: pine
pinecone accepting requests since Mon Mar 4 15:15:21 PST 1991
printer pinecone is idle. enabled since Mon Mar 4 15:15:26 PST 1991. available.
# lpsystem -A
000202038194180e000000000000000000
# pmadm -a -p tcp -s lp -i root -m `nlsadmin -o /var/spool/lp/fifos/listenS5`
-v `nlsadmin -V`
# pmadm -a -p tcp -s lpd -i root -m `nlsadmin -o /var/spool/lp/fifos/listenBSD
-A
'\x000202038194180e000000000000000000'` -v `nlsadmin -V`
# pmadm -a -p tcp -s 0 -i root -m `nlsadmin -c /usr/lib/saf/nlps_server -A
'\x00020ACE8194180e000000000000000000'` -v `nlsadmin -V`
pine# cat /var/saf/tcp/log
10/28/91 10:22:51; 178; @(#)listen:listen.c      1.19.9.1
10/28/91 10:22:51; 178; Listener port monitor tag: tcp
10/28/91 10:22:51; 178; Starting state: ENABLED
10/28/91 10:22:51; 178; Service 0: fd 6 addr \ \x00020ACE8194180e000000000000000000
10/28/91 10:22:51; 178; Service lpd: fd 7 addr \x000202038194180e000000000000000000
10/28/91 10:22:52; 178; Net opened, 2 addresses bound, 56 fds free
10/28/91 10:22:52; 178; Initialization Complete
# lp /etc/passwd
request id is pinecone-23
```

Printing Problems

When you set up a printer, you may find that nothing prints the first time you try to print a file. Or you may get a little further: Something prints, but it is not what you expect—the output is incorrect or illegible. Then, when you get past these problems, you may encounter other problems, such as the following:

- LP commands hang.

- Printers become idle.

- Users get conflicting messages.

NOTE. *Although many of the suggestions in this chapter are relevant to parallel printers, they are specific to the more common serial printers.*

No Output (Nothing Prints)

When nothing prints, there are three basic areas to check:

- The printer hardware

- The network

- The LP print service

Check the Hardware

The hardware is the first thing to check. As obvious as it sounds, make sure that the printer is plugged in and is turned on. In addition, refer to the manufacturer's documentation for information about hardware settings. Some computers use hardware switches that change the characteristics of a printer port.

The printer hardware includes the printer, the cable that connects it to the computer, and the ports at each end of the cable. As a general approach, work your way from the printer to the system.

Use the following checklist to troubleshoot hardware problems:

1. Check that the printer is plugged in and turned on.

2. Check that the cable is connected to the port on the printer and to the port on the workstation or server.

3. Check that the cable is the correct cable and that it is not defective.

4. Refer to the manufacturer's documentation.

5. Check that hardware switches for the ports are set properly.

6. Check that the printer is operational. Use the printer's self-test feature if the printer has one. (Check the printer documentation for information about printer self-testing.)

7. Check that the baud settings for the computer and the printer are correct. If the baud settings are not the same for both the computer and the printer, sometimes nothing will print, but more often you get incorrect output.

Check the Network

Problems with remote jobs—those going from a print client to a print server—are common. Make sure that network access between the print clients and the print server is enabled.

If the network is running NIS+, check NIS+ configurations and credentials. If the network is not running NIS or NIS+, check to make sure that names and IP addresses of each client are correctly entered in the /etc/hosts file on the print server. Also check to be sure that the name and IP address of the print server are correctly entered in the /etc/hosts file of each print client system.

Use the following steps to check for problems with the network:

1. On a print client or server, type **ping** *system-name* and press Return. This command helps you check that the network link between the print server and print clients is set up correctly.

```
elm% ping maple
maple is alive
elm% ping oak
oak not available
elm%
```

If the system is alive, the network connection is all right. Either a naming service or the local /etc/hosts file has successfully translated the host (system) name you entered into an IP address.

If the system is not available, check the NIS or NIS+ setup at your site. You may need to take additional steps so that print servers and print clients can communicate with one another. If your site is not running NIS or NIS+, check to make sure you have entered the IP address for the print server in the /etc/hosts file for each print client, and that you have entered all of the names and IP addresses of the client systems in the /etc/hosts file of the print server.

2. Check that the port monitor is configured correctly on the print server.

3. Check that the network listen services are registered with the port monitor on the print server.

Check the LP Print Service

For printing to work, the LP scheduler must be running on both the print server and print clients. In addition to the scheduler running, a printer must be enabled and accepting requests before it will produce any output. If the LP print service is not accepting requests for a printer, the submitted jobs (print requests) are rejected. Usually, in that instance, the user receives a warning message when a job is submitted. If the LP print service is not enabled for a printer, jobs remain queued on the system until the printer is enabled.

In general, analyze a printing problem as follows:

1. Follow the path of the print request step-by-step.

2. Examine the status of the LP print service at each step.

3. Is the configuration correct?

4. Is the printer accepting requests?

5. Is the printer enabled to process requests?

6. If the request is hanging on transmission, examine the lpNet log (/var/lp/logs/lpNet).

7. If the request is hanging locally, examine the lpsched log (/var/lp/logs/lpsched).

8. If the request is hanging locally, have notification of the printer device errors (faults) mailed to you, and re-enable the printer.

How to Check and Start the Scheduler   The print scheduler must be running both on the print server and on each print client system. On the print server and on each print client, type lpstat -r and press Return. Check the output of the command to make sure that the LP print service is running.

```
elm% lpstat -r
scheduler is running
elm%
```

If the scheduler is not running, become superuser and type **/usr/lib/lp/lpsched** and press Return.

How to Enable Printers and Accept Print Requests   You must enable printers and tell them to accept print requests.

Follow these steps both on the print server and on each print client to make sure that the printer is enabled and is accepting print requests:

1. Type **lpstat -a** and press Return to make sure that the printer is accepting requests.

```
elm% lpstat -a
oak accepting requests since Wed Mar 13 20:37:07 PST 1991
pinecone not accepting requests since Wed Apr 17 19:10:55 PDT 1991 unknown
reason
elm%
```

If the printer is not accepting requests, become superuser and then type **accept** *printer-name* and press Return. The printer you specify now accepts requests.

2. Type **lpstat -p** *printer-name* and press Return to make sure that the printer is enabled to print requests. In the following example, the printer pinecone is disabled.

```
elm% lpstat -p pinecone
printer pinecone disabled since Wed Apr 17 19:13:33 PDT 1991. available.
unknown reason
elm%
```

If the printer is disabled, become superuser and then type **enable** *printer-name* and press Return. The printer you specify is enabled.

```
pine% su
Password:
# enable pinecone
printer "pinecone" now enabled.
#
```

How to Check the Port Connection   Check to make sure that the cable is connected to the port the LP print service is using. To find out which port is configured for the LP print service, type **lpstat -t** on the print server and press Return. In the following example, the printer is connected to /dev/term/a.

```
elm% lpstat -t
scheduler is running
system default destination: pinecone
device for pinecone: /dev/term/a
elm%
```

If the cable is connected to the right port, type **ls -l /devices** and press return to check whether the device is owned by lp and that the permissions are set to 600. In the following example, the port is configured correctly.

```
oak% ls -l /devices
total 12
crw-rw-rw-    1 root      sys      28,   0 Mar 24 10:22
audio@1,f7201000:sound,audio
crw-rw-rw-    1 root      sys      28,128 Mar 24 10:22
audio@1,f7201000:sound,audioctl
crw-------    1 root      sys      68, 11 Mar 24 09:39 eeprom@1,f2000000:eeprom
brw-rw-rw-    1 root      sys      36,   0 Mar 24 09:39 fd@1,f7200000:a
crw-rw-rw-    1 root      sys      36,   0 Mar 24 09:39 fd@1,f7200000:a,raw
brw-rw-rw-    1 root      sys      36,   1 Mar 24 09:39 fd@1,f7200000:b
crw-rw-rw-    1 root      sys      36,   1 Mar 24 09:39 fd@1,f7200000:b,raw
brw-rw-rw-    1 root      sys      36,   2 Mar 24 09:39 fd@1,f7200000:c
crw-rw-rw-    1 root      sys      36,   2 Mar 24 09:39 fd@1,f7200000:c,raw
drwxr-xr-x    2 root      sys         4608 Mar 24 10:22 pseudo
drwxr-xr-x    3 root      sys          512 Mar 24 11:41 sbus@1,f8000000
crw-------    1 lp        sys      29,   0 Mar 24 09:39 zs@1,f1000000:a
crw-rw-rw-    1 root      sys      29,131072 Mar 24 09:39 zs@1,f1000000:a,cu
crw-rw-rw-    1 root      sys      29,   1 Mar 24 09:39 zs@1,f1000000:b
crw-rw-rw-    1 root      sys      29,131073 Mar 24 09:39 zs@1,f1000000:b,cu
oak%
```

If you are not certain which device is the serial port, you can type **ls -l /dev/term** and press Return to display the link to the /devices file.

```
oak% ls -l /dev/term
total 4
lrwxrwxrwx    1 root      root         29 Mar 24 10:23 a ->
../../devices/zs@1,f1000000:a
lrwxrwxrwx    1 root      root         29 Mar 24 10:23 b ->
../../devices/zs@1,f1000000:b
oak%
```

Use the following steps if you need to change the ownership or permissions for the device:

1. Become superuser.

2. Type **chown lp** *device-name* and press Return. The lp process now owns the port device file, and no other processes can use it.

3. Type **chmod 600** *device-name* and press Return. Only lp or root can access the printer port device file.

How to Check Printer Configurations   Check to make sure the printer type and file content type are configured properly on the print server and on each print client. Type **lpstat -p** *printer-name* **-l** and press Return. In the following example, a PostScript printer is configured properly and is available to process print requests on both the print server (pine) and the print client (oak).

```
pine% lpstat -p pinecone -l
printer pinecone is idle. enabled since Wed Feb 4
20:17:21 PST 1970. available.
        Content types: PS
        Printer types: PS
pine% rlogin oak
Password:
oak% lpstat -p pinecone -l
printer pinecone is idle. enabled since Wed Feb 4
20:17:21 PST 1970. available.
        Content types: PS
        Printer types: PS
oak% logout
pine%
```

If the printer type or file content type is incorrect, type **lpadmin -p** *printer-name* **-T** *printer-type* **-I** *file-content-type* and press Return. On the print client, try setting the print type to unknown and the content type to any.

How to Check for Printer Faults on the Print Server   Print jobs may be waiting in the queue because of a printer fault on the print server. Use the following steps to make sure that the printer is not waiting because of a printer fault:

1. Become superuser.

2. Type **lpadmin -p** *printer-name* **-F continue** and press Return. You have instructed the LP print service to continue if it is waiting because of a fault.

3. Type **enable** *printer-name* and press Return. This command forces an immediate retry.

4. (Optional) Type **lpadmin -p** *printer-name* **-A 'write root'** and press Return. You have instructed the LP print service to set a default policy of sending the printer fault message to the terminal on which root is logged in if the printer fails. This policy may help you to get quick notification of faults as you try to fix the problem.

It is easy to set up a printer port as a login terminal by mistake. To check that the printer port is not incorrectly set up as a login terminal, type **ps -ef** and press Return. Look for the printer port entry. In the example, port /dev/term/a is incorrectly set as a login terminal. You can tell by the "passwd\n## informa-tion at the end of the line.

```
pine% ps -ef
  root  169  167  0  Apr 04 ?        0:08 /usr/lib/saf/listen tcp
    root  939    1  0 19:30:47 ?      0:02 /usr/lib/lpsched
    root  944  939  0 19:30:47 ?      0:00 lpNet
    root  859  858  0 19:18:54 term/a  0:01 /bin/sh -c /etc/lp/interfaces/
pinecone pinecone-294 pine!winsor "passwd\n##
pine%
```

If the port is set up as a login port, follow these steps to disable the login:

1. Become superuser.

2. Type **cancel** *request-id* and press Return. The request ID is shown in the output of the ps -ef command. In the following example, request-id pinecone-294 is canceled:

```
pine% su
# cancel pinecone-294
request "pinecone-294" cancelled
#
```

3. Type **lpadmin -p** *printer-name* **-h** and press Return. The printer port is set to be a non-login device.

4. Type **ps -ef** and press Return. Verify that the printer port is no longer a login device.

If you do not find the source of the printing problem in the basic LP print service functions, continue to one of the following procedures for the specific client or server case that applies.

How to Check Printing from a Solaris 2.x Client to a Solaris 2.x Print Server   Before you follow the steps in this section, you should already have checked the basic functions of the LP print service on both the print server and the print client. Make sure that the printer works locally before trying to diagnose problems with a print client. Use the following steps to check for printing problems between a Solaris 2.x client and a Solaris 2.x print server.

On the print client, type **ping** *print-server-name* and press Return. This command checks to make sure the systems are connected and are available on the network.

```
oak% ping pine
pine is alive
oak% ping elm
```

```
elm not available
oak%
```

If you receive the message "*system* not available," you have a network connection problem.

1. On the print client, become superuser.

2. Type **lpsystem -l** and press Return. Check the output to make sure the print server is identified as type s5 (for Solaris 2.*x*). In the following example, the print server oak is properly identified as type s5:

```
# lpsystem -l
System:                      oak
Type:                        s5
Connection timeout:          never
Retry failed connections:    after 10 minutes
Comment:                     none
#
```

If the print server is not identified correctly, type **lpsystem -t S5** *print-server-name* and press Return, as follows:

```
# lpsystem -t S5 oak
#
```

Use the following steps to check the print queue on the print client:

1. Type **cd /var/spool/lp/requests/***system-name* and press Return. This directory contains a record of print requests still in the queue.

2. Type **ls -l** and press Return. A list of the print jobs is displayed.

3. For the print job you want to check, type **lpstat -o** *request-id* and press Return. In the following example, the job is queued successfully:

```
# cd /var/spool/lp/requests/clobber
# ls -l
total 12
-rw-rw----   1 lp       lp           43 May 22 19:44 11-0
# lpstat -o pinecone-11
pinecone-11               root         364   May 22 19:59
#
```

If the job is not queued successfully, the client–server connection may be faulty.

Use the following steps to make sure that the client–server connection is not faulty:

1. On the print client, type **tail /var/lp/logs/lpNet** and press Return. The output of this command shows you if lpNet can connect to the print server. In the following example, the log shows that a job from the print client elm could not connect to the print server:

```
# tail /var/lp/logs/lpNet
05/21/91 19:36 p  1780 <none> Starting.
05/21/91 19:36 p  1780 <none> Starting lpNetParent.
05/21/91 19:36 p  1/80 <none> Initialized & Polling.
05/21/91 19:36 c  1781 elm Starting.
05/21/91 19:36 p  1780 <none> Started child for elm, pid = 1781
***05/21/91 19:36 c  1781 elm Could not connect to remote child.
05/21/91 19:36 c  1781 elm Normal process termination.
#
```

2. If the connection is not being made, on the print server, type **lpstat -t** and press Return. The output of this command shows you if the print server is operating properly. In the following example, printers pinecone and red are up and running on the print server:

```
pine% lpstat -t
scheduler is running
system default destination: pinecone
device for pinecone: /dev/term/a
pinecone accepting requests since Thu May 23 20:56:26 PDT 1991
printer red is idle. enabled since Sun May 19 17:12:24 PDT 1991. available.
printer pinecone now printing pinecone-314. enabled since Fri May 24 16:10:39
PDT 1991. available.
pinecone-129              root              488    May 23 20:43 filtered
pine%
```

3. On the print server, type **tail /var/lp/logs/lpNet** and press Return. Examine the lpNet log to see if the print server is connecting to the client. If there is no entry, or if the server cannot complete the connection to the print client, lpNet is not transmitting correctly. The following example shows the log for two jobs. The first job, from the system elm, completed successfully. The second job could not be completed because the print server could not connect to the system opus.

```
papers% tail /var/lp/logs/lpNet
05/17/93 09:39 c   834 elm Starting.
05/17/93 09:39 c   834 elm Normal process termination.
05/17/93 09:41 p   162 <none> Started child for elm, pid = 902
05/17/93 09:41 c   902 elm Starting.
05/17/93 09:41 c   902 elm Connected to remote child.
05/17/93 09:41 c   341 opus Could not connect to remote child.
05/17/93 09:51 c   341 opus Could not connect to remote child.
```

```
05/17/93 10:01 c   341 opus Could not connect to remote child.
05/17/93 10:11 c   341 opus Could not connect to remote child.
05/17/93 10:21 c   341 opus Could not connect to remote child.
papers%
```

4. On the print server, type **lpsystem -l** and press Return. Check the output to make sure that the print client is correctly identified as type s5. In the following example, the print client oak is configured correctly:

```
# lpsystem -l
System:                       clobber
Type:                         s5
Connection timeout:           never
Retry failed connections:     after 10 minutes
Comment:                      none
```

If the print client configuration is incorrect, type **lpsystem -t s5** *client-system-name* and press Return, as follows:

```
# lpsystem -t s5 oak
```

5. On the print server, type **sacadm -l** and press return. Check to make sure that the port monitor and network listen service are set up properly. The following example shows a print server that is configured correctly:

```
# sacadm  l
PMTAG           PMTYPE        FLGS RCNT STATUS    COMMAND
tcp             listen        -    9999 ENABLED   /usr/lib/saf/listen tcp #
#
```

6. Type **pmadm -l** and press Return. The following example shows a print server that is configured for all three types of services:

```
# pmadm -l
PMTAG           PMTYPE        SVCTAG       FLGS ID       <PMSPECIFIC>
tcp             listen        lp           -    root     - - p -
/var/spool/lp/fifos/listenS5 #
tcp             listen        lpd          -    root
\x000202038194143a0000000000000000 - p - /var/spool/lp/fifos/listenBSD #
tcp             listen        0            -    root
\x00020ACE8194143a0000000000000000 - c - /usr/lib/saf/nlps_server #
#
```

If the service and port monitors are not configured correctly, refer to the instructions earlier in this chapter for how to configure SAF for printers.

How to Check Printing from a Solaris 2.x Client to a SunOS 4.x Print Server
The steps in this section describe how to check printing services if the Solaris 2.x client is receiving printing services from a SunOS 4.x print

server. Before you use the steps in this section, you should already have checked the basic functions of the LP print service.

Use the following steps to make sure the print server is accessible:

1. On the print client, type **ping** *print-server-name* and press Return. If you receive the message "*system* not available", you have a network problem.

2. On the print server, type **ps -ax | grep lpd** and press Return. If the lpd daemon is running, a line is displayed, as shown in the following example. If it is not running, no process information is shown.

```
maple% ps -ax | grep lpd
  126 ?  IW     0:00 /usr/lib/lpd
  200 p1 S      0:00 grep lpd
maple%
```

3. If lpd is not running on the print server, become superuser and type **/usr/lib/lpd &** and press Return. The lpd daemon is started.

Use the following steps to make sure the remote lpd daemon is configured properly:

1. On the print server, become superuser.

2. Type **/usr/etc/lpc** and press Return. The line printer control lpc> prompt is displayed.

3. Type **status** and press Return. Status information is displayed. In the following example, the daemon is not running and needs to be restarted:

```
maple% su
Password:
# /usr/etc/lpc
lpc> status
red:
queuing is enabled
printing is enabled
no entries
no daemon present
lpc>
```

4. If no daemon is present, at the lpc> prompt, type **restart** and press Return. The daemon is restarted.

5. Type **status** and press Return. Verify that the lpd daemon has started.

6. Type **quit** and press Return. You are returned to the shell prompt.

If you get this far without pinpointing the problem, the SunOS 4.*x* system is working properly.

To make sure that the connection to the remote lpd print daemon from the print client is made correctly, type **ps -ef | grep lp** and press Return. One lpNet and one lpsched daemon should be running, as shown in the following example:

```
# ps -ef | grep lp
  root   162   154 51   Jan 07 ?      0:01 lpNet
  root   154     1 80   Jan 07 ?      0:02 /usr/lib/lpsched
#
```

If many lpNet daemons are running, you are likely to have other printing problems.

If you have multiple lpNet daemons, follow these steps:

1. Become superuser.

2. Type **lpshut** and press Return.

3. Type **ps -ef | grep lpNet** and press Return. Note the process ID numbers for all lpNet daemons. You will use the PID as input to the next command.

4. Type **kill** *PID PID PID...* and press Return. You should not use the -9 option to kill lpNet daemons. Wait a full minute for the daemons to die.

5. Reset the listener ports.

6. Type **/usr/lib/lpsched** and press Return.

If this procedure does not remove the extra lpNet daemons, reboot the system.
If the lpNet daemon is not running, follow these steps to start it:

1. Become superuser.

2. Type **lpshut** and press Return. The LP print service is stopped.

3. Type **/usr/lib/lp/lpsched** and press Return. The LP print service is restarted, including the lpNet daemon.

Use the following steps to make sure that the remote print server is identified correctly as a SunOS 4.*x* system:

1. On the print client, become superuser.

2. Type **lpsystem -l** and press Return. In the following example, a SunOS 4.*x* print server (maple) is specified correctly, as shown by Type being set to bsd.

```
elm% su
Password:
# lpsystem -l
System:                      maple
Type:                        bsd
Connection timeout:          never
Retry failed connections:    after 10 minutes
Comment:                     none
#
```

3. If the print server is identified incorrectly, type **lpsystem -t bsd** *print-server-name* and press Return.

Use the following steps to check the print logs on the print client:

1. Type **tail -100 /var/lp/logs/lpNet** and press Return. The last 100 lines of the log file are displayed. By examining the lpNet log, you can tell if the print client (oak in the following example) is connecting properly to the print server. The following example shows a few typical lines from the /var/lp/logs/lpNet log file when connections are being made properly:

```
oak% tail -100 /var/lp/logs/lpNet
04/18/91 09:40 p  1097 <none> Starting.
04/18/91 09:40 p  1097 <none> Starting lpNetParent.
04/18/91 09:40 p  1097 <none> Initialized & Polling.
04/17/91 19:32 c   965 oak lpd connected to oak
04/17/91 19:32 c   965 oak lpd disconnecting from oak
oak%
```

The following example shows a few lines from a log file that show that a connection has not been successful. Usually, if there is a problem you will see retries to the BSD system.

```
oak% tail -100 /var/lp/logs/lpNet
05/23/91 14:39 c   120 oak lpd retrying connection to oak
05/23/91 14:51 c   120 oak lpd retrying connection to oak
05/23/91 15:02 c   120 oak lpd retrying connection to oak
oak%
```

2. On the print client, become superuser.

3. Type **lpsystem -l** *print-server-name* and press Return. The current retry and time-out parameters are displayed.

4. Type **lpsystem -T {n,0,N} -R {n,0,N}** *print-server-name* and press Return. The -T option specifies the length of time a network connection can be idle before it is dropped. Choose either n (never time out) or 0 (drop

immediately), or enter a number (wait *N* minutes, then drop connection). The default is n. The -R option specifies the length of time to wait before trying to re-establish a connection. Choose either n (do not retry until there is more work) or 0 (try to reconnect immediately), or enter a number (wait *N* minutes before trying to reconnect). The default is to wait 10 minutes before trying to reconnect. In the following example, the network connection is specified to never time out, and the retry time is specified to reconnect immediately.

```
elm% su
Password:
# lpsystem -T n -R Ø maple
"maple" has been modified.
#
```

Incorrect Output

If the printer and the print service software are not configured correctly, the printer may print, but it may provide output that is not what you expect.

Check the Printer Type

If you used the wrong printer type when you set up the printer with the LP print service, inappropriate printer control characters may be sent to the printer. The results are unpredictable: Nothing may print, output may be illegible, or output may be printed in the wrong character set or font.

Use the following steps to check the printer type:

1. Become superuser.

2. Type **lpstat -p** *printer-name* **-l** and press Return. A list of the printer characteristics is displayed.

```
elm% lpstat -p pinecone -l
printer pinecone is idle. enabled since Wed Jan  2 18:20:22 PST 1991. available.
        Content types: PS
        Printer types: PS
        Description:
        Users allowed:
                (all)
        Forms allowed:
                (none)
        Banner not required
        Character sets:
                (none)
        Default pitch:
        Default page size:
elm%
```

If the printer type is not correct, become superuser and type **lpadmin -p** *printer-name* **-T** *printer-type* and press Return.

Check the stty Settings

Many formatting problems can result when the default stty (standard terminal) settings do not match the settings required by the printer. The following sections describe what happens when some of the settings are incorrect. Read the printer documentation to determine the correct stty settings for the printer port.

NOTE. *If a printer is connected by a parallel port, the baud setting is irrelevant.*

Table 11.8 shows the default stty options used by the LP print service's standard printer interface program.

Table 11.8 **Default stty Settings Used by the Standard Interface Program**

Option	Meaning
9600	Set baud rate to 9600.
cs8	Set 8-bit bytes.
-cstopb	Send 1 stop bit per byte.
-parity	Do not generate parity.
ixon	Enable XON/XOFF (also known as START/STOP or DC1/DC3).
opost	Do "output post-processing" using the settings listed below.
-olcuc	Do not map lowercase to uppercase.
onlcr	Change line feed to carriage return/line feed.
-ocrnl	Do not change carriage returns into line feeds.
-onocr	Output carriage returns even at column 0.
nl0	No delay after line feeds.
cr0	No delay after carriage returns.
tab0	No delay after tabs.
bs0	No delay after backspaces.
vt0	No delay after vertical tabs.
ff0	No delay after form feeds.

Use Table 11.9 to choose stty options to correct various problems affecting print output.

Table 11.9 **stty Options to Correct Print Output Problems**

stty Values	Result	Possible Problem from Incorrect Setting
300, 600, 1200, 1800, 2400, 4800, 9600, 19200, 38400	Sets baud rate to the specified value (enter only one baud rate)	Random characters and special characters may be printed and spacing may be inconsistent.
oddp	Sets odd parity	Characters are randomly missing or appear incorrectly.
evenp	Sets even parity	
-parity	Sets no parity	
-tabs	Sets no tabs	Text is jammed against right margin.
tabs	Sets tabs every 8 spaces	Text has no left margin, is run together, or is jammed together.
-onlcr	Sets no return at the beginning of lines	Incorrect double spacing.
onlcr	Sets return at beginning of lines	Print zigzags down the page.

To display the current stty settings for the printer port, type **stty -a <** *device-name* and press Return. The current stty settings for the printer port are displayed.

```
elm# stty -a < /dev/term/a
speed 9600 baud;
rows = 0; columns = 0; ypixels = 0; xpixels = 0;
eucw 1:0:0:0, scrw 1:0:0:0
intr = ^c; quit = ^|; erase = ^?; kill = ^u;
eof = ^d; eol = <undef>; eol2 = <undef>; swtch = <undef>;
start = ^q; stop = ^s; susp = ^z; dsusp = ^y;
rprnt = ^r; flush = ^o; werase = ^w; lnext = ^v;
parenb -parodd cs7 -cstopb -hupcl cread -clocal -loblk -parext
-ignbrk brkint -ignpar -parmrk -inpck istrip -inlcr -igncr icrnl -iuclc
ixon -ixany -ixoff imaxbel
isig icanon -xcase echo echoe echok -echonl -noflsh
-tostop echoctl -echoprt echoke -defecho -flusho -pendin iexten
opost -olcuc onlcr -ocrnl -onocr -onlret -ofill -ofdel tab3
elm#
```

To change the stty settings, type **lpadmin -p** *printer-name* **-o** **"stty=***options***"** and press Return.

You can change more than one option setting by including the options in single quotation marks and separating them by spaces. For example, suppose the printer requires you to enable odd parity and set a 7-bit character size. You would type a command such as the following:

```
# lpadmin -p clobber -o "stty='parenb parodd cs7'"
```

The stty option parenb enables parity checking/generation, parodd sets odd parity generation, and cs7 sets the character size to 7 bits.

To send a document to the printer, type **lp -d** *printer-name filename* and press Return. Look at the document to verify that it is printing correctly.

Check the Baud Settings

When the baud setting of the computer does not match the baud setting of the printer, usually you get some output, but it does not look like what you submitted for printing. Random characters are displayed, with an unusual mixture of special characters and undesirable spacing. The default for the LP print service is 9600 baud.

NOTE. *If a printer is connected by a parallel port, the baud setting is irrelevant.*

Check the Parity Setting

Some printers use a parity bit to ensure that data received for printing has not been garbled during transmission. The parity bit settings for the computer and for the printer must match. If they do not match, some characters will not be printed at all, or they will be replaced by other characters. The output will look only approximately correct, with the word spacing all right and many letters in their correct place. The LP print service does not set the parity bit by default.

Check the Tab Settings

If Tabs are set but the printer expects no Tabs, the printed output may contain the complete contents of the file, but the text may be jammed against the right margin. Also, if the Tab settings for the printer are incorrect, the text may not have a left margin, may run together, may be concentrated in a portion of the page, or may be incorrectly double-spaced. The default is for Tabs to be set every eight spaces.

Check the Return Setting

If the output is double-spaced but should be single-spaced, either the Tab settings for the printer are incorrect or the printer is adding a line feed after

each Return. The LP print service adds a Return before each line feed, so the combination causes two line feeds.

If the print zigzags down the page, the stty option onlcr which sends a Return before every line feed is not set. The stty=onlcr option is set by default, but you may have cleared it while trying to solve other printing problems.

Hung LP Print Service Commands

If you type any of the lp commands (lpsystem, lpadmin, lpstat, lpshut) and nothing happens (no error message, status information, or prompt is displayed), chances are that something is wrong with the LP scheduler. Such a problem usually can be resolved by stopping and restarting the LP scheduler.

Use the following steps to free hung LP commands:

1. Become superuser.

2. Type **lpshut** and press Return. If this command hangs, press Control+C and proceed to the next step. If this command succeeds, skip to step 5.

3. Type **ps -el | grep lp** and press Return. Note the process ID numbers (PID) from the first column. You will use the PID numbers in the next step.

   ```
   # ps -el | grep lp
      103 ?          0:00 lpNet
      134 term/a     0:01 lpsched#
   ```

4. Type **kill -9** *pid1 pid2* and press Return. All the lp processes are terminated.

5. Type **rm /usr/spool/lp/SCHEDLOCK** and press Return. You have removed the SCHEDLOCK file so that you can restart the LP print service.

6. Type **/usr/lib/lp/lpsched** and press Return. The LP print service is restarted.

Idle (Hung) Printers

You may find a printer that is idle even though print requests have been queued to it. A printer may seem idle when it shouldn't be for one of the following reasons:

- The current print request is being filtered.

- The printer has a fault.

- Networking problems may be interrupting the printing process.

Check the Print Filters

Slow print filters run in the background to avoid tying up the printer. A print request that requires filtering will not print until it has been filtered. To check the print filters, type **lpstat -o** *printer-name* and press Return. See if the first waiting request is being filtered. If the output looks like the following example, the file is being filtered. The printer is not hung; it just is taking a while to process the request.

```
pine% lpstat -o pinecone
pinecone-10          fred        1261    Mar 12 17:34 being filtered
pinecone-11          iggy        1261    Mar 12 17:36 on pine
pinecone-12          jack        1261    Mar 12 17:39 on pine
pine%
```

Check Printer Faults

When the LP print service detects a fault, printing resumes automatically, but not immediately. The LP print service waits about five minutes before trying again, and continues trying until a request is printed successfully. You can force a retry immediately by enabling the printer.

Use the following steps to resume printing after a printer fault:

1. Look for a message about a printer fault and try to correct the fault if there is one. Depending on how printer fault alerts have been specified, messages may be sent to root by e-mail or may be written to a terminal on which you (root) are logged in.

2. Type **enable** *printer-name* and press Return. If a request was blocked by a printer fault, this command will force a retry. If this command doesn't work, continue with other procedures in this section.

Check Network Problems

When printing files over a network, you may encounter the following types of problems:

- Requests sent to print servers may back up in the client system (local) queue.

- Requests sent to print servers may back up in the print server (remote) queue.

Use the following steps to check that the printer is ready to print:

1. Type **lpstat -p** *printer-name* and press Return. The information displayed shows you if the printer is idle or active, enabled or disabled, or available or not accepting print requests. If everything looks all right, continue with other procedures in this section.

2. If the printer is not available (is not accepting requests), become superuser and type **accept** *printer-name* and press Return. The printer begins to accept requests into its print queue.

3. If the printer is disabled, type **enable** *printer-name* and press Return. This command re-enables the printer, so it will act on the requests in its queue.

Check for Jobs Backed Up in the Local Queue

Jobs earmarked for a print server may back up in the client system queue for the following reasons:

- The print server is down.

- The printer is disabled on the print server.

- The network between the print client and print server is down.

- Underlying Solaris 2.*x* network software was not set up properly.

While you are tracking down the source of the problem, stop new requests from being added to the queue.

Check for Jobs Backed Up in the Remote Queue
If jobs back up in the print server queue, the printer probably has been disabled. When a printer is accepting requests but not processing them, the requests are queued to print. Unless there is a further problem, once the printer is enabled, the print requests in the queue should print.

Use the following steps to send jobs to a remote printer when they back up in the local queue:

1. On the print client, type **reject** *printer-name* and press Return. Further queuing of print requests from the print client to the print server is stopped.

2. Type **ping** *print-server-name* and press Return to check that the print server and the network between the print client and the print server is up.

3. Type **tail /var/lp/logs/lpNet** and press Return. The information displayed may help you pinpoint what is preventing the transmission of print requests from the print client to the print server.

4. After you fix the problem, on the print client type **accept** *printer-name* and press Return. New jobs can begin to queue.

5. If necessary, on the print client type **enable** *printer-name* and press Return. The printer is enabled.

Use the following steps to free jobs from a print client that back up in the print server queue:

1. On the print server, type **reject** *printer-name* and press Return. Further print requests are not queued.

2. Type **tail /var/lp/logs/lpsched** and press Return. The information displayed may help you pinpoint what is preventing the print requests that have been transmitted from the print client to the print server from being printed.

3. After you fix the problem, on the print server type **accept** *printer-name* and press Return. The printer accepts new jobs in the print queue.

4. If necessary, on the print server type **enable** *printer-name* and press Return. The printer is enabled.

Conflicting Status Messages

A user may enter a print request and be notified that the client system has accepted it, then receive mail from the print server that the job has been rejected. These conflicting messages may occur for the following reasons:

- The print client may be accepting requests, but the print server is rejecting requests.

- The definition of the printer on the print client might not match the definition of that printer on the print server. More specifically, the definitions of the print job components, such as filters, character sets, print wheels, and forms, are not the same on the client and server systems.

Check to make sure that identical definitions of these job components are registered on both the print clients and print servers so that local users can access printers on the print servers.

Use the following steps to resolve conflicting status messages:

1. Type **lpstat -p** *printer-name* and press Return. Check that the printer connected to the print server is enabled and is accepting requests. Users will see conflicting status messages when the print client is accepting requests but the print server is rejecting requests.

2. On the print server and on each print client, type **lpstat -p -l** *printer-name* and press Return. Check that the definition of the printer on the print client matches the definition of the printer on the print server. Look at the definitions of the print job components, such as print filters, character sets, print wheels, and forms, to be sure they are the same on both the client and server systems, so that local users can access printers on print server systems.

The three chapters in this part describe how to install and delete application software.

Chapter 12 provides an overview of the installation process, introduces the package commands and the Software Manager for installation, recommends policy for installing software on an application server, and describes how to access files from a CD-ROM drive.

Chapter 13 describes how to use the package commands to administer application software, and how to set up the users' environment.

Chapter 14 describes how to use the Software Manager to administer application software.

Application Software

12

Installing and Managing Application Software

Overview of Installing and Managing Application Software

User Access to Applications

CD-ROM Mounts

WHEN YOU SUPPORT A NETWORK THAT PROVIDES APPLICATION software to users, your responsibilities include the following tasks:

- Setting up the software installation environment

- Installing the software on a server or on the users' local system

- Setting up the users' environment to access software

- Removing software that is obsolete or no longer used

This chapter introduces the package commands and Software Manager—two alternative ways to install and manage application software. It also describes how to set up an application server and access files from a remote and a local CD-ROM drive. Chapter 13 describes how to use the package commands. Chapter 14 describes how to use Software Manager. Although you can install application software on a user's local system, the information in this chapter describes how to set up the software on an application server and share the files so that they are available over the network.

Overview of Installing and Managing Application Software

With Solaris 2.x system software, installation is managed by packages of information. A software package contains the components of a software product that are delivered on the CD-ROM installation medium. The components typically contain groups of files such as compiled programs, files, and installation scripts.

Software packages are installed from the CD-ROM onto a system, and are removed from a system, in one of the following ways:

- Using the package commands from a command line.

- Using the Software Manager tool (which calls the package commands).

- Using an installation script provided by the application vendor (which calls the package commands). Some vendors may also provide a deinstallation script.

You can use the package commands and the Software Manager interchangeably. For example, you can install software using the Software Manager and remove the software using the pkgrm(1M) command. Alternatively, you can install software using the pkgadd(1M) command and remove that software using the Software Manager.

Using Package Commands

You manage software from a command line using the commands shown in Table 12.1.

Table 12.1 **Package Commands**

Task	Command
Set installation defaults	vi(1) admin(4)
Create a script to define installation parameters	pkgask(1M)
Install software package or store files for installation at a later time	pkgadd(1M)
Check accuracy of installation	pkgchk(1M)
List installed packages	pkginfo(1M)
Remove packages	pkgrm(1M)

These tasks are described in detail in Chapter 13.

Using the Software Manager

The Software Manager is an OpenWindows tool that you can use to perform the same tasks that you would perform from a command line using the package commands. Packages that are to be installed using the Software Manager may be grouped into clusters for easier administration. The Software Manager calls the package commands to perform the requested functions. Figure 12.1 shows the Software Manager base window. Refer to Chapter 14 for instructions on how to use this tool.

Using Installation Scripts

Although SunSoft recommends a policy on how to create packages for installation, some software products from application vendors provide their own installation scripts. The installation scripts must call the package commands to perform setup and installation of the software. Always read the installation instructions from the vendor to make sure that you follow the vendor's recommended installation procedure.

Figure 12.1

The Software
Manager base
window.

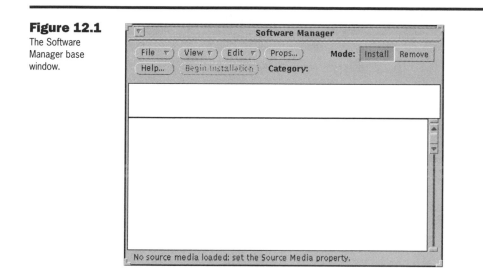

User Access to Applications

Making applications available to users is a major task of system administration. Most users depend on reliable access to application software to get their jobs done. A quarter or more of system administration time can easily be consumed by the demands of creating and maintaining user access to application software.

You may need to perform any or all of the following tasks to administer user access to applications:

- Acquire software.

- Locate space for it.

- Install it on multiple local systems.

- Set up user environments, such as paths, links, and environment variables.

- Revise user environments each time the software version changes or new software is added.

Anything that you can do to leverage these tasks will increase productivity.

You can use a variety of creative approaches to managing software access. One existing approach uses the automounter extensively to match up users with the proper binary version of applications. The principal drawback to using only an automounter approach is that it does not manage the environmental setup required by most packages.

Another existing approach uses scripts that are run once on each system to set up the user environment for an application. Subsequently, when the user starts the application, the environment is already properly prepared. A disadvantage to this approach is that it introduces additional command names that users have to learn to prepare for running an application. An additional drawback is that some programs use the same environment variable names as other programs with different values. When users run a script for a specific application but do not start the application until later, other packages that use the same environment variable may be affected. (See "Wrappers and Dot Files" later in this chapter for an example.)

Another approach uses wrappers to manage access to software. Wrappers are tailored application startup scripts. These scripts set up the user's environment at run time and start the application. Wrappers perform the setup that you would otherwise have to hard-code in individual users' "dot files."

Using wrappers together with standard application server layouts and simplified user mount and path setups can produce an environment in which you need to do very little, if any, administrative maintenance of the end user environment. Users can have as few as one software access mount and one software access path component.

Most application access at Sun is based on this last approach, which was developed by Sun Information Resources. SunSoft recommends that you consider dedicating servers to provide access to application software over the network, in the manner proposed in the following sections.

NOTE. *A comprehensive description of how to configure and manage application servers is beyond the scope of this book. However, the approaches and examples cited here will give you a foundation based on sound principles and real-world experience.*

Automating Your Application Environment

The information in the following sections provides suggestions for ways that you can automate your application environment. The key technologies and techniques are introduced in Table 12.2 and described in the following sections.

Table 12.2   **Key Elements for an Application Server**

Element	Used to
NFS/automounter	Share application file systems across the network; guarantee consistency and integrity with read-only access

Table 12.2   Key Elements for an Application Server (Continued)

Element	Used to
Online: DiskSuite™	Permit file systems larger than individual disks; enable a single mount to access a huge distribution
wrappers	Remove setup requirements from the end user environment; provide all users with consistent behavior
symbolic links	Allow one executable to have many startup names; permit generic path references to version-named locations; control default application versions
common command directory	Make all commands accessible with a single path component
rdist	Facilitate replication of file systems across application servers

When you set up an application server, you dedicate a single slice (partition) to contain the applications and wrappers. You create two (or more) directories in the slice. The application directory contains the applications and wrappers, as well as a symbolic link directory that you can use to determine the default version of the application. The common command directory contains symbolic links in the form of command names that link to the wrappers for each application. You can use a product such as SunSoft Online: DiskSuite™ to create a large file system that spans more than one slice or disk. When you have installed the application packages, you write a wrapper that sets up the environment for the application. If you want to copy the setup to another server, you can do so using the rdist command. Refer to "Designing an Application Server" later in this chapter for a detailed description of these tasks.

Benefits of a Standardized Application Server Setup

The information in the following section describes the administrative benefits you gain from a standardized application server setup.

Use NFS   Installing the same application for multiple users on local disks uses extra disk space, requires more time, and becomes a support burden. You must perform upgrades at multiple locations. When problems arise, you may have to deal with multiple versions of the same application.

When you provide an NFS-shared installation, you reduce local disk installations. You save time by reducing the number of systems that you must support. When multiple users share access to a single read-only copy of an application, you perform fewer installations and upgrades, and simplify troubleshooting by assuring that users are executing the same code.

Consolidate Your Installations Even NFS-shared applications can be difficult to maintain if they are scattered among too many locations. Sometimes applications have been installed on a user's system or on a server. As demand for the application develops, it is shared from the original location. Users frequently pass the word to other users about where they mount the application from. In such a situation, users may draw on inconsistent or unreliable sources and be confused about where they should get applications.

To solve this problem, designate dedicated application servers. Sharing all standard applications from the same server offers users a reliable source and lets you keep track of where maintenance must be done.

Hopefully, you are already using NFS and dedicated application servers in your application environment.

Standardize Server Layouts Your environment, like that at Sun, may require many application servers to service different networks, buildings, and regions. If so, commit to using the same file system layout on all application servers. Although the contents of different application servers may vary from one server to another, the locations of individual applications should be consistent. A unified file system naming scheme simplifies user paths and reduces the updates required when user moves dictate their change from one application server to another. This approach also simplifies the process of copying (distributing) applications from a master installation server to production servers, since the destination file system is the same.

Sometimes in comparing two locations where a product has been installed, you cannot tell whether the contents of like-named directories are intended to be the same or different; you have no outward clue. SunSoft recommends that you install applications in directories with names that identify both the product and the version. You and others will then know what the directories contain. In addition, you can maintain multiple versions of an application at the same directory level.

In some environments, you must perform maintenance at numerous locations for each change. Using wrappers and a common command directory reduces the number of locations where attention is needed, limits them to servers, and leverages the results for all users.

Synchronize Version Cutovers In the traditional UNIX environment, you may find it difficult to convert to a new application version quickly because of the number of changes to the user environment that may be required. Using symbolic links to control all the versioning at this level, and using wrappers that immediately provide any needed user setups, can help to speed up cutovers and to synchronize them. It can be difficult to know who is using particular applications, or whether some applications are being used at all.

Wrappers can increase usage visibility if you code them to report to a central location by e-mail each time the product is started.

Benefits of a Standardized User Environment

The information in these sections describes the administrative benefits you gain from a standardized user environment setup.

Simplify User Mount Points   When users access applications from a variety of locations or even from multiple file systems on a dedicated server, they need a variety of mount points. You, as system administrator, probably have to maintain the information that supports these mounts. Regardless of whether you perform this maintenance on individual user systems or by using automounter maps, the fewer times you need to update the user environment, the more time you save.

Simplify User Path Requirements   When you configure dedicated application servers so that all applications are accessible from a single file system, users need only one mount, which may not need to be updated. Even when the contents of the file system that users are mounting change, the mount point remains the same.

Maintaining path updates for users may be an unnecessary burden. If users have the "right" path, it does not need to be changed. The right path is one whose standard component(s) provide ongoing access to all applications.

Reduce Run Time Conflicts   The settings that some applications need at run time may be in conflict with those needed by others. Wrappers tailor one process environment without affecting others.

Simplify User Relocations   User moves can impose a tremendous burden, because many user setups in a nonstandard environment are customized. Using wrappers and simplified user mounts and paths can drastically reduce the updates required to reinstate application service after a move. In some cases, you need change only the server name for the user's mount.

Using Wrapper Technology

Wrappers are custom startup scripts for applications, and have been used for quite some time. Many application vendors such as Frame Technology use wrappers to tailor their application startup.

Vendors cannot, however, anticipate the full range of startup decisions and settings that will be needed in every customer environment. You can add value by developing wrappers that are truly customized to your own end user environment. It may be worth writing your own wrapper—even to front-end an application vendor-designed wrapper. Wrappers can leverage your system administration expertise and hard-won knowledge of the application requirements in a consistent way, to the benefit of all your users.

Wrappers and Dot Files

Ordinarily, user "dot files" (for example, .login and .cshrc for the C shell or .profile for the Bourne shell) try to provide for what users may do after they log in. The goal is to define a comprehensive environment that supports all requests to access applications. It is not only difficult, but in some cases impossible, to provide for all cases: Some applications need a different value for an environment variable than does another application that uses the same variable name.

For example, to run a given Sybase application, the users may need to set the DSQUERY variable to identify the back-end database server for the application. If this variable is set from dot files at login time, it extends throughout subsequent shell environments. However, other Sybase applications may require different DSQUERY values. If DSQUERY is set, instead, by a wrapper for the Sybase application, the DSQUERY value applies only to the application, and may be set to different values by other wrappers for other applications.

When you use wrappers, the environment for each application is set up as needed. Wrappers construct the needed environment at run time, before executing the application. In addition, the settings are visible to the resulting application process only; they do not interact with the rest of the user's environment. This encapsulation of run time environment is a significant advantage of wrappers.

Likewise, users' paths frequently must be updated as applications come and go, in an effort to provide for what the user may decide to run.

Consider this analogy: In a given year, you plan to go running, hiking, skating, scuba diving, and snow skiing. (Forget for a moment that as a system administrator you're too busy.) Doesn't it seem more practical to don the special equipment for each activity just before you need it (and take it off when you're done), rather than trying to put it all on at the beginning of the year, just "so you'll be ready"? Clearly, the latter approach can generate conflicts. And in choosing where to go skiing, for instance, you probably would prefer to choose your destination based on where the snow is at the time you are ready to go.

Additional Wrapper Advantages

With wrappers you can provide sensible default values for variables, while still allowing users the option to override those settings. You can automate user installation steps that some applications require when first run, and know that you are producing consistent results. You can also generate usage information about the application.

Wrapper Overhead and Costs

Some administrators question whether the merits of a wrapper approach justify the overhead imposed each time an application is started up. After all, an additional shell script is being run ahead of the normal application startup. Several years of experience with complex wrappers at Sun have shown that the delay in startup time is trivial and the benefits are overwhelming.

The biggest cost to consider is the flip side of the greatest benefit—wrappers are powerful, so they require care. Wrappers present consistent behavior to large numbers of users. If wrappers are well produced and maintained, they deliver gratifyingly reliable service and prevent many problems. On the other hand, if wrappers are broken, service to large numbers of users may be impacted.

Introduction of Wrappers into an Existing Environment

One of the great advantages of wrappers is that you can introduce them immediately into almost any application environment. Once you develop a wrapper for a given application, if the command names that link to it are installed in a location already in the users' paths (for example, /usr/local/bin), you can make the application immediately available without needing to do anything to set up the user environment.

To provide a limited implementation, you can decide how many wrappers you want to provide, and for which applications. You can write wrappers as you add new packages, and write wrappers for older applications as well. You can create links to the wrappers in a directory already in the users' paths. Alternatively, you can create a new directory that contains the links to the wrappers.

The tasks involved in setting up a limited implementation of an application server with wrappers include:

- Installing packages using vendor instructions

- Creating a "value-added" subhierarchy within each package

- Creating wrappers for applications, to eliminate or minimize any requirement for hard-coded setup by individual users

- Installing wrappers into their respective application "value-added" subhierarchy

- Creating all application command names as symbolic links in a directory that is already on the users' path (or in a new directory to be added to their paths)

- Creating symbolic links to point to the application wrapper

Designing an Application Server

To provide a complete implementation of these techniques throughout an environment, the tasks on the server include:

- Identifying servers to specialize in providing application access.

- Implementing the fewest possible slices (partitions) to contain the software packages.

- Performing software installations on these servers in a consistent file system layout.

- Sharing the application server file system read-only to users.

- Naming package directories in a way that reflects both the application name and the version.

- Installing packages initially per vendor instructions; then, adjusting them if necessary to simplify and encapsulate their structure.

- Creating a "value-added" subhierarchy within each application.

- Creating wrappers for applications, to eliminate or minimize any requirement for hard-coded setup by individual users.

- Installing wrappers into their respective application "value-added" subhierarchy.

- Creating all application command names as symbolic links in a common directory. Create symbolic links to point to the application wrapper.

- As applications are added to a server, updating other servers appropriately, using rdist.

The tasks in the user environment include (1) setting up users with the appropriate mount point and mount to access the application server and (2) setting up users with a path that includes the common command directory.

The following sections describe in greater detail the basic tasks involved in a general implementation. However, coverage of many topics necessarily is superficial, and the overall model is simplified.

Server Configuration

Consider the following points when designating servers to act as application servers:

- Choose server configurations that you believe to be robust. Consolidating applications into one location simplifies life only to the extent that the system provides ongoing, reliable service. Typically, when application service is down, users are down.

- Choose servers that can retain their identities for reasonable lengths of time. Hostname changes require mount maintenance, and hostid changes can make license passwords obsolete.

User Capacity

It is impossible to offer specific guidelines as to the number of servers you will require. Your goal is to provide reasonable NFS response time to all clients served. The user ratio you can support depends on many factors, such as the server characteristics, network characteristics, the types of applications being served, and the number of clients.

Try to locate application servers on the same network segments as the bulk of their clientele. As a rule, you obtain the best response if you minimize NFS traffic through routers and other store-and-forward network devices.

Compatible Services

It is probably simplest to dedicate a server exclusively as an application server. If, however, it is impossible or impractical to do so in your environment, you may need to implement a multipurpose server.

Certain services present little conflict with NFS service because of their light weight or typical scheduling. Examples include license service and backup service. Additional, nonapplication NFS roles, such as sharing client root or home directory file systems, may have some impact on application response time.

NOTE. *For its role as an NFS server, a platform need not be typical of the user base platforms. However, if an application server is also to act as a license server, it must be capable of running the license support binaries provided by the application vendors.*

Other functions are incompatible with optimum NFS performance because they make heavy CPU and I/O demands. Examples of incompatible functions include back-end database engine, development activity, and routing.

Disk Allocation

You need to allocate adequate space for applications on the server, allowing ample space to accommodate future additions. Also remember that you may need space for multiple versions of some applications as you transition users to newer versions.

As noted earlier, you want to serve applications from a single file system to minimize user mounts. If your overall application space requirements exceed the size of your largest disk, you may wish to use SunSoft's Online: DiskSuite.

This product lets you concatenate multiple physical disk slices into one logical metaslice. Online: DiskSuite offers other performance and high-availability enhancements such as striping, mirroring and "hot spare" capability.

File System Configuration

The following sections suggest a basic file system configuration for application servers. When you create one or more application servers, you generally provide a single file system with a consistent directory hierarchy. In that way, you create an environment that is consistent throughout your organization.

Basic Directories

When you have a server with a disk slice (partition) that you consider adequate for long-term use as an application server, you can begin to implement the file system itself. As a foundation, SunSoft recommends that you create a minimum of two standard directories, which, in this model, we name:

```
/usr/apps/exe
/usr/apps/pkgs
```

You install symbolic links that represent all the available commands used to execute applications in the /usr/apps/exe, the common command directory. You install all of the applications in the /usr/apps/pkgs directory.

Parallel Hierarchies

You may want to create one or more parallel file systems. For example, you might want to make a distinction between packages implemented by central administration and packages introduced by regional administration. You might also want to distinguish between production and beta versions of software.

If you want to create such parallel hierarchies, you could designate them as:

```
/usr/apps/local/pkgs
/usr/apps/local/exe
```

The /usr/apps/local/pkgs directory contains the applications, and the corresponding /usr/apps/local/exe directory would contain the symbolic links to the wrappers for those applications. With this type of arrangement you need to add a second path (/usr/apps/local/exe) to the users' environment. If you arrange the directory as a parallel hierarchy instead of a separate file system, you could use a single mount point. If you create a separate file system, users would need to have a second mount point.

Clearly there are more variations not presented here. It is important for you to determine your needs. Try to plan for the long term, and try to keep your setup as simple and as consistent as possible. At Sun it has, indeed, been possible to provide most application services through a single mount.

Transitory Names If you use wrappers, avoid the temptation to create a file system with directories that are named after architectures or other transitory distinctions, for example, /usr/apps/sun3. Packages are always present, but other distinctions come and go. Confine file system distinctions to individual application directories (which come and go themselves) where only the wrapper is impacted by changes.

Permissions Unless you have good reasons not to do so, permissions should be mode 755 for directories you create and for those within applications, so they are writable by owner, with read and execute for group and world. Sometimes vendors ship nonwriteable directories that interfere with your ability to transfer the contents to another system. In general, make other files writable by owner, and readable by all, while leaving execute permissions intact. You can change a directory hierarchy to the recommended permissions using the following commands:

```
$ /usr/bin/find directory-name -type d -exec /usr/bin/chmod 755 {} \;
$ /usr/bin/chmod -R u+w directory-name
$ /usr/bin/chmod -R ugo+r directory-name
$
```

Ownership If you set up or maintain an extensive network of application servers and update them using trusted host relationships, consider what account should own the software distribution. In general, you do not need to have root be the owner. You may find some security advantages to creating a special, nonprivileged ownership account to manage application servers.

File System Sharing

Before users can access files on the application server, you must share (export) the file system to make it available to other systems on the network. SunSoft strongly recommends that you share the applications file system read-only.

Follow these steps on the application server to share the file system:

1. Become superuser.

2. Edit the /etc/dfs/dfstab file and add the line

   ```
   share -F nfs -o ro pathname
   ```

3. Type **share** *pathname* and press Return.

In the following example, the pathname /usr/apps is shared:

```
oak% su
Password
# vi /etc/dfs/dfstab
[Add the following line]
```

```
share -F nfs -o ro /usr/apps
[Quit the file and save the changes]
# share /usr/apps
#
```

If you must start the NFS service manually, use the following steps. Otherwise, the services will be started at boot time.

1. Type **/usr/lib/nfs/nfsd 8** and press Return. You have started the NFS daemons.

2. Type **/usr/lib/nfs/mountd** and press Return. You have started the mount daemon.

3. Type **share -F nfs -o ro** *pathname* and press Return.

The *pathname* is the name of the mount point file system. For example, if you have mounted the partition as /usr/apps, type **share -F nfs -o ro /usr/apps** and press Return.

Installing and Configuring Packages

If the application is to be installed in a directory other than /opt, you need to set up either the package commands or the Software Manager to install the software in a different directory, and then install the software.

SunSoft suggests that you use a name for the application directory that reflects the actual product name (in lowercase for simplicity), with some sort of version suffix. For example, following the proposed naming convention, you might install version 2.0 of FooTool in the directory /usr/apps/pkgs/footool,v2.0.

Follow the vendor's directions to install the software. If the vendor's or developer's install procedure does not use the package commands, you may need to rename the directory after completing the vendor installation process. See Chapter 13 for instructions on how to use the package commands. See Chapter 14 for instructions on how to use the Software Manager.

Normally you should minimize any changes that you make to the original installed software. The flexibility of the wrapper helps you adapt to unusual requirements. You do, however, typically want to add some things to the package—at least, the wrapper itself. Create a subdirectory at the top level of the package to contain the wrapper and other possible additions. Such additions might include site-specific READMEs, announcements, and scripts that complete server-specific setup for the package. In the following example, the subdirectory is called dist.

```
$ cd /usr/apps/pkgs/footool,v2.0
$ /usr/bin/mkdir dist
$
```

Determine whether you think this directory needs to be subdivided further. If so, be sure to use a consistent naming convention. The location of the wrapper determines the form of the command name links that must connect to it. For the purpose of this illustration, we refer to the wrapper as being in the top level of this subdirectory, and named simply "wrapper." In other words:

```
/usr/apps/pkgs/footool,v2.0/dist/wrapper
```

In many application packages you must configure some of the files before the package can be run. If you are maintaining multiple application servers, consider the following:

1. Once you modify the original files, you may not have generic copies left. If you copy the package to another server, you may want the original files to match the vendor's setup documentation.

2. If you synchronize the package between servers after setup, be careful not to overwrite the server-specific setups with those from another server.

Consider how you want to handle such files. One way is to identify the files that are candidates for modification and to make copies of them where they reside, with a suffix such as ".orig." This convention preserves generic copies. You still must avoid shipping the modified versions of these files to other servers so that you do not overwrite local configurations that are already established.

Changes to the Default Package Version

Applications are installed into directories that identify their versions. Multiple versions can thus coexist at the same directory level. To identify the default version of a given application, create a generic directory name as a symbolic link pointing to the version-named directory you want to be the default.

In the following example, the /usr/apps/pkgs directory contains two versions of FooTool and a generic footool name link:

```
$ cd /usr/apps/pkgs
$ ls -ld footool*
lrwxrwxrwx   1 nobody    nobody        12 Jun 19  1992 /usr/apps/pkgs/footool ->
footool,v1.0
drwxr-xr-x   9 nobody    nobody       512 Jun 18  1992 /usr/apps/pkgs/footool,v1.0
drwxr-xr-x   9 nobody    nobody       512 May  3 21:23 /usr/apps/pkgs/footool,v2.0
$
```

The default version is footool,v1.0. If you want to change the default version to 2.0, remove the existing link and create a new link to version 2.0, as shown in the following example:

```
$ /usr/bin/rm footool
$ /usr/bin/ln -s footool,v2.0 footool
$ ls -ld footool*
lrwxrwxrwx   1 nobody    nobody         12 Jul 19 07:32 /usr/apps/pkgs/footool ->
footool,v2.0
drwxr-xr-x   9 nobody    nobody        512 Jun 18  1992 /usr/apps/pkgs/footool,v1.0
drwxr-xr-x   9 nobody    nobody        512 May  3 21:23 /usr/apps/pkgs/footool,v2.0
$
```

The version footool,v2.0 is the default for all users, because the symbolic links in /usr/apps/exe now point to a wrapper using a path that refers to the directory named footool. This path now leads to the wrapper in footool,v2.0.

Developing Wrappers

The information in the following sections describe some basic information about how to develop wrappers. Refer to Part VI of this book for an introduction to shell programming.

Interpreter Choice

You typically write wrapper scripts in an interpreted language so that they can execute on the various platform configurations in the environment. If you are going to write wrappers, you must decide which interpreter to use. Solaris 2.*x* provides three shells that make suitable interpreters for wrappers, as noted in Table 12.3.

Table 12.3   Available Shells

Shell	Description
/usr/bin/sh	Bourne shell
/usr/bin/ksh	Korn shell
/usr/bin/csh	C shell

SunSoft recommends that you use the Bourne shell to write wrappers. The Korn shell may not be available on some systems in the environment. Although the C shell is popular for interactive use, the Bourne shell is more advanced as a programming language. The Bourne shell supports functions—which result in code that is reusable in other wrappers—and the ability to pipe into and out of control constructs. The examples in this chapter use Bourne shell syntax.

NOTE. *In an environment that is so heterogeneous that even the Bourne shell is not universally available, you would have to seek yet another interpreter, possibly perl.*

The first line in a Bourne shell wrapper script is:

```
#!/bin/sh
```

Wrapper Directory and Naming

Create a subdirectory in the application directory, for example, /usr/apps/ pkgs/*application-name*/dist. Within that directory, create a wrapper that has the same name as the other wrappers. For example, name each wrapper "wrapper" (for example, /usr/apps/pkgs/*application-name*/dist/wrapper). When you use the same name for each application wrapper, it simplifies administration because you do not need to remember a host of different wrapper names. You can easily create links to any wrapper.

Command Name Evaluation

One of the first things a wrapper must do is evaluate the name that was used to invoke it. The wrapper has its own name. The wrapper name is different from any of the application command names, but the wrapper must know which command name it is being asked to represent.

For example, for package footool,v2.0, commands "foo" and "bar" are each links to the script called "wrapper" that is in the /usr/apps/pkgs/footool,v2.0/dist directory. When a user types **foo**, the wrapper learns the name used to invoke it from the construct $0. In this case $0 is /usr/apps/exe/foo. The /bin/basename command is used to strip the leading path, and "foo" is assigned to the variable "cmd," as follows:

```
cmd=`/bin/basename $0`
```

Environment Variables

Many applications require that environment variables be assigned before an application is executed. Environment variables are usually values that cannot be reliably predicted by the compiled code, such as the directory where the application is installed. Such variables must be set and exported to be available to subsequently executing processes, just as they would be from a user's dot files. In Bourne shell format, the syntax is as follows:

```
export FOOHOME
FOOHOME=/usr/apps/pkgs/footool,v2.0
```

NOTE. *You can export the environment variable either before or after you assign it a value.*

Platform Evaluation

Not all applications support all combinations of hardware platform and operating system that may be in your environment. Therefore, you need to evaluate the user's platform to see if service can be provided.

For example, if footool,v2.0 supports only the Sun4 platform, the code below (politely) declines service to all other platforms:

```
case $arch in
     sun4)
               ;;
     *)
               echo >&2 "Sorry, $cmd not available for $arch architecture."
               exit 1
               ;;
esac
```

Command Path Construction

Next, you define the variable command in terms of code that will yield the complete execution path to the application binary.

NOTE. *The wrapper may not, in fact, be executing the binary itself, but may be invoking a link that the vendor has routed through its own wrapper, as is the case with the product FrameMaker.*

In the footool,v2.0 wrapper, you might write a command path definition as shown below:

```
command=$FOOHOME/bin.$arch/$cmd
```

The command path definition could be more complex, or it could be as simple as that shown below:

```
command=$FOOHOME/bin/$cmd
```

Exec/Argument Passing

The wrapper has now made its assignments and calculations and has determined that the service is available for this user. It is time to hand off execution to the application and get out of the way, using the exec statement. The wrapper process has navigated to the correct binary and passed on the necessary environment. It then vanishes and imposes no further burden.

The last action of the wrapper is to make sure that any arguments the user included on the original command line get through exactly as expressed,

which is the purpose of the ${1+"$@"} construct at the end of the exec statement shown below:

```
exec $command ${1+"$@"}
```

A Basic Wrapper
At this point we have a wrapper that looks like this:

```
#!/bin/sh
        cmd=`/bin/basename $0`
        export FOOHOME
        FOOHOME=/usr/apps/pkgs/footool,v2.0
        case $arch in
            sun4)
                        ::
            *)
                        echo >&2 "Sorry, $cmd not available for $arch
                        architecture."
                        exit 1
                        ;;
        esac
        command=$FOOHOME/bin/$cmd
        exec $command ${1+"$@"}
```

The wrapper example is not quite complete; it does not consider how
$arch gets defined. The code necessary to assess architecture varies depend-
ing on the mix of platforms in the environment. However, in a given environment, you would need to use this same code for many wrappers. You can
create the code as a Bourne shell function that can be replicated in as many
wrappers as necessary.

In fact, for ease of maintenance, you might choose to make this code one
function among others in a library external to the wrappers themselves. The
wrappers requiring this function then merely source it from the library and
execute it at the appropriate point in the wrapper. In this way, you often can
carry out maintenance required by the wrappers by updating the library that
supports all the wrappers. Refer to Chapter 16 for some examples of wrapper
functions.

If you provide a function library, be sure to use a consistent naming convention so that the wrappers can access and source the wrapper functions.
You may want to apply the version-naming convention to this directory as
well. For example, you might create a directory named /usr/apps/library,v1.0.

When a function library exists, you use the functions in scripts by defining
the library location and sourcing the function script at the beginning of the
wrapper. Then, before you use the $arch variable, you set it, as defined in the
wrapper function. Then you would execute the function at the appropriate
point in the wrapper to return the values required. Remember, our wrapper
example here is very basic. The bold lines in the following example show the

additions made to the basic script. Refer to Chapter 16 for an example of the function arch.sh.fctn.

```
#!/bin/sh
library=/usr/apps/pkgs/library.v1.0
. $library/sh/arch.sh.fctn
cmd=`/bin/basename $0`
export FOOHOME
FOOHOME=/usr/apps/pkgs/footool.v2.0
arch=`Arch`
case $arch in
    sun4)
        ;;
    *)
        echo >&2 "Sorry, $cmd not available for $arch architecture."
        exit 1
        ;;
esac
command=$FOOHOME/bin/$cmd
exec $command ${1+"$@"}
```

Using a Common Command Directory

You want to create symbolic links for all application command names in the /usr/apps/exe directory. When you do so, users can access all of the software in the distribution with a single, unchanging path component.

If you choose to have a common command directory for a parallel hierarchy, as mentioned previously, two path components are sufficient to access the entire distribution.

The command names are symbolic links that point to the location of the wrapper for their application. For example, if the package FooTool 2.0 has the commands foo and bar, create these names as symbolic links in /usr/apps/exe as follows:

```
$ cd /usr/apps/exe
$ /usr/bin/ln -s /usr/apps/pkgs/footool/dist/wrapper foo
$ /usr/bin/ln -s /usr/apps/pkgs/footool/dist/wrapper bar
$ ls -l foo bar
lrwxrwxrwx  1 nobody   nobody        35 Apr  6  1992 foo ->
                                             /usr/apps/pkgs/footool/dist/wrapper
lrwxrwxrwx  1 nobody   nobody        35 Apr  6  1992 bar ->
                                             /usr/apps/pkgs/footool/dist/wrapper
```

Notice that the link destinations refer to the generic directory name link, footool, rather than explicitly to the footool.v2.0 directory. Use the generic directory name link for each package in this way to determine which version of the package the commands are connected to. The users start the default version of the software, and you can change the default version simply by changing the link that determines it.

You could link the command names via the specific version-named directory instead, but you would find that it requires more work and more exposure when you need to change from one version to another. This extra work might not be obvious when packages have only one or two commands, but some applications have many. FrameMaker, for instance, has more than 80 commands!

Setting User Configurations

The following sections describe what you need to do to set up the user environment to access files on the application server.

Mount Points

In a general implementation, each user system needs to have a mount point directory—for example, /usr/apps.

Mounts

You can mount files from an application server using NFS. You can mount files either by editing the /etc/vfstab or by using the automounter.

If you use the /etc/vfstab file, edit it on each user's system and add a line that looks like the following:

```
#device      device     mount     FS      fsck    mount      mount
#to mount    to fsck    point     type    pass    at boot    options
#
server-name:/usr/apps -  /usr/apps  nfs     -       yes        ro
```

For example, to mount from an application server named oak, become superuser and add the following line to the user's /etc/vfstab file:

```
oak:/usr/apps  -  /usr/apps  nfs  -  yes  ro
```

Refer to Part III of this book for information about setting up the automounter.

Path

Each user typically needs either one or two path components to access applications, depending on whether you implement a parallel hierarchy. The name of the second component depends on the naming scheme applied to the parallel hierarchy. Suppose the path components are:

```
/usr/apps/exe
/usr/apps/local/exe
```

The order in which you put the directories in the path is up to you. If you have applications with the same name in both directories, you may want priority applied to either the global or the local distribution. The placement in the path relative to the standard OS directories is significant only if you expect to encounter name conflicts with commands in those locations.

A path for Solaris 2.*x* users could conceivably be as simple as the following:

```
/usr/openwin/bin /usr/bin /usr/sbin /usr/apps/exe /usr/apps/local/exe
```

Migration Considerations

In migrating existing users to a new software scheme, you must (carefully) simplify their existing setups. Of course, they need the mount point and mount, and the path component(s). Beyond these, you must remove most of the other hard-coded settings, to allow the dynamic connections to operate. There are always exceptions, though, and some hard-coded setups remain appropriate.

Understanding Distribution Issues

If you must maintain multiple application servers and need to copy application packages (or entire file systems) from one to another, you probably want to become familiar with the rdist(1) command. It is a standard utility whose specialty is synchronizing file systems or portions of file systems between remote hosts. One of rdist's great advantages is that it compares the status of files between the source and destination systems and copies only those files that need updating. This procedure is more efficient in many cases than using tar, for example, which copies files unconditionally.

Unfortunately, the manual page for rdist does not provide clear guidelines for how to begin simply and scale to more sophisticated formats. The following paragraphs provide some suggestions for how to begin.

NOTE. *Be sure to begin with controlled experimentation and study of the rdist manual page so that you are not unpleasantly surprised by unexpected results.*

To be able to rdist from one system to another depends on some level of trusted host relationship. (That is, the UID using rdist must be able to log in to the remote system without a password.) You may want this account to be owned by a UID other than root.

Once this privilege exists, you can rdist a hierarchy from the local system to the same destination on the remote system with a command as simple as the following:

```
$ rdist -c /usr/apps remote-system
```

Perhaps the most common form of rdist is to refer to a file that lists the target host systems and the path names to be synchronized. When the file has been created, use the following syntax:

```
$ rdist -f distfile
```

You may encounter limitations because rdist distfiles cannot use actual shell variables for flexibility. However, you can work around this limitation by creating a script in which the shell expands variables before feeding the resulting syntax to rdist. The format of such a script is shown below, and is the beginning of the power needed to use rdist to perform flexible, selective updates.

```
#!/bin/sh
files="
pathname1
pathname2
. . .
"
hosts="
host1
host2
. . .
"
rdist -f - <<-EOrdist
("$files")
-> ("$hosts")
EOrdist
```

NOTE. *Beware of using rcp -r to copy hierarchies. In the process, symbolic links get converted to actual copies of their destination files. This conversion not only can affect the amount of space occupied, but can produce unexpected behavior. You may later make changes to link destination files, such as wrappers, not realizing that command names have become outdated copies of the script itself.*

Licensing

Many SunSoft unbundled products and application software packages require software licenses that control the number of users who can access the product at the same time. If the application software has a floating license system, you can also designate the application server as a license server. Alternatively, a single license server can manage licenses for multiple application servers, provided the license server is accessible to all the application servers across an existing network.

A full description of all the available types of licenses and license servers is beyond the scope of this book. Following are three possible configurations for setting up license servers:

1. Single independent license server: All licenses are handled by a single server.

2. Multiple independent license servers: You can have as many independent license servers as you have systems on the network. Each license server is configured independently, and you must obtain individual license passwords for each independent server system.

3. Multiple redundant license servers: You can define a set of servers that operate together to emulate a single independent license server configuration. A redundant license server configuration improves the stability of a license system and ensures that licensed products will not shut down as long as the majority of your license servers are running. You must obtain a license password for each set of redundant license servers. When you define a set of redundant license servers, you must administer them as a set. If you add a license password to one of the servers in the set, you must add it to all other license servers in the set.

CD-ROM Mounts

The following sections describe how to access files on a CD-ROM from a local drive on a system running Solaris 2.2 (and later) system software, from a local drive on a system running Solaris 2.0 and 2.1, and from a remote drive.

Using a Local CD-ROM Drive (Solaris 2.2 System Software)

With Solaris 2.2 system software (and later), the CD-ROM is automatically mounted for you when you insert a CD-ROM caddy into the CD-ROM drive. Use the following procedures if you are running Solaris 2.2 system software or later. (If you are running Solaris 2.0 or 2.1 system software, use the procedures described in the section "Using a Local CD-ROM Drive (Solaris 2.0 or 2.1 System Software).")

NOTE. *Diskettes are also automatically mounted using the Solaris 2.2 volume management software. See Appendix A for more information.*

To access files from a local CD-ROM drive with Solaris 2.2 (and beyond) system software, you do not need to have superuser privileges or create a mount point. Simply insert the CD-ROM disc into the disc caddy and insert the disc caddy into the CD-ROM drive. The /cdrom mount

point is created and the files are mounted. The /cdrom directory contains a cdrom0 subdirectory that is a symbolic link to the volume name of the CD-ROM. You can type either **cd /cdrom/cdrom0** or **cd /cdrom/*cdrom-name*** to access the files.

Using a Local CD-ROM Drive (Solaris 2.0 or 2.1 System Software)

Follow these procedures to mount a CD-ROM from a command line.

1. Become superuser.

2. Insert the CD-ROM disc into the caddy and insert the caddy into the CD-ROM drive.

3. Type **mkdir /cdrom** and press Return. You have created a mount point directory named /cdrom.

4. Type **mount -F** *file-system-type* **-o ro /dev/dsk/c0t6d0s2 /cdrom** and press Return. For UNIX file system type, use -F ufs; for High Sierra file system type, use -F hsfs. The files are mounted on the /cdrom mount point.

   If you want to simplify the mount process, you can add an entry to the /etc/vfstab file, as shown in the following steps:

1. Become superuser

2. Edit the /etc/vfstab file and add the following entry. If the *file-system-type* is UNIX, use ufs; if the *file-system-type* is High Sierra, use hsfs:

   ```
   /dev/dsk/c0t6d0s2  -  /cdrom   file-system-type  -  no  ro
   ```

3. Insert the CD-ROM disc into the caddy and insert the caddy into the CD-ROM drive.

4. Type **mount /cdrom** and press Return. The CD-ROM files are mounted.

Accessing Files from a Remote CD-ROM

These sections tell you how to set up a Solaris 2.*x* system with a remote CD-ROM drive to share files. The following procedure for sharing files works for Solaris 2.2 releases or greater.

How to Share CD Files from a Remote CD-ROM drive

Before you can share CD-ROM files from a command line, the mountd daemon must be running. To find out if the mountd daemon is running, and to start it, if necessary, you'll need to do the following:

1. On the system with the CD-ROM drive attached, type **ps -ef | grep mountd** and press Return. If the mountd daemon is running, other systems can access shared files. However, if the mountd daemon is not running, you will need to stop NFS services and restart them. Be sure to notify any users of the system that NFS services will momentarily be interrupted.

2. Become superuser.

3. Type **/etc/rc3.d/S15nfs.server stop** and press Return. The NFS services are stopped.

4. Type **/etc/rc3.d/S15nfs.server start** and press Return. The NFS services are restarted and the CD files are exported.

   Use the following steps to share CD files from a remote CD-ROM drive:

1. Insert the CD-ROM into the caddy and insert the caddy into the drive. The CD-ROM is mounted.

2. Become superuser on the Solaris 2.2 system with the CD-ROM drive attached.

3. Type **share -F nfs -o ro /cdrom/cdrom0** and press Return.

NOTE. *Volume management does not recognize entries in the /etc/dfs/dfstab file. With Solaris 2.3 volume management, you can set up remote CD-ROM mounts by editing the /etc/rmmount.conf file. Refer to the rmmount.conf manual page for more information.*

```
oak% ps -ef | grep mountd
    root   4571  4473  5 12:53:51 pts/3    0:00 grep mountd
oak% su
Password:
# /etc/rc3.d/S15nfs.server stop
# /etc/rc3.d/S15nfs.server start
# share -F nfs -o ro /cdrom/cdrom0
# ps -ef | grep mountd
    root   4655  4473  6 12:56:05 pts/3    0:00 grep mountd
    root   4649     1 47 12:55:25 ?        0:00 /usr/lib/nfs/mountd
```

How to Access Shared CD-ROM Files

You can use the /mnt directory as the mount point for the CD-ROM files, or create another directory.

NOTE. *Do not use the /cdrom mount point to mount local files. Volume management may interfere with accessing files on the volume management /cdrom mount point.*

Once the CD-ROM is in the remote drive and the files are shared, follow these steps to access the shared files on a local system:

1. On the local system, become superuser.

2. Type **mount** *remote-system-name***:/cdrom/cdrom0** */mount-point* and press Return. The files from the remote system directory /cdrom/cdrom0 are mounted on the */mount-point* directory. The cdrom0 subdirectory is symbolically linked to the actual name of the CD-ROM, which has a name assigned by the application vendor.

In the following example, the files from the remote system castle are mounted on the /mnt mount point.

```
oak% su
Password:
# mount castle:/cdrom/cdrom0 /mnt
# cd /mnt
# ls
SUNWssser  SUNWsssra  SUNWsssrb  SUNWsssrc  SUNWsssrd  SUNWsssstr
#
```

How to Unmount Shared CD-ROM Files

When you are through using the CD-ROM files, use the following steps to unmount the remote CD-ROM:

1. On the local system, become superuser.

2. Type **cd** and press Return.

3. Type **umount** */mount-point* and press Return. The files from the remote system directory /cdrom/cdrom0 are unmounted.

Package Commands

THIS CHAPTER DESCRIBES HOW TO USE THE SOLARIS 2.*X* PACKAGE COMMANDS to install, remove, and administer software.

Package Command-Line Utilities

You manage software from a command line using the commands shown in Table 13.1.The package commands are located in the /usr/sbin directory. You must have superuser privileges to use the pkgadd and pkgrm commands.

Table 13.1   **Package Commands**

Task	Command
Set installation defaults	vi(1) admin(4)
Create a script to define installation parameters	pkgask(1M)
Install software package or store files for installation at a later time	pkgadd(1M)
Check accuracy of installation	pkgchk(1M)
List installed packages	pkginfo(1M)
Remove packages	pkgrm(1M)

Before adding a package, insert the CD-ROM into its caddy and mount the CD-ROM following the instructions at the end of Chapter 12.

Setting Up Package Configuration Files

The pkgadd and pkgrm files, by default, use information from the /var/sadm/install/admin/default file, shown below.

```
oak% more /var/sadm/install/admin/default
#ident      "@(#)default1.492/12/23 SMI"/* SVr4.0  1.5.2.1*/
mail=
instance=unique
partial=ask
runlevel=ask
idepend=ask
rdepend=ask
space=ask
setuid=ask
conflict=ask
```

```
action=ask
basedir=default
oak%
```

The parameters in this file are a set of *parameter=value* pairs, each on a separate line. If you do not want to use the default values, you can create an admin file and set different values. Table 13.2 lists and describes the parameters and shows the available values.

Table 13.2   Package Administration Options

Parameter	Description	Possible Value
mail	Who will receive mail about installation or removal?	*user-name*
instance	Package already installed.	ask overwrite unique quit
partial	Partial package installed.	ask nocheck quit
runlevel	Is run level correct?	ask nocheck quit
idepend	Are package dependencies met?	ask nocheck quit
rdepend	Is there a dependency on other packages?	ask nocheck quit
space	Is disk space adequate?	ask nocheck quit
setuid	Ask permission to setuid?	ask nocheck quit nochange

Table 13.2 **Package Administration Options (Continued)**

Parameter	Description	Possible Value
conflict	Will overwriting a file cause conflict with other packages?	ask nocheck quit nochange
action	Check for security impact?	ask nocheck quit
basedir	Set base install directory. ($PKGINST creates a default directory with the same name as the package.)	default $PKGINST /path /path/$PKGINST

NOTE. *Do not edit the /var/sadm/install/admin/default file. If you want to change the defaults, create your own admin file.*

If you create a custom admin file and specify it from the command line using the -a admin option, the pkgadd and pkgrm commands automatically look for the file in the /var/sadm/install/admin directory. If you put the admin file in another directory, you must specify the absolute path name for the file as part of the command-line argument.

To create an admin file, use any editor. Define each parameter=value pair on a single line. You do not need to assign values to all 11 parameters. If you do not assign a value and pkgadd needs one, it will use the default value "ask."

NOTE. *You cannot define the value "ask" in an admin file for use with non-interactive installation. Installation will fail when a problem occurs.*

The following example shows an admin file created to automatically install files in the /usr/apps/pkgs directory and to use the default values for other parameters:

```
oak% more /var/sadm/install/admin/admin
mail=
instance=unique
partial=ask
runlevel=ask
idepend=ask
rdepend=ask
space=ask
```

```
setuid=ask
conflict=ask
action=ask
basedir=/usr/apps/pkgs/$PKGINST
oak%
```

Setting Up the Installation Base Directory

Before you begin software installation, decide where you want to install the software. If you want to install in a directory other than /opt, create an admin file in /var/sadm/install/admin/admin and set the basedir parameter to the directory where you want to install the software. If basedir is the only parameter you want to change, you can create an admin file that contains only one parameter. All other parameters use the default values. See Table 13.2, earlier in the chapter, for a description of the other parameters you can customize.

The following steps show how to create an admin file that installs files in the /usr/apps/pkgs directory and uses the name of the package as the directory name, and how to use the admin file to control installation:

1. Become superuser.

2. Type **cd /var/sadm/install/admin** and press Return.

3. Use any editor to create a file. Assign the file any name you like, other than the name "default." A suggested file name is "admin."

4. Type **basedir=/usr/apps/pkgs/$PKGINST** to the file.

5. Save the changes and quit.

Installing a Package with an Alternative Admin File

Unless you specify a different administrative file, the pkgadd command uses the /var/sadm/install/admin/default file, which specifies the base directory as /opt. To use an alternative admin file, use the following syntax:

```
pkgadd -d device -a admin-file pkgid
```

The following example installs the package SUNWssser from the CD-ROM device using an admin file named "admin":

```
# pkgadd -d /cdrom/cdrom0 -a admin SUNWssser
```

Adding Packages

Use the pkgadd command to install software packages. The default pkgadd command is interactive and can inform you of potential problems in the installation as they occur.

NOTE. *You must have superuser privileges to use the pkgadd command.*

The syntax of the pkgadd command is:

```
pkgadd -d device-name [ -a admin-file ] pkgid
```

For example, to interactively install a software package named SUNWpkgA from a directory named /cdrom/cdrom0, you would type **/usr/sbin/pkgadd -d /cdrom/cdrom0 SUNWssser** and press Return. To install the same software package using an alternative administrative file named admin, type **/usr/sbin/pkgadd -d /cdrom/cdrom0 -a admin SUNWssser** and press Return. See "Setting Up Package Configuration Files" earlier in this chapter for information about package administrative files.

You can install multiple packages from the command line by typing a list of *pkgids* separated by spaces. The following example shows an edited example of installation of SearchIt 2.0 software from the /cdrom/cdrom0 directory:

```
# pkgadd -d /cdrom/cdrom0 SUNWssser SUNWsssra SUNWsssrb SUNWsssrc SUNWsssrd
SUNWssstr

Processing package instance <SUNWssser> from </cdrom/cdrom0>

SearchIt Text Messages and Handbook
(sparc) 2.0

(C) 1992, 1993 Sun Microsystems, Inc. Printed in the United States of America.
2550 Garcia Avenue, Mountain View, California, 94043-1100
U.S.A.

(Additional copyright information not shown)

Using </opt> as the package base directory.
## Processing package information.
## Processing system information.
## Verifying package dependencies.
WARNING:
    The <SUNWsssra> package "SearchIt Runtime 1 of 3" is a
    prerequisite package and should be installed.

Do you want to continue with the installation of this package [y,n,?] y
## Verifying disk space requirements.
## Checking for conflicts with packages already installed.

The following files are already installed on the system and are being
```

used by another package:
        /opt <attribute change only>

Do you want to install these conflicting files [y,n,?,q] **y**
Checking for setuid/setgid programs.

Installing SearchIt Text Messages and Handbook as <SUNWssser>

Installing part 1 of 1.
/opt/SUNWssoft/SearchIt/share/locale/C/LC_HELP/Home.info
/opt/SUNWssoft/SearchIt/share/locale/C/LC_HELP/Index.info
/opt/SUNWssoft/SearchIt/share/locale/C/LC_HELP/Search.info
/opt/SUNWssoft/SearchIt/share/locale/C/LC_HELP/SearchIt.handbook
/opt/SUNWssoft/SearchIt/share/locale/C/LC_HELP/SearchIt.info
/opt/SUNWssoft/SearchIt/share/locale/C/LC_HELP/Viewer.info
/opt/SUNWssoft/SearchIt/share/locale/C/LC_MESSAGES/SUNW_SEARCHIT_LABELS.po
/opt/SUNWssoft/SearchIt/share/locale/C/LC_MESSAGES/SUNW_SEARCHIT_MESSAGES.po
/opt/SUNWssoft/SearchIt/share/locale/C/LC_MESSAGES/SUNW_SEARCHIT_XVBROWSER.po
[verifying class <none>]

Installation of <SUNWssser> was successful.

Processing package instance <SUNWsssra> from </cdrom/cdrom0>

SearchIt Runtime 1 of 3
(sparc) 2.0

(*Copyright information not shown*)

Using </opt> as the package base directory.
Processing package information.
Processing system information.
   3 package pathnames are already properly installed.
Verifying package dependencies.
WARNING:
    The <SUNWsssrb> package "SearchIt Runtime 2 of 3" is a
    prerequisite package and should be installed.
WARNING:
    The <SUNWsssrc> package "SearchIt Runtime 3 of 3" is a
    prerequisite package and should be installed.

Do you want to continue with the installation of this package [y,n,?] **y**
Verifying disk space requirements.
Checking for conflicts with packages already installed.
Checking for setuid/setgid programs.

Installing SearchIt Runtime 1 of 3 as <SUNWsssra>

Installing part 1 of 1.
/opt/SUNWssoft/SearchIt/README
/opt/SUNWssoft/SearchIt/bin/auto_index
/opt/SUNWssoft/SearchIt/bin/browseui

```
/opt/SUNWssoft/SearchIt/bin/catopen
/opt/SUNWssoft/SearchIt/bin/collectionui
(Additional files not shown)
[ verifying class <none> ]

Installation of <SUNWsssra> was successful.

Processing package instance <SUNWsssrb> from </cdrom/cdrom0>

SearchIt Runtime 2 of 3
(sparc) 2.0

(Copyright information not shown)

Using </opt> as the package base directory.
## Processing package information.
## Processing system information.
   4 package pathnames are already properly installed.
## Verifying package dependencies.
## Verifying disk space requirements.
## Checking for conflicts with packages already installed.
## Checking for setuid/setgid programs.

Installing SearchIt Runtime 2 of 3 as <SUNWsssrb>

## Installing part 1 of 1.
/opt/SUNWssoft/SearchIt/lib/fultext/fultext.ftc
/opt/SUNWssoft/SearchIt/lib/fultext/fultext.stp
/opt/SUNWssoft/SearchIt/lib/libft.so.1
[ verifying class <none> ]

(Additional package installations not shown)
```

When you do not use the -d option to pkgadd to specify the device, the command checks the default spool directory, /var/spool/pkg. If the package is not there, installation fails. You must specify a full (absolute) path name to a device or a directory following the -d option.

If pkgadd encounters a problem, information about the problem is displayed along with the prompt "Do you want to continue with this installation of the package?" Type **yes**, **no**, or **quit**. Typing "yes" continues with the installation. If you have specified more than one package, typing "no" stops the installation of the package that failed, but continues with installation of the other packages. Typing "quit" stops installation of all packages.

Checking the Installation of a Package

You can use the pkgchk command to check the completeness, specific path name, file contents, and file attributes of an installed package.

The syntax of the pkgcheck command is:

```
pkgchk pkgid
```

For example, to check the package SUNWman, the on-line manual pages, type **pkgchk SUNWman** and press Return. If the prompt is returned with no messages, the package is properly installed.

```
oak% pkgchk SUNWman
oak%
```

If messages are displayed, the package is not properly installed, as shown in the following example:

```
oak% pkgchk SUNWssoft
WARNING: no pathnames were associated with <SUNWssoft>
oak%
```

You can specify more than one package identifier by typing a list separated by spaces. If you do not specify a *pkgid*, the complete list of packages on a system is checked.

You can check the installation completeness of a specific path name using the -p option to pkgchk with the following syntax:

```
pkgchk -p pathname
```

If you want to check more than one path, provide them as a comma-separated list.

You can check the installation completeness of just the file attributes using the -a option to the pkgchk command. You can check the installation completeness of just the file contents using the -c option to the pkgchk command. The syntax is shown below:

```
# /usr/sbin/pkgchk [ -a | -c ] pkgid
```

To check the completeness of a spooled package, use the -d option to the pkgchk command. This option looks in the specified directory or on the specified device and performs a check of the package. For example:

```
# /usr/sbin/pkgchk -d spool-dir pkgA
```

In this example, the pkgchk command looks in the spool directory *spool-dir* and checks the completeness of the package named pkgA.

NOTE. *Spooled package checks are limited because not all information can be audited until a package is installed.*

Listing Packages

If you need to check which packages are installed on a system, use the pkginfo command. The default is to display information about currently installed packages. You can also use the pkginfo command to display packages that are on mounted distribution media.

Use the command pkginfo with no arguments to list all installed packages. The following example shows the first few packages from a system:

```
[48]castle{winsor}% pkginfo
system    SUNWadmap    System & Network Administration Applications
system    SUNWadmfw    System & Network Administration Framework
system    SUNWadmr     System & Network Administration Root
system    SUNWarc      Archive Libraries
system    SUNWaudio    Audio applications
system    SUNWbcp      Binary Compatibility
system    SUNWbtool    CCS tools bundled with SunOS
system    SUNWcar      Core Architecture, (Root)
(Additional packages not shown in this example)
```

You can display information about a single package using the following syntax:

```
pkginfo pkgid
```

In the following example, information is displayed for the SUNWsteNP package:

```
oak% pkginfo SUNWsteNP
application SUNWsteNP       NeWSprint
oak%
```

To display information about packages on a CD-ROM, mount the CD-ROM following the instructions at the end of Chapter 12. Then use the following syntax to display a complete list of packages on the CD-ROM:

```
oak% pkginfo -d /cdrom/cdrom-name
```

You can display information about single packages on a CD-ROM using the following syntax:

```
oak% pkginfo -d /cdrom/cdrom-name pkgid
```

Removing Packages

Under previous releases of SunOS, you could remove unbundled software packages using the rm(1) command. With Solaris 2.x system software, you should always use the pkgrm command to remove packages. The pkgrm command makes administration easier by removing a complete unbundled package with a single command.

Use the following syntax to remove a package in interactive mode:

/usr/sbin/pkgrm *pkgid*

In the following example, the package SUNWdiag is removed:

```
oak% su
Password:
# pkgrm SUNWdiag

The following package is currently installed:
   SUNWdiag        Online Diagnostics Tool
                   (sparc) 2.1

Do you want to remove this package [y,n,?,q] y

## Removing installed package instance <SUNWdiag>
## Verifying package dependencies.
## Processing package information.
## Removing pathnames in <none> class
/opt/SUNWdiag/lib/libtest.a
/opt/SUNWdiag/lib
/opt/SUNWdiag/include/sdrtns.h
/opt/SUNWdiag/include
/opt/SUNWdiag/bin/what_rev
/opt/SUNWdiag/bin/vmem
/opt/SUNWdiag/bin/tapetest
/opt/SUNWdiag/bin/sunlink
/opt/SUNWdiag/bin/sundials
/opt/SUNWdiag/bin/sundiagup
/opt/SUNWdiag/bin/sundiag.info
/opt/SUNWdiag/bin/sundiag
/opt/SUNWdiag/bin/sunbuttons
/opt/SUNWdiag/bin/sptest
/opt/SUNWdiag/bin/revision_ref_file
/opt/SUNWdiag/bin/rawtest
/opt/SUNWdiag/bin/prp
/opt/SUNWdiag/bin/probe
/opt/SUNWdiag/bin/pmem
/opt/SUNWdiag/bin/nettest
/opt/SUNWdiag/bin/music.au
/opt/SUNWdiag/bin/mptest
/opt/SUNWdiag/bin/lpvitest
/opt/SUNWdiag/bin/isdntest
/opt/SUNWdiag/bin/gttest.data
/opt/SUNWdiag/bin/gttest
/opt/SUNWdiag/bin/fstest
/opt/SUNWdiag/bin/fputest
```

```
/opt/SUNWdiag/bin/fbtest
/opt/SUNWdiag/bin/dispatcher
/opt/SUNWdiag/bin/diagscrnprnt
/opt/SUNWdiag/bin/cg6test
/opt/SUNWdiag/bin/cg12.data.gsxr
/opt/SUNWdiag/bin/cg12.data
/opt/SUNWdiag/bin/cg12
/opt/SUNWdiag/bin/cdtest
/opt/SUNWdiag/bin/cbrtest
/opt/SUNWdiag/bin/bpptest
/opt/SUNWdiag/bin/autest.data
/opt/SUNWdiag/bin/autest
/opt/SUNWdiag/bin/audbri
/opt/SUNWdiag/bin/57fonts.400
/opt/SUNWdiag/bin/57fonts.300
/opt/SUNWdiag/bin
/opt/SUNWdiag
## Updating system information.

Removal of <SUNWdiag> was successful.
#
```

To remove a package in noninteractive mode, use the -n option to the pkgrm command, as shown below:

/usr/sbin/pkgrm -n *pkgid*

To remove a package that was spooled to a directory, use the -s option to the pkgrm command, as shown below:

/usr/sbin/pkgrm -s *spooldir* [*pkgid*]

In this example, *spooldir* is the name of the spool directory where the unbundled package was spooled and *pkgid* is the name of the package to be removed. When you do not supply a package identifier, pkgrm interactively prompts you to remove or preserve each package listed in the spool directory.

Package System Log File

The package commands maintain a list of installed packages in the /var/sadm/install/contents file. No tools are available to list the files contained in a package. The following example shows the first ten lines of the /var/sadm/install/contents file:

```
oak% head contents
/bin=./usr/bin s none SUNWcsr
/dev d none 0775 root sys SUNWcsr SUNWcsd
/dev/conslog=../devices/pseudo/log:conslog s none SUNWcsd
/dev/console=../devices/pseudo/cn:console s none SUNWcsd
```

```
/dev/dsk d none 0775 root sys SUNWcsd
/dev/fd d none 0775 root sys SUNWcsd
/dev/ie=../devices/pseudo/clone:ie s none SUNWcsd
/dev/ip=../devices/pseudo/clone:ip s none SUNWcsd
/dev/kmem=../devices/pseudo/mm:kmem s none SUNWcsd
/dev/ksyms=../devices/pseudo/ksyms:ksyms s none SUNWcsd
oak%
```

If you need to determine which package contains a particular file, you can use the grep command to search the package system file. In the following example, using the grep command to search for information about the pkgadd command shows that the command is part of the SUNWcsu package and is located in /usr/sbin. A manual page for the pkgadd command is part of the SUNWman package, and is located in /usr/share/man/man1m.

```
oak% grep pkgadd /var/sadm/install/contents
/usr/sbin/pkgadd f none 0500 root sys 77472 53095 733241518 SUNWcsu
/usr/share/man/man1m/pkgadd.1m f none 0444 bin bin 3784 63018 732833371 SUNWman
# Last modified by pkgadd for SUNWsteNP package
oak%
```

14

Software Manager

SOFTWARE MANAGER (SWMTOOL) IS AN OPENWINDOWS APPLICATION that you can use to install and remove unbundled software packages on a Solaris 2.*x* system.

Software that is designed to be managed using the Software Manager groups the packages into a set of clusters to make software management easier. The Software Manager calls the package commands. You can use the package commands and the Software Manager interchangeably. For example, you can install software using the Software Manager and remove the software using the pkgrm command. Alternatively, you can install software using the pkgadd command and remove that software using the Software Manager. The Software Manager displays all packages installed on a system, regardless of how they were installed.

The Software Manager provides the following functionality:

- Displays a list of the software packages installed on a local system, showing the full title, package names, icons, and the size of each package

- Installs and removes software on a local or a remote Solaris 2.*x* system

- Lets you specify the directory from which to install the software

Starting the Software Manager

The Software Manager executable, swmtool, is in the /usr/sbin directory. Use the following steps to start the Software Manager.

NOTE. *You must run Software Manager as superuser to install or remove software. If you want to configure a remote system, you must have superuser access to that system.*

1. Become superuser. Log in as root, or become superuser, if you have not done so already.

```
oak% su
Password: <your root password>
oak#
```

2. Type **swmtool &** and press Return. The Software Manager window is displayed and Install mode is selected, as shown in Figure 14.1.

```
oak# /usr/sbin/swmtool &
```

Customizing Installation

Before you begin installing software, you can customize some of the installation parameters to minimize or maximize the amount of operator intervention required during installation.

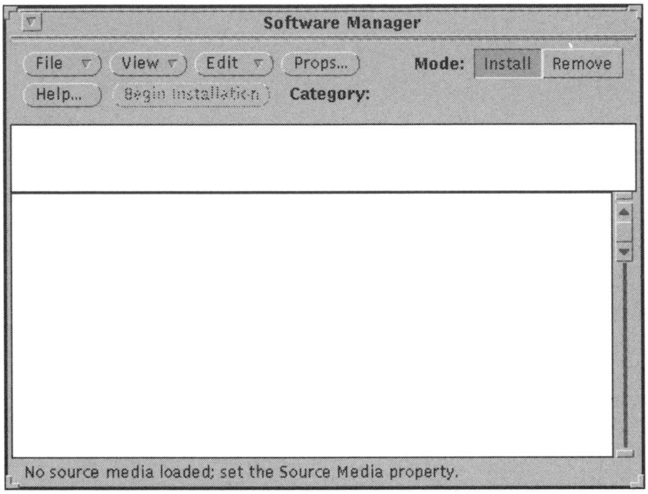

Figure 14.1
Software Manager
base window

Use the following steps to customize installation:

1. Click SELECT on the Props button. The Software Manager: Properties window is displayed, as shown in Figure 14.2.

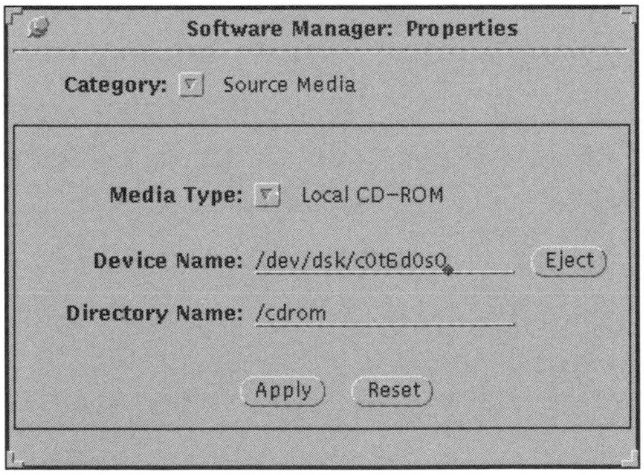

Figure 14.2
Display the Software
Manager: Properties
window.

2. Choose Package Administration from the Category menu, as shown in Figure 14.3. The Package Administration settings are displayed, as shown in Figure 14.4.

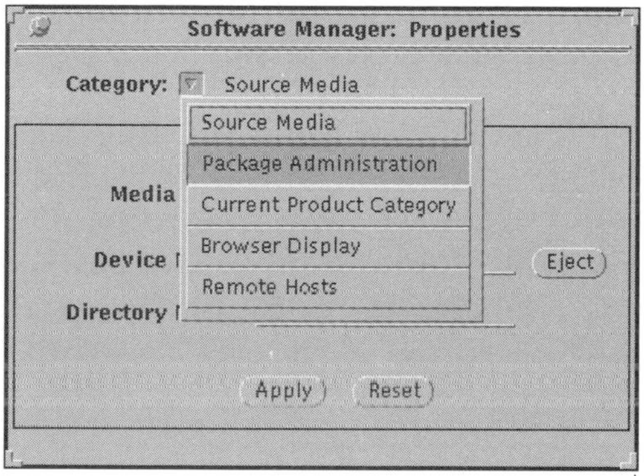

Figure 14.3

Choose Package
Administration from
the Category menu.

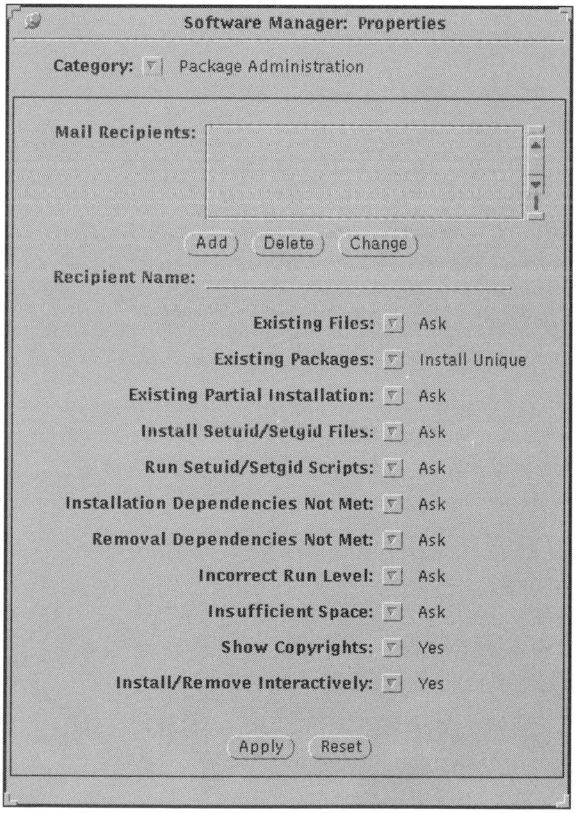

Software Manager: Properties

Category: ▽ Source Media

- Source Media
- Package Administration
- Current Product Category
- Browser Display
- Remote Hosts

Media

Device

(Eject)

Directory

(Apply)   (Reset)

Figure 14.4

The Package
Administration
control settings

Software Manager: Properties

Category: ▽ Package Administration

Mail Recipients:

(Add)   (Delete)   (Change)

Recipient Name:

Existing Files: ▽ Ask

Existing Packages: ▽ Install Unique

Existing Partial Installation: ▽ Ask

Install Setuid/Setgid Files: ▽ Ask

Run Setuid/Setgid Scripts: ▽ Ask

Installation Dependencies Not Met: ▽ Ask

Removal Dependencies Not Met: ▽ Ask

Incorrect Run Level: ▽ Ask

Insufficient Space: ▽ Ask

Show Copyrights: ▽ Yes

Install/Remove Interactively: ▽ Yes

(Apply)   (Reset)

You can specify who will receive mail about installation and removal by editing the contents of the scrolling list. To add a user, type the user name in the Recipient Name text field and click SELECT on the Add button. To delete an entry, click SELECT on the entry to select it and then click SELECT on the Delete button. To change an entry, click SELECT on the entry to select it, edit the entry in the Recipient Name text field, and click SELECT on Change.

Table 14.1 lists the settings that you can control. You can choose one of the available options for each setting. The first option for each setting is the default. The default settings are the most interactive.

Table 14.1   **Software Manager Package Administration Settings**

Setting	Available Options
Existing Files	Ask/Overwrite/Skip/Abort
Existing Packages	Ask/Overwrite/Install Unique/Abort
Existing Partial Installation	Ask/Ignore/Abort
Install Setuid/Setgid Files	Ask/Yes/No/Abort
Run Setuid/Setgid Scripts	Ask/Yes/Abort
Installation Dependencies Not Met	Ask/Ignore/Abort
Removal Dependencies Not Met	Ask/Ignore/Abort
Insufficient Space	Ask/Ignore/Abort
Show Copyrights	Yes/No
Install/Remove Interactively	Yes/No

3. When you have chosen the settings you want to use, click SELECT on the Apply button.

Installing Software

If necessary, click SELECT on the Install mode setting in the Software Manager base window to prepare for installation.

Accessing Files on a Local CD-ROM

Use the following steps to access files on a local CD-ROM:

1. If the Software Manager: Properties window is displayed, choose Source Media from the Category menu. Otherwise, Click SELECT on the Props button. The Software Manager: Properties window is displayed. If the Source Media settings shown in Figure 14.5 are not displayed, choose Source Media from the Category menu.

Figure 14.5

The Software Manager: Properties window

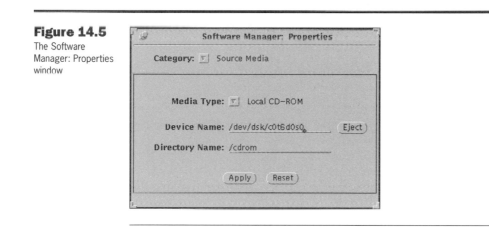

2. Choose Mounted Directory from the Media Type menu, as shown in Figure 14.6.

Figure 14.6

Choose Media Type.

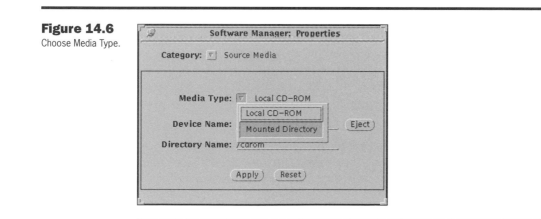

3. Type the name of the CD-ROM directory in the Directory Name text field. The /cdrom directory always has a /cdrom0 subdirectory that is a symbolic link to the name of the directory. You can type either **/cdrom/-cdrom0** or **/cdrom/*directory-name*** in the text field. If you are installing packages from the Solaris 2.*x* CD-ROM, the path is /cdrom/cdrom0/s0. In the example shown in Figure 14.7, the Directory Name is /cdrom/cdrom0.

Figure 14.7

Enter the mount point directory name.

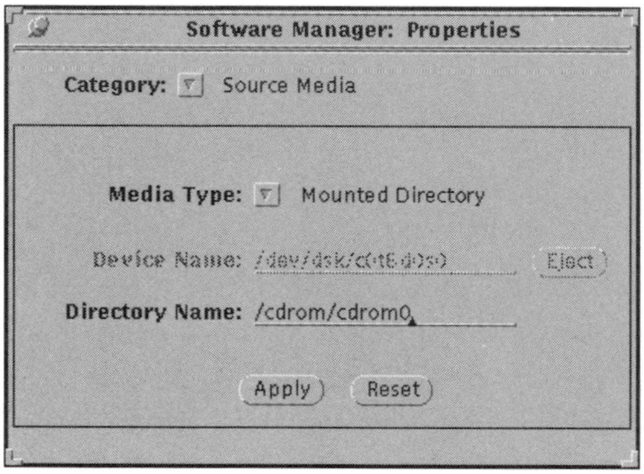

4. Click SELECT on the Apply button. The name of the cluster is displayed in the top pane of the Software Manager base window, and the available clusters and space requirements are displayed in the bottom pane. In the example shown in Figure 14.8, the name of the CD-ROM directory is un-named_cdrom#1, and three SearchIt™ clusters are available for installation.

Setting Up a Remote Host for Installation

You can use Software Manager to install files on a remote system using the local CD-ROM. Before you can use Software Manager to install or remove files on a remote system, however, you must first provide the name of the remote system to the Software Manager.

NOTE. *You will need superuser access to the remote system that you want to identify to the Software Manager. You can gain superuser access in two ways—knowing the superuser password for the remote system, or making sure that the remote systems has a .rhosts entry that allows unrestricted superuser access from the system on which you are running Software Manager.*

Figure 14.8
CD-ROM files are
displayed.

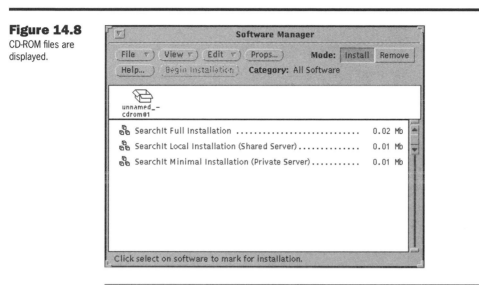

Use the following steps to access files on a local CD-ROM:

1. Click SELECT on the Props button. The Software Manager: Properties window is displayed.

2. Choose Remote Hosts from the Category menu, as shown in Figure 14.9. The Properties window display changes to show the settings for Remote Hosts, as shown in Figure 14.10. The local system is selected as the target host, by default.

Figure 14.9
Choose Remote
Hosts from the
category menu.

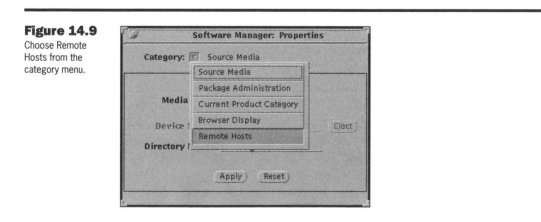

Figure 14.10
Remote Hosts
settings

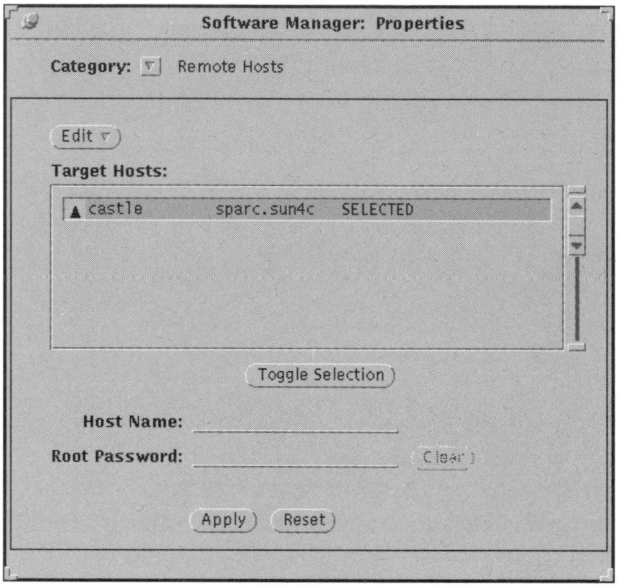

3. Type the name of the remote host in the Host Name text field, and the root password for the remote host (if required) in the Root Password text field, as shown in Figure 14.11. Note that, for security, the root password is not displayed. When the Root Password text field has information in it, the Clear button is active. (Click SELECT on the Clear button to clear the entry from the Root Password field.)

NOTE.　*A root password may not be required if the .rhosts file has an entry for that system. You can find out if you need a password by entering just the host name and adding the host. If a password is required, the required root password glyph (a circle with a line through it) is displayed. You can then enter the password and use the Change command from the Edit menu to modify the entry.*

4. Choose Add Entry, and a location from the Edit menu, as shown in Figure 14.12. The remote system is added to the scrolling list, as shown in Figure 14.13. Each entry in the list contains three fields: a glyph showing the status of the host system (up, down, requires a root password, or unknown), the name of the host, and its selection status.

Figure 14.11

Enter Remote Hosts information.

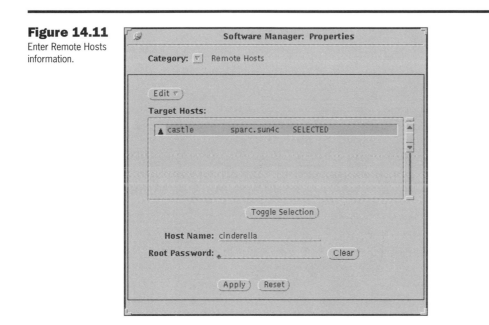

Figure 14.12

Choose Add Entry from the Edit menu.

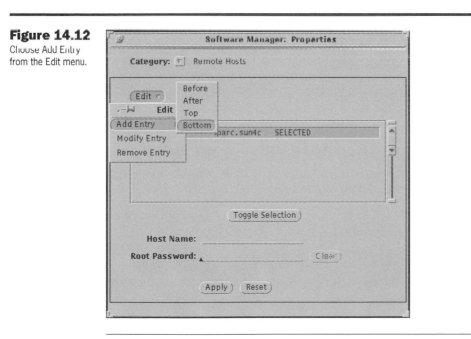

Figure 14.13

Remote Host is added to scrolling list.

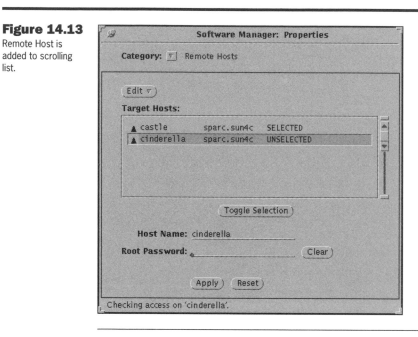

5. To select a remote host, click SELECT on the name of the target host in the scrolling list, and then click SELECT on Toggle Selection. You can install software on more than one system at a time, so be sure to unselect systems that you do not want to install. To unselect a system, click SELECT on the name of the host, and then click SELECT on Toggle Selection. The selection status is displayed in the last field. In the example shown in Figure 14.14, the remote host cinderella is selected and the local host castle is unselected.

Setting an Alternative Location for Installation

You can set an alternative path for installing packages or clusters. If you do not set an alternative path, Software Manager uses the default location, usually /opt.

NOTE. *If you set up an application server as described in Chapter 12, the following procedure is almost always required.*

Follow these steps to set an alternative path:

1. Position the pointer over the cluster or package you want to install.

2. Press MENU, and choose Set Base Directory from the pop-up menu, as shown in Figure 14.15. The Package Information window is displayed, as shown in Figure 14.16.

Figure 14.14

Toggle Selection

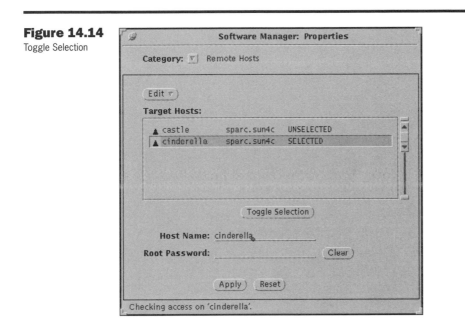

Figure 14.15

Choose Set Base Directory from the pop-up menu.

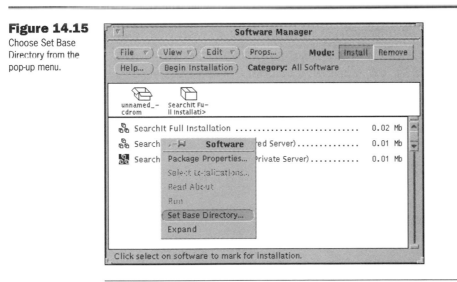

Figure 14.16
The Package
Information window

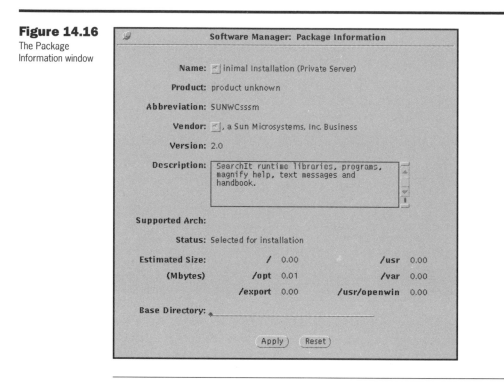

3. Type the name of the install directory in the Base Directory text field at the bottom of the window and click SELECT on the Apply button. For example, to install a package in the /usr/apps/pkgs directory using the default package name as the directory name, type **/usr/apps/pkgs/$PKGINST** in the Base Directory text field.

Beginning Installation

Before you follow the steps in this section, check to make sure that you have:

■ Set the package administration properties (if desired)

■ Set the source media properties to the CD-ROM mount point directory

■ Set the remote hosts properties (if installing software on a remote system)

■ Specified a base directory for installation (if you do not want to use the default installation directory)

When you have set up all properties and specified the base directory (if desired), you are ready to install software. Use the following steps to install software:

1. Click SELECT on the clusters or packages in the Software Manager base window that you want to install. In the example shown in Figure 14.17, the SearchIt Minimal Installation is selected for installation.

Figure 14.17
Select software
clusters.

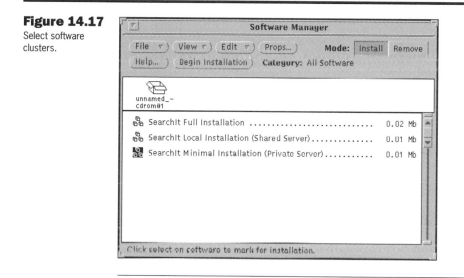

2. Click SELECT on the Begin Installation button. The button is inactive, as shown in Figure 14.18. Installation begins and a Command Input/Output window is displayed, as shown in Figure 14.19.

3. When prompted, answer the questions in the Command Input/Output window, as shown in Figure 14.20. Informational messages are displayed, showing you the status of the installation. When the installation is complete, a message is displayed in the Command Input/Output window, as shown in Figure 14.21.

Removing Software

You can use Software Manager to display installed packages and to remove software from a system.

Use the following steps to remove software from a system:

1. Become superuser.

Software Manager

| File ▽ | View ▽ | Edit ▽ | Props... | **Mode:** | Install | Remove |

Help...   Begin Installation   **Category:** All Software

unnamed_–
cdrom#1

🔳 SearchIt Full Installation .... 0.02 Mb

🔳 SearchIt Local Installation (Shared Server) .... 0.01 Mb

🔳 SearchIt Minimal Installation (Private Server) .... 0.01 Mb

Installing selected software...

Software Manager: Command Input/Output

Sun, Sun Microsystems, the Sun Logo, SunSoft, Solaris, SearchIt, NFS
SunCD, SunOS, SunInstall, OpenWindows, DeskSet, SunNet CDmanager are
trademarks or registered trademarks of Sun Microsystems, Inc. UNIX and
OPEN LOOK are registered trademarks of UNIX System Laboratories, Inc.

This product incorporates technology licensed from Fulcrum Technologies
Inc. All other product names mentioned herein are the trademarks of
their respective owners.

All SPARC trademarks, including the SCD Compliant Logo, are trademarks
or registered trademarks of SPARC International, Inc. SPARCstation,
SPARCserver, SPARCengine, SPARCworks, and SPARCompiler are licensed
exclusively to Sun Microsystems, Inc. Products bearing SPARC
trademarks are based upon an architecture developed by Sun
Microsystems, Inc.

The OPEN LOOK(R) and Sun(TM) Graphical User Interfaces were developed
by Sun Microsystems, Inc. for its users and licensees. Sun acknowledges
the pioneering efforts of Xerox in researching and developing the
concept of visual or graphical user interfaces for the computer
industry. Sun holds a non-exclusive license from Xerox to the Xerox

Figure 14.20

Respond to prompts displayed in the Command Input/Output Window.

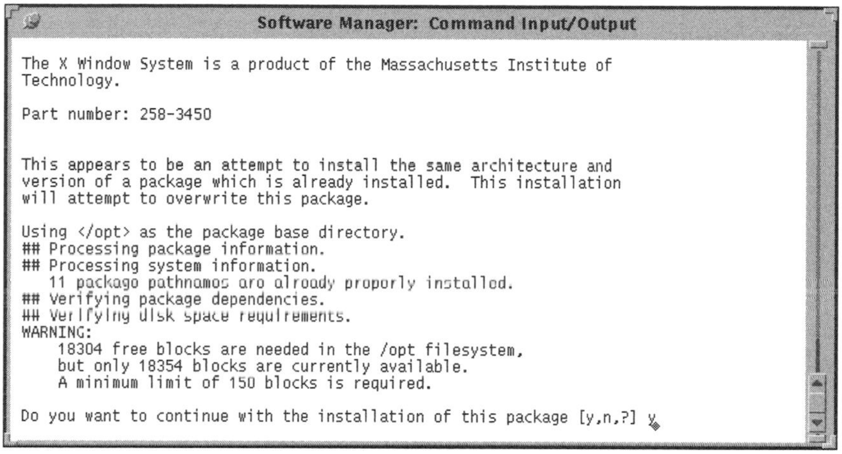

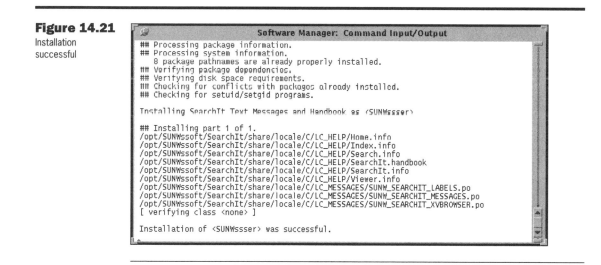

Figure 14.21

Installation successful

2. If Software Manager is not running, type **swmtool&** and press Return.

3. Click SELECT on the Remove mode setting. A list of installed software packages is displayed. Click SELECT to highlight each package you want to remove, as shown in Figure 14.22.

Figure 14.22

Select software packages for removal.

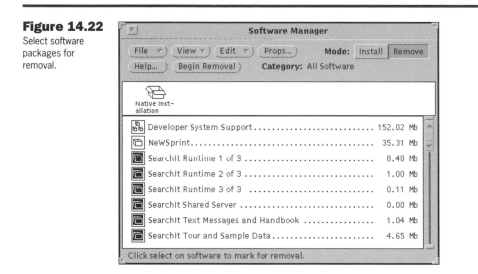

4. Click SELECT on Begin Removal. The Begin Removal button is inactive, as shown in Figure 14.23, and the Command Input/Output window is displayed, as shown in Figure 14.24. Respond to any prompts that are displayed in the Command Input/Output window.

Figure 14.23

Begin removing software.

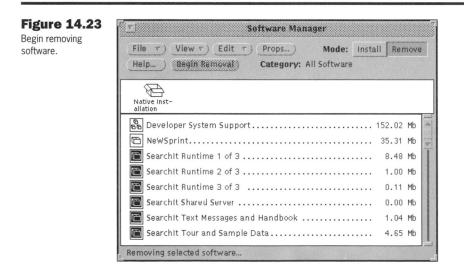

```
Software Manager: Command Input/Output
   SUNWssstr        SearchIt Tour and Sample Data
                    (sparc) 2.0

Do you want to remove this package [y,n,?,q] n
Removing <SUNWssser> package instance from host <castle>

The following package is currently installed:
   SUNWssser        SearchIt Text Messages and Handbook
                    (sparc) 2.0

Do you want to remove this package [y,n,?,q] y

## Removing installed package instance <SUNWssser>
## Verifying package dependencies.
WARNING:
    The <SUNWsssrd> package depends on the package
    currently being removed.
WARNING:
    The <SUNWssstr> package depends on the package
    currently being removed.
Dependency checking failed.

Do you want to continue with the removal of this package [y,n,?,q]
```

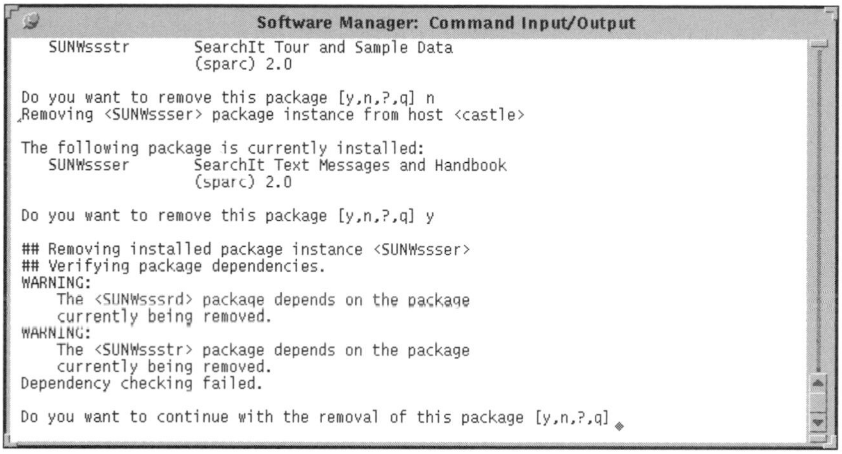

Figure 14.24 Command Input/Output window

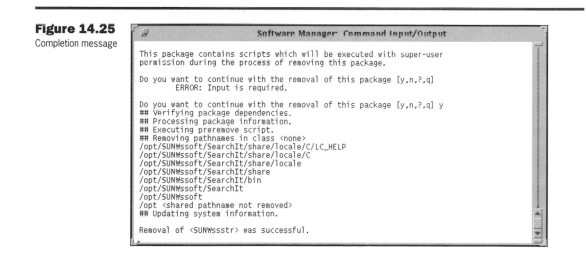

When software removal is complete, a completion message is displayed in the Command Input/Output window, as shown in Figure 14.25, and the packages are removed from the list displayed in the Software Manager base window, as shown in Figure 14.26.

```
Software Manager: Command Input/Output

This package contains scripts which will be executed with super-user
permission during the process of removing this package.

Do you want to continue with the removal of this package [y,n,?,q]
        ERROR: Input is required.

Do you want to continue with the removal of this package [y,n,?,q] y
## Verifying package dependencies.
## Processing package information.
## Executing preremove script.
## Removing pathnames in class <none>
/opt/SUNWssoft/SearchIt/share/locale/C/LC_HELP
/opt/SUNWssoft/SearchIt/share/locale/C
/opt/SUNWssoft/SearchIt/share/locale
/opt/SUNWssoft/SearchIt/share
/opt/SUNWssoft/SearchIt/bin
/opt/SUNWssoft/SearchIt
/opt/SUNWssoft
/opt <shared pathname not removed>
## Updating system information.

Removal of <SUNWssstr> was successful.
```

Figure 14.25 Completion message

Figure 14.26

Software is removed from the list.

This part introduces shell programming in two chapters: Chapter 15 introduces the basic concepts of shell programming and the three shells available with Solaris 2.x system software. It describes how shells work, describes the programming elements, and provides reference tables comparing shell syntax. Chapter 16 contains examples of shell scripts.

Refer to these two chapters if you want to familiarize yourself with the basics of shell programming and to decide which shell language you want to use to perform a specific task. This book does not provide in-depth instructions for writing scripts in the Bourne, Korn, and C shell programming languages. Refer to one of the many books that have been written on the subject for complete instructions on how to use any of the shell programming languages. Refer to the Bibliography at the back of this book for a partial list of references.

PART

6

Introduction to Shell Programming

CHAPTER

15

Writing Shell Scripts

SOLARIS 2.X SYSTEM SOFTWARE INCLUDES THREE SHELLS: BOURNE, KORN, and C. Each shell has its own high-level programming language that you can use to execute sequences of commands, select among alternative operations, perform logical tests, and repeat program actions. The Bourne and Korn shells use almost identical syntax, although the Korn shell is a superset of the Bourne shell and provides more functionality. The Bourne shell is used for most scripts that are distributed with Solaris 2.x system software. The C shell uses a syntax that is similar to C programming language syntax, and it has built-in capabilities not provided with the Bourne shell, such as history and array capability.

This chapter introduces the basic concepts of shell programming and the three shells, describes how shells work, and compares the syntax of the three shells; reference tables are provided throughout this chapter and are repeated in Chapter 16.

Basic Concepts

A shell is a specialized Solaris 2.x utility that provides an interface between the user and the operating system kernel. The kernel is the central core of the operating system that controls all aspects of a computer's operation. The kernel coordinates all of the executing utilities and manages the system's resources. The shell is a special command interpreter that invokes and interacts with the kernel to provide a way for users to execute utilities and other programs.

The shell is a special utility. Each user is assigned a default shell that is started each time the user logs into a system or opens a new Command Tool or Shell Tool window. The shell interprets the commands that it reads. You can type those commands directly into the shell at the prompt, or the shell can read the commands from a file. A file containing shell commands is called a shell program or shell script.

Shell programs are interpreted, not compiled: The commands are read and executed in sequence, one by one. A compiled program, on the other hand, is initially read and converted to a form that can be directly executed by the CPU, and thereafter executed all at once. Because shell scripts are interpreted, even the fastest shell script will always run more slowly than an equivalent program written in a compiled language, such as C.

Introducing Bourne, Korn, and C Shells

The Bourne, Korn, and C shells each have their own environment and syntax. Table 15.1 compares the initialization files that define the shell environment at startup.

Table 15.1	**Shell Initialization Files**			
Feature	**Bourne**	**Korn**		**C**
Read at login	.profile	.profile		.login
Read at invocation of shell		Any file specified in .profile with ENV=*.file*		.cshrc

The initialization files contain environment variables and other settings that configure the user's environment when a shell is started. Refer to the section "Environment Variables" later in this chapter for more information. The .profile (Bourne and Korn shells) and .login (C shell) files are executed when a user logs into a system. The Korn shell and .cshrc (C shell) environment files are executed each time a shell is started. Use these environment files to define aliases and functions for interactive use, and to set variables that you want to apply to the current shell.

Bourne Shell

The Bourne shell, written by Steve Bourne when he was at AT&T Bell Laboratories, is the original UNIX shell. This shell is preferred for shell programming because of its programming capabilities and its universal availability. It lacks features for interactive use, however, such as the ability to recall previous commands (history) and built-in arithmetic. The Bourne shell is the default login shell for the root account, and it is used as the default user login shell if you do not specify another shell in the user's passwd file. The Bourne shell is used for all system-supplied administration scripts.

The Bourne shell command is /bin/sh. The default prompt for the Bourne shell is a dollar sign ($). The root prompt is a pound sign (#).

Korn Shell

The Korn shell, written by David Korn of AT&T Bell Laboratories, was designed to be compatible with the Bourne shell and to offer interactive features comparable to the C shell. The Korn shell includes convenient programming features such as built-in integer arithmetic, arrays, and string-manipulation facilities. The Korn shell runs faster than the C shell, and runs virtually all scripts that are written for the Bourne shell.

The Korn shell command is /bin/ksh. The default prompt for the Korn shell is a dollar sign ($). The root prompt is a pound sign (#).

C Shell

The C shell, written by Bill Joy when he was at the University of California at Berkeley, was designed to incorporate features such as aliases and command history for interactive use. Its programming features have a syntax that is similar to the C programming language.

The C shell command is /bin/csh. The default prompt for the C shell is the system name followed by a percent sign (%). The root prompt is the system name followed by a pound sign (#).

Understanding How Shells Process Commands

Each shell creates subshells and child processes to interpret and execute commands. For example, the following list shows a simplified version of the order in which the Korn shell processes commands:

1. Parses (divides up) the command into units separated by the fixed set of metacharacters: Space Tab Newline ; ( ) < > | &. Types of units include words, keywords, I/O redirectors, semicolons, and others.

2. Checks the first part of each unit for shell keywords, such as function or if statements, with no quotes or backslashes. When a keyword is found, the shell processes the compound command.

3. Searches the list of aliases.

4. Expands any tilde (~) expressions.

5. Substitutes variables.

6. Substitutes commands.

7. Substitutes arithmetic expressions.

8. Splits the items that result from parameter, command, and arithmetic substitution and splits them into words again.

9. Expands wildcards.

10. Looks up built-in commands, functions, and executable files.

11. Sets up I/O redirection.

12. Runs the command.

The Bourne shell interprets commands in a similar way, but does not check for aliases, tildes, or arithmetic. The C shell interprets commands in a different order.

Naming Shell Scripts

When you assign a name to a shell script, follow the general rule for naming Solaris 2.x files. Make a script name as descriptive as possible so that you can easily remember what the script is supposed to do. Be careful to avoid names that are used by Solaris 2.*x* for its own programs unless you intend to replace those utilities with your own scripts.

Each shell has a list of built-in commands. You should also avoid using built-in shell commands as script names. If you name a file with one of the shell built-in commands—such as alias, break, case, cd, continue, echo, else, exit, or history for the C shell—the shell interprets the script name as a built-in shell command and tries to execute it instead of executing the script. For example, with the Bourne or Korn shell, you will run into trouble if you name a script "test," which you might easily do if you are testing something out, because "test" is a built-in Bourne and Korn shell command. Refer to the shell syntax sections in Chapter 16 and to the sh(1), ksh(1), and csh(1) manual pages for a complete list of built-in commands.

Identifying the Shell

The first line of each shell script determines the shell that runs—or inter-prets—the program. Always identify the interpreting shell on the first line of the script, using the information from Table 15.2.

Table 15.2	First Line of Script	
Shell	**Syntax**	
Bourne	#!/bin/sh	
Korn	#!/bin/ksh	
C	#!/bin/csh -f	

The -f (fast) option to /bin/csh runs the script without sourcing the .cshrc file.

If you do not specify the shell in the first line of the script, and the script is executable, the current shell interprets the contents of the script.

After the first line of a script, any line beginning with a pound sign (#) is treated as a comment line and is not executed as part of the script.

Making Scripts Executable

Before you can run a shell script, it is customary to change its permissions so that it has, at a minimum, read and execute permissions (chmod 555). While you are writing and debugging the script, give yourself write permission to the file (chmod 755) so that you can edit it. When assigning permissions to a completed shell script, consider the scope of access that you want to permit to this script. Use restrictive permissions if the script is proprietary or individual and more relaxed permissions if many users who are not in the same group will use the script.

Storing Shell Scripts

After you have created a shell script, you can execute it only from the directory where it resides or by using the full path name, unless you set your path variable to include the directory that contains the script.

If you write many scripts, you may want to create a ~/bin directory in your home directory and update your search path to include this directory. In this way, your scripts will be available regardless of where you are in the directory hierarchy. If you are providing scripts for more general use, be sure to debug them before you put them in a directory where they are more accessible.

Writing Shell Scripts (the Process)

The following checklist describes the process to follow when writing any shell script:

1. Decide what you want the script to do. Come up with a list of the commands that will accomplish the desired task.

2. Use an editor to put the commands into a file. Give the file a name that indicates what the script does.

3. Identify the shell in the first line of the script.

4. Include comments at the beginning of the script to describe its purpose and to annotate each individual part of the script. These comments can be useful when you debug the script and to interpret a script that may be used only occasionally. Comments are also invaluable in helping others to interpret scripts you have written.

5. Save the file and quit the editor.

6. Change the permissions so that the file has, at a minimum, read and execute permissions.

7. Check your path or PATH variable to make sure that the directory containing the script is in the search path.

8. Type the name of the script as a command. The script is executed one line at a time.

9. If errors occur, debug the script.

10. When the script is complete, decide where you want to store the command (for example, in your home directory, your local ~/bin directory, or in a directory that is more globally available).

Variables

A variable is a name that refers to a temporary storage area in memory. A variable holds a value. Changing a variable's value is called assigning a value to the variable. Shell programming uses two types of variables: shell variables and environment variables. By convention, shell variables are written in lowercase and environment variables are written in uppercase letters.

Shell Variables

Shell variables are maintained by the shell and are known only to the shell. Shell variables are always local and are not passed on from parent to child processes.

Displaying Variables from a Command Line

You use the set command with no arguments to display a list of current shell and environment variables. The Bourne and Korn shells display variables in the format shown in the following example:

```
$ set
CALENDAR=/home/winsor
DVHOME=/home/winsor/docudisc/dd.alpha
DVPATH=/home/winsor/docudisc/dd.alpha
ERRNO=10
FCEDIT=/bin/ed
FMHOME=/home2/frame
HELPDIR=$SUNDESK/help
HOME=/home1/winsor
HZ=100
IFS=

LD_LIBRARY_PATH=/usr/openwin/lib:/usr/lib:/usr/ucblib
LINENO=1
LOGNAME=winsor
MAIL=/var/mail/winsor
MAILCHECK=600
MANSECTS=\1:1m:1c:1f:1s:1b:2:\3:3c:3i:3n:3m:3k:3g:3e:3x11:3xt:3w:3b:9:4:5:7:8
OPENWINHOME=/usr/openwin
OPTIND=1
PATH=.:/home1/winsor:/usr/openwin:/usr/openwin/bin/xview:/home2/frame/bin:/usr/d
ist/local/exe:/usr/dist/exe:/home1/winsor/bin:/etc:/usr/etc:/usr/sbin:/usr/bin:/
usr/ucb:.
PPID=9139
```

```
PS1=$
PS2=>
PS3=#?
PS4=+
PWD=/home1/winsor
RANDOM=23592
SECONDS=1
SHELL=/bin/csh
TERM=sun
TMOUT=0
TZ=US/Pacific
USER=winsor
$
```

The C shell displays its variables in the following format:

```
[26]castle{winsor}% set
argv      ()
cwd       /home1/winsor
history 25
home      /home1/winsor
ignoreeof
noclobber
noglob
path      (. /home1/winsor /usr/openwin /usr/openwin/bin/xview /home2/frame/bin
/usr/dist/local/exe /usr/dist/exe /home1/winsor/bin /etc /usr/etc /usr/sbin
/usr/bin /usr/ucb .)
prompt    [!]castle{winsor}%
savehist          25
shell     /bin/csh
status    0
term      sun
time      15
user      winsor
[27]castle{winsor}%
```

Setting and Displaying Shell Variables

To create a Bourne or Korn shell variable, you simply assign the value of the variable to the name, using the following syntax. If the value contains spaces or characters that the shell interprets in a special way, you must enclose the value in quotes. Refer to the section "Quoting" later in this chapter for more information.

```
variable=value
```

In the following Bourne or Korn shell example, the variable *today* is set to display the output of the date command.

```
$ today=Tuesday
$ echo $today
Tuesday
$
```

To display the value for a variable for any shell, type **echo $*variable*.** Although the echo command is recognized by the Korn shell, print $*variable* is the preferred syntax. Optionally, you can enclose the name of the variable in curly braces ({}). You may want to use curly braces if you are concatenating strings together and want to separate the name of the variable from the information that follows it. In the following example, a variable named *flower* is set to rose. If you want to add an "s" at the end of the variable name when it is displayed, you must enclose the variable in curly braces.

```
$ flower=rose
$ echo $flower
rose
$ echo $flowers

$ echo ${flower}s
roses
$
```

You can set local variables from the command line, as shown in the previous examples, or within a script.

Use the following syntax to set a C shell variable. If the value contains spaces or characters that the shell interprets in a special way, you must enclose the value in quotes. Refer to the section "Quoting" later in this chapter for more information.

```
set variable=value
```

You can also set the value of a variable to return the output of a command. To do so, enclose the name of the command in backquotes (` `). The Korn shell also supports the notation $(*command*). In the following C shell example, the variable *today* is set to display the output of the date command:

```
oak% set today = `date`
oak% echo $today
Thu Jul 8 12:41:27 PDT 1993
oak%
```

Refer to the section "Quoting" later in this chapter for more information.

Unsetting Shell Variables

You can use the unset command to remove any shell variable, as shown in the following Bourne shell example:

```
$ unset today
$ echo $today

$
```

Stripping File Names

Sometimes you want to modify a path name to strip off unneeded parts. With the Bourne shell you can use the basename(1) utility to return only the file name, and the dirname(1) utility to return only the directory prefix. The Korn and C shells provide a built-in way for you to modify path names.

Korn Shell Path Stripping

The Korn shell provides pattern-matching operators, shown in Table 15.3, that you can use to strip off components of path names.

Table 15.3 **Korn Shell Pattern-Matching Operators**

Operator	Description
${variable#pattern}	Delete the shortest part at the beginning of the variable that matches the pattern and return the rest.
${variable##pattern}	Delete the longest part at the beginning of the variable that matches the pattern and return the rest.
${variable%pattern}	Delete the shortest part at the end of the variable that matches the pattern and return the rest.
${variable%%pattern}	Delete the longest part at the end of the variable that matches the pattern and return the rest.

The following example shows how all of the operators work, using the pattern /*/ to match anything between two slashes, and .* to match a dot followed by anything.

```
$ pathname=/home/winsor/Design.book.new
$ echo ${pathname#/*/}
winsor/Design.book.new
$ echo ${pathname##/*/}
Design.book.new
$ echo ${pathname%.*}
/home/winsor/Design.book
$ echo ${pathname%%.*}
/home/winsor/Design
$
```

C Shell Path Stripping

The C shell provides a set of modifiers that you can use to strip off unneeded components. These modifiers are quite useful in stripping path names, but can also be used to modify variable strings. Table 15.4 lists the C shell variable modifiers.

Table 15.4   **C Shell File Name Modifiers**

Modifier	Description
:e	Extension—remove prefix ending with a dot.
:h	Head—remove trailing pathname components.
:r	Root—remove trailing suffixes beginning with a dot (.).
:t	Tail—remove all leading pathname components.
:q	Quote—force variable to be quoted. (Used to quote $argv.)
:x	Like q, but break into words at each space, tab, or newline.

The following example shows the results of the first four variable modifiers:

```
oak% set pathname = /home/winsor/Design.book
oak% echo $pathname:e
book
oak% echo $pathname:h
/home/winsor
oak% echo $pathname:r
/home/winsor/Design
oak% echo $pathname:t
Design.book
```

Built-In Shell Variables

All three shells have a set of single-character variables that are set initially by the shell, as shown in Table 15.5. You can use these variables to access words in variables and return other information about the variable. These variables are used differently in the C shell than they are in the Bourne and Korn shells.

Table 15.5 **Variables Initialized by Shell**

Variable	Explanation
$*	Bourne or Korn shell: List the value of all command-line parameters. This variable is useful only in scripts because the login shell has no arguments associated with it.
	C Shell: Not used. Use $argv instead.
$#	Bourne or Korn shell: Return the number of command-line arguments (in decimal). Useful only in scripts.
	C shell: Count the number of words (in decimal) in a variable array.
$?	Bourne or Korn shell: Return the exit status (in decimal) of the last command executed. Most commands return a zero exit status if they complete successfully; otherwise a non-zero exit status is returned. This variable is set after each command is executed.
	C shell: Check to see if a variable of that name has been set.
$$	All shells: Return the process ID (PID) number of the current shell (in decimal).
$!	Bourne or Korn shell: Return the process number (in decimal) of the last process run in the background.

For the Bourne and Korn shells, you can use the $* variable to list the values of command-line arguments within a script, and the $# variable to hold the number of arguments. In the following example, the shell expands the $* variable to list all of the command-line arguments to the script:

```
#!/bin/sh

echo $#
for var in $*
do
        echo $var
done
```

If you named the script tryit and executed it with three arguments, the value of arguments from $# is echoed, and the list of arguments from $* is displayed next, one on each line. The input string may contain quotes. Refer to the sh(1) manual page for information about how quoted strings are interpreted.

```
$ tryit one two three
3
one
two
```

```
three
$
```

For the C shell, the $#*variable* command holds the number of words in a variable array, as shown in the following example:

```
oak% set var = (a b c)
oak% echo $#var
3
oak%
```

For the Bourne shell, the $? variable displays exit status for the last command executed in the same way that the C shell status variable does. Refer to the section "Exit Status" later in this chapter for an example.

For the C shell, you can use the variable $?*variable* to test if a variable is set. $?*variable* returns a 1 if a named variable exists, or 0 if the named variable does not exist.

```
oak% set var="a b c"
oak% echo $?var
1
oak% unset var
oak% echo $?var
0
oak%
```

NOTE. *The numbers returned by $?*variable *are the opposite from status numbers, where 0 is success and 1 is failure.*

For all shells, the $$ variable returns the PID number of the current shell process, as shown in the following examples. Because process numbers are unique, you can use this string to generate unique temporary file names. For example, when a script assigns a file name of tmp.$$, that file is rarely confused with another file.

NOTE. *If you are concerned about generating unique filenames, you can use the format feature of the date(1) command to generate a temporary filename that includes both a process ID and a time and date stamp.*

```
oak% echo $$
364
oak% sh
$ echo $$
392
$
```

Each shell also includes built-in commands for efficiency. Table 15.6 lists the built-in commands. The Bourne shell relies more on using external commands to do the work, and thus has the fewest built-in commands. The additional built-in commands for the Korn shell are shown by (K) following the command name. The job control variant of the Bourne shell, jsh, has the same job control features as the Korn shell.

CAUTION! *Do not use any of the built-in commands as names for shell scripts. If you use one of the built-in commands as a shell script name, the shell will execute the built-in command instead of running the script.*

Table 15.6 **Shell Built-In Commands**

Purpose	Bourne or Korn Shell	C Shell
Null command	:	:
Create a command name alias	alias (K)	alias
Run current command in background	bg (K)	bg
Exit enclosing for or while loop	break	break
Break out of a switch		breaksw
Change directory	cd	cd
Continue next iteration of for or while loop	continue	continue
Default case in switch		default
Print directory stack		dirs
Write arguments on stdout	echo, print (K)	echo
Evaluate and execute arguments	eval	eval
Execute the arguments	exec	exec
Return or set shell variables		@
Exit shell program	exit	exit
Create an environment variable	export	setenv
Bring a command into foreground	fg (K)	fg
Execute foreach loop	for	foreach
Perform filename expansion		glob
Go to label within shell program		goto

Table 15.6 **Shell Built-In Commands (Continued)**

Purpose	Bourne or Korn Shell	C Shell
Display history list	fc (K)	history
If-then-else decision	if	if
List active jobs	jobs (K)	jobs
Send a signal	kill	kill
Set limits for a job's resource use	ulimit	limit
Terminate login shell and invoke login		login
Terminate a login shell		logout
Change to a new user group	newgrp (K)	
Change priority of a command		nice
Ignore hangup		nohup
Notify user when job status changes		notify
Control shell processing on receipt of a signal	trap	onintr
Pop the directory stack		popd
Push a directory onto the stack		pushd
Read a line from stdin	read	$<
Change a variable to read-only	readonly	
Repeat a command *n* times		repeat
Set shell environment variables	=	setenv
Set a local C shell variable		set
Shift positional parameters $* or $argv	shift	shift
Read and execute a file	. (dot)	source
Stop a background process		stop
Stop the shell	suspend (K)	suspend
CASE statement	case	switch
Evaluate conditional expressions	test	

Table 15.6 **Shell Built-In Commands (Continued)**

Purpose	Bourne or Korn Shell	C Shell
Display execution times	times	time
Set default security for creation of files and directories	umask	umask
Discard aliases	unalias (K)	unalias
Remove limitations on resources	ulimit	unlimit
Unset a variable	unset	unset
Unset an environment variable		unsetenv
UNTIL loop	until	
Wait for background process to complete	wait	
WHILE loop	while	while

Environment Variables

Environment variables are often used to define initialization options such as the default login shell, user login name, search path, and terminal settings. Some environment variables are set for you each time you log in. You can also create your own variables and assign values to them. By convention, environment variable names are in capital letters.

Environment variables are passed on from parent to child processes. For example, an environment variable set in a shell is available to any program started in that shell, to any additional program started by the initial program, and so on. In other words, environment variables are inherited from parent to child, from child to grandchild, and so on. They are not inherited backward from parent to grandparent.

Use the env command to display a list of current environment variables. Consult the *Solaris System Administrator's Guide* for more information about environment variables.

For the Bourne and Korn shells, use the following syntax to assign environment variables and export them. You must export the variable for it to be put into the environment of child processes.

```
VARIABLE=value;export VARIABLE
```

For the Korn shell, you can also use the following syntax:

```
export VARIABLE=value
```

For the C shell, use the setenv command with the following syntax to assign environment variables:

```
setenv VARIABLE value
```

Use the unsetenv command with the following syntax to remove the environment variable:

```
unsetenv VARIABLE
```

Input and Output

When you write shell scripts, you want to be able to obtain input from sources outside your scripts, for example, from another file or from keyboard input. You also want to be able to generate output both for use within the script and for display on the screen.

The following sections describe how to control input and output of a shell script using standard input, output, error, and redirection; how to accept user input (input from the keyboard) to a script; how to create "here" documents; and how to generate output to the screen.

Standard In, Standard Out, and Standard Error

When writing shell scripts, you can control input/output redirection. Input redirection is the ability to force a command to read any necessary input from a file instead of from the keyboard. Output redirection is the ability to send the output from a command into a file or pipe instead of to the screen.

Each process created by a shell script begins with three file descriptors associated with it, as shown in Figure 15.1.

Figure 15.1

File descriptors

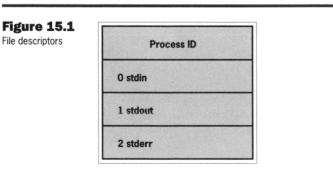

These file descriptors—standard input, standard output, and standard error—determine where input to the process comes from, and where the output and error messages are sent.

Standard input (STDIN) is always file descriptor 0. Standard input is the place where the shell looks for its input data. Usually data for standard input comes from the keyboard. You can specify standard input to come from another source using input/output redirection.

Standard output (STDOUT) is always file descriptor 1. Standard output (default) is the place where the results of the execution of the program are sent. Usually, the results of program execution are displayed on the terminal screen. You can redirect standard output to a file, or suppress it completely by redirecting it to /dev/null.

Standard error (STDERR) is always file descriptor 2. Standard error is the place where error messages are sent as they are generated during command processing. Usually, error messages are displayed on the terminal screen. You can redirect standard error to a file, or suppress it completely by redirecting it to /dev/null.

You can use the file descriptor numbers 0 (standard input), 1 (standard output), and 2 (standard error) together with the redirection metacharacters to control input and output in the Bourne and Korn shells. Table 15.7 shows the common ways you can redirect file descriptors.

Table 15.7   Bourne and Korn Shell Redirection

Description	Command
Take STDIN from file	<file, or 0<file
Redirect STDOUT to file	> file, or 1> file
Redirect STDERR to file	2> file
Append STDOUT to end of file	>> file
Redirect STDERR to STDOUT	2>&1
Pipe standard output of cmd1 as standard input to cmd2	cmd1	cmd2
Use file as both STDIN and STDOUT	<> file
Close STDIN	<&-
Close STDOUT	>&-
Close STDERR	2>&-

When redirecting STDIN and STDOUT in the Bourne and Korn shells, you can omit the file descriptors 0 and 1 from the redirection symbols. You must always use the file descriptor 2 with the redirection symbol.

The 0 and 1 file descriptors are implied, and not used explicitly for the C shell, as shown in Table 15.8. The C shell representation for standard error (2) is an ampersand (&). STDERR can only be redirected when redirecting STDOUT.

Table 15.8 **C Shell Redirection Metacharacters**

Description	Command
Redirect STDOUT to file	> file
Take input from file	< file
Append STDOUT to end of file	>> file
Redirect STDOUT and STDERR to file	>& file
Append STDOUT and STDERR to file	>>& file

Command-Line Input

You can ask users to provide input to a script as part of the command-line argument when the script is run. All three shells use the positional parameter $n to specify as many as nine command-line arguments (for example, $1, $2, $3, and so on). $0 is a legitimate variable, and returns the name of the command. Consider the following Bourne shell script, named tryit:

```
#!/bin/sh

echo $#
for var in $*
do
        echo $var
done
```

NOTE. *With the Korn shell, you can use ${10}, ${11} ... notation to recognize more than nine command-line arguments.*

This script can be rewritten in the following way to work with any of the three shells. Each of these command-line arguments can be used to pass filenames or other information into a shell script from a command line.

NOTE. *For the C shell, you cannot use the echo $# statement in the script. Instead, you can use $#argv to hold the number of command-line arguments.*

Instead of using $#argv, which is shown in later examples, echo $0 (which displays the name of the script) is substituted in the following example:

```
echo $Ø
echo $1
echo $2
echo $3
```

The resulting screen display lists the command-line arguments, as shown below:

```
oak% tryit one two three
tryit
one
two
three
oak%
```

NOTE. *The $n notation does not return an error if no parameters are provided as part of the command. Users do not need to supply command-line arguments, so you cannot be sure that $n will contain a value unless you check the number of positional parameters using $# for the Bourne and Korn shells.*

The C shell provides additional syntax for positional parameters, as shown in Table 15.9.

Table 15.9   **C Shell $argv Notation**

Notation	Description
$#argv	Count the number of command line arguments.
$*	Return the value of all arguments.
$argv	Return the value of all arguments.
$argv[1-3]	Return the value of arguments 1 through 3.
$0	Return the command used to run the shell script.
$argv[n]	Return the nth argument.
$argv[$#argv}	Return the last argument.

The shell performs range checking on the $argv[n] syntax, but it does not on the $n syntax. If the word is not found, the message "Subscript out of range" is displayed.

NOTE. *$argv[0] is not defined and does not return the name of the script as $0 does.*

Table 15.10 shows an example script and the output.

Table 15.10   A Sample $argv Script and Its Output

#!/bin/csh -f	oak$ **argdemo one two three four**
echo Number of args = $#argv	Number of args = 4
echo All args = $*	All args = one two three four
echo All args = $argv	All args = one two three four
echo Args 1-3 = $argv[1-3]	Args 1-3 = one two three
echo Name of script file = $0	Name of script file = argdemo
echo Script file\? = $argv[0]	Script file? =
echo Second arg = $argv[2]	Second arg = two
echo Last arg = $argv[$#argv]	Last arg = four
echo Fifth arg = $5	Fifth arg =
echo Fifth arg = $argv[5]	Subscript out of range

Shifting Command-Line Arguments

You can use the shift command, which is built into all three shells, to manipulate the positional parameters in a script. The shift command moves each argument from $1 through $n to the left, changing the previous argument list. The shift command is particularly useful in processing positional parameters in while loops; you can use these commands together to process each positional parameter in turn.

In the following Bourne shell example, each argument is displayed in turn. The shift command shifts the list to the left, removing the leftmost value in the list, as shown in the following script:

```
#!/bin/sh
while [ $# -ne 0 ]
```

```
do
    echo argument: $1
    shift
done
```

The following example shows the output of this script:

```
$ tryit one two three
argument: one
argument: two
argument: three
$
```

Because the shift command shifts the positional parameters, you only need to use $1 in the script to display (or process) the command-line arguments. The following example shows how positional parameters are shifted from a Bourne shell command line:

```
$ set a b c d e f g h i
$ while [ $# -gt 0 ]; do
> echo $*
> shift
> done
a b c d e f g h i
b c d e f g h i
c d e f g h i
d e f g h i
e f g h i
f g h i
g h i
h i
i
$
```

Refer to the section "Using While Loops" later in this chapter for more information about while loops.

Interactive Input

You can ask for a single line of input anywhere in a script. For the Bourne and Korn shells, use the read command followed by a variable name for interactive input.

NOTE. *You do not need to assign the variable before you use it as an argument to the read command. The following example shows the Bourne and Korn shell syntax for interactive input.*

New with SVR4.

NOTE. *To suppress the newline at the end of the prompt so that users type the input on the same line as the string that is displayed, use "\c" at the end of the string when /usr/bin is in the path before /usr/ucb. The SunOS 4.x echo -n command works only if you have /usr/ucb in the path before /usr/bin. Refer to the echo(1) manual page for more information.*

```
#!/bin/sh

echo "Enter search pattern and press Return: \c"
read filename
```

When the prompt is displayed, the script waits for input from the keyboard. When the user types input and presses Return, the input is assigned to the variable and the script continues to execute.

NOTE. *Be sure to always include a descriptive screen prompt as part of the script before you request input so that users know that the script is waiting for screen input before it continues.*

For the C shell, the special variable $< waits for a value from STDIN. You can use $< anywhere you would use a variable.

For the C shell, use $< as a value to a variable, as shown below:

```
#!/bin/csh -f
echo "Enter search pattern and press Return: \c"
set pattern = $<
```

When the prompt is displayed, the script waits for input from the keyboard. When the user types input and presses Return, the input is assigned to the variable and the script continues to execute.

Here Documents

Sometimes a shell script requires data. Instead of having the data in a file somewhere in the system, you can include the data as part of the shell script. Including the data in the script makes it simpler to distribute and maintain the script. Such a collection of data is called a here document—the data (document) is right here in the shell script. Another advantage of a here document is that shell parameters can be substituted in the document as the shell is reading the data.

The general format of a here document is shown as follows. The format is the same for all three shells.

```
    lines of shell commands
    ...
command << delimiter
lines of data belonging
to the here document
delimiter
    ...
    more lines of shell commands
```

The here document operator << signals the beginning of the here document. The operator must be followed by a special string that delimits the input, for example <<DONE. Follow the here document operator with the list of input you want to use. The input can be any text, and may include variables because the shell does variable substitution on a here document. At the end of the here document, you must include the delimiter at the left margin on a single line. The shell sends everything between the two delimiters to be processed as standard input.

In the following example, the mail message specified in the here document is sent to members of the staff whose names are contained in a file named stafflist inviting them to a party. The delimiter used is EOF.

```
#!/bin/sh

time="7:00 p.m."
mail -s "staff party" `cat stafflist` << EOF
Please come to our staff party being held
in the cafeteria at $time tomorrow night
EOF
```

Generating Output

The following sections describe how to use the echo command, quoting, and command substitution.

NOTE. *Although the echo command works in Korn shell scripts, the print command is preferred. The syntax for the print command is the same as for the echo command.*

The Echo and Print Commands

Use the echo command to generate messages to be displayed on a terminal screen. You have already seen some examples of using the echo command to display the value for a variable. You can also use the echo command to display text messages, as shown in the following portion of an interactive Bourne shell script:

```
#!/bin/sh
echo "Enter a pathname and press Return:"
read pathname
```

If you want to echo more than one message on the same line, use the \c string at the end of the line to leave the cursor at the end of the output line and to suppress the newline. The following example modifies the previous Bourne shell script so that the user types the input following the colon, instead of on the line beneath the prompt message:

```
#!/bin/sh
echo "Enter a pathname and press Return: \c"
read pathname
```

If you need to display control characters or metacharacters, you can escape them (that is, get the shell to interpret the character literally) by putting a backslash (\) in front of the character. Refer to the echo(1) manual page for information about special backslash characters (for example, \c, \n). The Bourne and Korn shell echo command has fewer restrictions on quoting metacharacters than does the C shell echo command. In the following Bourne shell script, an error message is displayed only for the parentheses in the last line, which are not escaped with backslashes. Note that the dollar sign ($) followed by a space does not need to be escaped.

```
$ more echodemo
#!/bin/sh

echo Type a pathname and press Return:
echo You owe me \$35 \(Please pay\).
echo This is a $ sign (not a variable)
$ echodemo
Type a pathname and press Return:
This is a $ sign (Not a variable).
anything: syntax error at line 6: `(' unexpected
$
```

Quoting

All three shells use the same syntax for quoting, as shown in Table 15.11. Quoting a string incorrectly can cause many unexpected results.

NOTE.   *The bang (!) is not used as a metacharacter in the Bourne and Korn shells. If it is not quoted properly, it is likely to cause problems mostly in the C shell.*

Table 15.11 **Quoting**

Character	Term	Description
\	Backslash	Nullifies the special meaning of any shell metacharacter, including another backslash.
``	Backquotes	The output is substituted as if it were typed in place of the command. Refer to the shell manual pages for more information.
''	Single quotes	Nullifies the special meaning of all characters except bang (!), the backslash (\), and the single quote itself ('). Single quotes are more restrictive than double quotes and do not permit variable or backquote expansion.
""	Double quotes	Nullifies the special meaning of all special characters except bang (!), backquote (``), and dollar sign ($). Permits variable and backquote expansion.

The following examples demonstrate the result of different forms of quotation:

```
$ name=Fred
$ echo "My name is $name"
My name is Fred
$ echo 'My name is $name'
My name is $name
$ echo "Today is `date`"
Today is Fri Jul  9 12:12:35 PDT 1993
$ echo 'Today is `date`'
Today is `date`
$ echo 'Use metacharacters * ? < > | & and $ often'
Use metacharacters * ? < > | & and $ often
$ echo "It's hard to turn off"!
It's hard to turn off!
```

Command Substitution

You can substitute the output of the command in place of the command itself. This process is called command substitution. Use backquotes (``) to surround the desired command. You can use command substitution to return the output of the command, or to use it as the value for a variable.

NOTE. *In the Korn shell, the $(command) syntax can be used instead of backquotes.*

In the first example following, the output of the date command is used as part of a larger output string, and the output of the who command is filtered through wc, which counts the number of lines in the output of who to determine how many users are logged in. The second example pipes the output of the who command to the cut command to display only the list of user names and uses the uname -n command to display the name of the system.

```
$ echo Today is `date` and there are `who | wc -l` users logged in
Today is Fri Jul 9 13:12:41 PDT 1993 and there are 5 users logged in

$ echo `who | cut -f1 -d" "` logged onto `uname -n`
winsor newton fred george anna logged onto seachild
$
```

Testing Conditions

When writing scripts, you frequently want to test for conditions. The simplest test is to determine whether a condition is true or false. If the expression is true, execute any subsequent commands; if not, continue with the script. Table 15.12 shows the syntax for conditional tests.

Table 15.12   **Conditional Test Syntax**

Bourne and Korn Shells	C Shell
if *command*	if (*cond*) then
then	*commands*
commands	else if (*cond*) then
elif *command*	*commands*
commands	else
else	*commands*
commands	endif
fi	

If-Then-Else-Elif

For the Bourne and Korn shells, use the if-then-else-elif-fi syntax to test for conditions. You can follow the if statement with the test command and its argument(s) to test for conditions. As an alternative to typing the test command, you can enclose the test condition in square brackets []. You must put a space after the first bracket and before the last one for the characters to be interpreted correctly—for example:

```
if [ -r filename ]
then
```

The results of test -r *filename* and [-r *filename*] are identical. Refer to the section "Test and C Shell Built-in Test" in Chapter 16 for test command options.

The Bourne shell fragment shown next uses the simplest form of the if statement to test if a user entered at least one command-line argument following the name of the script:

```
#!/bin/sh
#
# Test for at least one command-line argument
#
if test $# -lt 1
then
    echo Usage: $0 name requires one command-line argument
    exit 1
fi
```

If you want the script to perform additional actions if the first conditional test fails, use the else clause, as shown in the following Bourne shell fragment:

```
#!/bin/sh

if test $# -lt 1
then
    echo Usage: $0 name requires one command-line argument
    exit 1
else
    echo "Thank you for entering arguments"
    echo "You entered $# arguments"
fi
```

You can test for additional conditions within the if statement using the elif conditional (a combination of else and if). The elif clause is only performed if the previous if or else fails. Each elif clause lists another command to be tested. The following Bourne shell example has one elif and one else clause:

```
#!/bin/sh
#
# Time of day greetings
#
```

```
hour=`date +%H`

if [ $hour -H 12 ]
then
    echo "Good Morning!"
elif [ $hour -H 17 ]
then
    echo "Good Afternoon!"
else
    echo "Good Night!"
fi
```

If-Else-Else If-Endif

The C shell has built-in constructs that you can use to test conditions. Refer to the section "Test and C Shell Built-in Test" in Chapter 16 for C shell test command options.

The C shell fragment shown next tests to see if a user entered one or more command-line arguments following the name of the script:

```
#!/bin/csh -f

if ($#argv == 0) then
    echo Usage: $0 name requires one command-line argument
    exit 1
endif
```

NOTE. *The then statement for the C shell, if present, must be positioned at the end of the if line.*

If you want the script to perform additional actions if the first conditional test fails, use the else clause, as shown in the following C shell fragment:

```
#!/bin/csh -f

if ($#argv == 0) then
    echo Usage: $0 requires command-line arguments
    exit 1
else
    echo "Thank you for entering arguments"
    echo "You entered $# arguments"
endif
```

You can test for additional conditions within the if statement using the else if conditional. The else if clause is performed only if the previous if or else if fails. Each else if statement lists another command to be tested. The following C shell example has one else if and one else statement:

```
#!/bin/csh -f
#
# Time of day greetings
#
set d=`date +%H`
set hour = $d[4]

if ($hour < 12) then
    echo "Good Morning\!"
else if ($hour < 17) then
    echo "Good Afternoon\!"
else
    echo "Good Night\!"
endif
```

Nested If Constructs

If statements can contain additional if statements. When you write a script with nested if statements, be sure to indent the statements to make it easier to follow the logic of the statements and to check that you have included all the required elements.

The syntax for nesting if statements in the Bourne and Korn shells is shown below:

```
if command
then
    if command
    then
        command
        ...
    else
        command
        ...
    fi
elif command
then
    command
    ...
else
    command
```

```
    ...
fi
```

The syntax for nesting if statements in the C shell follows:

```
if (expression) then
    if (expression) then
        if (expression) then
            command
            ...
        else
            command
            ...
        endif
    else if (expression) then
        command
        ...
    else
        command
        ...
    endif
endif
```

Multi-Branching

You may want to take several different types of action depending on the value of a variable or a parameter. Although you can use conditional testing to test each value and take action, you can more easily perform such tests using the case statement or the C shell switch statement, as shown in Table 15.13.

Table 15.13   Switch and Case Syntax

Bourne and Korn Shells	C Shell
case *value* in	switch (*value*)
pattern1)	case *pattern*:
command	*commands*
command ;;	breaksw
pattern2)	default:
command ;;	*commands*

Table 15.13   **Switch and Case Syntax (Continued)**

Bourne and Korn Shells	C Shell
*)	breaksw
default action ;;	endsw
esac	

The value of the variable is successively compared against patterns until a match is found. The commands immediately following the matching pattern are executed until ;; (for the Bourne and Korn shells) or until breaksw (for the C shell) is found. The last test *) (Bourne or Korn shell) or default: (C shell) is a default action. If no other values match, then the shell executes the default action. In many scripts, the default action displays an error message and exits from the shell.

Case statements can be especially helpful for processing parameters to a function.

The following Bourne script example sets the terminal type:

```
#!/bin/sh
#
# Set the terminal type
#
case $TERM in
    tvi???)
        echo $TERM
        echo Probably the system console ;;
    vt[12][02]0)
        echo Just like a shelltool ;;
    Wyse40 | Wyse75)
        echo A Wyse terminal ;;
    sun)
        echo Aha!! a workstation ;;
    *)
        echo surprise! it's a $TERM
esac
```

The following example shows an interactive C shell script to set the terminal type:

```
#!/bin/csh -f
#
```

```
# Set the terminal type
#
echo "Do you want to see the present setting? \c"
set input = $<
switch ("$input")
    case [Yy]*:
        echo "term =" $TERM
        breaksw
endsw
echo "Terminal type? \c"
set term = $<
switch ($term)
    case tvi950:
    case vt100:
    case sun:
        setenv TERM $term
        breaksw
    default:
        echo "I don't know that one."
        breaksw
endsw
```

Controlling the Flow

You can use loops to control the flow of execution in a script. A loop is an iterative mechanism that repeats a sequence of instructions until a predetermined condition is satisfied. You can use different forms of loops. The for/foreach loop executes a list of commands one time for each value of a loop variable. The while loop repeatedly executes a group of commands within the body of the loop until the test condition in the expression is no longer true. The Bourne and Korn shells provide an until loop that continues to execute until a command executes successfully. Table 15.14 shows the syntax for for/foreach, while, and until loops.

Table 15.14   Looping Syntax

Feature	Bourne/Korn Shell	C Shell
for/foreach loops	for *variable* in *list*	foreach *variable* (*list*)
	do	*commands*

Table 15.14   Looping Syntax (Continued)

Feature	Bourne/Korn Shell	C Shell
	commands	end
	done	
while loops	while *command*	while (cond)
	do	*commands*
	commands	end
	done	
until loops	until *command*	
	do	
	commands	
	done	

Using For/Foreach Loops

Use the for loop to process items from a fixed list or from a command-line argument. The Bourne and Korn shell for loop executes the commands between the do and the done statement as many times as there are words or strings listed after "in".

The for loop's basic syntax is:

```
for variable in word1 word2 word3 . . . wordn
    command $variable
    command
done
```

A special format of the first line of the for loop, for variable, uses the values of positional parameters $1, $2, and so on and is equivalent to using for variable in "$@" as the first line of the for loop.

The following Bourne shell script contains two examples of for loops. The first example copies files into a backup directory. The second removes all files that contain a .o suffix.

```
#!/bin/sh
#
# Backup files
#
dir=/home/winsor/backup
for file in ch1 ch2 ch3 ch4
do
    cp $file $dir/${file}.back
    echo $file has been backed up in directory $dir
done

for file in *.o
do
    echo removing $file
    rm $file
done
```

In the C shell, use the foreach loop to process items from a fixed list or to execute commands interactively from a command line. In the C shell, the foreach construct executes a list of commands one time for each value specified in the (*list*).

The following C shell script contains two examples of foreach loops. The first example copies $file into a backup directory. The second example removes all files that contain a .o suffix.

```
#!/bin/csh -f
#
# Backup files
#
set dir=/home/winsor/backup
foreach file (ch1 ch2 ch3 ch4)
    cp $file $dir/${file}.back
    echo $file has been backed up in directory $dir
end

foreach file (*.o)
    echo removing $file
    rm $file
end
```

You can type the foreach loop statement at the command-line prompt. The secondary prompt (?) is displayed. At the prompt, type the commands you want to execute in the loop. When you have completed the list of commands, type **end**. The commands are executed in sequence and the C shell prompt is redisplayed. In the following example, the name of each C source file in the directory is displayed and compiled, and the binary output file renamed. The :r modifier removes the .c extension. If there are 10 source files in the current working directory, the loop is executed 10 times. When there are no more C source files, the loop ends.

```
oak% foreach file (*.c)
? echo $file
? cc -o $file:r $file
? end
oak%
```

The following example converts raster files to gif format, strips off the .rs suffix, and adds a .gif suffix:

```
oak% foreach file (*.rs)
? cat $file | rasttoppm | ppmtogif > ${file:r}.gif
? end
oak%
```

Using While Loops

Use while loops to repeatedly execute a group of commands within the body of a loop until the test condition in the expression is no longer true. In other words, the while loop says, "While the expression is true, execute these commands."

For the Bourne and Korn shells, the while loop executes the commands between the do and the done statements as long as the initial command exits with a status of zero.

The basic syntax for the while loop is:

```
while command
do
      command
      command
done
```

In the following Bourne shell script, the first example sets num equal to 0 and adds 1 to it as long as the number is less than or equal to 4.

```
#!/bin/sh

num=0
while [ $num -le 4 ]
do
        num=`expr $num + 1`
```

```
        echo number: $num
done
```

The next example displays the command-line arguments in sequence when any arguments are given. Refer to the section "Shifting Command-Line Arguments" earlier in this chapter for information about the shift command. Refer to the section "Mathematical Operations" later in this chapter for information about the expr command.

```
#!/bin/sh

while [ $# -ne Ø ]
do
        echo argument: $1
        shift
done
```

For the C shell, the while loop executes the commands between the while and the end statement as long as the expression is true.

The basic syntax for the while loop is:

```
while (expression)
    command
    command
end
```

In the following C shell script, the first example sets num equal to 0 and adds 1 to it as long as the number is less than or equal to 4:

```
#!/bin/csh -f

@ num = Ø
while ($num <= 4)
    @ num++
    echo "number: $num"
end
```

The output of this script follows:

```
oak% tryit
number: Ø
number: 1
number: 2
number: 3
number: 4
```

The next example displays the command-line arguments in sequence when any arguments are given:

```csh
#!/bin/csh -f
#
while ($#argv != 0)
        echo "argument: $1"
        shift
end
```

Using Until Loops

Use Bourne or Korn shell until loops to test until the command returns a successful status. The syntax for the until loop is similar to the while loop:

```
until command
do
    command
    command
done
```

NOTE. *The until condition is checked at the top of the loop, not at the bottom.*

The following example prints out the numbers 1 through 5:

```sh
#!/bin/sh

num=0
until [ $num -gt 4 ]
do
        num=`expr $num + 1`
        echo number: $num
done
```

The results of this script are the same as the example shown using the while loop. Refer to the section "Mathematical Operations" later in this chapter for a description of the expr command used in the preceding example.

Breaking Loops

All three shells have built-in break and continue commands that you can use to break out of a for/foreach, while, or until loop. The break command forces termination of the loop and transfers control to the line after the done (for the Bourne and Korn shells) or end (for the C shell) statement. In the following C shell example, the script continues running the while loop until the user answers Yes (or yes, y, or Y). When the user does answer yes, the break terminates the while loop and, in this case, exits because there are no additional commands to execute.

```
#!/bin/csh -f
#
while (1)
        echo "Finished yet? \c"
        set answer = $<
        if ($answer =~ [Yy]*) break
end
```

You can use the continue command in a similar way to control for/foreach and while loops. The continue command operates on the innermost loop with which it is associated. The continue statement transfers execution immediately back to the while test, skipping all subsequent commands in the innermost loop. If continue is used with a foreach loop, the continue statement quits the current iteration of the loop and processes the next item in the list.

Exit Status

When a command or shell function terminates, it returns an exit status to the invoking shell. The exit status is a numeric value that indicates whether or not the program ran successfully.

Every command that runs has an exit status, which is set by the programmer when the command is written. Usually, an exit status of 0 means that the program executed successfully. Any non-zero value (usually 1 or –1) means that the program failed. Programmers may not always follow this convention. Check the manual page for a given command to determine its exit status. For example, the grep command returns one of three exit status values: 0 means that the search pattern was found, 1 means that the pattern could not be found, and 2 means that the grep command could not open or find the file(s) to be searched.

For the Bourne shell, the $? variable holds exit status for the last command executed in the same way that the C shell status variable does. Usually, 0 indicates success and 1 indicates failure.

```
$ pwd
/home/seachild/winsor
$ echo $?
0
$ cd /home3
/home3: bad directory
```

```
$ echo $?
1
$
```

The C shell variable status is automatically set by the shell to the exit status of the last command executed. You can use the echo command to display the exit status at the prompt.

```
oak% grep root /etc/passwd
root:x:0:1:0000-Admin(0000):/:/sbin/sh
oak% echo $status
0
oak% grep anthonly /etc/passwd
oak% echo $status
1
oak% grep root /etc/password
grep: can't open /etc/password
oak% echo $status
2
oak%
```

When writing shell scripts, you can add an exit 0 to the end of the script to indicate successful completion. Exiting with any other value shows that something went wrong.

Mathematical Operations

You can do mathematical operations only on integers (whole numbers) for all three shells. If you want to do more complicated arithmetic, you can use the awk command.

To perform mathematical operations in the Bourne shell, you can use the expr command. The syntax is:

```
expr arguments
```

You must separate the mathematical operators (shown in Table 15.15) and the operand with white space.

Table 15.15   Mathematical Operators

Operator	Description
+	Addition

Table 15.15   Mathematical Operators (Continued)

Operator	Description
-	Subtraction
*	Multiplication
/	Division
%	Remainder

Multiplication, division, and remainder have higher precedence than do addition or subtraction. Use parentheses for grouping.

The following example uses the expr command:

```
$ i=4
$ expr $i + 1
5
$ expr $i - 1
3
$ expr $i \* 2
8
$ expr $i / 2
2
$ expr $i % 2
0
$ j=2
$ expr $i + $j
6
$
```

The Korn shell has let and built-in $(()) expressions to do arithmetic.

The C shell @ command is similar to the Bourne and Korn shell expr command. The @ command evaluates an expression mathematically and then assigns the resulting value to a shell variable, as shown in Table 15.16.

Table 15.16   C Shell Mathematical Operators

Syntax	Description
@ *variable* = (*expression*)	Set value of variable equal to the expression.

Table 15.16 **C Shell Mathematical Operators (Continued)**

Syntax	Description
@ *variable* += (*expression*)	Addition.
@ *variable* -= (*expression*)	Subtraction.
@ *variable* *= (*expression*)	Multiplication.
@ *variable* /= (*expression*)	Division.
@ *variable* ++	Add 1.
@ *variable* –	Subtract 1.

The expressions can be mathematical or logical. Mathematical expressions typically use the operators shown in Table 15.15. Logical expressions typically use one of the following operators, and yield a 1 (true) or 0 (false) value:

```
> < >= <= == !=
```

The following example shows C shell numeric values:

```
oak% @ total = 5 + 3
oak% echo $total
8
oak% @ total++
oak% echo $total
9
oak% @ total += 4
oak% echo $total
13
oak% @ newtotal = ($total > 5)
oak% echo $newtotal
1
oak%
```

User-Defined Functions

You can write your own functions in the Bourne and Korn shells and use them as part of other scripts.

NOTE. *Not all Bourne shells support functions. However, the Solaris 2.x Bourne shell supports functions.*

User-defined functions are useful if you have a series of commands that you want to use repeatedly. The functions written for an application server are an example of user-defined functions. Some examples of functions are provided in the section "Example Scripts" in Chapter 16. When you define a function, you use the name of the function at the place where you want to execute the series of commands contained in the function.

Typically, you define functions at the beginning of a script, but you can define them in separate files and share them between scripts. Once the function has been defined, you can use it any number of times.

Use the following syntax to define functions:

```
function_name() {
    (body of the function)
}
```

Shell functions use positional parameters and special variables such as * and # in the same way that shell scripts do. Typically, you define several shell functions within a single shell script. Each function receives arguments as positional parameters. These positional parameters "overlay" command-line parameters.

To call the function, use the function_name as if it were a normal command at the place in the script where you want to use the function. The following Bourne shell script defines and uses a simple function:

```
#!/bin/sh
#
printlist() {
        echo The current list of arguments is:
        echo $*
}
while [ $# -gt 0 ]
do
        printlist $*
        shift 2
done
```

The result of running this script is:

```
oak% doit one two three four
The current list of arguments is:
one two three four
The current list of arguments is:
three four
oak%
```

Debugging Shell Scripts

The following sections provide some suggestions for debugging shell scripts.

Using Debugging Flags

A common problem when writing shell scripts is that the shell does not interpret the command in exactly the way that you expect. When the shell interprets a command line, it substitutes variables with values, replaces filename wildcards with the appropriate file names, and performs command substitution. If the interpretation transforms a command line into something unexpected, the command most likely will not execute the way you intended it to.

All three shells provide -x (echo) and -v (verbose) options that you can use to help pinpoint where problems are occurring in a script. The -v option displays each line of the script as it is read from the file. The -x option shows each line after it has been processed by the shell and is ready for execution. The combination of these two options provides you with much useful information to debug your scripts.

You can use the options from the command line, as shown:

```
oak% csh -xv script-name
$ sh -xv script-name
$ ksh -xv script-name
```

Alternatively, you can set the flag options in the first line of the script, as:

```
#!/bin/sh -xv
#!/bin/csh -f -xv
#!/bin/ksh -xv
```

The following example shows the time-of-day greeting script with the -x option in the command line, followed by the screen output:

```
#!/bin/sh -x
#
# Time of day greetings
#
hour=`date +%H`

if [ $hour -le 12 ]
then
        echo "Good Morning!"
elif [ $hour -le 17 ]
then
        echo "Good Afternoon!"
```

```
else
        echo "Good Night!"
fi
```
$ greetings
```
+ date +%H
hour=11
+ [ 11 -le 12 ]
+ echo Good Morning!
Good Morning!
$
```

The following example shows the output for the same script with the -v option set:

$ greetings
```
#!/bin/sh -v
#
# Time of day greetings
#
hour=`date +%H`

if [ $hour -le 12 ]
then
        echo "Good Morning!"
elif [ $hour -le 17 ]
then
        echo "Good Afternoon!"
else
        echo "Good Night!"
fi
Good Morning!
$
```

The following example shows the screen output of the same script with -xv set:

$ greetings
```
#!/bin/sh -xv
#
# Time of day greetings
#
hour=`date +%H`
+ date +%H
hour=11
```

```
if [ $hour -le 12 ]
then
        echo "Good Morning!"
elif [ $hour -le 17 ]
then
        echo "Good Afternoon!"
else
        echo "Good Night!"
fi
+ [ 11 -le 12 ]
+ echo Good Morning!
Good Morning!
$
```

Understanding Shell Parsing Order

Each shell analyzes commands, whether from the command line or in a script, and parses them (divides them up) into recognizable parts. Shells can perform many kinds of substitutions and expansions. These operations are carried out in a very specific order for each shell. The parsing order for a shell can have a definite impact on shell programs that you write. Understanding the parsing order can help you determine where a script may be broken. Figure 15.2 shows a simplified version of Korn shell parsing order. When a command or string is quoted, the parsing order is affected. It can be difficult to understand exactly how the evaluation process works. Nevertheless, sometimes understanding the order in which a shell performs its operation can provide some insight into a problem. The Bourne shell parses in a similar order to the Korn shell, omitting history and alias substitution.

Figure 15.3 shows a simplified version of C shell parsing order.

The Bourne shell script that follows fails because variable expansion is done after redirection:

```
$ moreit='| more'
$ cat   /etc/passwd $moreit
ppp:x:12881:1:PPP:/tmp:/usr/etc/ppp-listen
root:x.:0:1:Operator:/:/bin/csh
nobody:x:65534:65534::/:
(Lines omitted from example)
+::0:0:::
cat: |: No such file or directory
cat: more: No such file or directory
$
```

Figure 15.2

Korn shell parsing order

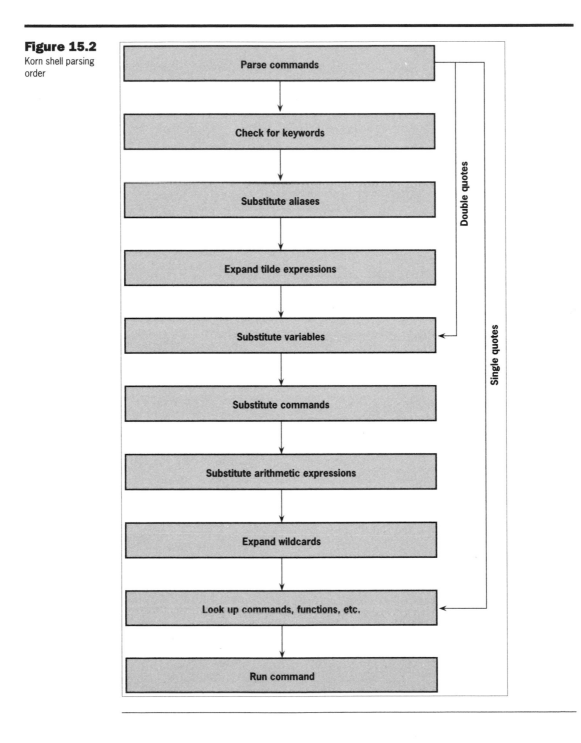

Figure 15.3

C shell parsing order

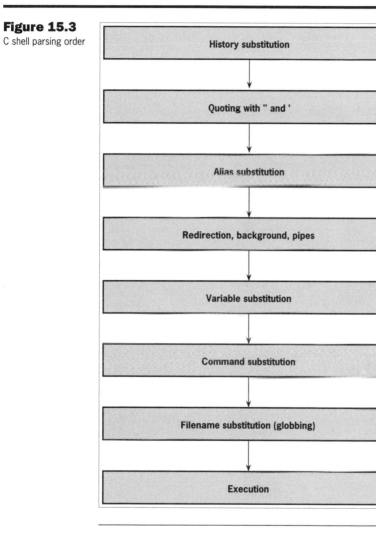

16

Reference Tables and Example Scripts

Reference Tables

Example Scripts

Reference Tables

This chapter contains tables of syntax elements for all three shells and examples of shell scripts.

Environment Files

Feature	Bourne	Korn	C
Read at login	.profile	.profile	.login
Read at invocation of choll		Any file specified in .profile with ENV=.*file*	.cshrc

First Line of Script

Shell	Syntax
Bourne	#!/bln/sh
Korn	#!/bin/ksh
C	#!/bin/csh -f

Korn Shell Path Operators

Operator	Description
${*variable#pattern*}	Delete the shortest part at the beginning of the variable that matches the pattern and return the rest.
${*variable##pattern*}	Delete the longest part at the beginning of the variable that matches the pattern and return the rest.
${*variable%pattern*}	Delete the shortest part at the end of the variable that matches the pattern and return the rest.
${*variable%%pattern*}	Delete the longest part at the end of the variable that matches the pattern and return the rest.

C Shell Path Modifiers

Modifier	Description
:e	Extension—remove prefix ending with a dot.
:h	Head—remove trailing pathname component.
:r	Root—remove trailing suffixes beginning with a dot (.).

Modifier	Description
:t	Tail—remove all leading pathname components.
:q	Quote—force variable to be quoted. Used to quote $argv.
:x	Like q, but break into words at each space, tab, or newline.

Variables Initialized by Shell

Variable	Explanation
$*	Bourne or Korn shell: List the value of all command-line parameters. This variable is useful only in scripts because the login shell has no arguments associated with it.
	C shell: Not used. Use $argv instead.
$#	Bourne or Korn shell: Return the number of command-line arguments (in decimal). Useful only in scripts.
	C shell: Count the number of words (in decimal) in a variable array.
$?	Bourne or Korn shell: Return the exit status (in decimal) of the last command executed. Most commands return a zero exit status if they complete successfully; otherwise a non-zero exit status is returned. This variable is set after each command is executed.
	C shell: Check to see if a variable of that name has been set.
$$	All shells: Return the process ID (PID) number of the current shell (in decimal).
$!	Return the process number (in decimal) of the last process run in the background.

Shell Built-In Commands

Purpose	Bourne or Korn Shell	C Shell
Null command	:	:
Create a command name alias	alias (K)	alias
Run current command in background	bg (K)	bg
Exit enclosing for or while loop	break	break
Break out of a switch		breaksw
Change directory	cd	cd
Continue next iteration of for or while loop	continue	continue
Default case in switch		default
Print directory stack		dirs

Purpose	Bourne or Korn Shell	C Shell
Write arguments on STDOUT	echo, print (K)	echo
Evaluate and execute arguments	eval	eval
Execute the arguments	exec	exec
Return or set shell variables	set	@
Exit shell program	exit	exit
Create an environment variable	export	setenv
Bring a command into foreground	fg (K)	fg
Execute foreach loop	for	foreach
Perform filename expansion		glob
Go to label within shell program		goto
Display history list	fc (K)	history
If-then-else decision	if	if
List active jobs	jobs (K)	jobs
Send a signal	kill	kill
Set limits for a job's resource use	ulimit	limit
Terminate login shell and invoke login		login
Terminate a login shell	exit	logout
Change to a new user group	newgrp	
Change priority of a command		nice
Ignore hangup		nohup
Notify user when job status changes		notify
Control shell processing on receipt of a signal	trap	onintr
Pop the directory stack		popd
Push a directory onto the stack		pushd
Read a line from stdin	read	$<
Change a variable to read only	readonly	
Repeat a command *n* times		repeat
Set shell environment variables	=	setenv
Set a local C shell variable		set

Purpose	Bourne or Korn Shell	C Shell
Shift positional parameters $* or $argv	shift	shift
Read and execute a file	. (dot)	source
Stop a background process		stop
Stop the shell	suspend (K)	suspend
CASE statement	case	switch
Evaluate conditional expressions	test	
Display execution times	times	time
Set default security for creation of files and directories	umask	umask
Discard aliases	unalias (K)	unalias
Remove limitations on resources	ulimit	unlimit
Unset a variable	unset	unset
Unset an environment variable		unsetenv
UNTIL loop	until	
Wait for background process to complete	wait	
WHILE loop foreground	while	while

Bourne and Korn Shell Redirection

Description	Command
Take standard input from file	*<file*, or 0*<file*
Redirect STDOUT to file	*> file*, or 1*> file*
Redirect STDERR to file	2*> file*
Append STDOUT to file	>> *file*
Redirect STDERR to stdout	2>&1
Pipe standard output of *cmd1* as standard input to *cmd2*	*cmd1*	*cmd2*
Use *file* as both STDIN and STDOUT	<> *file*
Close STDIN	<&-
Close STDOUT	>&-

C Shell Redirection Metacharacters

Description	Command
Redirect STDOUT to file	> *file*
Take input from file	< *file*
Append STDOUT to end of file	>> *file*
Redirect STDOUT and STDERR to file	>& *file*
Append STDOUT and STDERR to file	>>& *file*
Close STDERR	27&-

C Shell $argv Notation

Notation	Description
$#argv	Count the number of command-line arguments.
$*	Display all arguments.
$argv	Display all arguments.
$argv[1-3]	Display arguments 1 through 3
$0	Display the command used to run the shell script.
$argv[n]	Display the *n*th argument.
$argv[$#argv}	Display the last argument.

Quoting

Character	Term	Description
\	Backslash	Nullifies the special meaning of any shell metacharacter, including another backslash.
``	Backquotes	The output is substituted as if it were typed in place of the command. Refer to the shell manual pages for more information.
''	Single quotes	Nullifies the special meaning of all characters except bang (!), the backslash (\), and the single quote itself ('). Single quotes are more restrictive than double quotes and do not permit variable or backquote expansion.
""	Double quotes	Nullifies the special meaning of all special characters except bang (!), backquote (``), and dollar sign ($). Permits variable and backquote expansion.

Metacharacter Shell Syntax

Feature	Bourne and Korn	C
Single-character wildcard	?	?
Any number of characters	*	*
Set of single characters	[abc]	[abc]
Range of single characters	[a-c]	[a-c]
Inverse range of single characters	[!a-c]	N/A

Variable Shell Syntax

Feature	Bourne	Korn	C
Assigning regular variables	x=1	x=1	set x = 1
Accessing regular variables	echo $x	echo $x	echo $x
Assigning arrays	N/A	y[0]=1; y[1]=2	set y=(1 2)
Accessing array elements	N/A	echo $y	echo $y[1] $y[2]
		echo ${y[1]}	
Accessing entire array	N/A	echo ${y[*]}	echo $y
Exporting variables (make global)	export var	export var	use setenv command
Command-line arguments	N/A	N/A	$argv, $#argv, $argv[1]
Positional parameters	$*, $#, $1	$*, $#, $1	$*, $1
Setting positional params	set a b c	set a b c	N/A

I/O Redirection and Piping

Feature	Bourne	Korn	C
STDOUT to file	> *filename* 1> *filename*	> *filename* 1> *filename*	> *filename*
STDIN from file	< *filename* 0< *filename*	< *filename* 0< *filename*	< *filename*
STDERR to file	2> *filename*	2> *filename*	N/A
Output and errors to file	2>&1	2>&1	>& *filename*
Output to next command		cmd		cmd		cmd

Feature	Bourne	Korn	C
Output and errors to next command	2>&1 |	2>&1 |	|&

Printing to the Screen

Feature	Bourne	Korn	C
Display text and variables	echo	print echo	echo

Reading from the Keyboard

Feature	Bourne	Korn	C
Read keyboard input	read *name1 name2* . . .	read *name1 name2* . . .	set var = $<

Math and Calculations

Feature	Bourne	Korn	C
Perform a calculation	var=`expr a + b`	let var= a + b	@ var = (a + b)
Test a relational condition	var=`expr a < b`	let var=a < b	@ var = (a < b)

Command Substitution

Feature	Bourne	Korn	C
Command substitution	`command`	$(command) `command`	`command`

Tilde Expansion

Feature	Korn	C
Tilde represents user's home directory	~ ~loginid	~ ~loginid
Tilde represents current and previous directories	~+ ~-	N/A

Alias Syntax

Feature	Korn	C
Create new alias	alias name=value	alias name value
Display current list of values	alias	alias
Remove alias from list	unalias name	unalias name

History Syntax

Feature	Korn	C
Turn on history	automatic	set history = num
Display history list	history or fc	history
Display partial listing	history *n m*	history *n*
	history *-n*	
Reexecute a command	r *string*	!*string*
	r *number*	!*number*
	r	!!

Function Syntax

Feature	Bourne and Korn	C
Create a function	*func*() {	*func*() {*commands* }
	function *func* {*commands* }	
Use a function	Use *func* as a command	Use *func* as a command

Programming Statement Syntax

Feature	Bourne and Korn	C

If conditional	if *command*
	then
	  commands
	elif *command*
	  commands
	else
	  commands
	fi
		if (*cond*) then
		  commands
		else if (*cond*) then
		  commands
		else
		  commands
		endif

Switch and case
 	
pattern
	case *thing* in
	  pattern)
	    commands;;
	  *)
	    commands;;
	esac
		switch (*thing*)
		  case *pattern*:
		    commands
		  default:
		    commands
		endsw

While loops	while *command*
	do
	  commands
	done
		while (*cond*)
		  commands
		end

For/foreach loops	for *variable* in *list*
	do
	  commands
	done
		foreach *variable* (*list*)
		  commands
		end

Test and C Shell Built-in Test

What Is Tested	Test Command	csh Built-in
file is block device	-b *file*	N/A
file is character device	-c *file*	N/A
file is directory	-d *file*	-d *file*
file or directory exists	N/A	-e *file*
file is *file*	-f *file*	-f *file*
file has set-group-id bit set	-g *file*	N/A
file has sticky bit set	-k *file*	N/A
file is owned by executing user	N/A	-o *file*
file is a named pipe	-p *file*	N/A
current user can read *file*	-r *file*	-r *file*
file exists and has size >0	-s *file*	N/A

What Is Tested	Test Command	csh Built-in
n is a terminal file descriptor	-t *n*	N/A
file has set-user-id bit set	-u *file*	N/A
current user can write to *file*	-w *file*	-w *file*
current user can execute *file*	-x *file*	N/A
file has zero size	N/A	-z *file*
string is NULL	-z *string*	*string* == ""
string is NOT NULL	*string* != ""	-n *string, string*
strings are equal	*string* = *string*	*string* == *string*
strings are not equal	*string* != *string*	*string* != *string*
string matches filename wildcard pattern	N/A	*string* =~ *pattern*
string does not match filename wildcard pattern	N/A	*string* !~ *pattern*
num1 is equal to *num2*	*num1* -eq *num2*	*num1* == *num2*
num1 is not equal to *num2*	*num1* -ne *num2*	*num1* != *num2*
num1 is less than *num 2*	*num1* -lt *num2*	*num1* < *num2*
num1 is less than or equal to *num2*	*num1* -le *num2*	*num1* <= *num2*
num1 is greater than *num2*	*num1* -gt *num2*	*num1* > *num2*
num1 is greater than or equal to *num2*	*num1* -ge *num2*	*num1* >= *num2*
logical AND	-a	&&
logical OR	-o	||
logical NEGATION	!	!!

Bourne Shell Mathematical Operators

Operator	Description
+	Addition
-	Subtraction
*	Multiplication
/	Division
%	Remainder

C Shell Mathematical Operators

Syntax	Description
@ *variable* = (*expression*)	Set value of variable equal to the expression.
@ *variable* += (*expression*)	Addition.
@ *variable* -= (*expression*)	Subtraction.
@ *variable* *= (*expression*)	Multiplication.
@ *variable* /= (*expression*)	Division.
@ *variable* ++	Add 1.
@ *variable* --	Subtract 1.

Example Scripts

These sections contain some examples of Bourne shell scripts.

Anonymous ftp Script

A script named fez performs an anonymous ftp get or list.

```
#! /bin/sh
#
#       @(#)fez,v1.0                      (mc@anywhere.EDay.Sun.COM) 08/29/92
#
PATHNAME=anywhere.EBay:/home/me/bin/fez
MYNAME=`basename $0`
#
# Author:
#     Wayne Thompson
#
# Synopsis:
usage=`/bin/sed -e "s/^ *//" << endusage
      usage: $MYNAME [-h] [-abfglmprR] [[login@]hostname:[sourcepath]]
endusage`
#
# Description:
#     This script will perform an anonymous ftp get or list.
#
#     If the hostname is not specified on the command line, then
#     it is derived from the basename(1) of the current directory.
#     This provides for a hierarchy of hostnames within which to
#     get files or directory listings.
#
#     If no flags and arguments are given or a single argument of
#     the form "hostname:" is given, the default action will be
```

```
#       to retrieve a recursive directory listing from the remote
#       host into the file "./ls-lR.".
#
#       Directory listings are named in the following manner:
#           <the command used to produce the listing w/spaces collapsed>
#           followed by the path it was produced from with slashes(/)
#           transliterated to dots(.). e.g.
#               ls-1.              (ls -1 /)
#               ls-lR.a.b          (ls -lR /a/b)
#
#       When mirroring is enabled(default), the directory listing
#       "ls-lR.a.b" would be placed in the directory "./a/b" which
#       would be created if necessary.
#       Likewise, "fez export.lcs.mit.edu:/contrib/3dlife.c" would
#       get "/contrib/3dlife.c" from "export.lcs.mit.edu" and place
#       it into "./contrib/3dlife.c".
#       An alternative behaviour is provided by the "-f" flag, which
#       serves to flatten the destination hierarchy.
#       "fez -f export.lcs.mit.edu:/contrib/3dlife.c" would get
#       "/contrib/3dlife.c" into "./3dlife.c"
#
#       The default user is "anonymous".
#       The default password is one of:
#           internal to Sun = $USER@hostname
#           external to Sun = $USER@Sun.Com
#       You may override these in $HOME/.netrc (see netrc(5))
#       or from the command line.
#
# Options:
#       -a       ascii mode
#       -b       binary mode                      (default)
#       -f       flatten hierarchy
#       -g       get                              (default w/arg)
#       -h       print command description.
#       -l       list                             (default w/o arg)
#       -m       mirror hierarchy                 (default)
#       -p passwd password
#       -(r|R)   recursive                        (default w/o arg)
#
# Environment:
#
# Files:
#       $HOME/.netrc                 file for ftp remote login data
#
# Diagnostics:
#       Exit Status:
#           Ø       normal termination
#           1       abnormal termination
#
#       Errors (stderr):
#           usage
#
```

```
#       Warnings (stderr):
#
#       Info (stdout):
#
# Dependencies:
#       Fez only knows how to talk to UNIX(R) hosts.
#
# Caveats:
#       A recursive directory get will not fetch subdirectories unless
#       they already exist.
#
# Bugs:
#

# >> BEGIN parse options >>>>>>>>>>>>>>>>>>>>>>>>>>>>>>>>>>>>>>>>>> #

while [ $# -gt 0 ]
do
    case $1 in
        -??*)                                   # bundled options
            opts=$1
            while [ $opts ]
            do
                opts=`/bin/expr $opts : '.\(.*\)'`
                case $opts in
                    a*)                         # ascii mode
                        mode=asci
                        ;;

                    b*)                         # binary mode
                        mode=binary
                        ;;

                    f*)                         # flatten remote hierarchy
                        flat=true
                        ;;

                    g*)                         # get
                        ;;

                    l*)                         # list
                        list=true
                        ;;

                    p)
                        passflg=true
                        shift
                        if [ $# -eq 0 ]
                        then
                            echo >&2 "$MYNAME: error: no passwd"
                            echo >&2 "usage"
                            exit 1
```

```
                        fi
                        passwd=$1
                        ;;

                p*)
                        echo >&2 "$MYNAME: error: p: must be last element of
bundled options"
                        exit 1
                        ;;

                [rR]*)                              # recursive
                        recurse=true
                        ;;

                ?*)
                        echo >&2 "$MYNAME: error: -`/bin/expr $opts : '\(.\)'`:
unknown option."
                        echo >&2 "$usage"
                        exit 1
                        ;;
            esac
        done
        shift
        ;;

    -a)                                 # ascii mode
        mode=ascii
        shift
        ;;

    -b)                                 # binary mode
        mode=binary
        shift
        ;;

    -f)                                 # flatten remote hierarchy
        flat=true
        shift
        ;;

    -g)                                 # get
        shift
        ;;

    -h)                                 # help
        /bin/awk '
            /^$/ {
                exit;
            }

            /^[# :]/ && NR > 1 {
                print substr ($0, 3);
```

```
            }
    ' $0 |
    /bin/sed "
        /^$/{
            N
            /^\n$/D
        }
        s/\$MYNAME/$MYNAME/
    "
    exit 0
    ;;

-l)                                     # list
    list=true
    shift
    ;;

-m)                                     # mirror remote hierarchy
    mirror=true
    shift
    ;;

-p)
    passflg=true
    shift
    if [ $# -eq 0 ]
    then
        echo >&2 "$MYNAME: error: no passwd"
        echo >&2 "usage"
        exit 1
    fi
    passwd=$1
    shift
    ;;

-[rR])                                  # recursive
    recurse=true
    shift
    ;;

--)                                     # end of options
    shift
    break
    ;;

-*)
    echo >&2 "$MYNAME: error: $1: unknown option."
    echo >&2 "$usage"
    exit 1
    ;;

*)                                      # end of options
```

```
            break
            ;;
    esac
done

# << END parse options <<<<<<<<<<<<<<<<<<<<<<<<<<<<<<<<<<<<<<<<<< #

# >> BEGIN parse arguments >>>>>>>>>>>>>>>>>>>>>>>>>>>>>>>>>>>>>> #

case $# in
    0)
        list=true
        recurse=true
        ;;

    1)
        case $1 in
            *:)
                list=true
                recurse=true
                ;;
        esac
        ;;

    *)
        echo >&2 "$MYNAME: error: unexpected argument(s)."
        echo >&2 "$usage"
        exit 1
        ;;
esac

# << END parse arguments <<<<<<<<<<<<<<<<<<<<<<<<<<<<<<<<<<<<<<<< #

# >> BEGIN initialization >>>>>>>>>>>>>>>>>>>>>>>>>>>>>>>>>>>>>>> #

[ umask -ge 700 ] && umask `/bin/expr \`umask\` - 0700`

# return unrooted dirname
dirname () {
    expr \
    './'${1-.}'/' : '\(\.\)/[^/]*/$' \
    \| ${1-.}'/' : '/*\(.*[^/]\)//*[^/][^/]*//*$' \
    \| .
}
[ ${1-.} = / ] && set .
host=`/bin/expr \
    "$1" : '[^@]*@\(.*\):' \
    \| "$1" : '\(.*\):' \
    \| \`/bin/basename \\\`pwd\\\`\``

path=`/bin/expr "$1" : '[^:]*:\(.*\)' \| $1. : '[^:]*:\(.*\)' \| ${1-.}`
dir=`dirname $path`
```

```
file=`/bin/basename $path`
login=`/bin/expr "$1" : '\([^@]*\)@' \| anonymous`
if /bin/ypmatch $host hosts.byname 2>&- 1>&- ||
    /bin/ypmatch $host hosts.byaddr 2>&- 1>&-
then
    port=21
    passwd=${passwd-USER@`hostname`}
else
    port=4666
    passwd=${passwd-USER@Sun.COM}
    machine=$host
    host=sun-barr.EBay
fi

if [ $list ]
then
    cmd="ls -l${recurse+R}"
    file=ls-l${recurse+R}`expr \
        $path : '\(\.\)$' \
        \| $dir$file : '\(\..*\)' \
        \| /$dir/$file | tr / .
        `
    dir=$path
else
    cmd=${recurse+m}get
    [ $recurse ] && dir=$path && file=\*
fi

case $1 in
    *@*:*)
        ;;
    *)
        [ $passflg ] ||
        eval `
            /bin/awk '
                /machine *'"${machine-$host}"'/ {
                    for (i = 1; i <= NF; i++) {
                        if ($i == "login") print "login="$++i";";
                        if ($i == "password") print "passwd="$++i";";
                    }
                    exit;
                }
            ' $HOME/.netrc 2>&-
        `
        ;;
esac

# << END initialization <<<<<<<<<<<<<<<<<<<<<<<<<<<<<<<<<<<<<<<< #

# >> BEGIN verify prerequisites >>>>>>>>>>>>>>>>>>>>>>>>>>>>>>>> #

if [ ! "$flat" ]
```

```
then
    /bin/mkdir -p $dir 2>&-
    cd $dir
fi

# << END verify prerequisites <<<<<<<<<<<<<<<<<<<<<<<<<<<<<<<<<<<<< #

# >> BEGIN main >>>>>>>>>>>>>>>>>>>>>>>>>>>>>>>>>>>>>>>>>>>>>>>>>> #

/usr/ucb/ftp -i -n -v $host $port << EOFTP
    user $login${machine+@$machine} $passwd
    ${mode-binary}
    cd $dir
    $cmd $file
    quit
EOFTP
echo ""

# << END main <<<<<<<<<<<<<<<<<<<<<<<<<<<<<<<<<<<<<<<<<<<<<<<<<<<< #
```

arch.sh.fctn Function

The arch.sh.fctn script emulates SunOS 4.*x* system architecture.

```
#
#   %M%:      Version: %I%     Date:       %G%
#

[ $_Arch_loaded ] || {


# Function:
#     @(#)Arch                        (Wayne.Thompson@Sun.COM) 05/14/92
#
# Description:
#     This function emulates 4.x arch(1).
#
# Variables:
#
# Usage:
#     Arch
#     Arch -k
#     Arch archname
#
# Return:
#     0 success
#     1 non-success
#
# Dependencies:
#     This function works under SunOs 3.x - 5.x.
#
```

```
# Bugs:
#

Arch () {
    case $1 in
        '')
            /bin/arch $* 2>&- || /bin/expr `/bin/uname -m` : '\(sun[0-9]*\)'
            ;;

        -k)
            /bin/arch $* 2>&- || /bin/uname -m
            ;;

        *)
            if [ -x /bin/arch ]
            then
                /bin/arch $*
            else
                [ $* = `/bin/expr \`/bin/uname -m\` : '\(sun[0-9]*\)'` ]
            fi
            ;;
    esac
}

_Arch_loaded=1
}
```

array.sh.fctn Function

The following function extends the functionality of the Bourne shell to in-clude associative arrays:

```
## >> BEGIN package: arrays >>>>>>>>>>>>>>>>>>>>>>>>>>>>>>>>>>>>>>>> ##

# Package:
#       @(#)arrays,v1.0                    (Wayne.Thompson@Sun.COM) 05/02/93
#
# Description:
#       This package contains functions that emulate associative arrays.
#       Keys are limited to letters, digits, underscores, hyphens and periods.
#
# Variables:
#       __array_size_<array>
#       __array_keys_<array>
#       __array__<array>_<key>
#       __array_filename
#       __array_name
#       __array_key
#       __array_keys
#       __array_cell
#
```

```
# Usage:
#     setarray array key [value ...]
#     getarray array key
#     unsetarray array [key ...]
#     keys array
#     sizearray array
#     defined array [key]
#     dumparray pathname [array ...]
#
# Dependencies:
#     Array names and keys are combined to form strings which are
#     evaluated as parameters.
#
# Bugs:
#

### >> BEGIN function: setarray >>>>>>>>>>>>>>>>>>>>>>>>>>>>>>>>>>>> ###

# Function:
#     @(#)setarray.v1.0               (Wayne.Thompson@Sun.COM) 05/16/93
#
# Description:
#     This function assigns values to array elements. If more than one
#     value is provided and the key is an integer, values will be
#     assigned to successive elements beginning with the initial key.
#
# Variables:
#     __array_size_<array>
#     __array_keys_<array>
#     __array__<array>_<key>
#     __array_name
#     __array_key
#     __array_cell
#
# Usage:
#     setarray array key [value ...]
#     setarray pathname
#
# Return:
#
# Dependencies:
#
# Bugs:
#

setarray () {
    case $# in
        0)
            echo >&2 setarray: error: "$@"
            echo >&2 usage: setarray array key '[value ...]'
            exit 1
            ;;
```

```
    1)
        if [ -f $1 ]
        then
            while read __array_name __array_key __array_value
            do
                setarray $__array_name $__array_key $__array_value
            done < $1
            return
        else
            echo >&2 setarray: error: $1: no such file
            exit 1
        fi
        ;;

    2|3)
        ;;

    *)
        case $2 in
            [0-9]*)
                ;;

            *)
                echo >&2 setarray: error: "$@"
                echo >&2 setarray: error: 2nd argument must be an integer
                exit 1
                ;;
        esac
        ;;
esac
__array_name=$1
__array_key=$2
case $2 in
    *[-.]*)
        __array_cell=`echo $2 | /bin/tr '[-.]' __`
        shift 2
        set $__array_name $__array_cell "$@"
        ;;
esac
eval "
    if [ \${__array_size_$1+1} ]
    then
        [ \${__array__$1_$2+1} ] || {
            __array_size_$1=\`/bin/expr \$__array_size_$1 + 1\`
            __array_keys_$1=\"\$__array_keys_$1 \$__array_key \"
        }
    else
        __array_size_$1=1
        __array_keys_$1=\$__array_key
    fi
    __array__$1_$2=\$3
```

```
        "
        case $# in
            2)
                    shift 2
                    ;;

            *)
                    shift 3
                    ;;
        esac
        while [ $# -gt 0 ]
        do
                array_key=`/bin/expr $__array_key + 1`
                eval "
                    [ \${__array__${__array_name}_$__array_key+1} ] || {
                            __array_size_$__array_name=\`/bin/expr
\$__array_size_$__array_name + 1\`
                            __array_keys_$__array_name=\"\$__array_keys_$__array_name
\$__array_key\"
                    }
                    __array__${__array_name}_$__array_key=\$1
                "
                shift
        done
}


### << END function: setarray <<<<<<<<<<<<<<<<<<<<<<<<<<<<<<<<<<<<< ###

### >> BEGIN function: getarray >>>>>>>>>>>>>>>>>>>>>>>>>>>>>>>>>> ###

# Function:
#       @(#)getarray.v1.0               (Wayne.Thompson@Sun.COM) 05/02/93
#
# Description:
#       This function prints array values.
#
# Variables:
#       __array__<array>_<key>
#       __array_name
#
# Usage:
#       getarray array [key ...]
#
# Return:
#
# Dependencies:
#
# Bugs:
#

getarray () {
        case $# in
```

```
            0)
                echo >&2 getarray: error: "$@"
                echo >&2 usage: getarray array '[key ...]'
                exit 1
                ;;

            1)  # entire array
                set $1 `keys $1`
                ;;
    esac
    __array_name=$1
    shift
    while [ $# -gt 0 ]
    do
        case $1 in
            *[-.]*)
                eval echo \$__array__${__array_name}_`echo $1 | /bin/tr '[-.]'

                ;;

            *)
                eval echo \$__array__${__array_name}_$1
                ;;
        esac
        shift
    done
}
```

```
### << END function: getarray <<<<<<<<<<<<<<<<<<<<<<<<<<<<<<<<<<< ###

### >> BEGIN function: unsetarray >>>>>>>>>>>>>>>>>>>>>>>>>>>>>>>> ###

# Function:
#     @(#)unsetarray,v1.0              (Wayne.Thompson@Sun.COM) 05/02/93
#
# Description:
#     This function unsets (undefines) one or more array elements
#     or an entire array.
#
# Variables:
#     __array_size_<array>
#     __array_keys_<array>
#     __array__<array>_<key>
#     __array_name
#     __array_key
#     __array_keys
#
# Usage:
#     unsetarray array [key ...]
#
# Return:
#
```

```
# Dependencies:
#
# Bugs:
#

unsetarray () {
    case $# in
        0)
            echo >&2 unsetarray: error: "$@"
            echo >&2 usage: unsetarray array '[key ...]'
            exit 1
            ;;

        1)  # entire array
            set $1 `keys $1`
            ;;
    esac

    __array_name=$1
    shift

    while [ $# -gt 0 ]
    do
        eval "
            __array_keys=
            [ \${__array__${__array_name}_$1+1} ] &&
            for __array_key in \$__array_keys_$__array_name
            do
                case \$__array_key in
                    \$1)
                        case \$1 in
                            *[-.]*)
                                unset __array__${__array_name}_\`echo \$1 |
/bin/tr '[-.]' __\`
                                ;;

                            *)
                                unset __array__${__array_name}_$1
                                ;;
                        esac
                        __array_size_$__array_name=\`/bin/expr
\$__array_size_$__array_name - 1\`
                        ;;

                    *)
                        case \$__array_keys in
                            '')
                                __array_keys=\$__array_key
                                ;;

                            *)
                                __array_keys=\"\$__array_keys \$__array_key\"
```

```
                                  ;;
                         esac
                          ;;
                esac
            done
            __array_keys_$__array_name=\$__array_keys
        "
        shift
    done
    eval "
        case \$__array_size_$__array_name in
            0)
                unset __array_size_$__array_name __array_keys_$__array_name
                ;;
        esac
    "
}


### << END function: unsetarray <<<<<<<<<<<<<<<<<<<<<<<<<<<<<<<<<< ###

### >> BEGIN function: keys >>>>>>>>>>>>>>>>>>>>>>>>>>>>>>>>>>>>>> ###

# Function:
#     @(#)keys,v1.0                    (Wayne.Thompson@Sun.COM) 05/02/93
#
# Description:
#     This function prints the keys of an array.
#
# Variables:
#     __array_keys_<array>
#
# Usage:
#     keys array
#
# Return:
#
# Dependencies:
#
# Bugs:
#

keys () {
    case $# in
        1)
            eval echo \$__array_keys_$1
            ;;

        *)
            echo >&2 keys: error: "$@"
            echo >&2 usage: keys array
            exit 1
            ;;
```

```
        esac
}

### << END function: keys <<<<<<<<<<<<<<<<<<<<<<<<<<<<<<<<<<<<<<< ###

### >> BEGIN function: sizearray >>>>>>>>>>>>>>>>>>>>>>>>>>>>>>>> ###

# Function:
#     @(#)sizearray,v1.0               (Wayne.Thompson@Sun.COM) 05/02/93
#
# Description:
#     This function prints the number of defined array elements.
#
# Variables:
#     __array_size_<array>
#
# Usage:
#     sizearray array
#
# Return:
#
# Dependencies:
#
# Bugs:
#

sizearray () {
    case $# in
        1)
                eval echo \${__array_size_$1:-0}
                ;;

        *)
                echo >&2 sizearray: error: "$@"
                echo >&2 usage: sizearray array
                exit 1
                ;;
    esac
}

### << END function: sizearray <<<<<<<<<<<<<<<<<<<<<<<<<<<<<<<<<<< ###

### >> BEGIN function: defined >>>>>>>>>>>>>>>>>>>>>>>>>>>>>>>>>>> ###

# Function:
#     @(#)defined,v1.0                 (Wayne.Thompson@Sun.COM) 05/02/93
#
# Description:
#     This function returns whether an array element or array is defined.
#
# Variables:
#     __array_size_<array>
```

```
#       __array__<array>_<key>
#
# Usage:
#     defined array [key]
#
# Return:
#     Ø          defined
#     1          undefined
#
# Dependencies:
#
# Bugs:
#

defined () {
    case $# in
        1)
            eval set \${__array_size_$1+Ø} 1
            ;;

        2)
            case $2 in
                *[-.]*) set $1 `echo $2 | /bin/tr '[-.]' __`;;
            esac
            eval set \${__array__$1 $2+Ø} 1
            ;;

        *)
            echo >&2 defined: error: "$@"
            echo >&2 usage: defined array '[key]'
            exit 1
            ;;
    esac
    return $1
}


### << END function: defined <<<<<<<<<<<<<<<<<<<<<<<<<<<<<<<<<<<<< ###

### >> BEGIN function: dumparray >>>>>>>>>>>>>>>>>>>>>>>>>>>>>>>>> ###

# Function:
#     @(#)dumparray.v1.Ø              (Wayne.Thompson@Sun.COM) Ø5/Ø2/93
#
# Description:
#     This function dumps arrays in file in a format readable by
#     shell dot (.) command.
#
# Variables:
#     __array_filename
#
# Usage:
#     dumparray pathname [array ...]
```

```
#
# Return:
#    Ø         success
#    1         failure
#
# Dependencies:
#
# Bugs:
#    Since this depends on the output of set, and set does not preserve
#    quoting, the resultant file may be unusable. Use of
#    storearray/setarray is safer, albeit slower.
#

dumparray () {
    case $# in
        Ø)
            echo >&2 dumparray: error: "$@"
            echo >&2 usage: dumparray pathname '[array ...]'
            exit 1
            ;;
    esac

    __array_filename=$1
    shift

    set |
    /bin/awk '
        /\(\){$/ { exit }                    # functions follow parameters

        /^__array_(filename|name|key|keys|cell)=/ { next }     # temp storage

        /^__array_(size|keys)*_(`echo ${*:-.\*} | /bin/tr " " \|`')(_|=)/ {
            if (NF > 1) {
                n = index($Ø, "=");
                print substr($Ø , 1, n)"'\''"substr($Ø, n+1)"'\''";
            }
            else {
                print;
            }
        }
    ' > $__array_filename
}

### << END function: dumparray <<<<<<<<<<<<<<<<<<<<<<<<<<<<<<<< ###

## << END package: arrays <<<<<<<<<<<<<<<<<<<<<<<<<<<<<<<<<<<<<<< ##
```

The function scripts arch.sh.fctn (displayed earlier in this chapter), hostname.sh.fctn, osr.sh.fctn, and whoami.sh.fctn are used to help in the transition from SunOS 4.*x* to Solaris 2.*x*.

hostname.sh.fctn Function

The hostname.sh.fctn script emulates the SunOS 4.*x* hostname command:

```
#
#  %M%:    Version:  %I%    Date:    %G%
#

[ $_Hostname loaded ] || {


# Function:
#     @(#)hostname                    (Wayne.Thompson@Sun.COM) 02/15/92
#
# Description:
#     This function emulates 4.x hostname(1) given no arguments.
#
# Variables:
#
# Usage:
#     Hostname
#
# Return:
#
# Dependencies:
#     This funcion works under SunOs 3.x - 5.x.
#
# Bugs:
#

Hostname () {
    /bin/hostname 2>&- || /bin/uname -n
}

_Hostname_loaded=1
}
```

osr.sh.fctn Function

The osr.sh.fctn script outputs the numeric portion of the current operating system release, for example 5.2 for Solaris 5.2 system software:

```
#
#  %M%:    Version:  %I%    Date:    %G%
#

[ $_Osr_loaded ] || {

# Function:
#     @(#)Osr                        (Wayne.Thompson@Sun.COM) 02/08/92
#
```

```
# Description:
#     This function outputs the numeric portion of the current OS release.
#
# Variables:
#
# Usage:
#     os=`Osr`
#
# Return:
#     0 success
#     1 non-success
#
# Dependencies:
#     This funcion works under SunOs 3.x - 5.x.
#
# Bugs:
#

Osr () {
    /bin/expr `
        {
            /bin/uname -r ||
            /bin/cat /usr/sys/conf*/RELEASE
        } 2>&- ||
        /etc/dmesg |
        /bin/awk '
            BEGIN { status = 1 }
            /^SunOS Release/ { print $3; status = 0; exit }
            END { exit status }
        ' ||
        /bin/expr "\`
            /usr/ucb/strings -50 /vmunix |
            /bin/egrep '^SunOS Release'
        \`" : 'SunOS Release \([^ ]*\)'
    ` : '\([.0-9]*\)'
}

_Osr_loaded=1
}
```

whoami.sh.fctn Function

The whoami.sh.fctn emulates the SunOS 4.x whoami command:

```
#
#  @(#)  whoami.sh.fctn      1.2     Last mod: 6/4/93
#

[ $_Whoami_loaded ] || {

# Function:
```

```
#       @(#)whoami                      (Wayne.Thompson@Sun.COM) 03/20/92
#
# Description:
#     This function emulates 4.x whoami(1).
#
# Variables:
#
# Usage:
#     whoami
#
# Return:
#
# Dependencies:
#     This funcion works under SunOs 3.x - 5.x.
#
# Bugs:
#

Whoami () {
    /usr/ucb/whoami 2>&- ||
    /bin/expr "`/bin/id`" : '[^(]*(\([^)]*\)'
}


_Whoami_loaded=1
}
```

Volume Management

Volume management is a new feature with Solaris 2.2 system software. Volume management automates mounting of CD-ROMs and diskettes; you no longer need to have superuser permissions to mount a CD-ROM or a diskette.

CAUTION! *The Solaris 2.0 and 2.1 procedures for mounting CD-ROMs and diskettes will not work for Solaris 2.2 and later releases. Volume management controls the /dev/dsk/c0t6d0s0 path to a CD-ROM drive and the /dev/diskette path to the diskette drive. If you try to access a CD-ROM or diskette using these paths, an error message is displayed.*

Volume Management Files

Volume management consists of the /usr/sbin/vold volume management daemon, the /etc/vold.conf configuration file used by the vold daemon to determine which devices to manage, the /etc/rmmount.conf file used to configure removable media mounts, and actions in /usr/lib/rmmount. The volume daemon logs messages in the /var/adm/vold.log file.

The default /etc/vold.conf file is shown as:

```
# @(#)vold.conf 1.13    92/10/28 SMI
#
# Volume Daemon Configuration File
#

# Database to use (must be first)
db db_mem.so

# Labels supported
label dos label_dos.so floppy
label cdrom label_cdrom.so cdrom
label sun label_sun.so floppy

# Devices to use
use cdrom drive /dev/dsk/c0t6 dev_cdrom.so cdrom0
use floppy drive /dev/fd0 dev_floppy.so floppy 0

# Actions
insert /vol*/dev/fd[0-9]/* user=root /usr/sbin/rmm
insert /vol*/dev/dsk/* user=root /usr/sbin/rmm
eject /vol*/dev/fd[0-9]/* user=root /usr/sbin/rmm
eject /vol*/dev/dsk* user=root /usr/sbin/rmm
notify /vol*/rdsk/* group=tty /usr/lib/vold/volmissing -c
```

```
# List of file system types unsafe to eject
unsafe ufs hsfs pcfs
```

If you want additional CD-ROM and diskette drives on a system, you must edit the /etc/vold.conf file and add the new devices to the "Devices to use" list. The syntax for a "Devices to use" entry is shown as:

```
use device type special shared-object symname options
```

Table A.1 describes each of the fields for the "Devices to use" syntax.

Table A.1　　**Device Control Syntax Descriptions**

Field	Supported Default Values	Description
device	cdrom, floppy	The removable media device.
type	drive	The type of device—multiple or single media support.
special	/dev/dsk/c0t6 /dev/diskette	Pathname of the device to be used in the /dev directory.
shared-object	/usr/lib/vold/*shared-object-name*	Location of the code that manages the device.
symname	cdrom0, floppy0	The symbolic name that refers to this device. The *symname* is placed in the device directory (either /cdrom or /floppy).
options	user=nobody group=nobody mode=0666	The user, group, and mode permissions for the inserted media.

The /etc/rmmount.conf file is shown as:

```
# @(#)rmmount.conf 1.2     92/09/23 SMI
#
# Removable Media Mounter configuration file.
#

# File system identification
ident hsfs ident_hsfs.so cdrom
ident ufs ident_ufs.so cdrom floppy
ident pcfs ident_pcfs.so floppy
```

```
# Actions
action cdrom action_filemgr.so
action floppy action_filemgr.so
```

The files in the /usr/lib/vold directory are listed as:

```
oak% ls -1 /usr/lib/rmmount
action_filemgr.so.1
action_workman.so.1
oak%
```

If you encounter problems with volume management, check the /var/adm/vold.log file for information. An example of this file follows:

```
oak% more /var/adm/vold.log
Tue Jun  1 17:34:24 1993 warning: dev_use: couldn't find a driver for drive
cdrom at /dev/dsk/c0t6
Tue Jun  1 17:39:12 1993 warning: dev_use: couldn't find a driver for drive
cdrom at /dev/dsk/c0t6
Tue Jun  1 18:24:24 1993 warning: dev_use: couldn't find a driver for drive
cdrom at /dev/dsk/c0t6
Wed Jun 23 15:08:47 1993 warning: check device 36.2: device not managed
Wed Jun 23 15:09:58 1993 warning: check device 36.2: device not managed
Wed Jun 23 15:11:08 1993 warning: check device 36.2: device not managed
Thu Jul 15 13:51:23 1993 warning: check device 36.2: device not managed
Thu Jul 15 13:52:53 1993 warning: check device 36.2: device not managed
Thu Jul 15 14:04:37 1993 warning: check device 36.2: device not managed
Thu Jul 15 14:05:52 1993 warning: check device 36.2: device not managed
Thu Jul 15 14:06:16 1993 warning: check device 36.2: device not managed
Wed Jul 21 16:33:33 1993 fatal: svc tli create: Cannot create server handleThu
Jul 22 16:32:28 1993 warning: cdrom: /dev/rdsk/c0t6d0s2; Device busy
castle%
```

If you want to display debugging messages from the volume daemon, you can start the daemon by typing **/usr/sbin/vold -v -L 10**. With these flags set, the volume daemon logs quite a bit of information in /var/adm/vold.log.

Another way to gather debugging information is to run the rmmount command with the debug flag. To do so, edit /etc/vold.conf and change the lines that have /usr/sbin/rmmount to include the -D flag, as shown in the following example:

```
insert /vol*/dev/diskette[0-9]/* user=root /usr/sbin/rmmount -D
```

Volume Management Mount Points

Volume management automatically mounts CD-ROM file systems on the /cdrom mount point when you insert the media into the drive. When you insert a diskette in the diskette drive, you must either use the volcheck(1) command or choose Check for Floppy from the File menu of the File Manager before files are mounted on the /floppy mount point. Table A.2 describes the mount points and how volume management uses them.

Table A.2   **Volume Management Mount Points**

Media	Mount Point	State of Media
Diskette	/floppy/floppy0	Symbolic link to mounted diskette in local diskette drive
	/floppy/*floppy-name*	Mounted named diskette
	/floppy/unnamed_floppy	Mounted unnamed diskette
CD-ROM	/cdrom/cdrom0	Symbolic link to mounted CD-ROM in local CD-ROM drive
	/cdrom/*CD-ROM-name*	Mounted named CD-ROM
	/cdrom/*CD-ROM-name/partition*	Mounted named CD-ROM with partitioned file system
	/cdrom/unnamed_cdrom	Mounted unnamed CD-ROM

If the media does not contain a file system, volume management provides block and character devices in the /vol file system, as shown in Table A.3.

Table A.3   **Solaris 2.3 CD-ROM and Diskette Device Locations When No File System Is Present**

Media	Device Location	State of Media
Diskette	/vol/dev/diskette0/unnamed_floppy	Formatted unnamed diskette-block device access
	/vol/dev/rdiskette0/unnamed_floppy	Formatted unnamed diskette—raw device access
	/vol/dev/diskette0/unlabeled	Unlabeled diskette—block diskette-raw device access
CD-ROM	/vol/dev/dsk/c0t6/unnamed_cdrom	CD-ROM—block device access
	/vol/dev/rdsk/c0t6/unnamed_cdrom	CD-ROM—raw device access

CD-ROMs and Volume Management

The following sections describe how to access files from local and remote CD-ROM drives.

Mounting a Local CD-ROM

Use the following procedure to mount a CD-ROM from a local drive:

1. Remove the protective film and remove the CD-ROM from its plastic case.

2. Place the CD-ROM into its caddy so that the CD label is visible.

3. Insert the caddy into the drive slot. The CD-ROM is automatically mounted on the /cdrom mount point. If File Manager is running, a window displays the contents of the CD-ROM, as shown in Figure A.1.

Figure A.1
The File Manager
CD-ROM window

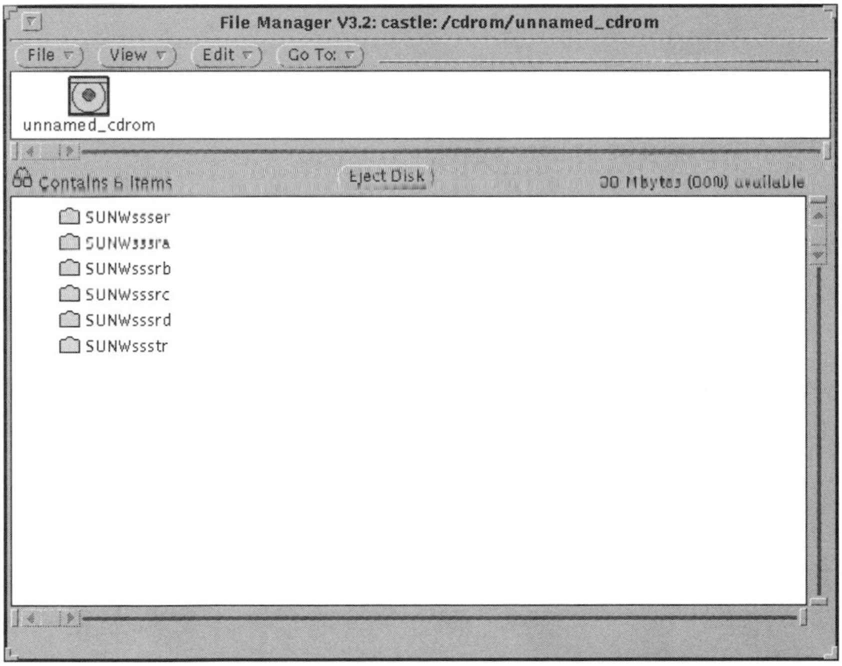

4. To access files on the CD-ROM from a command line, type **cd/cdrom/cdrom0** and press Return.

5. Type **ls** and press Return. The list of files in the /cdrom/cdrom0 directory is displayed.

You can use the File Manager CD-ROM window and the command line interchangeably. For example, you can eject a CD-ROM either from a command line by typing **eject cdrom** or by clicking SELECT on the Eject button in the File Manager CD-ROM window.

Sharing Files from a Remote CD-ROM Drive

Before you can share CD-ROM files from a command line, the mountd daemon must be running. On the system with the CD-ROM drive attached, type **ps -ef | grep mountd** and press Return.

If the mountd daemon is running, other systems can access shared files. If the mountd daemon is not running, you need to stop NFS services and restart them. Be sure to notify any users of the system that NFS services will be interrupted momentarily when you use the following procedure.

Use the following steps to start the mountd daemon:

1. Become superuser.

2. Type **/etc/rc3.d/S15nfs.server stop** and press Return. NFS services are stopped.

3. Type **/etc/rc3.d/S15nfs.server start** and press Return. NFS services are re-started and the CD files are exported.

```
oak% ps -ef | grep mountd
    root  4571  4473  5 12:53:51 pts/3    0:00 grep mountd
oak% su
Password:
# /etc/rc3.d/S15nfs.server stop
# /etc/rc3.d/S15nfs.server start
```

Use the following steps to share CD files from a remote CD-ROM drive:

1. Insert the CD-ROM into the caddy and insert the caddy into the drive. The CD-ROM is mounted.

2. Become superuser on the Solaris 2.2 (or later) system with the CD-ROM drive attached.

3. Type **share -F nfs -o ro /cdrom/cdrom0** and press Return.

NOTE. *Volume management does not recognize entries in the /etc/dfs/dfstab file. With Solaris 2.3 volume management, you can set up remote CD-ROM* *mounts to be automatically shared by editing the /etc/rmmount.conf file. Refer to the rmmount.conf manual page for more information.*

```
oak% su
Password:
# share -F nfs -o ro /cdrom/cdrom0
# ps -ef | grep mountd
   root 4655 4473  6 12:56:05 pts/3   0:00 grep mountd
   root 4649    1 47 12:55:25 ?       0:00 /usr/lib/nfs/mountd
#
```

How to Access Shared CD-ROM Files

You can use the /mnt directory as the mount point for the CD-ROM files, or create another directory.

NOTE. *Do not use the /cdrom mount point to mount local files. Volume management may interfere with accessing files on the volume management /cdrom mount point.*

Once the CD-ROM is in the remote drive and the files are shared, follow these steps to access the shared files on a local system:

1. On the local system, become superuser.

2. Type **mount** *remote-system-name:/cdrom/cdrom0 /mount-point* and press Return. The files from the remote system directory /cdrom/cdrom0 are mounted on the */mount-point* directory. The cdrom0 subdirectory is symbolically linked to the actual name of the CD-ROM that has a name assigned by the application vendor.

In the following example, the files from the remote system castle are mounted on the /mnt mount point.

```
oak% su
Password:
# mount castle:/cdrom/cdrom0 /mnt
# cd /mnt
# ls
SUNWssser  SUNWsssra  SUNWsssrb  SUNWsssrc  SUNWsssrd  SUNWssstr
#
```

How to Unmount Shared CD-ROM Files

When you are through using the CD-ROM files, use the following steps to unmount the remote CD-ROM:

1. On the local system, become superuser.

2. Type **cd** and press Return.

3. Type **umount /*mount-point*** and press Return. The files from the remote system directory /cdrom/cdrom0 are unmounted.

Diskettes and Volume Management

When you insert a diskette into the diskette drive, Volume Manager does not mount the diskette automatically; this prevents excessive reads, which can quickly wear out the diskette drive. You must use a command that checks for the presence of a diskette in the diskette drive.

Command-Line Access

Follow these steps to format a diskette from a command line:

1. Insert a diskette into the diskette drive.

2. Type **volcheck** and press Return. The system has access to the unformatted diskette.

3. Type **fdformat** and press Return to format a ufs file system or **fdformat -d** to format an MS-DOS file system.

4. When prompted, press Return to begin formatting the diskette.

5. For ufs file systems, you must also make a new file system on the diskette.

   a. Become superuser.

   b. Type **newfs /vol/dev/rdiskette0/unnamed_floppy** and press Return.

Follow these steps to access files on a formatted diskette:

1. Insert a formatted diskette in the diskette drive.

2. Type **volcheck** and press Return. If there is a formatted diskette in the drive, volume management mounts it on the /floppy mount point. If no diskette is in the drive, no error message is displayed. The volcheck command redisplays the prompt. Once the diskette is mounted on the /floppy mount point, you can access files on it either from the command line or from the File Manager Floppy window, described in the section on "File Manager Access."

3. Type **cd /floppy** and press Return.

4. Type **ls** and press Return. The name of the diskette is displayed.

5. Type **cd *diskette-name*** and press Return.

6. Type **ls** and press Return. The names of the files on the diskette are displayed. You can copy files to and from the diskette using the cp command.

In the following example, the diskette is not mounted, so the only directory in /floppy is ms-dos_5. After volcheck mounts the diskette, the directory with the name of the diskette is displayed. The diskette in this example contains only a lost+found directory.

```
oak% cd /floppy
oak% ls
ms-dos_5
oak% volcheck
oak% ls
ms-dos_5            unnamed_floppy
oak% cd unnamed_floppy
oak% ls
lost+found
oak% cp /home/winsor/Appx/appxA.doc .
oak% ls
appxA.doc lost+found
oak%
```

You cannot unmount a file system whose current working directory is in use. If you get the message "Device busy" a process has its current working directory on the diskette. Use the fuser command to find out what process is using the diskette. See the fuser(1M) manual page for information.

Use the following steps to eject the diskette:

1. Type **cd** and press Return. You have changed out of the /floppy directory.

2. Type **eject** and press Return. After a few seconds, the diskette is ejected from the drive.

File Manager Access

If you are running File Manager, you can use it to format a diskette, display the contents, and copy files to and from the diskette. Follow these steps to format a diskette, display its contents, and eject it:

1. Insert the diskette into the diskette drive.

2. Choose Check for Floppy from the File menu, as shown in Figure A.2.

Figure A.2
Choose Check for
Floppy from the File
menu.

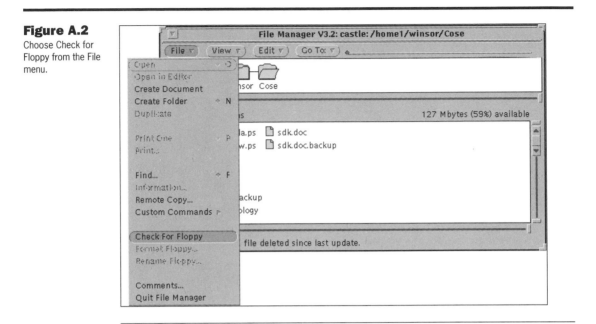

3. If the diskette is not formatted, a window is displayed, as shown in Figure A.3. Click SELECT on the Cancel & Eject button if you want to eject the diskette without formatting it.

4. Click SELECT on the format you want to use, then click on Format Disk. The diskette is formatted and a new file system is created.

5. When the diskette is formatted and contains the file system, the File Manager Floppy window displays the contents of the diskette, as shown in Figure A.4.

You can drag and drop files to and from the Floppy window in the same way that you manipulate other files using the File Manager.

To eject the diskette, click SELECT on the Eject Disk button. After a few seconds, the diskette is ejected and the File Manager Floppy window is dismissed.

Using the tar and cpio Commands with Diskettes

If a diskette contains tar or cpio files, volume management does not mount it. You cannot access files on the diskette from the old /dev/rdiskette device name because volume management provides access to the media, not to the device.

Figure A.3

File Manager floppy format

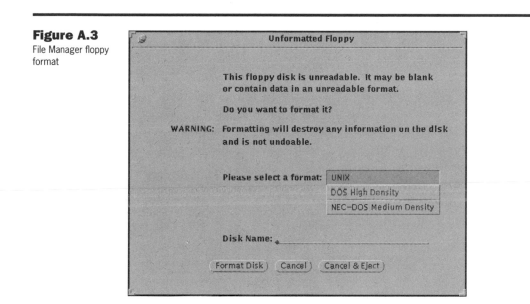

Figure A.4

File Manager Floppy window

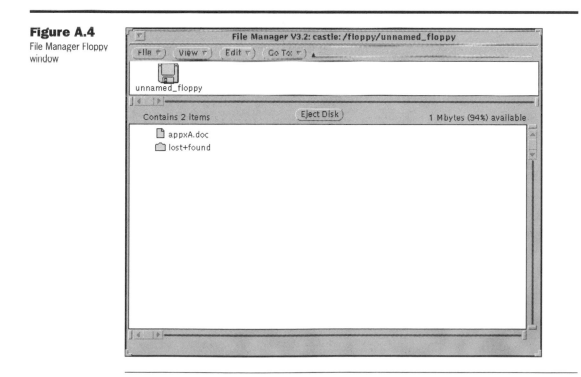

You can access tar and cpio files on a diskette using the symbolic link to the character device for the media that is in floppy drive 0, as:

```
/vol/dev/aliases/floppy0
```

Use the following steps to copy a file to a formatted diskette using the tar command:

1. Insert a formatted diskette into the diskette drive.

2. Type **volcheck** and press Return.

3. Type **tar cvf /vol/dev/aliases/floppy0** *filename* and press Return. The files are copied to the diskette.

4. Type **eject** and press Return. After a few seconds, the diskette is ejected.

Use the following steps to copy all tar files from a diskette:

1. Insert a formatted diskette into the diskette drive.

2. Change to the directory where you want to put the files.

3. Type **volcheck** and press Return. The diskette is mounted.

4. Type **tar xvf /vol/dev/aliases/floppy0** and press Return. The files are copied to the diskette.

5. Type **eject** and press Return. After a few seconds, the diskette is ejected.

Alternatively, with Solaris 2.2 (and later) systems, you can access tar or cpio files using the following device name syntax:

```
/vol/dev/rfd0/media-name
```

The most common *media-name* is "unlabeled".

With Solaris 2.3, the device name syntax is changed. You access tar or cpio files using the following device name syntax:

```
/vol/dev/rdiskette0/media-name
```

The most frequent *media-name* for media without a file system is "unlabeled".

For example, to copy a tar file to a diskette, type **tar cvf /vol/dev/rdiskette0/unlabeled** *filename* and press Return. To retrieve all tar files from a diskette, type **tar xvf /vol/dev/rdiskette0/unlabeled** and press Return.

Troubleshooting

From time to time, you may encounter problems with mounting diskettes (or, less frequently, a CD-ROM). If you encounter a problem, first check to find out if volume management knows about the diskette. The best way to check is to look in /vol/dev/rdiskette0 to see if something is there. If the files are not mounted, you may have forgotten to run the volcheck command, or you may have a hardware problem. If references to /vol hang, the /usr/sbin/vold daemon has probably died, and you should restart it.

If you find a name in /vol/dev/rdiskette0 and nothing is mounted in /floppy/*media-name*, it is likely that the data on the media is not a recognized file system. It may be a tar, cpio, or Macintosh file system. You can access these media through the block or character devices found in /vol/dev/rdiskette0 or /vol/dev/diskette0, and use your own tools to interpret the data on them.

Using Workman with Volume Management

Many people use the workman program to play music from their CD-ROM drive. Workman is not a Sun product, but it is in wide use. To use workman with volume management, add the line shown in bold to the /etc/rmmount.conf file. Be sure the line comes before the action_filemgr line.

```
# @(#)rmmount.conf 1.2      92/09/23 SMI
#
# Removable Media Mounter configuration file.
#

# File system identification
ident hsfs ident_hsfs.so cdrom
ident ufs ident_ufs.so cdrom floppy
ident pcfs ident_pcfs.so floppy

# Actions
action cdrom action_workman.so pathname
action cdrom action_filemgr.so
action floppy action_filemgr.so
```

The *pathname* is the name of the path where users access the workman program, for example, /usr/apps/pkgs/exe/workman.

When you have made this change, audio CD-ROMs are automatically detected and the workman program is started when the CD-ROM is inserted into the CD-ROM drive.

NOTE. *When you set up workman in the way described here, users should not try to start workman from the application, as volume management may get confused. In addition, with Solaris 2.2 (and later) volume management, if you are using workman, you must eject the CD-ROM from the workman application. If you eject the CD-ROM from another window, workman hangs. This problem will be fixed in Solaris 2.3 system software.*

Changes with Solaris 2.3 System Software

With Solaris 2.2, you cannot automatically export CD-ROM and diskette drives or use the /etc/vfstab file. You must use the share command to export the file system after every reboot.

NOTE. *You cannot share a pcfs file system with Solaris 2.2 system software.*

With Solaris 2.3 system software, a share cdrom* instruction will be provided in the /etc/rmmount.conf file so that a CD-ROM is automatically shared when it inserted into the CD-ROM drive. You will be able to specify flags in the same way as you do for the share command. You will also be able to use the name of a particular piece of media, if desired. When Solaris 2.3 system software is available, refer to the rmmount.conf manual page for more details.

With Solaris 2.3, the device names for the physical device will change to be consistent with /dev. In Solaris 2.2 system software, the device names are /vol/dev/rfd0 and /vol/dev/fd0. With Solaris 2.3 system software, the device names are /vol/dev/rdiskette0 and /vol/dev/diskette0. The symbolic link in /vol/dev/aliases will always point to the correct device.

Disabling Volume Management

You may want to disable volume management for some users. To do so, use the following steps:

1. Become superuser.

2. Remove or rename the /etc/rc2.d/S92volmgt script.

3. Type **/etc/init.d/volmgt stop** and press Return.

You can disable part of volume management and leave other parts functional. You may, for example, want to automatically mount CD-ROMs, but use the Solaris 2.0 method for accessing files on a diskette. You can do so by commenting out the lines for diskettes in the /etc/vold.conf file, as shown:

```
# @(#)vold.conf 1.15      93/01/18 SMI
#
# Volume Daemon Configuration file
#

# Database to use (must be first)
db db_mem.so

# Labels supported
label dos label_dos.so floppy
label cdrom label_cdrom.so cdrom
label sun label_sun.so floppy

# Devices to use
use cdrom drive /dev/dsk/c0t6 dev_cdrom.so cdrom0
# use floppy drive /dev/diskette dev_floppy.so floppy0

# Actions
# insert /vol*/dev/fd[0-9]/* user=root /usr/sbin/rmmount
insert /vol*/dev/dsk/* user=root /usr/sbin/rmmount
# eject /vol*/dev/fd[0-9]/* user=root /usr/sbin/rmmount
eject /vol*/dev/dsk/* user=root /usr/sbin/rmmount
notify /vol*/rdsk/* group=tty /usr/lib/vold/volmissing  c

# List of file system types unsafe to eject
unsafe ufs hsfs pcfs
```

Serial Port Manager

With Solaris 2.3 system software, Administration Tool provides a Serial Port Manager that you can use to set up and configure SAF for character terminals and for modems. This appendix introduces the Serial Port Manager and describes how to use it. On-line help is also available for this new tool.

The Serial Port Manager and SAF

You can configure a serial port for use with a modem or terminal, using either the Administration Tool (admintool), Serial Port Manager or the SAF commands described in Part 4 of this book. SunSoft recommends that you use the Serial Port Manager graphical user interface for these tasks.

The Serial Port Manager uses the pmadm command to configure the serial port software to work with terminals and modems. It provides templates for common terminal and modem configurations, and provides a quick visual status of each port. You can also set up multiple ports, modify them, or delete port services.

Once a serial port is configured, use the SAF commands to administer the port.

Templates

The Serial Port Manager provides five templates for the most common terminal and modem configurations, which you can then modify for a particular device.

- Terminal—hardwired

- Modem—dial-in only

- Modem—dial-out only

- Modem—bidirectional

- Initialize Only—no connection

When you choose one of these templates from the Use Template menu, a set of default values is displayed that are optimized for the service that you choose.

Security

You may use the Serial Port Manager to configure either a local or a remote system. Because the Serial Port Manager must modify system information, you need special privileges to use it on a system. Table B.1 describes the user privileges you need to run Administration Tool.

Table B.1 **User Privileges Needed to Run Administration Tool**

System	Privileges
Local	Run Administration Tool as root, or be a member of the UNIX sysadmin group (GID 14) for that system
Remote	Be a member of the UNIX sysadmin group (GID 14) for that system

Starting the Serial Port Manager

You start the Serial Port Manager from the Administration Tool window. To start Administration Tool, type **/usr/bin/admintool &** and press Return. Figure B.1 shows the Administration Tool window.

Figure B.1
Administration Tool

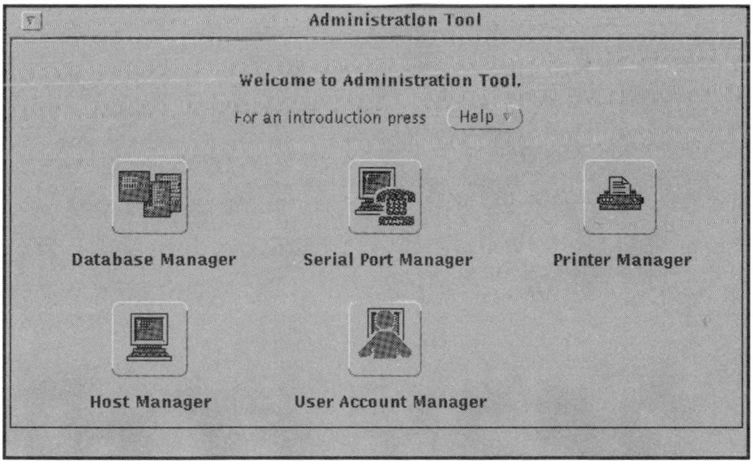

To start the Serial Port Manager, click on the Serial Port Manager icon in the Administration Tool window. The Serial Port Manager window is displayed, as shown in Figure B.2.

Figure B.2
Serial Port Manager
window

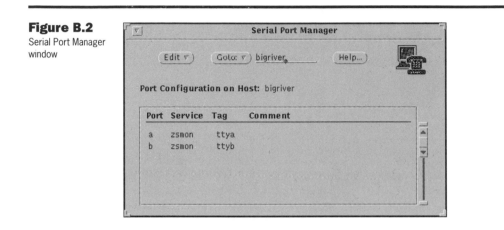

Specifying a Remote System

To look at ports on a remote system, type the name of the remote system in the Goto text field and press Return.

Using the Serial Port Manager

You can use the serial port manager for the following tasks:

- Initialize a port without configuring the service

- Add a service

- Modify a service

- Disable a service

- Delete a service

You perform each task by clicking SELECT on the name of each port you want to configure, and then choosing an item from the Edit menu. You choose Modify Service for the first four tasks, and Delete Service if you want to delete the service for the selected port(s).

When you choose Modify Service from the Edit menu, the Modify Service window is displayed, as shown in Figure B.3.

The Modify Service window provides access to the port templates and lets you show three different levels of information about a port. When you click on the More setting, additional information about the port is displayed, as shown in Figure B.4.

Figure B.3

The Modify Service window

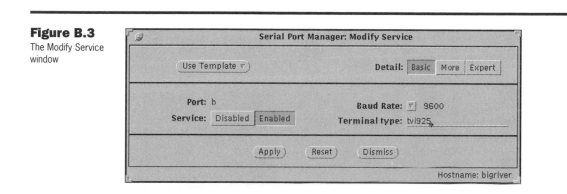

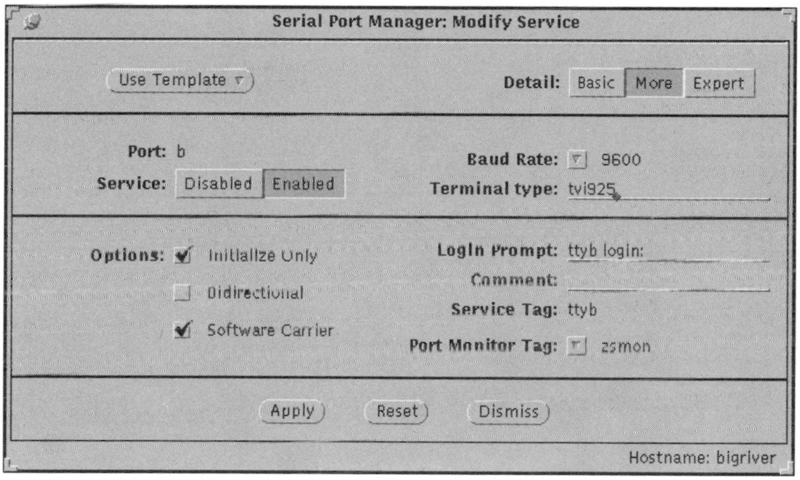

When you click on the Expert setting, additional information is displayed, as shown in Figure B.5.

Figure B.4

More Port Manager information

Figure B.5
Expert information

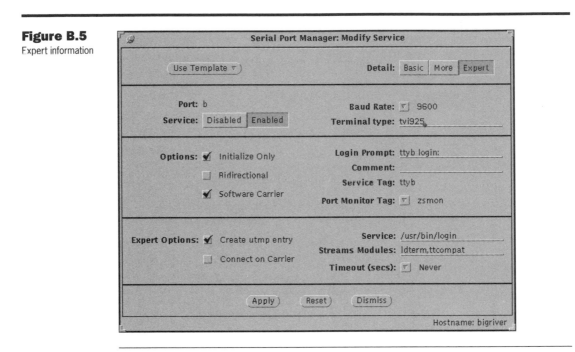

Table B.2 describes each of the settings in the Modify Service window.

Table B.2   Modify Service Window Items

Item	Description
Basic:	
Port	Lists the port or ports you selected from Serial Port Manager window.
Service	Shows whether the service for the specified port is turned on (Enabled) or turned off (Disabled).
Baud rate	Shows the line speed used to communicate with the terminal. The line speed represents an entry in /etc/ttydefs.
Terminal type	Shows the abbreviation for the type of terminal, such as wyse50, ansi, or vt100. Similar abbreviations are found in /etc/termcap. This value is set in the environment variable $TERM.
More:	
Option: Initialize only	Shows whether port software is initialized but not configured.

Table B.2 **Modify Service Window Items (Continued)**

Item	Description
Option: Bidirectional	Shows whether the port line is used in both directions.
Option: Software carrier	Shows if the software carrier detection feature is used. If the option is *not* checked, the *hardware* carrier detection signal is used.
Login prompt	Shows the prompt displayed to a user after a connection is made.
Comment	Shows the comment field for the service.
Service tag	Lists the service tag associated with this port—typically, an entry in the /dev/term directory.
Port monitor tag	Specifies the name of the port monitor to be used for this port. Note: The default monitor typically is correct.
Expert:	
Create utmp entry	Specifies that a utmp entry is created in the accounting files upon login. Note: This item must be checked if a login service is used. See the Service item, following.
Connect on carrier	Specifies whether the service associated with a port is invoked immediately when a connect indication is received.
Service	Shows the program that is run on connection.
Streams modules	Shows the STREAMS modules that are pushed before the service is invoked.
Timeout (secs)	Specifies the number of seconds before a port is closed if the open process on the port succeeds and no input data is received.

Adding a Character Terminal

Table B.3 shows the default settings for adding a character terminal.

Table B.3 **Terminal—Hardwired Default Values**

Item	Default Value
Port	—
Service	enabled
Baud rate	9600

Table B.3 **Terminal—Hardwired Default Values (Continued)**

Item	Default Value
Terminal type	—
Option: Initialize only	no
Option: Bidirectional	no
Option: Software carrier	yes
Login prompt	login:
Comment	Terminal—hardwired
Service tag	—
Port monitor tag	zsmon
Create utmp entry	yes
Connect on Carrier	no
Service	/usr/bin/login
Streams modules	ldterm,ttcompat
Timeout (secs)	never

Use the following steps to configure SAF for a character terminal:

1. Select the port(s) that will be used with a terminal.

2. Choose Modify Service from the Edit menu. The Modify Service window is displayed, showing the Basic settings. Select either More or Expert to display more settings.

3. Choose Terminal—Hardwired from the Use Template menu, as shown in Figure B.6.

    The Modify Service window displays default settings for the Terminal—Hardwired template shown in Table B.3.

4. Change values of template entries if desired. If you change the values, be sure to change the comment field so that other users will know that you have changed the default values.

5. Click on Apply to configure the port.

Figure B.6

Use Template menu

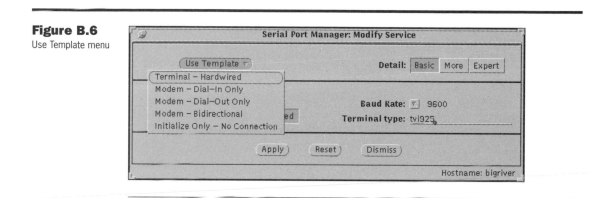

Configuring SAF for a Modem

Table B.4 shows the choices that you can make to configure modems.

Table B.4 **Modem Templates**

Modem Configuration	Description
Modem—dial-in only	Users may dial in to the modem but cannot dial out.
Modem—dial-out only	Users may dial out from the modem but cannot dial in.
Modem—bidirectional	Users may either dial in or dial out from the modem.

Table B.5 shows the default values for a dial-in modem.

Table B.5 **Modem—Dial-In Only Default Values**

Item	Default Value
Port	—
Service	enabled
Baud rate	9600
Terminal type	—
Option: Initialize only	yes
Option: Bidirectional	no

Table B.5   **Modem—Dial-In Only Default Values (Continued)**

Item	Default Value
Option: Software carrier	no
Login prompt	login:
Comment	Modem—dial-in only
Service tag	—
Port monitor tag	zsmon
Create utmp entry	yes
Connect on carrier	no
Service	/usr/bin/login
Streams modules	ldterm,ttcompat
Timeout (secs)	never

Table B.6 shows the default values for a dial-out modem.

Table B.6   **Modem—Dial-Out Only Default Values**

Item	Default Value
Port	—
Service	enabled
Baud rate	9600
Terminal type	—
Option: Initialize only	no
Option: Bidirectional	no
Option: Software carrier	no
Login prompt	login:
Comment	Modem—dial-out only
Service tag	—

Table B.6 **Modem—Dial-Out Only Default Values (Continued)**

Item	Default Value
Port monitor tag	zsmon
Create utmp entry	yes
Connect on carrier	no
Service	/usr/bin/login
Streams modules	ldterm,ttcompat
Timeout (secs)	never

Table B.7 shows the default settings for bidirectional modem service.

Table B.7 **Modem—Bidirectional Default Values**

Item	Default Value
Port	—
Service	enabled
Baud rate	9600
Terminal type	—
Option: Initialize only	no
Option: Bidirectional	yes
Option: Software carrier	no
Login prompt	login:
Comment	Modem—bidirectional
Service tag	—
Port monitor tag	zsmon
Create utmp entry	yes
Connect on carrier	no
Service	/usr/bin/login

Table B.7   **Modem—Bidirectional Default Values (Continued)**

Item	Default Value
Streams modules	ldterm,ttcompat
Timeout (secs)	never

Use the following steps to configure SAF for a modem:

1. Select the port(s) that will be used with a modem in the Serial Port Manager window.

2. Choose Modify Service from the Edit menu.

3. Choose the modem configuration from the Use Template menu that meets or most closely matches your modem service.

4. Change values of template entries if desired. If you change the values, be sure to change the comment field so that other users will know that you have changed the default values.

5. Click on Apply to configure the port.

The equivalent commands and steps for adding a dial-out only modem, as specified by the Modem—dial-out only default values, are shown here.

Initializing Ports without Configuring

Table B.8 shows the default values for initializing a port without configuring it.

Table B.8   **Initialize Only—No Connection Default Values**

Item	Default Value
Port	—
Service	enabled
Baud rate	9600
Terminal type	—
Option: Initialize only	yes
Option: Bidirectional	no

Table B.8   **Initialize Only—No Connection Default Values (Continued)**

Item	Default Value
Option: Software carrier	no
Login prompt	login:
Comment	Initialize only—no connection
Service tag	—
Port monitor tag	zsmon
Create utmp entry	yes
Connect on carrier	no
Service	/usr/bin/login
Streams modules	ldterm,ttcompat
Timeout (secs)	never

To initialize ports without configuring for a specific device, follow these steps:

1. Select the port(s) that you want to initialize.

2. Choose Modify Service from the Edit menu.

3. Choose Initialize Only—No Connection from the Use Template menu, as shown in Figure B.7.

Figure B.7

Initialize port

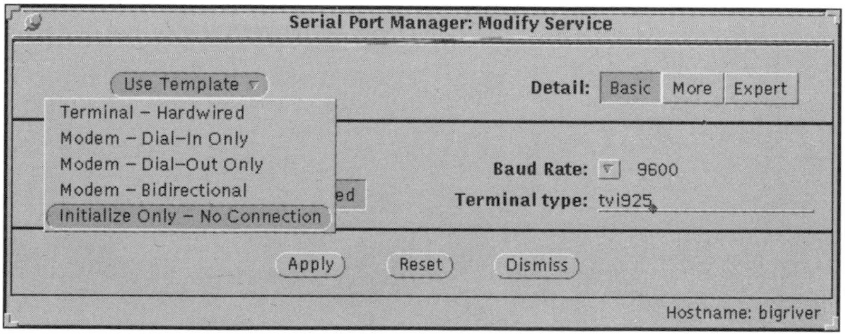

4. Click on Apply to initialize the port.

Disabling Ports

To disable service on configured ports, follow these steps:

1. Select the port(s) that you want to disable.

2. Choose Modify Service from the Edit menu.

3. Select Disable in the Modify Service window, as shown in Figure B.8.

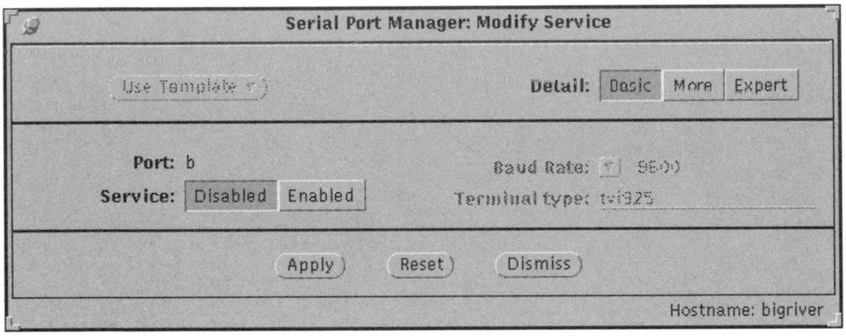

Figure B.8

Disabling ports

4. Click on Apply to disable the port.

Removing Port Services

To delete services on configured ports, follow these steps:

1. Select the port(s) that has a service you want to delete.

2. Choose Delete Service from the Edit menu, as shown in Figure B.9.

3. You are asked if you really want to delete the service for the specified port or ports. You may cancel the delete operation or continue with it.

Figure B.9

Removing port
services

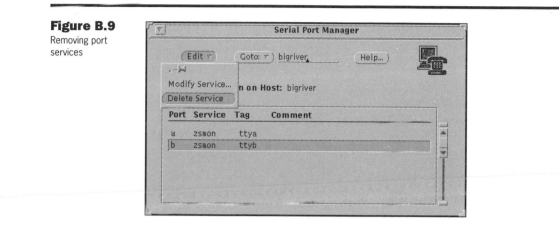

GLOSSARY

access rights   The four types of operations—read, modify, create, and destroy—that control access to NIS+ objects for each of the authorization rights categories.

Administration Tool   An OpenWindows tool from which you can access Host Manager and Database Manager applications. With the Solaris 2.1 (and later) environment, Printer Manager and User Manager applications are also available. See also **Database Manager**.

alias   An alternative name or names assigned to a program or to an electronic mail address.

application server   A server set up and administered exclusively to provide application services to users over the network.

authorization rights   The four categories—nobody, owner, group, and world—that control access to NIS+ tables.

Auto_home database   The database that you use to add home directories to the automounter. You access the Auto_home Database using the Database Manager. In SunOS 4.*x* releases, this database was a file named auto.home.

automounter   Solaris 2.*x* software that automatically mounts a directory when a user changes into it and unmounts the directory when it is no longer in use.

automount maps   The local files or name service tables that the automounter consults to determine which directories to mount, which system to mount them from, and where to mount them on the user's local system.

bang   An exclamation point (!) that acts as a single-character UNIX command or as a separator between the routes of a route-based electronic mail address.

base directory   The directory in which the package commands and Software Manager install software packages. The default base directory is /opt.

baud rate   The transmission speed of a serial communications channel.

Bourne shell   One of the three Solaris 2.*x* command interpreters. The Bourne shell is the default user shell, and the shell language used to write most system administration shell scripts. See also **C shell**, **Korn shell**.

breakout box A diagnostic device that plugs into an RS-232-C cable and is used to test whether a signal is present on each cable pin.

cache A small, fast memory area that holds the most active part of a larger and slower memory.

CD-ROM An acronym for compact disc, read-only memory. CD-ROM is a read-only storage medium for digital data.

character terminal A serial port device that displays only letters, numbers, and other characters such as those produced by a typewriter.

child process A subordinate process that is executed within an environment created by another process. The process that creates the environment for the child is called the *parent*.

client A system that receives system resources from a remote system over the network.

compiler A program that translates source code into a machine-readable form in preparation for creating directly executable programs.

concatenation The combining of two or more files to create one larger file. Also, with Online: DiskSuite, the combining of separate component disks into a sequential system of disk blocks.

C shell One of the three Solaris 2.*x* command interpreters. See also **Bourne shell**, **Korn shell**.

daemon A special type of program that, once activated, starts itself and carries out a specific task without any need for user intervention. Daemons typically are used to handle jobs that have been queued, such as printing, mail, and communication.

Database Manager An OpenWindows tool accessed from Administration Tool, which is used to administer NIS+ tables and ufs files in the /etc directory. You can also use the Database Manager to look at (but not edit) the contents of NIS maps.

direct map An automount map that specifies absolute paths as the mount point.

diskette   A nonvolatile storage medium used to store and access data magnetically. SunOS 5.*x* system software supports 3.5-inch double-sided high density (DS, HD) diskettes.

domain   A directory structure for electronic mail addressing, network address naming, and NIS+ hierarchy naming. Within the United States, top-level Internet domains include *com* for commercial organizations, *edu* for educational organizations, *gov* for governments, *mil* for the military, *net* for networking organizations, and *org* for other organizations. Outside of the United States, top-level Internet domains designate the country. Subdomains designate the organization and the individual system.

domain addressing   Using a domain address to specify the destination of an electronic mail message or NIS+ table.

electronic mail   A set of programs that transmit mail messages from one system to another, usually over communications lines. Electronic mail is frequently referred to as *e-mail*.

e-mail   See **electronic mail**.

environment variable   A system- or user-defined variable that provides information about the operating environment to the shell.

exit status   A numeric value assigned in a program or a shell script to indicate whether it ran successfully. An exit status of 0 means that the program executed successfully. Any non-zero value means that the program failed.

export   See **share**.

file descriptor   An integer that designates an open file. The file descriptor for STDIN is 0, for STDOUT is 1, and for STDERR is 2.

file system   A hierarchical arrangement of directories and files.

floppy diskette   See **diskette**.

fork   To copy one process into a parent process and a child process, with separate but initially identical text, data, and stack segments.

fully qualified domain name   A domain name that contains all of the elements needed to specify where an electronic mail message should be delivered or where an NIS+ table is located. NIS+ fully qualified domain names always have a dot at the end. See also **domain**.

gateway   A connection between differing communications networks. Also a system that handles electronic mail traffic between differing communications networks.

GID   The group identification number used by the system to control access to information owned by other users.

Group database   The database that you use to create new group accounts or to modify existing group accounts. You access the Group database from the Database Manager.

here document   A format used within a shell script to provide a collection of data within the shell script.

home directory   The part of the file system that is allocated to an individual user for private files.

Hosts database   A directory service used to look up names and addresses of other hosts on a network. You access the Hosts database from the Database Manager.

indirect map   An automount map that contains simple path names as the mount point.

init states   One of the seven states, or run levels, a system can be running. A system can run in only one init state at a time.

inode   An entry in a predesignated area of a disk that describes where a file is located on that disk, the size of the file, when it was last used, and other identifying information.

interpreter   A program that reads and executes programming commands in sequence, one by one as they are encountered. Shell scripts are an example of interpreted programs.

IP address   A unique Internet address number that identifies each system in a network.

kernel   The master program set of SunOS software that manages all the physical resources of the computer, including file system management, virtual memory, reading and writing files to disks and tapes, scheduling of processes, printing, and communicating over a network.

Korn shell   One of the three Solaris 2.*x* command interpreters. The Korn shell is upwards compatible with the Bourne shell and provides an expanded set of features. See also **Bourne shell**, **C shell**.

license server   A server that provides users access to software licenses.

listenBSD   An LP print service daemon that is run on a SunOS 5.*x* print server to listen for print requests from SunOS 4.*x* print clients on the network.

listenS5   An LP print service daemon that is run on a print server to listen for print requests from SunOS 5.*x* print clients on the network.

login name   The name assigned to an individual user and that controls access to a system.

mail address   The name of the recipient and the location to which an electronic mail message is delivered.

mail alias   See **alias**.

mailbox   A file on a mail host where mail messages are stored.

mail client   A system that does not provide mail spooling for its users. Mail is spooled on a mail server.

mailer   A protocol that specifies the policy and mechanics used by sendmail when it delivers mail.

mailhost   The main mail system on a network that receives and distributes mail outside of the network or the domain. A mailhost can also be a mail server.

mail server   Any system that stores mailboxes in the /var/mail directory. A mail server can also serve as a mailhost.

mail services   Services provided by a set of programs and daemons that transmit electronic mail messages between systems and distribute them to individual mailboxes.

master map   The automount map consulted by the automounter when a system starts up. The automount map contains the default mount points /net and /home and the names of the direct and indirect maps that the automounter consults.

metadevice   A logical device that is created by using the SunSoft Online: Disk Suite product to concatenate or stripe one or more disks into a single logical device unit.

modem   A peripheral device that modulates a digital signal so that it can be transmitted across analog telephone lines and then demodulates the analog signal to a digital signal at the receiving end. The name is a contraction for *mod*ulate/*dem*odulate.

mount   To extend the directory hierarchy by attaching a file system from somewhere else in the hierarchy on a mount point directory.

mount point   A directory in the file system hierarchy where another file system is attached to the hierarchy.

mount table   The system file (/etc/mnttab) that keeps track of currently mounted file systems.

name space   A hierarchical arrangement of domains and subdomains, similar to the hierarchical UNIX file system, used by NIS+ and the automounter.

NFS (network file system)   The default Solaris 2.*x* distributed file system that provides file sharing among systems. NFS servers can also provide kernels and swap files to diskless clients.

NIS   The SunOS 4.*x* network information service.

NIS+   The Solaris 2.*x* network information service.

null modem cable   A cable that swaps lines 2 and 3 so that the proper transmit and receive signals are communicated between two data termination equipment (DTE) devices. Line 7 goes straight through.

OpenWindows   A windowing system based on the OPEN LOOK® graphical user interface.

package commands The set of Solaris 2.*x* commands—pkgadd, pkgask, pkgchk, pkginfo, and pkgrm—that are used to install, query, and remove software packages.

parent process A superior or controlling process that executes subordinate processes, called *children.*

parse To resolve a string of characters or a series of words into component parts to determine their collective meaning. Virtually every program that accepts command input must do some sort of parsing before the commands can be acted upon. For example, the sendmail program divides an e-mail address into its component parts to decide where to send the message.

partially qualified domain name An NIS+ domain name that specifies the local directory only and does not contain the complete domain name. For example, hosts.org_dir is a partially qualified domain name that specifies the hosts table in the org_dir directory of the default NIS+ domain. See also **domain**.

partition A discrete portion of a disk, configured using the format program. A partition is the same as a slice.

Passwd database The database that you use to add, modify, or delete user accounts. You access the Passwd database from the Database Manager.

path The list of directories that are searched to find an executable command. The path is a shell environment variable.

path name A list of directory names, separated with slashes (/), that specifies the location of a particular file.

port A physical connection between a peripheral device such as a terminal, printer, or modem and the device controller. Also, an access point on a system that is available on the network.

port monitor A program that continuously watches for requests to log in or requests to access printers or files. The ttymon and listen port monitors are part of the Service Access Facility (SAF).

positional parameter A shell script notation—$1, $2, $*n*—used to access command-line arguments.

principals Individuals or systems within the NIS+ namespace that have been "registered" with the NIS+ service.

process A program in operation.

relay host A system that transmits to and receives mail from outside your network or domain using the same communications protocol.

RFC Request for Comments, specify Internet protocols and standards. RFCs are submitted to SRI-NIC, where they are assigned numbers and are distributed by electronic mail to the Internet community. The most important RFCs (through 1985) are available in a three-volume publication, The DDN Protocol Handbook, which is available from SRI International in Menlo Park, California.

run level See **init state**.

SAC See **Service Access Controller**.

SAF See **Service Access Facility**.

script See **shell script**.

sendmail The mailer transport agent used by Solaris 2.*x* system software. See also **transport agent**.

server A system that provides network service such as disk storage and file transfer, or a program that provides such a service.

service A process that is started in response to a connection request.

Service Access Controller (SAC) The process that manages access to system services provided by the Service Access Facility.

Service Access Facility (SAF) The part of the system software that is used to register and monitor port activity for modems, terminals, and printers. SAF replaces /etc/getty as a way to control logins.

share To make a file system available (mountable) to other systems on the network.

shell   The command interpreter for a user, specified in the Passwd database. The SunOS 5.*x* system software supports the Bourne (default), C, and Korn shells.

shell script   A file containing a set of executable commands that are taken as input to the shell.

shell variable   Local variables maintained by a shell, which are not passed on from parent to child processes.

slice   An alternate name for a partition. See also **partition**.

Software Manager   An OpenWindows tool that you can use to install, remove, and query software packages. Software Manager calls the package commands to perform its functions.

spooling directory   A directory where files are stored until they are processed.

spooling space   The amount of space allocated on a print server for storing requests in the printer queue.

stand-alone system   A system that has a local disk and can boot without relying on a server.

standard error   The part of a process that determines where error messages are displayed. The file descriptor for stderr is 2. The default device for stderr is the terminal screen.

standard input   The part of a process that determines where input is received from. The file descriptor for stdin is 0. The default device for stdin is the keyboard.

standard output   The part of a process that determines where the results of commands are displayed. The file descriptor for stdout is 1. The default device for stdout is the terminal screen.

stderr   See **standard error**.

stdin   See **standard input**.

stdout   See **standard output**.

striping   Interlacing two or more disk partitions that make a single logical slice of up to 1 terabyte. With the SunSoft Online: DiskSuite product, the addressing of blocks is interlaced on the resulting metadevice to improve performance.

superuser   A user with special privileges granted if the correct password is supplied when logging in as root or using the su command. For example, only the superuser can edit major administrative files in the /etc directory. The superuser has the user name root.

symbolic link   A file that contains a pointer to the name of another file.

system   A computer with a keyboard and a terminal. A system can have either local or remote disks, and may have additional peripheral devices such as CD-ROM players, tape drives, diskette drives, and printers.

terminfo database   The database that describes the characteristics of TTY devices and printers.

third-party software   Application software that is not included as part of the basic system software.

transport agent   The program that is responsible for receiving and delivering e-mail messages. The Solaris 2.*x* transport agent is sendmail.

ufs (UNIX file system)   The default disk-based file system for the SunOS 5.*x* operating system.

UID number   The user identification number assigned to each login name. UID numbers are used by the system to identify, by number, the owners of files and directories. The UID of root is 0.

uncommitted interface   An interface in the sendmail.cf file that is a de facto industry standard. Uncommitted interfaces have never had a formal architectural review, and may be subject to change.

unmount   To remove a file system from a mount point so that the files are no longer accessible.

user account   An account set up for an individual user in the Passwd database that specifies the user's login name, password, UID, GID, login directory, and login shell.

User Account Manager   An OpenWindows tool accessed from the Solaris 2.1 or later versions of Administration Tool; it is used to add users to an NIS+ environment or to a local system.

value   Data, either numeric or alphanumeric.

variable   A name that refers to a temporary storage area in memory. A variable holds a value.

virtual file system table   The file (/etc/vfstab) that specifies which file systems are mounted by default. Local ufs file systems and NFS file systems that are mounted automatically when a system boots are specified in this file.

virtual memory   A memory management technique used by the operating system for programs that require more space in memory than can be allotted to them. The kernel moves only pages of the program currently needed into memory, while unneeded pages remain on the disk. Virtual memory extends physical memory over disk. See also **kernel**.

volume management   System software available with Solaris 2.2 and later releases that mounts CD-ROM and diskettes automatically.

wrapper   A shell script for an application installed on an application server that sets up the user's environment and points to the executables that are suitable for that user.

BIBLIOGRAPHY

General References

Coffin, Stephen. *UNIX System V Release 4: The Complete Reference.* Osborne McGraw-Hill, 1990.

Garfinkel, Simson, and Gene Spifford. *Practical UNIX Security.* O'Reilly & Associates, 1991.

Loukides, Mike. *System Performance Tuning.* O'Reilly & Associates, 1990.

Nemeth, Evi, Garth Snyder, and Scott Seebass. *UNIX System Administration Handbook.* Prentice Hall Software Series, 1989.

Rosen, Kenneth H., Richard R. Rosinski, and James M. Farber. *UNIX System V Release 4: An Introduction.* Osborne McGraw-Hill, 1990.

Stern, Hal. *Managing NFS and NIS.* O'Reilly & Associates, 1991.

Winsor, Janice. *Solaris System Administrator's Guide.* SunSoft Press/Ziff-Davis Press, 1993.

Electronic Mail References

DDN Protocol Handbook, The. 1985. Three-volume set of RFCs, available from SRI International, 333 Ravenswood Avenue, Menlo Park, CA 94025.

Frey, Donnalyn, and Rick Adams. *!%@:: A Directory of Electronic Mail Addressing & Network,* 2d ed. O'Reilly & Associates, 1990.

RFC 822 *Standard for the Format of ARPA INTERNET Text Messages.*

RFC 1211 Problems with Maintaining Large email Lists.

NIS+ Reference

Ramsey, Rick. *All About Administering NIS+.* SunSoft Press/Prentice Hall, 1992.

Printing Reference

PostScript Language Reference Manual. Adobe Systems Incorporated, October 1990.

Shell References

Anderson, Gail, and Paul Anderson. *The UNIX C Shell Field Guide.* Prentice Hall, 1986.

Arick, Martin R. *UNIX C Shell Desk Reference.* QED Technical Publishing Group, 1992.

Arthur, Lowell Jay. *UNIX Shell Programming,* 2d ed. John Wiley & Sons, Inc., 1990.

Bolsky, Morris I., and David G. Korn. *The Kornshell Command and Programming Language.* Prentice Hall, 1989.

Olczak, Anatole. *The Korn Shell User & Programming Manual.* Addison-Wesley Publishing Company, 1992.

Rosenblatt, Bill. *Learning the Korn Shell.* O'Reilly & Associates, 1993.

Programming Languages

Aho, Alfred V., Brian W. Kernighan, and Peter J. Weinberger. *The AWK Programming Language.* Addison-Wesley Publishing Company, 1988.

Dougherty, Dale. *sed & awk.* O'Reilly & Associates, 1991.

INDEX

B

Imagination.
Innovation. Insight.

The How It Works Series from Ziff-Davis Press

"... a magnificently seamless integration of text and graphics ..."

Larry Blasko, The Associated Press, reviewing *PC/Computing How Computers Work*

No other books bring computer technology to life like the *How It Works* series from Ziff-Davis Press. Lavish, full-color illustrations and lucid text from some of the world's top computer commentators make *How It Works* books an exciting way to explore the inner workings of PC technology.

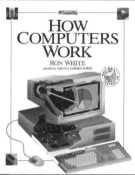

ISBN: 094-7 Price: $22.95

PC/Computing How Computers Work

A worldwide blockbuster that hit the general trade bestseller lists! *PC/Computing* magazine executive editor Ron White dismantles the PC and reveals what really makes it tick.

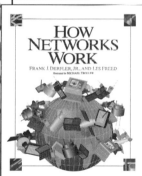

ISBN: 129-3 Price: $24.95

How Networks Work

Two of the most respected names in connectivity showcase the PC network, illustrating and explaining how each component does its magic and how they all fit together.

ISBN: 133-1 Price: $24.95

ISBN: 166-8 Price: $15.95

How Macs Work

A fun and fascinating voyage to the heart of the Macintosh! Two noted *MacUser* contributors cover the spectrum of Macintosh operations from startup to shutdown.

How Software Works

This dazzlingly illustrated volume from Ron White peeks inside the PC to show in full-color how software breathes life into the PC. Covers Windows™ and all major software categories.

How to Use Your Computer

Conquer computerphobia and see how this intricate machine truly makes life easier. Dozens of full-color graphics showcase the components of the PC and explain how to interact with them.

All About Computers

This one-of-a-kind visual guide for kids features numerous full-color illustrations and photos on every page, combined with dozens of interactive projects that reinforce computer basics, making this an exciting way to learn all about the world of computers.

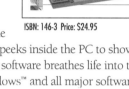

ISBN: 146-3 Price: $24.95

ISBN: 155-2 Price: $22.95

Available at all fine bookstores or by calling 1-800-688-0448, ext. 100. Call for information on the Instructor's Supplement, including transparencies, for each book in the How It Works Series.

ZIFF-DAVIS
ZD
PRESS

Arrrgh!

Don't you just hate it when software doesn't work the way you expect? When simple problems block your progress for hours? When your resident techie isn't around, the technical support hotline is constantly busy, on-line help is no help at all, the manual is hopeless, and the book you have tells you everything except what you really need to know?

ISBN: 099-8
Price: $29.95

Don't you just hate it?

We do too. That's why we developed **HELP!**, a ground-breaking series of books from Ziff-Davis Press.

HELP! books mean fast access to straight answers. If you're a beginner, you'll appreciate the practical examples and skill-building exercises that will help you work confidently in no time. If you're already an experienced user, you'll love the comprehensive coverage, highly detailed indexes, and margin notes and sidebars that highlight especially helpful information.

ISBN: 014-9
Price: $27.95

ISBN: 039-4
Price: $27.95

ISBN: 151-X
Price: $29.95

We're launching the **HELP!** series with these all-new books:

HELP! WordPerfect 6.0—WordPerfect insider Stephen G. Dyson has created the most complete single source of techniques, examples, and advice that will help you clear the hurdles of WordPerfect 6.0 quickly and easily.

HELP! Microsoft Access—Best-selling author Miriam Liskin gives you fast access to the complete feature set of Microsoft's leading-edge Windows database program. Sample databases included on disk!

HELP! Paradox for Windows—Popular database and spreadsheet authority Lisa Biow provides one-stop solutions to the challenges of Borland's high-powered new database manager.

HELP! Windows NT 3.1—Windows authority Ben Ezzell has the answers to your NT questions in this highly effective quick-access format.

HELP! Lotus Notes 3.0—Learn how to harness the power of Lotus Notes with this easy-access reference guide from the ultimate Notes guru, John Helliwell.

So if you hate struggling with software as much as we do, visit your favorite bookstore and just say **HELP!**

ISBN: 160-9
Price: $29.95
Avail.: November

Available at all fine bookstores or by calling 1-800-688-0448, ext. 101.

ZIFF-DAVIS ZD PRESS

Ziff-Davis Press Survey of Readers

Please help us in our effort to produce the best books on personal computing.
For your assistance, we would be pleased to send you a FREE catalog
featuring the complete line of Ziff-Davis Press books.

1. How did you first learn about this book?

Recommended by a friend . . . . ☐ -1 (5)

Recommended by store personnel . . . . ☐ -2

Saw in Ziff-Davis Press catalog . . . . ☐ -3

Received advertisement in the mail . . . . ☐ -4

Saw the book on bookshelf at store . . . . ☐ -5

Read book review in: _____ ☐ -6

Saw an advertisement in: _____ ☐ -7

Other (Please specify): _____ ☐ -8

2. Which THREE of the following factors most influenced your decision to purchase this book? (Please check up to THREE.)

Front or back cover information on book . . . ☐ -1 (6)

Logo of magazine affiliated with book . . . . . . ☐ -2

Special approach to the content . . . . ☐ -3

Completeness of content . . . . ☐ -4

Author's reputation. . . . . ☐ -5

Publisher's reputation . . . . ☐ -6

Book cover design or layout . . . . ☐ -7

Index or table of contents of book . . . . ☐ -8

Price of book . . . . ☐ -9

Special effects, graphics, illustrations . . . . . . ☐ -0

Other (Please specify): _____ ☐ -x

3. How many computer books have you purchased in the last six months? _____ (7-10)

4. On a scale of 1 to 5, where 5 is excellent, 4 is above average, 3 is average, 2 is below average, and 1 is poor, please rate each of the following aspects of this book below. (Please circle your answer.)

Depth/completeness of coverage	5	4	3	2	1	(11)
Organization of material	5	4	3	2	1	(12)
Ease of finding topic	5	4	3	2	1	(13)
Special features/time saving tips	5	4	3	2	1	(14)
Appropriate level of writing	5	4	3	2	1	(15)
Usefulness of table of contents	5	4	3	2	1	(16)
Usefulness of index	5	4	3	2	1	(17)
Usefulness of accompanying disk	5	4	3	2	1	(18)
Usefulness of illustrations/graphics	5	4	3	2	1	(19)
Cover design and attractiveness	5	4	3	2	1	(20)
Overall design and layout of book	5	4	3	2	1	(21)
Overall satisfaction with book	5	4	3	2	1	(22)

5. Which of the following computer publications do you read regularly; that is, 3 out of 4 issues?

Byte . . . . ☐ -1 (23)

Computer Shopper . . . . ☐ -2

Corporate Computing . . . . ☐ -3

Dr. Dobb's Journal . . . . ☐ -4

LAN Magazine . . . . ☐ -5

MacWEEK . . . . ☐ -6

MacUser . . . . ☐ -7

PC Computing . . . . ☐ -8

PC Magazine . . . . ☐ -9

PC WEEK . . . . ☐ -0

Windows Sources . . . . ☐ -x

Other (Please specify): _____ ☐ -y

Please turn page.

6. What is your level of experience with personal computers? With the subject of this book?

	With PCs	With subject of book
Beginner	☐ -1 (24)	☐ -1 (25)
Intermediate	☐ -2	☐ -2
Advanced	☐ -3	☐ -3

7. Which of the following best describes your job title?

Officer (CEO/President/VP/owner) ☐ -1 (26)
Director/head ☐ -2
Manager/supervisor ☐ -3
Administration/staff ☐ -4
Teacher/educator/trainer ☐ -5
Lawyer/doctor/medical professional ☐ -6
Engineer/technician ☐ -7
Consultant ☐ -8
Not employed/student/retired ☐ -9
Other (Please specify): _____ ☐ -0

8. What is your age?

Under 20 ☐ -1 (27)
21-29 ☐ -2
30-39 ☐ -3
40-49 ☐ -4
50-59 ☐ -5
60 or over ☐ -6

9. Are you:

Male ☐ -1 (28)
Female ☐ -2

Thank you for your assistance with this important information! Please write your address below to receive our free catalog.

Name: _____

Address: _____

City/State/Zip: _____

Fold here to mail.   1315-08-11

_____
_____
_____